Martin Walker is the *Guardian*'s first resident correspondent in Moscow for fifty years. He covered the
revolution in Portugal for the paper in 1975. He is also
the author of an acclaimed book on the National Front
and *Powers of the Press*, an authoritative assessment
of the world's most influential newspapers.

The Waking Giant

MARTIN WALKER

SPHERE BOOKS LTD

Published by the Penguin Group
27 Wrights Lane, London W8 5TZ, England
Viking Penguin Inc., 40 West 23rd Street, New York, New York 10010, USA
Penguin Books Australia Ltd, Ringwood, Victoria, Australia
Penguin Books Canada Ltd, 2801 John Street, Markham, Ontario, Canada L3R 1B4
Penguin Books (NZ) Ltd, 182–190 Wairau Road, Auckland 10, New Zealand

Penguin Books Ltd, Registered Offices: Harmondsworth, Middlesex, England

First published in Great Britain by Michael Joseph Ltd 1986
Published in Abacus by Sphere Books Ltd 1987
Reprinted 1988 (twice)

Printed and bound in Great Britain by
Cox & Wyman Ltd, Reading
Set in Sabon

Contents

Preface and Acknowledgements

I never expected to become any kind of expert on Soviet affairs. I had studied history at Oxford, and international relations at Harvard, and had a reasonable knowledge of the forces which had shaped the Soviet Union's past, and of the policies it pursues in the present. Perhaps appropriately, it was at the beginning of that symbolic year of 1984 that the *Guardian* decided I should become its third resident Moscow correspondent. My predecessors were a hard act to follow. The first was Arthur Ransome, now perhaps best known for his marvellous stories for children, but a man who had first arrived in the country in Tsarist days, and who had lived through the revolutionary turbulence that gave birth to the Soviet system. He shared a flat with Karl Radek, a Politburo member, played chess with Lenin, and enjoyed a stormy affair with Leon Trotsky's secretary before marrying her and carrying her back to Britain. The second was Malcolm Muggeridge, at once the gadfly and the grand old man of the British media establishment. He had lived in Moscow in the early 1930s, gone to the Ukraine to report on the desperate famine that marked the infancy of Mikhail Gorbachev, and left the country to file his exclusive and shattering account of the disaster Stalin was inflicting on the Russian peasantry. He was not allowed to return.

Fifty years later, having spent months reading the available books (in English) on the Soviet Union, having assiduously listened to my Linguaphone tapes of the Russian language, and having gone through a three-week crash course in the language that seemed at the time to be having little effect, I arrived by sea at Leningrad, to embark on the long drive south and east to Moscow. It was an illuminating and rather baffling journey. The ship on which I had travelled, owned by a joint Swedish–Soviet company, was modern and well appointed, with a casino, and notable vintage clarets on its wine list. The approaches up the long Gulf of Finland, past the old naval base of Kronstadt, where the rebellious sailors had been so bloodily crushed in the name of the revolution in 1921, were vastly impressive. Modern warships and a succession of cargo vessels joined our convoy into the elegant port. That night, I checked into the grandly marbled Prebaltiskaya hotel, paying £90 by credit card for the privilege, and watched a television programme about Soviet high technology and computers.

The next day's drive was like moving into another and much more backward world. At times, the main road between Moscow and Leningrad degenerated into a narrow two-lane track. There were villages where chickens and the occasional pig trundled across the narrow road, while bowed, lumpish women in boots and headscarves hauled sacks from horse-drawn carts. I stopped in one of the villages and went into the only store to buy something for lunch. There were several piles of iron buckets, endless jars of pickled cucumbers, some scraggy radishes and tinned fish and bread. The only beverage available was mineral water or vodka. The village's water supply came from a public tap outside the store, and women came by to fill two buckets, which they carried away balanced on a long pole across their shoulders.

This was my introduction to the contradictions of Soviet life, the huge gap between its aspirations and its achievements, between the modern cities and the rural backwardness, between the high-tech systems that produce rockets and space stations and the lumbering economy that produces shortages and queues. A thoughtful Russian friend, who had worked as a journalist in London, once told me that he had been equally bewildered by the differences between the elegance of London's Bond Street and the burned-out shell of Brixton, the suburb which had become an angry ghetto. 'We have grown up with the failings and inconsistencies of our own societies,' he said. 'We are only shocked by the contradictions of others.'

I am grateful to Yuri and to many other Soviet friends and acquaintances for their help and guidance in introducing me to their way of life. Peter Preston, Richard Gott and Martin Woollacott – respectively, editor, features editor and foreign editor of the *Guardian* – wisely asked me from the beginning to try and report the place as if it were any other country in the world. I thank them for their unfailing help and support, for giving me the opportunity to get to know the country, and for insisting that

Preface and Acknowledgements

I try to write about arts and the theatre as well as Kremlinology, the life of ordinary people as well as the policies announced in *Pravda*. It would have been impossible even to try without the kindness of many Russians who took me to their dachas, to their wedding feasts and into their homes, studios and workshops, who took me skiing and fishing through the ice, hunting in Siberia, to unauthorised rock concerts and private poetry readings and underground art exhibitions, and to midnight church services. They are a marvellously warm people, and it has been a privilege to get to know them.

All foreign journalists in Moscow are accredited to the press department of the ministry of foreign affairs. Under the direction of Vladimir Lomeiko, a former Novosti journalist in Bonn, it has become an efficient and sophisticated operation, wise in the ways of the Western media, familiar with the deadlines of the US television news shows and the Fleet Street front pages. I am grateful to Mr Lomeiko and his staff, some of whom have become personal friends. A particular debt is due to Sasha Sazonov and Nikolai Krivoshein; my work as a journalist would have been impossible without their help. Much more than thanks are due to my Russian staff at the *Guardian* office, Nina Petrova and Slava Yevteyev, who have put up with my foreign habits and my idiosyncratic way of seeing things, guided me through the toils of Moscow bureaucracy, and kept the office running. They have adopted the entire Walker family, and we are all deeply fond of them.

Moscow being the city it is, and East–West relations being in the state they are, the Western community lives and works closely together. Having lived and worked widely abroad, I do not think I have ever met a more impressive press and diplomatic corps than those serving in Moscow during my time. All of my colleagues from the British press helped me and my family to settle in, and we all exchanged gossip, analysis and information in a way that would probably appal competition-minded editors back in Fleet Street. One of the great pleasures of the job has been working closely with foreign colleagues. It is invidious to single out a few, but Pierre Bocev of AFP, Charles Lambroschini of *Le Figaro*, Fernando Mezzetti of *Il Giornale Nuovo*, Hartwig Nathe of DPA, Walter Rogers of ABC-TV, Steve Hurst of NBC-TV, Mike McIver of CBC, Dusko Doder of the *Washington Post*, Serge Schmemann, Philip Taubman and Seth Maidans of the *New*

York Times and Dusko Pesic of *Politika* have all helped me enormously. They have a colleague's deepest respect and affection.

Anyone who has glanced at Western news stories datelined Moscow will know how often we quote diplomatic sources. This is not simply because of the difficulty of finding Russian sources but because, for obvious reasons, most countries tend to send some of their best people to Moscow. The two British ambassadors of my time were Sir Iain Sutherland and Sir Bryan Cartledge; the Maclaren of Maclaren and the Madame Maclaren have become close chums, as well as the best and most popular press attachés in Moscow. I am also deeply grateful to Mr and Mrs Arthur Hartman, the American ambassador and his wife, for their insights into superpower politics and some marvellous parties. The ambassador of Singapore, Tony Saddique, gave me the benefit of one of the best analytical minds in Moscow, and the envoys of Jamaica, Egypt, Pakistan, Greece, Canada, the Netherlands, Luxemburg, Sweden and Australia know how much my work has depended on their unfailing help and goodwill.

Most thanks of all are due to my own family, my wife Julia, herself a journalist, who scooped me on the story of Beatles records going on official sale in Moscow, and our daughters, Katie and Fanny. Katie was aged two when we arrived, and Fanny first came to Moscow when she was nine days old, in a chill February. Her first words were in Russian and, with luck, she and Katie will be able to speak that lovely tongue for the rest of their lives. It was through Julia's forbearance and loving support that I was able to write this book, and many of the insights are hers. During the manic months of the Geneva summit, the twenty-seventh party congress and the Chernobyl nuclear disaster, it was my family that kept me fed and sane and loved. This book is therefore for them, for Julia and Katie and Fanny, who shared the Russian adventure with me, and who gave it meaning.

Martin Walker
Moscow

Introduction

This book is written from the ghetto. We foreigners who live in
Moscow, the journalists, diplomats, businessmen and bankers,
are assigned to one of a series of apartment blocks that are
surrounded by wire fences. The gates are guarded by a sentry
box, where a policeman stands day and night. He is supposed to
be there for our security, but his presence does not seem to prevent
the occasional burglary, nor the more frequent vandalism inflicted
on our cars. Indeed, his main duty seems to be to monitor and
check the names of any Russian who seeks to visit us, and to
make reports of our movements whenever we leave by car.

This is easily done. In the Soviet Union all foreigners' car
numberplates are coded. Russian numberplates consist of black
numbers on a white background. Foreigners are assigned different
colours. A diplomat has a red plate, a journalist or businessman
a yellow plate. The numbers of diplomats' cars always begin with
a D; journalists are assigned the letter K (for *korrespondent*), and
businessmen have M; cars hired by a foreigner from the state
agency are given the letter H, and those with a permit to leave
the country P. The codes do not stop there. After the first letter
comes a second group of numbers, which identifies the driver's
nationality. Britain, for example, has 001, the USA 004, France
007 – all the way down to the new diplomatic mission from
Zimbabwe, which has 115. There is then a final group of three
numbers which identifies the individual driver. So, whenever a
policeman reports by radio to the officials at the central moni-
toring station that K 001 819 has been seen parked somewhere
in Moscow, they can begin to work out which Russian the British
journalist from the *Guardian* may have been visiting.

Each time we leave the compound by car, the report is phoned
in. If our cars are not checked into another of the regular moni-
toring points – another residential compound, an embassy, an

assigned office area or Soviet ministry – the first alerts go out to check exactly where we might be. We cannot go far. We are limited to the city itself, a 40-kilometre radius from the Kremlin, unless we obtain prior approval to travel on those roads which are open to foreigners. Officially, since the Helsinki agreement, journalists do not require permission from the foreign ministry to travel outside Moscow. We need only to inform them of our travel plans two days in advance. The difference is largely academic. On all the roads leading from Moscow, and at regular intervals on every road we are entitled to use, there are the GAI posts, the traffic police stations, which monitor our movements. As we pass, each post phones ahead to the next, and if we do not pass the next checkpoint within a reasonable time, they come looking for us – as we found when we stopped for a picnic on the road near the old town of Vladimir.

By Soviet standards, we live well. The flat for myself, my wife and two children is made of two standard-size Russian flats knocked together to give us three bedrooms. A Russian would pay about 10 roubles a month in rent. (At the official exchange rate, a rouble is approximately equivalent to one pound.) We pay over 500 roubles a month, in hard currency. We must also use hard currency at the two small supermarkets made available to us, where there is hardly ever a meat shortage, and where the biggest counters are for imported wines, spirits and Western cigarettes. The existence of the supermarkets means that we do not have to rely on the usual Russian shops, that we do not have to queue, and that we are shielded from the ups and downs of Soviet food supplies. We can even use our credit cards.

We have a special hospital assigned for our use, where the facilities are rather better, and the supply of drugs more reliable, than in the standard Russian health service. We can, by writing formal letters, obtain tickets to the Bolshoi ballet, the theatre, the circus and other entertainments in short supply. We can buy, again for hard currency, Russian-printed books that are so rare in Soviet shops that they command a hefty premium on the black market. We can usually get a room in a reasonable hotel, by reserving in advance and by paying in hard currency; and where a Russian would pay 5 roubles for his room, we will pay 50 or more. When we fly on Aeroflot, we are assigned to a separate departure lounge from the Russian passengers, who are frequently bumped off the plane to make room for us. We are, therefore, less popular with the locals than we might be. Privilege is a clever mechanism to keep people apart.

Among the foreigners who live in Moscow, there are various cynical explanations for all this. Certainly, the way we are treated is designed to keep us from getting too close to the realities of Soviet life and to the ordinary life of Soviet people. But this cannot be the sole purpose behind it. The system is too easy to circumvent. We can travel by metro to visit our Russian friends, or park our cars at some distance from their flats. Or we can drive friends into our own compounds, straight past the police box, and rush them up to our flat so that their identity papers are not checked – and only the microphones in the walls and telephones can monitor our conversations. We can easily evade the 40-kilometre limit by using public transport, the excellent electric trains around the Moscow countryside, the buses and trams to the city beaches at Serebrianny Bor. We can use the Russian shops, depend on our roubles, and learn the art of Russian queuing.

Doubtless, our lives are restricted in this way in order to increase the state's foreign currency earnings. The 10,000 foreigners in Moscow must contribute something over $100 million a year to the state bank in rents and purchases. But it must cost the state a vast amount to police and service us in this way. The purpose is not simply economic. It is partly traditional. Foreigners have always been treated this way in Russia. In the days of Ivan the Terrible, the foreign merchants were assigned to the ghetto known as Kitaigorod, or Chinatown – probably because so much of the trade at the time was connected with the old silk routes to China. Kitaigorod was a walled city within the city, and occupied the eastern flank of Red Square, right under the guns of the Kremlin.

There is also an evident attempt to show us the better side of Soviet life. The odd thing about the system is that it seems designed to replicate for us the life of a senior, though not top-rank, party official. The large apartments, the police security on our gates, the special numberplates that can get us through most ordinary police checks and roadblocks, the exclusive food shops and hospitals, the access to air and theatre tickets – this is how the *vlasti*, the powerful ones, live.

When we go on our travels around the Soviet Union, we are again given the *vlasti* treatment, a Russian version of the West's public relations machine – Russian, rather than Soviet, because it stems from an old national trait. When the short-sighted Catherine the Great went sailing down the Volga to view her dominions, the influential courtier Potemkin constructed mock villages on the riverbanks, complete with smiling and prosperous peasants, that served to obscure the occasional famine behind them. When foreigners travel, they get the Potemkin treatment: the good hotels, the better food, the carefully restored churches and historic monuments. We are escorted only to the better collective farms, those that have won state prizes for their achievements, and the factories that have overfulfilled the plan or brought in the new bonus payments system or possess an impressive computer room.

But then, this is how the *vlasti* make their tours – or, at least, it reflects the same sanitised and Potemkinised version of life that the *vlasti* were shown until Mikhail Gorbachev broke the pattern. Shortly after he came to power, Gorbachev made the usual brisk tour of Moscow. Every other leader had done the same. Chernenko had gone briefly to the prestigious Hammer and Sickle steel factory in Moscow and chatted with the shock workers. These are the industrial version of shock troops – they are awarded similar medals for their heroism on the shop floor – a legacy of Stalin's militarisation of even the Russian language in his drive to industrialise the state.

Gorbachev's tour of Moscow's Proletarsky district dispensed with tradition. First, he took only two cars, rather than the usual cavalcade with motorcycle outriders. Second, he did not bother to tell Viktor Grishin, the Moscow party chieftain, of his plans – a disregard for protocol akin to the Queen of England making a visit to the City of London without informing the Lord Mayor. Third, he did not go to one model factory. He simply pottered about – into a supermarket to ask the shoppers what they thought about shortages, into a kindergarten to meet the mothers who were picking up their children; and then he invited himself back to the home of one young couple for a cup of tea. He admired their furniture and impressive bookshelves, their collection of records, and waved aside the wife's apologies for untidiness. Had she but known, she said . . . In fact, the place was spotless. It all seemed spontaneous, refreshingly open – a rare glimpse of real life for one of the *vlasti* . . . Until, while idly chatting, he turned over his empty cup and saw the stamp that showed it had come from the central committee cafeteria. He had been Potemkinised.[1]

Introduction

Furious, Gorbachev left the apartment and proceeded to a part of the tour that he knew had been scheduled, at a local hospital. The doctors and administrators assured him that all was fine. By now, he was suspicious, and he began to probe. Do you have bandages? What about gut for sewing stitches – I know that's always in short supply. Then he rattled off the names of several drugs – did they have those? Emboldened, the doctors started to explain what the shortages really were, and to reveal that operations had to be delayed, that there were insufficient sheets to change the bedding often enough, that antiquated kitchens made the patients' meals cold and inadequate. You have to learn to tell us the truth, Gorbachev said. We can't help you if we don't know what you need. Then he turned to a little old lady who was peering round a corner at him. He beckoned her in, calling her *babushka*, or granny. Gently he questioned her. What did she do? A ward assistant and cleaner. What did she earn? Eighty roubles a month – the minimum wage. How did she live on that? The hospital director broke in to say that she could always get a second job in the evenings. Gorbachev rounded on him angrily and snapped, 'You have to start paying people enough so they don't need to do a second job.'[2]

Gorbachev's walkabout entered Moscow legend. The *vlasti* were not meant to behave like this, to want to discover what was really going on. There had been widespread relief when he became general secretary – not because people expected anything radically new, nor because his speeches on reform and his previous political career had made a great impact (they had not, beyond the small but influential elite who keep up with such things). The relief stemmed from his relative youth, from the fact that at last the Soviet people had a leader who could walk unaided, who was not an elderly invalid, who could deliver his speeches in a clear, strong voice, rather than hesitantly wheezing through the pages and losing his place on the way – as both Brezhnev and Chernenko had done on Soviet television. That in itself seemed enough.

The walkabout made people talk; more significantly, it did not make them joke. Russian humour is rich and wide-ranging. But there were no jokes about Gorbachev. Even his crackdown on alcohol provoked only tame and far from hostile nicknames such as 'Lemonade Joe' and '*Sok-Sek*' instead of *Gyen-Sek* ('fruit juice secretary' rather than general secretary). Then, just after the Moscow tour, I was at a party with Russian friends and I heard a retread of an old joke. Stalin, Khrushchev and Brezhnev are sitting in a carriage on a Trans-Siberian train in midwinter, and the train suddenly stops. Stalin says, Shoot the engine driver. And they do, but the train does not move. Khrushchev says, Rehabilitate the engine driver. And they do, but the train does not move. Brezhnev closes the curtains, settles back comfortably in his seat and says, Let's pretend the train is moving. That is how the joke used to go, but now I heard a new ending. Mikhail Gorbachev is sitting in the carriage, and when Brezhnev has finished young Mikhail leaps to his feet and runs up and down the corridors ordering all the passengers out onto the track. Then he leaps onto the platform of the train, adopts a heroic pose and yells at the bewildered passengers, Right, you lot, start pushing.

Then there was Gorbachev's visit to Leningrad, and his televised speech to the massed ranks of the local party officials. He spoke without notes, in his educated but pleasantly provincial Stavropol accent; he grinned a lot and talked straight. This was not how the Soviet people were accustomed to hearing their leaders; and, above all, it was not how they were accustomed to hearing top officials addressed. While talking about waste in the economy and the need to reduce it, he suddenly paused, looked steadily around at the audience and said, 'You know what the trouble really is?' He tapped his pockets, jangling the coins. 'You don't feel it here. Not personally. And it's about time you did.'[3]

This was new. Russian friends began to ask me for copies of my articles about Gorbachev and for copies of profiles that had appeared in Western magazines. There was a sudden hunger for information about the man, for the kind of biographical details that the Soviet press never provides. People wanted to know about his wife Raisa, about her trip to London, what the West had thought of her clothes, what she had bought. When they heard that I had met Raisa and the Gorbachevs' daughter Irina and their granddaughter Oksana at the May Day ceremony in Red Square, they wanted to know about the family. Suddenly, there was a human interest in the man at the top and those close to him, born not just of curiosity but of fascination – a fascination that in the West has been fuelled by a million articles and instant books and television profiles about our own new leaders.

In the West, we have something to go on. Nobody becomes a national leader without having been prominent in politics for years, having built up a public record, and a public image on television and in the press. We know the leader and the leader's family long before he or she assumes office. Not so in the Soviet Union. When Gorbachev came to power, the papers published the bare biographical details, mentioning where he was born, his university education, his Red Banner of Labour medal, his posts in the party hierarchy: a dry chronicle of an apparatchik's steady rise through the party ranks. It was not a human being in the Kremlin; it was a set of statistics. Now the Russians wanted to know more.

They did not find out only from us Westerners. Perhaps the most startling single aspect of the new leader was that, for a party man, he was reasonably well known in Moscow. He was the first Soviet leader since Lenin with a university education (which says much for the last sixty years of Soviet rule); he had several hundred classmates scattered around Moscow who had attended the city's prestigious university with him. There were even more citizens who knew Raisa, who continued to teach and lecture at Moscow University even while her husband was in the Politburo. She lectured in philosophy, and had been a pioneer of sociological research, one of the first Soviet scholars to use interview and polling techniques in her survey of the living standards of peasants in the Stavropol district, where her husband had been a local party official when she wrote her thesis in the early 1960s.[4] There were others again who knew the Gorbachevs' daughter Irina, a qualified doctor and medical researcher in Moscow, and her husband, a young surgeon.

Gorbachev himself had studied law, just at the time when the legal profession had started to grow in the Soviet Union. He graduated in 1955, and the following year Khrushchev made his famous 'secret speech' about Stalin's crimes against the party, attacking the old dictator's cult of personality and his 'violations of socialist legality'. This was a phrase that helped, in its own small way, to bring about a social revolution in the Soviet Union. Khrushchev began, hesitantly and even spasmodically, to bring the rule of law to a Soviet society that had been subject to Stalin's arbitrary whim. The KGB were no longer legally entitled to make an arrest; they were supposed to convince a public legal official, the procurator, to make out a warrant. Soviet courts became rather more serious places than they had been, and the defendant had a right to a lawyer, cowed and cautious as that lawyer might be. The legal forms were established, and lawyers began to use them, and to prosper financially from the private practice they were allowed, and indeed encouraged, to undertake.

The state was still supreme. When the KGB found to their horror that there were no legal charges that they could bring to incarcerate the first two dissident writers, Daniel and Sinyavsky, they invented new ones. But they made a travesty of Soviet justice to do it (see pages 140–141).[5] And Soviet justice was not only being taken rather more seriously by the public, who tripled the number of private legal actions brought before the courts in the Khrushchev years, but it had also spawned its own interest group – the Soviet legal profession. Soviet lawyers were hired by the ministry of foreign affairs for international work. They were hired by various ministries who were squabbling over which bureaucracy had the right to govern what. They were hired by municipalities who wanted to stop local factories polluting the environment. Like lawyers everywhere, they began to creep steadily into the national establishment. They campaigned to widen their powers in their own magazines such as *Chelovyek i Zakon* (*Man and Law*), which, when Gorbachev assumed office, was campaigning for the introduction of that grand old principle, the presumption of innocence, to be granted to anyone who appeared before a Soviet court.[6]

The theme of this book is, in a way, encapsulated in the above paragraph. The Gorbachev family are classic examples of the social revolution that has been taking place in the Soviet Union since the death of Joseph Stalin in 1953. University educated, a lawyer husband, an academic wife, and a daughter and son-in-law in medicine: this could be an archetypal family of the professional upper-middle classes of the West.

The forty years of peace since 1945 have allowed the Soviet Union to return to normal in a social sense. The 1917 revolution beheaded the old ruling and administrative classes. Twenty years later, Stalin wiped out the new ruling and administrative class the Bolsheviks had put in their place. He wiped out the army's officer corps and the literary intellectuals, and the more prosperous peasantry as well. This decimation of all the best educated and best trained in both the old Tsarist Russia and the new revolutionary Soviet Union was a sociological disaster that has no parallel in history. The population that survived was then subjected to a war which left 20 million dead. Every tenth inhabitant of the Soviet Union died during the Second World War; of the male babies born from 1920 to 1925, the peak fighting generation, only 3 per cent survived.

Stalin ripped out the nation's brains; and, when he went for the writers and the artists and the intellectuals, he ripped out its heart and soul. The evil that he inflicted on Russia has gone too deep for it to be honestly confronted and analysed in the country even today, except by a handful of brave and thoughtful men such as Roy Medvedev, Anton Antonov-Ovseyenko and Alexander Solzhenitsyn.[7] Even the marvellous Russian language has yet to recover from the dead and militarised phrases and pompous clichés in which Stalin locked it.

Yet the nation slowly recovers, the body politic heals and has brought forth a new intelligentsia, new writers, a vast new audience hungry for literature, a new professional class of lawyers, doctors, sociologists, economists, journalists and academics who know the system well enough to campaign for their own intellectual prerogatives and freedoms within it. Such people knew the Gorbachevs long before he took over the Kremlin. They had been students together, had argued late into the night about books and art and truth and, after Stalin fell, about politics too. In their middle age, when they said late at night in their kitchens over vodka and snacks of cheese and sardines on bread that the Misha they had known at university was a decent type, and that his wife was a fine and humane woman, they were speaking not just to me but to others like themselves, academics and professionals who had not been at Moscow University with the Gorbachevs, but who would spread the word around the Soviet intellectual community. Within months of taking office, Gorbachev had a degree of personal loyalty and familiarity among the new Soviet professional classes that was without precedent since Lenin's death.

'We have our Kennedy,' one Gorbachev contemporary, a journalist who had served in Washington, confided to me one night at a party in Moscow's Arbat district. 'You remember the relief that young America felt when Jack and Jackie Kennedy went into the White House, that after all those years of Eisenhower there was youth and style and promise and decision at the top? That's us. Moscow as Camelot. Camelot on ice.'

This was fanciful rambling, significant less for the bizarre parallel with Washington DC in 1960 than for the mood it conveyed, the sense that interesting people in Moscow thought of

Gorbachev as one of them, rather than as a machine politician from the party apparat. But the echoes of Kennedy were the flavour of the month in Moscow. It was during that evening that I first heard of Fyodor Burlatsky's new play, *Burden of Decision*, set in the White House during the Cuban missile crisis.

Burlatsky is a political commentator on the weekly literary newspaper *Literaturnaya Gazeta*, sometime consultant to the central committee on foreign affairs, and a personal friend of the Gorbachevs. His play is a remarkably sympathetic portrait of Kennedy, as a man desirous of peace and sincere in his religious faith. A moving scene of Kennedy at prayer contrasts sharply with the sudden appearance of Frank Sinatra in the White House, complete with brassy girlfriend. The real villain is the FBI chief J. Edgar Hoover, who is shown trying to blackmail Jackie Kennedy into persuading her husband to go to war on pain of the FBI's publicising the president's infidelities. The play was given a stylish production, rendered peculiarly Russian in the way that the ruling counterparts in Moscow were referred to simply as 'the leadership'; Khrushchev's name was never mentioned.

The people who flocked to Moscow's Satyr theatre to see the play seemed to be drawn predominantly from this Gorbachev generation, men and women old enough to have been frightened half to death during the missile crisis of 1962 but young enough to have been part of the social transformation which the Gorbachev family embodies. The size of this educated, culturally inclined new class is suggested by the circulations of literary newspapers and magazines. *Literaturnaya Gazeta* is read, or at least bought, by 3.1 million people; the newspaper is the voice of the writers' union, and deals largely with cultural affairs. The monthly *Novy Mir* literary magazine sells 420,000 copies; and *Yunost* (*Youth*), another monthly from the writers' union, which describes itself as a 'literary and socio-political journal', sells 3.2 million. The cultural newspaper *Sovyetskaya Kultura* has a circulation of 545,000. *Pravda*, by comparison, has a circulation of just over 10 million, and *Izvestia* 6.4 million. The daily sports paper sells 4.6 million. It would be unwise to draw too firm a conclusion from these figures. The bestselling newspaper *Trud* (*Labour*), the mouthpiece of the Soviet trade union organisation, has built the country's biggest daily circulation of 18.6 million by the standard Grub Street method of sensation – albeit a very soft and moderate Soviet-style sensation; it runs articles on UFOs and the search for

Atlantis and folk medicine. But, by Western standards, the size of the readership for the cultural and literary papers and magazines is remarkably high.

The increasingly prominent role of the law and lawyers in Soviet life is dramatically illustrated by the circulation of *Chelovyek i Zakon*, which sells 10.2 million copies a month. Whereas in 1940 Soviet universities were producing only 5700 economists and lawyers each year, by 1974 they were graduating 70,000 annually. A million trained lawyers and economists have been produced since 1970. This is just a fraction, but a socially significant one, of the phenomenal growth in Soviet higher and university education. The country had 1.2 million university students in 1950, and 5.2 million in 1984. Its full-time science research workers in 1984 totalled 1.5 million – or a quarter of all the world's scientists. A young Soviet's chance of receiving a university education is almost twice as high as that of his British or West German counterpart.[8]

These raw figures say little about the comparative quality of education or the productivity of the scientists. But, combined with the circulation statistics, they point to the achievement of the Soviet Union, and to its enormous investment, in establishing an educated and cultured society. The circulation figures for magazines and periodicals suggest that the average citizen buys twelve copies a year; and the daily sale of 180 million newspapers means that about four out of five adults buy a paper each day. The country's theatres sell 124 million tickets a year, and the cinemas sell almost 4000 million – which means that the average citizen goes to see a film fourteen times a year.[9]

The point is that Mikhail Gorbachev did not come out of nowhere. He is a product of the surging growth in Soviet education and new professions, and of the new social mix that has resulted. He was a country boy, not the son of a well-established and well-educated urban family. He went from a collective farm near the Black Sea to Moscow University; like many millions more around the country, he was able to take advantage of the opportunities in Soviet education – opportunities that have been spread far and wide across the nation, into the traditionally Muslim republics of the deep south, the Baltic states and far Siberia alike.

It is in the old Muslim lands where the provision of education has made the most difference. This is Russia's own Third World, and it must be admitted that the Russians have done a better job of educating and industrialising their Third World than the West ever tried to do with the underdeveloped countries of Africa, Asia and Latin America. For all the faults of the Soviet system, all the legacies of an ancient Russian xenophobia and racism, and all the continued dominance of Slavs in key official positions, achievements in the deep south have been remarkable.

Some five years ago, I saw the Soviet frontier from both the Turkish and the Iranian sides. Near Mount Ararat, I drove through mile after mile of bare pasture, where the Turkish peasants lived in what amounted to mud huts, scratching some kind of living from thin soil and thinner sheep and goats. In Iran, north of Tabriz, there had been a similar poverty, a similar failure of development. Then, since coming to live in the Soviet Union, I have seen the Turkish and Iranian borders from the Soviet side, from Armenia and Azerbaijan.

It was not quite like looking from the First World into the Third. There were still donkeys pottering through the Azerbaijan villages, women in the brightly coloured Armenian headscarves drawing water from the public wells. It was still peasant country, but visibly more prosperous. There were irrigation canals, schools, bookshops, public libraries. There were tractors in the fields, and acres of glasshouses. Whereas on the Turkish side the old Armenian churches were being pillaged for their huge stone blocks, on the Soviet side they had been carefully restored and the church possessions preserved for show in the cathedral museum. Among these objects was a piece of petrified wood, which church tradition claimed had come from Noah's original Ark. Certainly it had been found on the barren slopes of Mount Ararat. Soviet scientists had tested it with carbon dating and solemnly reported in writing to the Armenian church that the approximate date was 4400 BC. The scientists declined to comment on Noah, prehistoric shipbuilding, or even on the Old Testament as a documentary source. Still, they had helped.

Not long before my visit to Armenia, I had been thousands of miles to the north-east, in the centre of Siberia, at the new city of Ust-Ilimsk, which had been built on the empty taiga over the previous twelve years. Based around a huge hydroelectric dam, an aluminium smelter and a timber-processing complex, it is an industrial bridgehead in a vast featureless landscape. But one of the first buildings to have been completed was the local palace of culture, and there I watched the city's ballet class perform the chorus dance from *Swan Lake*. Doubtless, it was a Potemkin performance laid on for a visiting journalist; but, in spite of the propaganda and the sense of the artificial, there is something undeniably heroic about a community that can stage *Swan Lake* in a place where ten years earlier only wolves had howled.

The new Siberian cities and their ballet classes, the libraries, the expansion of education and the modernisation of the old Muslim lands, are impressive because they represent the fulfilment of at least some of the Soviet system's promises. But they may in the long run turn out to be less significant than the social revolution which the state never intended nor expected to happen. The emergence of the intelligentsia and professional classes first showed its capacity to disturb the Soviet system with the *samizdat* (literally, self-published) phenomenon of underground literature. Simply by existing as an audience for books the state did not want people to read, the new classes became a potential challenge to the old patterns of party control.

The challenges have become more pointed since. Lawyers campaign openly to change the law to give defendants better rights in the courts. Journalists campaign for the right to publish bad news as well as good, criticisms as well as the hackneyed salutations to heroes of socialist labour. Academics have managed to regain much of the freedom of research and enquiry that Stalin and his heirs removed from them with their absurd insistence that cybernetics was 'a bourgeois pseudo-science' and that genetics had to conform to the Marxist rule that environment was of more importance than heredity.

Members of each of these groups – scientists, lawyers, journalists and cultural celebrities – came together in the 1970s to form the first mass movement of public opinion the country had seen. The cause that united them was the need to preserve the ecological purity of Lake Baikal. They wrote letters to the press, and scientists gave up their free time to monitor the damage being done to the world's largest body of fresh water by the cellulose plants that had been erected on the lake shore. Prominent writers such as Valentin Rasputin put their names behind the campaign, and steadily the argument was won. The state was persuaded to instal purification equipment in the factories, and then to stop all discharges into the lake. The same coalition of public opinion came together again to fight the proposals to reverse the flow of

Siberian rivers so that their water could be used to irrigate the dry lands of the Muslim south. A gigantic scheme of great ecological risk, the river-reversal project was steadily and carefully criticised in what became a remarkable public debate in the Soviet media. Historians wrote of the national monuments and old churches that would be flooded by the new dams. Scientists warned that the Arctic ice cap could creep far to the south if the rivers stopped flowing into the Arctic Ocean. While Chernenko was general secretary, the plan was scheduled to go ahead. When Gorbachev succeeded to the leadership, one of the first people he summoned to Moscow was the economist from the Siberian think-tank of Novosibirsk, Professor Abel Aganbegyan, many of whose colleagues had joined the campaign against the project. Gorbachev himself was rumoured to be dubious about it. He had talked frequently in his speeches of ecological problems, and indeed the thrust of his disarmament policy, as expressed at the press conference he gave after the Geneva summit, was the need to save the planet for future generations. His wife Raisa, it was said by colleagues at Moscow University, had been against the project from the beginning. In February 1986, Professor Aganbegyan co-authored a long article in *Pravda* which attacked the economics of the scheme.[10] The party leadership of Uzbekistan, the project's strongest supporters within the party establishment, had been weakened and demoralised by a separate campaign against local corruption. The plan to reverse the rivers was effectively dead.

In his keynote speech to the party congress later in the month, Gorbachev made himself the personal spokesman for this new coalition of academics, intellectuals and media figures who had begun to perceive their own potential as a political force in Soviet society. His speech contained a series of promises to lift the remaining ideological restrictions upon their research work, restrictions with which his wife had been forced to contend in her own academic career. But his statement also came close to being an open bid for their support:

> We feel a pressing need for serious philosophical generalisations, well-founded economic and social forecasts, and profound historical researches. We cannot escape the fact that our philosophy and economics, as indeed our social sciences as a whole, are some distance removed from the imperatives of life. Scholasticism, doctrinaire thinking and dogmatism have been shackles for any genuine advance to knowledge. They lead to stagnation of thought, put a solid wall around science,

keeping it away from real life and inhibiting its development. The atmosphere of creativity is particularly productive for the social sciences. We hope that it will be used actively by our economists and philosophers, lawyers and sociologists, historians and literary critics for a bold and innovative formulation of new problems and for their creative theoretical elaboration.

No previous Soviet leader had publicly espoused such an intellectuals' charter, least of all in the party's most prestigious forum. Gorbachev had recognised the nature of the new social forces emerging in Soviet life, identified their component professions, and told them to think and work more freely.

There was another kind of social revolution under way, which the party had neither planned nor foreseen, and which it could never bring itself to embrace. It stemmed from the economic successes of the preceding thirty years, the steady growth in living standards and, above all, from the steep climb in incomes and personal savings. These developments were not restricted to those professional, educated groups which the Gorbachev family now typified. The growth in bonus payments had sharply increased the real wages of skilled industrial workers, and much of their new spending power had been funnelled into the booming black markets and into the free markets for foods grown on the private plots of the collective farmers. Those farmers in a position to grow fruits and vegetables and flowers out of season could make a killing in Moscow by flying to the capital from the sunny south with their produce in their suitcases. The black marketeers, and the Georgians and Armenians in the food trade, were becoming the new rich of Soviet life. In winter, people with money in Moscow would pay 20 roubles for a kilo of tomatoes or 8 roubles for a single cucumber; and, in the first week of March, to provide the obligatory flowers for their ladies on Women's Day, the men of Moscow were paying 5 roubles for a single flower. All this was legal, so long as the flowers and foodstuffs came from private plots. But as demand increased with the real incomes of the urban customers, supplies began to come from the storehouses of the state farms. In autumn 1985, a Moscow-based group of Armenians went on trial, charged with buying onions at the state shops at subsidised prices and then cleaning them carefully and selling them in the free markets for four times the state price.

In a rare survey of the black economy, *Izvestia* reckoned that it generated some 7000 million roubles a year.[12] Most observers and, privately, most Soviet economists reckon that this is a gross underestimate. After all, the black economy was, and is, perhaps the most efficient sector of all Soviet service industries. If you wish to get a car serviced, to obtain spare parts, to buy pharmaceutical drugs (and medicines are not prescribed free in the Soviet health service) or to obtain imported Western jeans or records or videos, the black market can provide, at a price.

It was all remarkably open. The black market in Western electrical goods functioned outside the second-hand shop next to the Moscow planetarium. A black market in spare parts for cars was conducted from the back door of the state service station in Ziyuzino – until the staff were arrested in 1985. In Lithuania, another market functioned in summer on the nudist beaches reserved for women, which kept the police away.[13] The black market in pirated tapes of the latest Western rock music was based inside Moscow University, and the rouble millionaires who ran the business flaunted their wealth, driving imported Western cars and living it up at the risqué cabaret of the Soyuz hotel in north Moscow. The Soyuz was not an Intourist hotel, and took roubles rather than foreign currency (although a dollar bill would never be rejected); consequently it was popular with Russians and a handful of foreigners in the know. It provided the best cabaret show for 5000 miles west of Tokyo.[14]

The hit movie of 1984 was a Soviet-made comedy called *The Blonde Around the Corner*, which was based on the lives of people on the fringes of the black economy. It was an affectionate portrait of the life of easy money and lavish parties. Although it ended in approved Soviet style, with the loose-living blonde married to a devout young research worker who wanted to settle in Siberia, build the future and raise a family, the reason for the film's success was that it portrayed a life that so many Russians could recognise.

On account of the black market, Moscow in the 1970s began increasingly to resemble other European cities. The street scenes remained dull, the colours drab, the roads pot-holed and the party slogans tediously repetitive. But the Western woollen ski caps, the Adidas shoes, the knee-high stiletto-heeled boots of the women, the Levi jeans, the plastic bags from German supermarkets, the sweat shirts with American university crests emblazoned on their chests and the popularity of Marlboro cigarettes – all testified to the effectiveness of the black market as a retail operation.

Introduction

These were emblems of a social transformation that Mikhail Gorbachev could never uphold; indeed, he continued with the brisk anti-corruption campaigns that Yuri Andropov had launched after Brezhnev's death, and widened them to include a crackdown on the peasants' free markets in Moscow and road checks on the lorries that trundled north to the Moscow markets from the farms of the sunny south. In March 1986, prices for flowers before Women's Day skidded sharply downwards as the state flower plantations made extra stocks available for sale in the free markets, to undercut the black marketeers and drive them out of business.[15]

Probably correctly, Gorbachev saw the black market as a symptom rather than a cause of social change: it was an inevitable reaction to the inadequacy of the Soviet service sector and its retailing systems, and to the way that increasing real incomes were burning holes in the pockets of a population frustrated by the lack of goods in the shops. In the long term, the only solution was to transform Soviet industry so that it produced better quality goods and was more responsive to consumer demand. In the medium term, this meant improving the retail sector, making shops attractive, cutting down on queues, improving the courtesy of shop service, and making the product lines more varied and the repair and servicing systems more reliable. It also meant somehow legalising individual initiative and allowing it to prosper in conjunction with the state, rather than to its detriment. With his promises to legalise small cooperatives in the service sector, Gorbachev had pointed to at least a possible solution. But, in the short term, it meant trying to find a way of making all these reforms ideologically acceptable to a party machine that was already beginning to grumble at the pace of change that Gorbachev had set out to impose.

This was perhaps Gorbachev's greatest problem. He was confronting the weight of a party tradition that was the stronger because the party itself was still, at heart, so insecure. Until Gorbachev came to power, the party had been run by men with personal memories of Stalin's time, when mistakes had proved fatal and salvation lay only in unswerving loyalty to whatever line *Pravda* laid down that day. Even after Stalin had gone and his Gulags had begun to empty, the party veterans had had to contend with the chaos that Khrushchev's reforms had caused, and they remembered the way in which he too had purged their ranks.

Khrushchev's victims lost their posts rather than their lives, but the posts and the privileges that went with them were precious to the party hierarchy. They had enjoyed the era of Brezhnev, under whom party chieftains in the distant republics were given wide latitude to run their own fiefs, even if this meant a steady increase in corruption. Something close to the guarantee of a lifetime job was a feature of the Brezhnev years, and Khrushchev's dangerous rules that called for strictly limited terms in office and a regular turnover of party committees were quietly buried. It may have been sensible to allow the country and the party officials a taste of stability after the terror of Stalin and the chaos of Khrushchev, but this interlude persisted for too long. By the time of Brezhnev's death, a social revolution was under way beneath this almost inert layer of a party leadership which governed and administered a land they no longer understood.

When Brezhnev died, the country was gravid with change – change that had been inordinately delayed, and which could be implemented only by a leader who was himself a part of the forces for change. In Gorbachev, the system finally produced such a man, of the right generation, the right educational background and professional training – someone with the kind of family and personal friends who could enlighten him to the real state of the Soviet nation independently of the party's own tightly structured information network. But the bureaucratic machine that he had inherited, and on which he would rely to administer the transformation, was still a product of the bad old ways.

Like every other reforming leader that Russia had known – like Ivan the Terrible and Peter the Great, and perhaps like Joseph Stalin too – Gorbachev's first task was to weaken the grip of the ruling elite that he had inherited, and then re-shape it to his own will. But those awesome predecessors in the Kremlin had inflicted a terrible price for the reforms they had imposed upon the land. They had been authoritarian leaders, ready to use terror and massacre to enforce their will. The social and intellectual background from which Gorbachev came, and the alteration in the temper of the population, foreclosed such an option. It would anyway have gone against Gorbachev's personal grain, and the population was no longer a nation of docile or demoralised peasants. They would not stand for it. When he was elected general

Introduction

secretary of the Communist Party of the Soviet Union on 11 March 1985, Mikhail Gorbachev faced a task that had been set no other Russian leader: to bring about fundamental change by consent.

1

The Rise of Mikhail Gorbachev

Mikhail Sergeyevich Gorbachev was born into a nightmare. In the spring of 1931, the peasants of Russia were being coerced into the collective farm system. The coercion was most intense where the land was richest, most capable of producing grain to feed the hungry mouths of the urban population, already starting to explode under the spur of the first five-year plan. The village of Privolnoye, where he was born on 2 March, lies in some of the richest land of all, the vast grain fields of Stavropol in the fertile plain between the Black and Caspian Seas. Gorbachev was born at a time of bizarre, almost surreal, abundance. The harvest of the previous year had been one of the best in Russia's history, and the threat of collectivisation led the peasantry to slaughter their livestock en masse, on the understandable assumption that it was better to eat your pigs and cattle while you had the chance than to surrender them to the anonymous collective. In the five years up to 1933, just over one half of the country's cows, horses and pigs and about one third of the sheep were slaughtered.[1]

But in the first months of Mikhail Gorbachev's life, the famine set in. The wonderful 83 million ton harvest of 1930 had allowed the government to export 4.7 million tons of grain. In 1931, grain exports rose to 5.06 million tons – but the harvest itself had collapsed to just under 70 million tons. The state seized the grain by force. The next year was even worse. The harvest was 14 per cent below average, but state procurements from the farmers rose by 44 per cent. Starvation began. The death penalty was enacted for those guilty of pilfering grain on the collective farms, and was later extended to those withholding food. Yuri Moshkov, the Soviet historian of collectivisation, recounts that 'Some kolkhozes in the north Caucasus [of which the Stavropol region is part] and the Ukraine ceased to come under the organising influence of the party and the state' – a euphemism for outright rebellion.[2]

The local Communist Party was purged, with 43 per cent of all investigated members expelled, including more than half of the party secretaries throughout the northern Caucasus. This was a rehearsal for the full-scale purges that were to devastate the party, the army and the nation at large over the next seven years. The difference was that the northern Caucasus had to suffer them twice. But the ruthless reimposition of party authority could not prevent the man-made famine that swept the country in 1932–33. Estimates based on demographic trends during the period suggest that between 5 and 10 million people died of hunger and privation. This was the infancy of Mikhail Gorbachev.[3]

On the face of it, Gorbachev might seem to have little reason to support the Soviet system, let alone embrace it. But he was born into the rural elite. His grandfather Andrei was the founder and chairman of the collective farm, a believer in the system. His father Sergei was a trained operator of tractors and combine harvesters, and a party member of some standing. Gorbachev's official biography describes his father as 'a modest man, deeply respected for his skills and knowledge of economic matters and his wisdom and even-handedness in party affairs'. Something of a mystery emerges here: the official biography states only that his father 'had fought at the front in the Great Patriotic War';[4] but in conversations in Britain during his official visit in December 1984, Gorbachev said that his father had died in the war, and that he had been brought up mainly by his grandparents. Clearly, his family had been fortunate to escape the purges of the party and the collective farm management in the early 1930s. Their loyalty to the system must have been beyond reproach. But Gorbachev was not raised in a dogmatic Marxist home. His mother, Maria Panteleyevna, who was twenty when he was born, still lives in the region. She was in the winter of 1985 a devout and regular churchgoer, according to Orthodox priests who claim to have seen her in the congregation.

The later 1930s saw a slow recovery on the farms, as some of the benefits of collectivisation began to appear, in the form of tractors, health care and schools. Conditions were not good. Collective farmers were paid in bread by the farm, with a tiny cash supplement – on average, enough to buy a pair of shoes over the course of a year. But the farmers' private plots provided extra food, and a potential source of income from produce sold in the free markets. Mikhail Gorbachev's endorsement, when in power, of the individual farmer's right to supplement his income from selling his privately grown fruit and vegetables harks back to his own childhood memories of how vital this tiny extra stipend could be to a rural family.

Soviet education in the 1930s was efficient, in terms of eradicating illiteracy and equipping the future working class with the basic numeric skills, but relentlessly ideological (one popular textbook of the period was entitled *I Want to Be Like Stalin*). However, the rural village school which began the education of the future Soviet leader had only three years to form him before Hitler's war came to conscript his father and, in the summer of 1942, bring his village and his home under enemy occupation. Whether young Mikhail stayed on the farm or was evacuated away from the advancing Germans is unknown, though a university contemporary later recorded that, for the student Gorbachev, 'the war had been a fundamental experience', based largely on the suffering of the civilian population in a theatre where the Nazis behaved with particular barbarity.

The war certainly disrupted Gorbachev's schooling, and the needs of postwar reconstruction meant that, throughout the Soviet Union, children were taken from the classroom to help with the sowing and the harvests. The women, the old and the young had to take on the labour of the adult males who, like Gorbachev's father, had died in the fighting and of those other millions lost in Stalin's camps.

According to his official biography, the young Gorbachev began work immediately after the war, at the age of fourteen, as an assistant to a combine harvester operator at a machine tractor station (MTS). This was an elite job in the countryside, a reflection of his father's prestige. The MTS was the key to Soviet control and transformation of the rural areas. Each MTS served a large area, contained scores of collective farms, and provided the tractors and the harvesters and the mechanical aids needed by each farm. In return, the MTS was paid in grain, and became the state's grain collection agency for its area. It also provided agronomists, evening classes and the inevitable lectures on party ideology. While their machinery and their life of travel made the MTS operators the envy of rural youth, they were also the state's chosen mechanism for bringing the countryside within the Soviet system.

Mikhail Gorbachev proved a model worker. At an exceptionally early age, he was awarded the Order of the Red Banner of Labour, a medal reserved for those who had worked prodigiously hard. It distinguished him from his fellow students at Moscow University when he began his studies there in September 1950. Indeed, given the disrupted nature of his schooling, it probably helped him gain admittance to what was then (as it remains) the most prestigious educational establishment in the country. It is not clear how much of the five years before university he spent at the MTS. One local newspaper biography implies that he continued at school, and that his MTS work was part-time.[5] The official biography says that he graduated from secondary school with the prize of a silver medal. Whatever the details, it was a remarkable leap from a north Caucasus village school to Moscow's law faculty, and the transition provides a vital clue to the evident loyalty that young Gorbachev felt to a system which gave him such an opportunity. His own career is proof of the equality of opportunity that existed in the country that Stalin still ruled.

Moscow in 1950 was a city in the throes of rebuilding; much of the work was performed by German prisoners of war, and by Russian convicts, one of whom was the future novelist Solzhenitsyn. At that time Stalin's personal taste had moved into its gothic phase, and the granite spires that are now characteristic of Moscow's skyline were rising steadily, including the largest of them all, that of Moscow University. But it was not a happy period for Soviet scholarship. Literary and history departments were reeling under the impact of Stalin's dabbling in the theory and ideology of linguistics, and the science faculties were coming to grips with Lysenko's perversion of genetics.

The department of law, in which young Gorbachev enrolled, was a curious choice. In the Soviet Union the law is not the stepping stone to a political or official career, as it is in the West. At the time, it was not even common for members of the College of Advocates to become party members. The best known Soviet lawyer of the day was Andrei Vyshinsky, the prosecutor-general who orchestrated the great show trials of the 1930s, and whose peroration 'Shoot the mad dogs' became a national catchphrase of the day. Vyshinsky later rose to be foreign minister, and died, possibly by his own hand, in 1955, the year of Gorbachev's graduation. Gorbachev may have owed his place at Moscow to the sudden expansion of the Soviet legal profession after the war. The number of law graduates rose from 2000 in 1947 to 8000 by 1955, as new law faculties were opened in universities around the country.[6]

Gorbachev was an exemplary student, the *komsorg kursa* or Komsomol official of his year in the law faculty, and, according to Zdenek Mlynar, a Czech student who was on the same course and lived in the same student residence, passed his final exams with distinction. Mlynar adds that he was intelligent, bright, popular and open-minded. Mlynar himself was a communist of decidedly liberal bent. He rose to become a member of the Czech Politburo in 1967, was a passionate supporter of the Prague Spring under Dubček, and was expelled from the party after the Russian occupation in 1968. In 1977, Mlynar went into exile in the West.[7] That he and the 'open-minded' Gorbachev became personal friends as students suggests that the young man from Stavropol was hardly a typical Stalinist. He was, however, convinced enough to join the party as a full member in 1952, the year before Stalin died.

The death of Stalin in 1953 came as a traumatic shock to a country that had been drilled into his worship. His replacement by Lavrenti Beria, the secret police chief, led to a threat of something close to civil war, as the rest of the Politburo joined with the army to oust him. Tanks appeared at key crossroads in the city as Marshal Zhukov and General Moskalenko arrested Beria in the room where the praesidium was meeting. With this incident following so hard on Stalin's death, the atmosphere of crisis in the city must have been palpable.

A sense of relief followed, whose spirit is captured by Ilya Ehrenburg's aptly titled novel *The Thaw*, published in the spring 1954 editions of *Novy Mir* magazine, under the editorship of Alexander Tvardovsky. *The Thaw* condemned the vaunted 'New Soviet Man' as a self-serving toady, and the approved social realist artist as a barely talented hack. Vera Panova's novel *The Seasons* attacked the corruption of the new upper class of party officials, and Leonid Zorin's play *The Guests* showed that the theatre too was freeing itself of the rigid grip of the Zhdanov decrees. The atmosphere at the university lightened, and discussion became more open, intellectual and cultural life more lively, until the thaw cooled again as 1954 wore on, and Tvardovsky was dismissed from the editorship of *Novy Mir*.[8]

Mikhail Gorbachev never experienced the giddy mood that intoxicated young intellectual Moscow after 1961, when the mass poetry readings began, abstract art suddenly mushroomed and each issue of *Novy Mir* (once again edited by Tvardovsky) was passionately awaited. But in a sense, the false thaw of 1954 was more intense because it had followed two long decades of Stalin's cultural permafrost. The sense of liberation and of boundless new possibilities was particularly strong at the university, in part because of the presence of so many foreign students (albeit from other socialist countries). According to his fellow students, the keen young communist Gorbachev joined happily in the general ferment of what was evidently a seminal period of his life.

In the summer of 1955 Gorbachev went back to the plains of Stavropol to begin his career as a full-time party worker. Doubtless his father's and grandfather's records, and perhaps contacts in the local party hierarchy, helped shape his choice. His first job was deputy head of the propaganda and agitation department of the regional committee of the Komsomol. His responsibility was to watch over the communist morale and training of the teenagers and young people of a region the size of Ireland containing rather fewer than 2 million people.

Recruitment into the Komsomol begins at the age of fourteen, but it is not universal. Only about 70 per cent of those eligible actually join. According to the official statutes its job is:

> to help the party educate youth in the communist spirit, to draw it into the work of building a new society, and to train a rising generation of harmoniously developed people who will live and work and administer public affairs under communism.

The Komsomol is the main avenue of recruitment into the Communist Party, and to be a Komsomol official is the first step on the ladder to a party career. The Komsomol is also a potential workforce; it provides brigades of volunteers to work on major state projects, such as the dams and steel plants of the 1930s, or the BAM railway across Siberia in the 1980s. On his return to Stavropol, Gorbachev was pitchforked into a campaign to recruit Komsomol volunteers for the huge Bratsk dam and power station in central Siberia.

Komsomol 'volunteers', like so much of the rest of the Soviet population, help out with the harvests, and provide voluntary *subbotniks* (literally 'little Saturdays') to the state. Members play a key role in the party machine within the armed forces, because of the high proportion of young conscripts, and they help to organise the younger workforces in the factories. They are represented on the governing bodies of schools and trade unions and in the groups which regulate local culture and education – and, inevitably, given its age range of fourteen to twenty-eight, the Komsomol acts as a kind of vast national marriage bureau.

In the agitation and propaganda section, Gorbachev had to organise lectures, parades and elections. The vast turnouts of 98 and 99 per cent of voters at Soviet elections are not faked. But to get them to the polls, it is normal practice for Komsomol volunteers to visit the homes of every voter, to remind or persuade them to vote. This is the point at which the Soviet political system begins to respond to voters' needs. A citizen unhappy with his housing conditions will say that he would love to vote but cannot make it to the polls because of his worry over the leaking roof. A harassed young mother will say she wants to vote but cannot leave the children because there are no kindergartens. To get 'his' voter out, the Komsomol volunteer will start to badger the bureaucracy on the voter's behalf, by writing letters; or, if need be, enlist the support of a local Komsomol official who is already plugged into the bureaucracy, as was the young Gorbachev.[9]

The young Gorbachev had his own quotas to fulfil. To make a success of his job meant ensuring that his Komsomol teams delivered a uniformly high proportion of voters, that they produced a large number of volunteers for state construction projects, that juvenile delinquency was low. It also meant each year fulfilling his plan for the number of lectures delivered, the number of recruitment and agitation sessions conducted at collective farms around the region and the number of volunteers marching on official parades. It meant organising the local 'agitprop' posters proclaiming 'Glory to Labour' or 'We shall fulfil the five-year plan in four years'. In the Khrushchev era, when almost every year saw radical new reorganisations of the administrative structure of farming and industry, it also meant explaining and justifying the changes to his young farmers and workers.

After less than nine months in the job, in March 1956, Mikhail Gorbachev was called to a meeting held under strict security in the Stavropol party headquarters, where the local first secretary read aloud Khrushchev's 'secret speech', exposing the crimes against the party committed by Joseph Stalin, the man Gorbachev had been brought up to believe was a demigod. He heard of Stalin's incompetence in the early months of the war, and of his refusal to take seriously the constant warnings he received of Hitler's plans to invade. He heard, and heard with a trained lawyer's ear, of the mockery of the 1930s trials, and the gross violations of Soviet law and elementary human decency that marked Stalin's assault on the party cadres. The experience must have been traumatic: the speech has not to this day been published in the Soviet Union; it was kept secret within the bosom of the party.

But the speech neither shook Gorbachev's faith nor interrupted his career. Now married to Raisa, a fellow Moscow graduate with a degree in philosophy who was working on her thesis on the sociology of Stavropol, he was quickly promoted from the agit-prop department to be first secretary of the Komsomol organisation in the city of Stavropol. The local capital and rail centre, with a population of some 200,000, the city was in effect run by its party committee, of which Gorbachev was now a member. The speed of his rise doubtless owed much to his family connections and to what must have seemed, in the sleepy steppes of Stavropol at the time, the awesome qualification of a Moscow University diploma. But it must also have come through his own merits, and through his personal charm, which has struck everyone who has met him, Russian or Western, communist or capitalist.

In 1958, he was promoted again, to be second secretary of the entire regional Komsomol, where his main task was to create the technical education facilities that would train a new generation of workers to exploit the vast natural gas deposits that had been discovered in the area. Traditionally an agricultural region, Stavropol was fast developing into part of a complex providing 40 per cent of the country's gas supplies. In 1960, to ensure that this vital natural resource was properly exploited, Moscow assigned a new party first secretary to the area, Fyodor Kulakov, who was to become the key patron of Gorbachev's career.[10] In the same year, Gorbachev was appointed first secretary of the Komsomol, with a seat on the party's ruling regional council. Again, his charm and undoubted talent made their impression and, in 1962, at the age of thirty-one, he was promoted out of the Komsomol and into the full party hierarchy as organiser of the production administration of the state and collective farms. Gorbachev's new job took him back to the farmland of his boyhood.

When Gorbachev had first returned to Stavropol with his new bride from Moscow, there had been marked improvements in rural life and prosperity. In the five years after Stalin's death, the amount of money available for the collective farms to pay their workforce increased fourfold – although, as much of the pay was in kind, this was less of a startling rise than it seemed. But those five years also saw a series of measures to encourage the use of private plots and livestock. The output of private meat rose by 35 per cent and of milk by more than 25 per cent, and in 1958 private plots were no longer forced to pay a tax on their produce. The opening up to the plough of the virgin lands – hitherto uncultivated soil in central Asia whose combined area was larger than the entire agricultural acreage of Canada – increased the grain harvest from just over 80 million tons in 1953 and 1954 to an average of 120 million tons in the years 1956 to 1958.[11]

Conditions in the rich grain-growing region round Stavropol were particularly prosperous. The state paid 25 roubles a quintal for grain up to the planned production target of each farm, and 80 roubles a quintal for all grain produced above the plan. The fertile Stavropol steppes regularly produced well above the plan, and the farms' incomes rose sharply. But, in 1958, Khrushchev had pushed through a major structural change. After years of collective farms being combined into larger units, he decided that the farms were now big enough to operate their own farm machinery, and the MTS network of centrally held tractors and combines was abolished. The MTS stations became repair shops, and the day-to-day maintenance of the sophisticated equipment was left in the clumsy and barely trained hands of the collective farms. Many of the skilled drivers and mechanics moved to the cities rather than to the farms, and the farms themselves were forced to pay for the 'gift' of this equipment, which meant that less cash was available for other investment or to pay their own farmers. The collective farms were much less powerful than the state-backed MTS organisation had been, and overall production of farm machinery began to fall sharply.

The result was not agricultural disaster but a failure to profit from the huge investments that had been poured into agriculture. Harvests stagnated, peasants trickled steadily away from the land, and Moscow's spasmodic interference in the farming process continued to cause chaos. Khrushchev's sudden passion for growing maize was followed by a determination to stop Stalin's old system of crop rotation, which led to lunacies such as the ploughing up of clover fields in order to report back to Moscow that the area under grass had been successfully reduced.[12]

These blunders and sudden fits and starts in policy, which also afflicted the industrial sector and indeed the very structure of government under Khrushchev, were less onerous in the fertile north Caucasus than elsewhere. They were nevertheless highly tiresome for a keen and ambitious young official such as Gorbachev, who knew that his future would depend on producing good results. But his career was progressing well. In 1961, he went back to Moscow as one of the 5000 delegates to the twenty-second congress of the Communist Party, and found the city transformed.

While a student, Gorbachev had not been allowed inside the walls of the Kremlin, a zone guarded for the privacy of Stalin and dignity of his government. But Khrushchev had thrown open large parts of the Kremlin grounds and the churches and Tsarist apartments as a public museum. He had also launched the Kremlin's biggest building project for 150 years: the erection of a new Palace of Congresses. A vast auditorium capable of seating the 5000 congress delegates and another 1000 guests and foreign dignitaries, it is a modernistic building of glass, steel and concrete whose contemporary roofline peeps incongruously over the old brick Kremlin battlements. When not in use for party rallies, the Palace of Congresses serves as a supertheatre for the Bolshoi company. Indeed, its penthouse buffet, to which an array of escalators can whisk 6000 people for canapes, sandwiches and (until Mr Gorbachev's new dry law) glasses of champagne, is the pride of Moscow's otherwise grim public catering system. To the young Gorbachev, it must have seemed the very image of the bright communist future.

1961 was the year when the Soviet Union sent the first man into space, reinforcing the international prestige it had won with the first Sputnik launched four years earlier; and Yuri Gagarin, the first cosmonaut and the living symbol of communism's achievements, was, like Gorbachev, a delegate to the party congress. As the young delegate from Stavropol gazed from the buffet windows at the Moscow skyline, at the seven gothic towers bequeathed by Stalin's architectural plans, at the streets busy with cars and the shops filled with consumer goods that had not been available in his student days, he must have been awed by the achievements of the system of which he was now a rising young representative. More than that, as one of 5000 delegates in a party of 10 million members, he must have felt proud to be an heir to the future which the transformed Moscow seemed to embody.

It was one of the best of times to be a communist. In the rest of the world, the colonial empires of France and Britain were passing away, just as Lenin had prophesied they would. The newly independent nations were sympathetic to the Soviet Union, and in these last months before the Sino-Soviet split, the onward march of socialism seemed to be proceeding according to plan. The crimes of Stalin had been exposed to the party in 1956, and were to be exposed more publicly at this congress of 1961 – publicly enough to inspire Alexander Solzhenitsyn to send his novel of the gulag *A Day in the Life of Ivan Denisovich* to Tvardovsky, reinstalled as editor of *Novy Mir*. Gorbachev himself was to vote for the resolution that wrenched Stalin's corpse from pride of place beside Lenin in the Red Square mausoleum; it read:

> . . . the grave violations by Stalin of Lenin's behests, his abuses of power, mass repressions of honest Soviet people and other actions at the time of his personality cult make it impossible to leave the coffin with his body inside the Lenin mausoleum.

The mood of heady confidence gripped the whole congress. It was a time of youth and reform, and the party rules were amended to limit party officials to no more than three terms, or fifteen years, of office, and to require that at least a third of the members of every party committee be changed at each election. And it was time for a new party programme, a manifesto of the party's visions and strategy for the future. The first party programme had been adopted with the foundation of the Bolshevik Party in 1903, and called for the planning and achievement of the revolution that would overthrow the Tsar. Once installed in power, Lenin drew up a second programme, which called for the establishment of the dictatorship of the proletariat and the industrialisation of the country. That too, it seemed, had been accomplished, and it was time for the party to set itself new goals.

The third party programme, adopted at the congress which Gorbachev attended, was a frankly utopian document. Socialism had been achieved, it claimed, and Marx's dream of full communism lay in wait, just beyond the horizon. Within twenty years, the third party programme enthused, the Soviet people would be outproducing the USA. It concluded: 'The party solemnly proclaims – the present generation of Soviet people shall live in communism.'[14]

With Yuri Gagarin sitting in the same hall as him, Gorbachev may have felt that such miracles were now within the party's grasp. But a moment's reflection must have taught him better. He knew how poorly the collective farmers still lived, even in a zone as prosperous as Stavropol. As a career-minded party worker, the new rules must have given him considerable pause for thought. If he could hold an elected party rank for no more than ten years, what would this imply for his future? And what would it imply for his patron, Fyodor Kulakov, to whose good offices he owed his place at the party congress? Would he not be replaced by a new man, with protégés of his own?

Over the next three years, thoughts such as these gripped the minds, and the self-interest, of party officials around the country. Not only had Khrushchev set them an impossible target; he was also striking at their career patterns, at their livelihoods and their job security. At the same time, he was making an increasing mess of his own job at the Kremlin. The state of foreign affairs looked grim, even through the pages of *Pravda*, with the Sino-Soviet split widening and the Cuba missile crisis of 1962 making thermonuclear war loom suddenly and desperately close. However great the merits of socialism might seem in the Kremlin Palace of Congresses, they were not enough to keep the East German comrades from fleeing into West Berlin until the Warsaw Pact was put to the humiliation and expense of erecting the Wall.

On the domestic front, Khrushchev's constant interference in the work of local officials and his spasmodic agricultural enthusiasms were becoming more than tiresome. When his Czech friend Mlynar came to visit him in Stavropol in 1967, Gorbachev himself criticised Khrushchev strongly for the constant reorganisations of the farms and industry.[15]

From 1963, when he took over running the party organs department of the Stavropol region, Gorbachev was in a position to monitor the growing grumbles of the party officials. The trade union and Komsomol chiefs reported to him, and he was custodian of the local *Nomenklatura* catalogue, the list of the key jobs in administration, farms and industry that were appointed by the party, and of the even more crucial list of the names of party members deemed suitable and qualified for these posts when vacancies occurred. Gorbachev had to report regularly on the mood and concerns of party officials to his first secretary and patron, Kulakov; and those concerns centred chiefly on the implications that Khrushchev's new rules had for their party careers.

This came as little surprise to Kulakov. As a member of the central committee, and a regular visitor to Moscow, he knew that such worries were widespread – and as 1964 wore on, he learned that there were some senior Politburo figures who were planning to do something about them. The speed with which Kulakov moved to a top job in the central committee secretariat after Khrushchev's fall strongly implies that he was privy to the party coup which toppled Khrushchev in October. The coup had been plotted by Leonid Brezhnev and the party's ideologist Mikhail Suslov. Suslov, as a former first secretary of the Stavropol region, was Kulakov's patron. Leonid Brezhnev's close friend Konstantin Chernenko was another powerful ally at court for Kulakov; the two men had worked together in the party committee in Penza in the immediate postwar years. Through Kulakov, Gorbachev could count on some extremely influential friends in the new Moscow hierarchy that replaced Khrushchev.[16] And in the next few years, Kulakov himself became a powerful man, elected a full member of the Politburo in 1971, while still retaining his post as a secretary of the central committee.

It may have been Kulakov's influence, or it may have been pure chance, but Gorbachev's career benefited at this time from a stroke of remarkable luck. The post of first secretary of a rich farming and natural-gas-producing region such as Stavropol is an important one in the Soviet Union. It carries with it an almost automatic seat on the central committee, and its holder has an influential voice in all policy decisions concerning agriculture. Kulakov had been promoted to Moscow as head of the agricultural department in the central committee secretariat, leaving the first secretaryship free. This is a perfect post for a young man on the way up; it was Gorbachev's good fortune that it was also suitable for an older man on the way down.

Leonid Yefremov had been appointed a candidate (non-voting) member of the Politburo by Khrushchev two years earlier, and Khrushchev's fall meant that another, lesser post had to be found for him. He was sent to Stavropol as first secretary to await his eventual retirement, which finally came in 1970, the year before the twenty-fourth party congress. The timing is important here. The party congress, held every five years, elects the central committee and had Yefremov still been first secretary of Stavropol at the time of the congress, he would inevitably have been re-elected to the central committee for another five years. Rather than this being permitted, Yefremov was retired in 1970, and replaced by Mikhail Gorbachev, who was thus elected to the central committee in 1971, at the remarkably young age of thirty-nine.

Gorbachev did not waste the six years waiting for Yefremov's inevitable eclipse. Doubtless with the distant support of Kulakov, he moved steadily up the party ladder, becoming first secretary of Stavropol city in 1966 and, two years later, second secretary of the region and Yefremov's deputy. He also used this time to obtain a second degree, in agronomy, at the local Stavropol college, just as Kulakov had done before him.[17] He was thus both a trained lawyer and a qualified specialist in agriculture, a rare and useful combination in the Soviet Union. His rise through the party ranks had groomed him for the succession, and his degree meant that there could be little objection to his taking over the first secretaryship of such a key farming region.

The Stavropol area has other natural attractions. Some of the finest spas in the Soviet Union, and some of the most delightful summer retreats, are to be found in the south of the region, where the foothills begin their slow and awesome rise to the great Caucasus mountain chain. Krasny Kamny (or 'red rocks') has been a favoured summer resort of Russia's rulers for over a century. But few enjoyed it more than Yuri Andropov, who took his summer vacation in the discreet comfort of the Politburo rest house in the hills that loom over Narzan and produce the finest mineral water in the Soviet Union.

Andropov became the director of the KGB in 1967, and one of the most powerful men in the country. Protocol required that his regular visits to Krasny Kamny be marked by a courtesy call from the region's first secretary, Mikhail Gorbachev. Andropov must have been intrigued by this bright young man with influential friends in Moscow. Doubtless he would have checked the KGB files and found not a whiff of scandal or corruption. Like so many people before and after him, the KGB chief was charmed by his engaging personality. As Gorbachev's official biography puts it, in an unusual foray into personal matters:[18]

Gorbachev was able to captivate people with his brilliance, and to interest them. He was not embarrassed to learn from friends, to adopt better ideas and to support new ones. His originality of thought and his charm attracted people to him.

Furthermore the forty-year-old man with his two degrees, his intellectual wife and pretty, intelligent daughter must have seemed to Andropov and his generation living proof that their work so far had been justified. The education of the men in their sixties and seventies who were then running the Politburo had been scraped together at night school and party colleges while they were simultaneously pushing through five-year plans, fighting world wars and worrying about the purges. A rising young scion of the system such as Gorbachev may have inspired a touch of envy, but also some self-congratulation. This was exactly the kind of new Soviet man they had been trying to produce.

Andropov came to know him well, seeking him out at central committee sessions in Moscow, and spending hours walking with him in the woods around Kislovodsk each summer. Gorbachev became a friend of the family, and not only of Andropov's family. At the numerous Politburo funerals of the 1980s, it was striking how often Gorbachev was the only senior figure who would personally embrace the bereaved widow and family and sit with them beside the bier where another once vigorous old man lay in state with his medals.

Gorbachev was invited to Andropov's Moscow home, a remarkably modest single-bedroomed flat in the Politburo block at 26 Kutuzovsky Prospekt. Above and below Andropov, other top officials occupied whole floors. One was Brezhnev; the other was the corrupt police chief and interior minister Nikolai Shchelokov, who was to be disgraced almost as soon as Andropov came to power.

A pleasant and promising companion, Gorbachev was also producing some impressive results from his agrarian region; this was all the more important as the era of massive Soviet grain imports began in the early 1970s. Gorbachev's success could be attributed partly to the fact that Soviet fertiliser production was finally coming on stream and the Stavropol region was able to make excellent use of it. But it was mainly on account of his readiness to use daring methods of incentive payments to encourage farms to overfulfil their plans. Gorbachev did not pioneer these working methods, nor at first did he trumpet them abroad – particularly after the minister of agriculture in 1970 criticised the way they divided farm workers into the new rich and the traditional poor.

In effect, the reform Gorbachev adopted allowed a handful of farm workers to sign a contract with their collective under which they would take on responsibility for a patch of land. They would plough, sow, weed, fertilise it, and supervise the harvest. They would be paid by results – a strong incentive – and they would be responsible for the same patch of land each year, which gave them a further incentive to treat and prepare the land well, rather than exhaust it, and to supervise drainage throughout the winter. 'As a rule, these teams obtain 20–30 per cent more produce from a given area, with lower outlays of labour and resources,' Gorbachev later wrote.[19] In 1976, he pushed through a resolution on the Stavropol central committee which set the goal of restricting the working of all the arable land in the region to mechanised teams of this type.

Then the whole process was thrown into reverse. There were ideological doubts about the principle behind the system, which was seen as undermining the very justification of the collective farm. Other supporters of the incentive-team system found themselves sacked and even disgraced. Gorbachev moved too fast for that. He announced another new principle, known as the Ipatovo method, after the district where it was pioneered. It was a throwback to the Stalin-style dream of the 1930s, the MTS stations on which he had worked as a boy. Huge fleets of tractors and combine harvesters were centralised and sent off like so many land armadas across the corn fields. In the first year, used on land that had been lovingly prepared and sown by the old incentive teams, the Ipatovo method scored excellent results across the whole of Stavropol. Brezhnev sent his personal congratulations, and Mikhail Gorbachev was summoned to Moscow as the farming superstar, the new secretary for agriculture on the central committee.[20]

But back on the plains of Stavropol, the harvests were dwindling as the farmworkers ceased to tend the fields that were no longer theirs to profit from. The great fleets of machinery looked wonderful on television news, but they worked at their own preordained pace, rather than when a particular plot of land was ripe for harvest. The Ipatovo method is heard of no more; and, four years after Gorbachev's triumphant departure for Moscow, *Izvestia* reported that the harvesting system in Stavropol was in poor shape, with 19,000 workers drafted in from the towns to help out on the fields.

In 1978, Fyodor Kulakov died. Gorbachev succeeded him as the central committee's secretary for agriculture at Moscow's Staraya Ploshadz, the real seat of power in the Soviet Union. The yellowish baroque building that houses the central committee secretariat is the heart of the party bureaucracy. If the ministers have the burden of day-to-day administration of the industries, the relevant central committee secretary sets the strategy and sees that it is carried out. By custom the secretaries attend Politburo meetings, although they do not vote, and they prepare the briefs which the Politburo discusses. They also transmit the Politburo decisions down through the system.

Gorbachev began with a bang. The harvest of 1978–79 was the finest the Soviet Union had ever known, producing 237 million tons of grain. Long-term purchase arrangements meant that 15 million tons still had to be imported,[21] but almost 20 million tons were stockpiled for the future. His success led to his being appointed a candidate member of the Politburo in November 1979 – which was exactly the point when his career might have started to go wrong.

As the harvests in Stavropol began to decline, so did the general agricultural output of the country. The harvest of 1979–80 was one of the worst of the decade, producing less that 180 million tons. The foreign exchange reserves had to be raided to buy 31 million tons of grain abroad, just as the American grain embargo after the invasion of Afghanistan had precluded a turn to the usual supplier. At 189 million tons, the following year's harvest was little better, and the 1981–82 harvest was the worst of all, a bare 160 million tons, and 46 million more tons had to be imported.

This dismal record took some explaining. Gorbachev not only survived; he convinced the Politburo that he knew what was wrong and how to put it right. First, he argued, Soviet agriculture was in the long term a considerable success. In the thirty years since 1950, agricultural output had grown by a steady 3 per cent a year (better than the US or EEC record), in spite of a shortage of good farmland and a desperately hard climate. The Soviet people were eating better than ever before, and in this sense the problems of agriculture were the problems of success. Higher living standards meant that people were eating only two thirds as much bread as they had in 1960 but much more meat, eggs, milk and vegetables. The problem with the grain harvest lay not in producing wheat for bread – the Soviet Union was self-sufficient in bread – but in providing fodder for the ever-swelling livestock herds.

Second, Gorbachev went on, anybody who had spent time on the land recently knew perfectly well what was needed. It was not any grandiose new scheme to bring more virgin land under the plough or to divert rivers to make the barren deserts bloom. It was much simpler than that. Country roads were so bad that a lorry lost at least a tenth of its load travelling from field to farm, and another tenth between farm and railhead. The Politburo had to provide funds to build an efficient rural transport system.

Third, there was the storage problem. There were no warehouses at the railhead, so that fertiliser that came in was soaked by rain until it cemented together in vast slag heaps all over the country. The grain waiting to be shipped out was nibbled by vermin, rotted by rain or blown away by the wind.

The cheap way to solve the storage and the rural transport problems together, the future party leader suggested, was to process the food much closer to the places where it was grown. The canning factories, the slaughter houses and the grain mills ought to be concentrated in regional agro-industrial centres. This would save railway space, cut losses in transit and ease the growing population pressures on the cities. Such concentrations would also provide urban and cultural centres within easy reach of the farms, thereby improving the leisure opportunities for the farm workers and stemming their disastrous drift from the land. It would give farmers' sons and daughters better and wider job opportunities and reduce the great cultural rift between town and country.

Gorbachev's presentation was clear and well argued, based on his authority as a qualified agronomist and as one who was nearer the countryside and the seat of a tractor than any other man around the Politburo table. He had two further points to make, but they had to be made with caution, dealing as they did with the vexed problems of private enterprise and supplementary earnings. From his boyhood, Gorbachev had known that the private plot was essential to the peasant's survival in hard times, and to his modest comfort even when the harvests were good. The private plots, he told the Politburo, took up about 3 per cent of the country's arable land, but they produced something like a quarter of the food. This was a smaller share than ten years ago, as the output of the big state farms in basic foodstuffs such as grain, milk and meat was rising steadily. But private produce was still an essential element of the Soviet diet.

This was a difficult subject to raise with Leonid Brezhnev, who saw himself as the saviour of the private plots after Khrushchev's spasmodic attempts to eradicate them. Immediately after toppling Khrushchev, Brezhnev had issued a decree halting the confiscation of private plots and authorising the state banks to lend peasants money in order to buy cows. Gorbachev argued that matters had to go further. He wanted the maximum acreage of the private plot to be increased beyond 0.5 hectare, and in this he failed. He wanted the limits on the numbers of private cattle owned by each household to be abolished, and he wanted the collective farms themselves to be authorised to provide fodder, veterinary and other services to the privately owned livestock. In these aims he was successful, and a decree giving effect to them was passed in 1981.[22]

Gorbachev also sought to extend the principle of team incentive labour which had served him so well in Stavropol. He did not win acceptance of this proposal, but the overall package of reforms that he put forward was endorsed by the Politburo and launched with considerable fanfare as the food programme of 1982. Oddly enough, Gorbachev did not himself present the plan to the plenary meeting of the full central committee in May 1982. In a subsequent article published in party journals to explain the implications of the programme, he made a point of stressing Brezhnev's 'leading role' in its composition, as if deliberately avoiding responsibility for a programme he knew to be flawed.[23]

In the event, Gorbachev did not have to wait long. Within six months, Brezhnev was dead, and in one of his first speeches as party leader, Yuri Andropov promised 'a wider independence and autonomy for industrial associations and farms'. The following spring, Gorbachev himself announced that the missing link in the food programme had been effectively restored. He called it the 'collective contract in farm production': giving autonomous teams of farm workers the right to draw up long-term contracts with management that would let them organise their own work, and decide their own pay packets, which would be linked to the amount of food they produced. Moreover, Gorbachev added, these teams should be allowed to elect their own leaders.

When an influential man like Gorbachev says that such things 'should be allowed to happen', it does not necessarily mean that they will. The capacity of the Russian bureaucracy for smothering good ideas has been legendary since Peter the Great gave the country its first professional civil service nearly 300 years ago. In Russia, a job in the bureaucracy has always meant prestige and status. Indeed, Peter the Great institutionalised the system of status by establishing a series of quasi-military ranks for the civil services that led, above a certain level, into the nobility. It was under this system, curiously enough, that the father of Vladimir Lenin, as an inspector of schools, was raised to the ranks of the aristocracy.

Almost by definition, any reform in Russia has involved tampering with the powerful tradition of bureaucratic status – which meant that a considerable proportion of the bureaucracy was bound to be against reform and seek to frustrate it. The communist reforms of the system of administration have modified this tradition, but not eradicated it. The sheer size of the Soviet Union has always given a wide degree of latitude to the local administration, so very far from Moscow. The 146 first secretaries of the party in the various *oblasts* and *krais* into which the country is divided have powers analogous to those of the Tsarist governor-generals. Indeed, it was the breadth of powers that Gorbachev enjoyed as first secretary of Stavropol that enabled him to make his reputation as an agricultural miracle worker by authorising the use of the team incentive system.

But the ministries have powers too. Regions without cooper-ative friends in the right ministry (and there are eighty-five sepa-tare ministries) will find it difficult to get enough stocks of fertiliser or to secure any increase in the number of tractors and threshing machines they are authorised to buy. If a collective farm manager wants to give his farm workers something to strive for, he has not only to obtain more money to pay them, he has to induce the local trade organisations to ship some decent consumer goods to the farm shop. So the local trade organisations have to persuade the ministry of light industry to allocate them more products. At every link in the endless chain, one bureaucrat can frustrate the process.

The Brezhnev years clogged this system into virtual immobility, because his policy of 'stability of cadres' (see page 26) meant that it was very difficult to fire or shift a party official or bureaucrat who was not up to the job. To penetrate this vast bureaucratic log-jam (which, the bureaucracy itself has calculated, produces 30,000 million documents each year[24]) required a network of personal contacts and, increasingly, outright corruption. Even if the entire bureaucracy was wholeheartedly behind Gorbachev's call for an extension of the team incentive system on the farms, the vast administrative machine was simply not flexible enough to cope.

First, the system involved a revolution in the method of financing the 26,000 collective farms and the 13 million households which lived and worked on them. To pay them all in accordance with the plan was complex enough. When arrangements had to be made to pay them by results, for crops that could not be calculated in advance, an accountant's nightmare ensued. How many extra roubles should be printed? Which account at the state banks should hold the sums for payment? How much should be paid in advance, and how long would it take to calculate the crop totals to find out how much each farm had to receive? Then there was the railway problem. How many extra trains and grain wagons should be reserved for harvest time? Where should the extra crops be stored, and how many thousands or millions of extra tons would there be?

A very large part of the administrative burden for the Gorbachev reform would fall on the shoulders of the collective farm chairman and his own management staff. These people were already trying to cope with the changes involved in the rest of the food programme, adjusting the traditional supply and delivery patterns to make them compatible with the new regional agro-industrial centres. Now they had to decide whether to go over to the complex new system, to supervise the elections of the team leaders, arrange a method to calculate how much each team had produced at harvest time, and work out how much cash to subtract for the team's use of the farm's machinery and other services. And, worst of all, whatever extra cash this new system produced was going into the pockets of the farm labourers. There were no such incentives for the farm managers and chairmen. The result was that many of them gave up their white collars and went back to the land to earn the extra money in the incentive teams, leaving the farm administration in utter chaos.[25]

One of the vital tasks of the Communist Party is to prevent this kind of chaos. There are almost two million full-time party workers round the country, and their role as a parallel state administration includes riding hard on administrative reforms to see that they are pushed through. A reform which does not have the party's support and commitment is doomed to dwindle away into the Russian earth. While there were many self-seeking reasons for the party machine not to throw itself wholeheartedly into implementing the team incentive system, there was one ideological problem which gave even the most honest party member pause for thought. Was this genuine communism, this system which was dividing the farm workers into the hard-working, almost self-employed rich and the rest?

This point was raised repeatedly as Gorbachev and Andropov tried to spread the doctrine of economic reforms throughout the economy. In the vital electronics industry, they attempted to develop an economic experiment that had been launched in Georgia in the 1970s, giving individual factories the right to retain up to 40 per cent of their profits and distribute those profits as incentives to the workforce. The money could be paid in direct cash bonuses or into the factory's social fund to provide extra holidays or other benefits; it could even be used to invest in more modern machinery to boost production and generate more profits in the future. The plan did not work quite as intended. Directors of electronics plants in Latvia and Lithuania, where the 'economic experiment' had been greeted with enthusiasm, were frank in explaining to foreign journalists why the standard cash incentives were having little effect. 'If a worker gets more money that's fine, but what does he do with it?' Aris Kokars of the Straume factory asked. 'If he wants to buy a car or to get a new apartment, money is not going to help. We have to try and get special authorisation from the city housing committee or the trade organisation, and that will mean getting approval from the party, which does not always see things our way.'[26]

For Mikhail Gorbachev in Moscow, promoted by Andropov to the position of central committee secretary with broad responsibilities for the economy, his mandate for reform was a challenge that involved a cruel paradox. To be in office in Moscow did not necessarily mean to have power. This cannot have come as a surprise to a man who had spent the previous twenty-five years rising through the ranks of the party hierarchy, learning the prerogatives and limitations of each job he held, and developing an intimate acquaintance with the capacity of the local party machine to initiate, to delay and to survive. But Gorbachev was now, in a curious way, a victim of the very system which had helped him to rise. He was at the controls, but the machine did not respond as he wished.

It was a lesson that both Khrushchev and Stalin had learned before him. In order to achieve change in the Soviet Union, the party itself must be reformed. Khrushchev had tried to force through change – and had built a coalition of opposition that toppled him from his job. In the 1930s, Stalin had succeeded in remaking the party to his own specification, but at the ruinous cost of the mass purges which had discredited and brutalised his entire reign. As he waited for what was already looking like an inevitable succession to the leadership, Mikhail Gorbachev from the Stavropol collective farm knew that he had to find a better way.

2

The New Generation of the Party Leadership

In February 1984, the third in a sad line of elderly invalids was elevated to the general secretaryship of the Communist Party, the job which Stalin had built into a synonym for Soviet leadership. Konstantin Chernenko was seventy-two, with a full head of carefully groomed white hair, and he wheezed his way through the public speeches he was required to deliver. Western doctors quickly diagnosed chronic emphysema, a disease of the lungs which is neither necessarily nor speedily fatal, but is certainly debilitating. It was a pathetic front to present to the Soviet people, and to the rest of the world.

Leonid Brezhnev had at least enjoyed ten vigorous years as Soviet leader before declining into the long illness that reduced him to the image seen on Western television screens of the barely mobile man being lifted from his chair and half carried by his aides. His successor, Yuri Andropov, had appeared relatively healthy for eight months before succumbing to the kidney disease that was to keep him from the public eye for the last six months of his reign. But Chernenko was visibly ill when he came to power.

The Soviet Union seemed to be governed by a gerontocracy, and the Politburo itself might have been an adjunct of the Kremlin hospital. A superpower ruled by old and ailing men, it was based on an economy whose dependence on Western grain imports made it seem as tired and moribund as its leaders. The country, and the Soviet system, could hardly have presented a more vulnerable target to its Western critics. With its armies fighting guerillas in Afghanistan, and tens of thousands of its citizens campaigning to leave the country, President Reagan's jibe about 'the evil empire' struck hard. The sad parade of old men hauling themselves painfully up the last steps to the podium above Lenin's tomb on Red Square seemed to embody a system whose time was spent.

On May Day 1984, Konstantin Chernenko walked slowly through the tiny postern gate in the Kremlin's east wall and into Lenin's tomb – resembling as much bunker as mausoleum, the tomb's squat bulk is composed of huge slabs of red and black, granite and marble. The vastness of Red Square was already half filled by the crowds waiting to see the parade of workers carrying paper flowers and pulling floats that boasted of their factory's achievements. Flower stalls and trolleys sold tea and buns. Before the march-past began, the crowd looked up at the podium to see the old men who ruled them.

The elderly Chernenko was followed by the seventy-five-year-old defence minister, Marshal Dmitri Ustinov, and by Premier Nikolai Tikhonov, who was seventy-nine, by Boris Ponomarev, seventy-nine, who had looked after relations with non-ruling Communist Parties since the end of the Second World War. After him came the deputy head of state, Vassily Kuznetsov, who was eighty-three, and foreign minister Andrei Gromyko, seventy-four.

These were men who remembered everything. They had been just starting their party careers when Stalin launched his purges, so they remembered fear. They were already in positions of responsibility when Hitler's armies reached the gates of Moscow, so they remembered the imminence of defeat, and the kind of sacrifices the Soviet people could make and still survive. And they remembered, perhaps most clearly of all, the victory of 1945, which seemed to justify beyond all question the system to which they had pledged their lives.

Ustinov had run the biggest arms factory in the country as the German tanks raced towards Leningrad, and had then organised the most staggering evacuation in history as some 1500 entire factories were packed up, loaded onto trains and trans-shipped to the Urals and the far dry lands of Kazakhstan to be reassembled and start work again.[1] Kuznetsov, the man in charge of metallurgy on the state defence committee, had somehow found the high-quality armoured steel to build the tanks and the guns that stopped Hitler.[2] Gromyko, as ambassador in Washington in the war years, had persuaded the Americans to send the trucks and the food and the lend-lease equipment that made the Red Army mobile, and had helped draft the map of the transformed postwar world with Stalin, Roosevelt and Churchill at Yalta in 1945.[3]

They were formidable men, in spite of their years. In another country or another system, they might by that time have been in honourable and comfortable retirement, their experience and their wisdom still available at the state's request, their memoirs being drafted to pass on to another generation their insights and the memories of the staggering times through which they had lived. But part of their memories, and an abiding fear of the Stalin years, told them of the iron law of Soviet power: thou shalt not retire.

They had helped establish that law. They had survived under Stalin, when execution was a conventional way to end a political career. They had known Khrushchev and supported him when he exposed Stalin's crimes to the party and made it clear that a man could lose his job without necessarily losing his head. They had seen Khrushchev toppled and sent into a retirement that was a long disgrace, with his family sacked from their plush jobs. And they had prospered through the two decades of Brezhnev, whose precept was 'faith in the cadres, stability of cadres' (confidence in and stability of the party officials). It was a confidence that worked both ways. Officials were kept secure in their jobs and their privileges; while Brezhnev was given party support, made the subject of lavish speeches of gross flattery and awarded endless medals testifying to his wartime exploits. They were not heroic days, under Brezhnev, but they were stable. For anyone who had lived under Stalin, or who had tried to administer the country while Khrushchev was making sudden calls for every peasant to plant maize, or for all the tractors to be given to the farmers, or for all the ministries to be relocated far from Moscow, or some such harebrained scheme, there was a lot to be said for stability.

No great threats loomed to breach that stability. The country had the missiles and the warheads that meant security from the kind of attacks it had lived through in 1941. The army had been given the tanks and guns it needed to ward off other menaces. While the KGB had been tamed from the ravenous beast it had become under Stalin, it was effective enough to control internal dissent – and there was little enough of that. The Soviet people were living better than ever before, and were confident that, every year, life would improve slightly, that holidays would be lengthened or the shops stock more food and more consumer goods. Basic foods were cheap, and children were being given a decent education. The Russians all had jobs, which was more than Western leaders could say for their people. The system worked. The old men could feel that they had succeeded.

But on the same podium stood a group of seven much younger men, ranging in years from fifty-three to sixty-one. The eldest was the former party chieftain of Leningrad, Grigory Romanov, who was now a secretary of the central committee, in charge of the defence industries, while also being a full member of the Politburo. Custom and the realities of power had made the simultaneous tenure of both these jobs a prerequisite for appointment to the leadership as general secretary.[4] The only other man who was both a full member of the Politburo and a central committee secretary was the youngest man on Lenin's tomb, Mikhail Gorbachev, who was fifty-three. His portfolio, which included overseeing the economy, ideology and senior party appointments, made him in effect the second most influential man in the country, after Chernenko.[5] But his eventual succession was not guaranteed. Chernenko might live for some years, enough time for others to consolidate their positions.

One man whose origins in the traditionally Muslim republic of Azerbaijan made it unlikely he would ever succeed to the top post was Geidar Aliev, sixty, a full member of the Politburo and the only career KGB officer among them.[6] Over the previous fifteen years, Aliev had become a party official, first secretary of Azerbaijan and now the deputy prime minister. The head of the KGB, sixty-one-year-old Viktor Chebrikov, had been brought into the management structure of the KGB from a professional party career when he was in his forties. He was only a candidate member of the Politburo, able to attend meetings, but not entitled to a vote. The need for a vote rarely arose, however, in a system where decisions were usually reached by consensus, and Geidar Aliev had seen no formal vote being taken since he had been brought onto the Politburo eight years earlier.[7]

There was only one other full member among the group of younger men, fifty-eight-year-old Vitaly Vorotnikov, who had been brought into the Politburo as a candidate eight months earlier and suddenly promoted to full membership immediately before Andropov's death. An honest and efficient administrator, Vorotnikov had been sent off to Cuba as ambassador after falling foul of one of Brezhnev's corrupt cronies who had been misruling the important grain district of Krasnodar. When Brezhnev fell, so did the crony, and Vorotnikov had been brought back to replace him. After cleaning up the Krasnodar district, Vorotnikov was summoned to Moscow by Yuri Andropov to become premier of the vast Russian republic, by far the largest of the fifteen republics that make up the USSR. Under Andropov, Vorotnikov's rise had been dramatic in its speed, but his career was unlikely to prosper under Chernenko.[8]

Vladimir Dolgikh, on the other hand, had high hopes of the Chernenko succession. He was a brilliant engineer and technocrat who had made his name by developing the mining complex of Norilsk near the Arctic Ocean, and had then sharply increased output and productivity in the important Siberian heavy industrial zone of Krasnoyarsk, where Chernenko's own party career had begun. A leading troubleshooter in the Soviet economy, he had next been ordered to solve the looming energy crisis in the western Siberian gas fields, which he had done with considerable success. Dolgikh would probably have risen on his merits, but he was one of the few Politburo members to have come from a powerful family – his father had been a high official in the ministry of internal affairs. After Dolgikh's achievements in Krasnoyarsk, Chernenko had become his patron, and the month before the 1984 May Day parade Chernenko had shown the fifty-nine-year-old technocrat a signal mark of favour by inviting him to be present at the new general secretary's first public appearance, among the workers at Moscow's Hammer and Sickle factory.[9]

The last of the seven younger men was Eduard Shevardnadze, from the relaxed southern republic of Georgia. Fifty-six years old, Shevardnadze was a former police chief who had risen to power in Georgia through purging the previous party leadership and the vast network of corruption it had bred.[10] A plain-living man, and more abstemious than most of his countrymen, he was given to haranguing his fellow Georgians, reminding them that they came from a great race of heroes and poets and honest farmers and accusing them of degenerating into conmen and black marketeers. Like Geidar Aliev of the neighbouring republic of Azerbaijan, who had also risen to power by purging a corrupt local party regime, he had been a protégé of Yuri Andropov, and could expect few favours from Chernenko.

As the two groups of the old men and the young raised their hands in salute to that May Day parade, they could have been characters in a Shakespeare play. Like the Montagues and Capulets, or like the Yorkists and Lancastrians in the Wars of the Roses, they were divided less by their relative age than by their allegiance to two dead men.

Some owed their careers and their prominence to Leonid Brezhnev, others owed their rise to Yuri Andropov; all had lived through the years of Kremlin guerilla warfare between the two men. It had never become an open breach but, in the last months of Brezhnev's life, Andropov had been exposing scandal after scandal and bringing the taint of corruption ever closer to Brezhnev himself. Brezhnev's daughter had been questioned, and some of her friends arrested. Brezhnev's brother-in-law, himself a deputy head of the KGB, had been found dead in mysterious circumstances. And in the republics far beyond Moscow, the provincial party leaders who had given Brezhnev their support and entertained him to lavish parties and hunting trips were being investigated and even arrested by the hard-faced young men with accountancy skills who made up Yuri Andropov's fraud squad and anti-corruption task force.[11]

Most of the old men were from the Brezhnev faction, and most of them had served with him during his rise to power, when he built the party machine in Moldavia, where Chernenko had joined him, and rebuilt the war-shattered industrial complex of Dnepropetrovsk. Tikhonov owed his influence to the Dnepropetrovsk mafia, as did the first secretary of the Ukraine party, Vladimir Shcherbitsky. The other regional party boss on the Politburo was the seventy-two-year-old Dinmukhamed Kunayev, the party chief of the second largest republic of Kazakhstan. He had first worked with Brezhnev in the 1950s. Flushed with success from Dnepropetrovsk, Brezhnev had been sent to northern Kazakhstan to run the virgin lands scheme, bringing the untilled steppes under plough. These two mighty provincial barons had reason to fear the Andropov group. Shcherbitsky had lost nine of his twenty-five regional party secretaries to Andropov's anti-corruption squads, and Kunayev had been ordered to purge a third of his own.[12] In the Communist Party, power comes from the ability not only to promote your own supporters but also to protect them. Andropov's purges struck at the very roots of power.

The Brezhnev group did not consist entirely of the old guard with decades of political debts and deals behind them. No whiff of scandal attached to Vladimir Dolgikh, who was suited in every way to be the crown prince of the Brezhnev faction. He was relatively young, able and had an excellent record. He was a full secretary of the central committee; and if he could be promoted from candidate to full member of the Politburo, he would then be eligible to succeed Chernenko. But he fell victim to a crude political squeeze.

Grigory Romanov, a marine engineer from Leningrad, had no reason to support the Brezhnev group, for they had kept him stalled in Leningrad for thirteen years. It was Yuri Andropov who had summoned him to Moscow as a secretary of the central committee. Romanov should have been one of the leaders of the Andropov faction, but political jealousy is as strong in Moscow as elsewhere. There was not room for two youngish men to lead the Andropov faction, and Gorbachev seemed to have the greater support. If the Andropov group went to Gorbachev, then Romanov would have to try for the support of the Brezhnev faction – which was grooming Dolgikh for the succession. Romanov had to stop Dolgikh, and the way to do that was to block any move to have him promoted to full Politburo membership. Since Gorbachev also saw Dolgikh as a potentially serious rival, the result was an unholy alliance between the two rivals to stop Dolgikh.[13]

The Andropov loyalists did not comprise as deep-rooted and widespread a mafia as the Brezhnev group, but the links between them strengthened as Andropov lay dying in the winter of 1983–84 and it became plain that the Brezhnev men were rallying. It was during this period that Gorbachev established his leadership of the Andropov group. He went constantly to Andropov's sickbed, or rather to the study fitted with a dialysis machine at the Kuntsevo hospital, and Andropov virtually governed through him. Andropov put Gorbachev in charge of the crisis management group after the air force had shot down the Korean airliner in September 1983, and also made him acting chairman of the special task force on economic reform that Andropov had founded. Gorbachev was made manager of the election campaign that would choose 140 regional and district party committees – which gave him a crucial opportunity to consolidate his own position in the party machine.[14] Aided by Andropov's latest appointment to the central committee, Yegor Ligachev, Gorbachev brought about the biggest shake-up in the regional committees for twenty years.

Andropov's decline may have established Gorbachev as his chosen heir apparent, but it came too quickly. The Brezhnev faction was still in place, and the Andropov supporters were too few to insist on Gorbachev's immediate succession, but the nucleus of the group was loyal enough. Aliev had owed his rise to Andropov's support, as had Vorotnikov and Shevardnadze. Their strength had been given a considerable boost by the support of Viktor Chebrikov, the head of the KGB. A member of the original Dnepropetrovsk mafia, he ought to have been a Brezhnev loyalist, and indeed had been appointed to the KGB as one of Brezhnev's men, but his thirteen years working with Yuri Andropov had changed his allegiance.

Furthermore, Brezhnev had made some powerful enemies in his time. Mikhail Solomentsev had been sacked from his job as second secretary of Kazakhstan in 1964, when Brezhnev was making room for Dinmukhamed Kunayev and his friends. But Solomentsev, a rather old-fashioned Russian nationalist, worked his way back up the hierarchy with the support of the party's *éminence grise*, the high priest of ideology and Russophile, Mikhail Suslov. Solomentsev was a gifted administrator, and was made chairman of the council of ministers of the Russian republic, but he became the only holder of that post to be refused promotion to the full Politburo. He spent thirteen years as a candidate member, with Brezhnev refusing to promote him further. Solomentsev joined the Andropov group out of revenge.

The two sides were fairly evenly balanced, and the key was held by the group in the middle, whose loyalties were less clearly defined. The two most important, on account of age and reputation, were Marshal Ustinov and Foreign Minister Gromyko. Two of the most impressive men in the Politburo, who owed their places to sheer ability rather than allegiance to any one group, they had been faithful to Brezhnev and to Andropov in turn. Their real loyalties were to country and party (probably in that order).

The eighty-three-year-old Vassily Kuznetsov had been deputy foreign minister for years, and would most likely follow Gromyko. The minister of culture, Pyotr Demichev, had probably never forgiven Brezhnev for demoting him after he had been promoted far and fast by Khrushchev. He would go with the centre group, as would cautious old Boris Ponomarev.

The lines were drawn up not only in the Politburo. Yuri Andropov had made two key appointments to the central committee. One was the economist and technocrat Nikolai Ryzhkov, fifty-four, who had run Uralmash, the country's biggest industrial enterprise. And running the department for the organisation of party work was sixty-three-year-old Yegor Ligachev, a teetotaller and puritan who despised the corruption and lavish life style associated with the Brezhnev family.

When Andropov died, it took the Politburo an unusually long four days to decide the succession. A deal was reached, under which Chernenko became general secretary, and Gorbachev became not just the agreed heir but the second general secretary, as the editor of *Pravda* was to describe it.[15] As a symbol of the deal, and of its constitutional novelty, the plenary meeting of the central committee which ratified the Politburo's decision was closed with a speech, not by the new general secretary as was the custom, but by Gorbachev.[16]

Chernenko's own speech spelled out the terms on which he had been allowed his brief tenure of office. He promised to continue with the reforms begun by Yuri Andropov, referring to him by name eleven times; he did not mention Brezhnev's name at all. This was no triumphant resumption of control by Brezhnev's old guard. It was, in retrospect, a rather stable method of transition through compromise, with Marshal Ustinov and Andrei Gromyko putting their support behind a solution which accepted the need for the changes and reforms launched by Andropov without wholesale disruption. These two old men – both of whom had been influential in the hierarchy when a change of regime had meant guns being drawn in the Politburo after the toppling of Beria – believed that one of the last great services they could render their country was to help assure a smooth transition of power.

The other remarkable feature of the struggle was the high calibre of some of the candidates for the leadership. Gorbachev's merits are well known, but Dolgikh's record as a technocrat and administrator made him a credible alternative. Since his fall, within three months of Gorbachev's coming to power, Grigory Romanov has been the victim of a campaign of denigration about his drinking habits, his authoritarian ways as party boss in Leningrad and his gratuitous rudeness to foreigners. He was, however, an able administrator who had encouraged some far-reaching economic reforms in Leningrad, bringing together design bureaus, research institutes and several factories into large productive combines, similar to the East German model.

Romanov was a man who had come up the old, hard way,

obtaining his professional qualifications as an engineer through a correspondence course. The new men such as Gorbachev and Dolgikh, Nikolai Ryzhkov and Vitaly Vorotnikov, were products of the huge investment the party had poured into the education system. Graduates of universities and established institutes, rather than of the correspondence courses and party schools which had produced Chernenko and Andropov, the first entirely Soviet generation of formally educated men was ready to take control.

This shared experience of higher education may have been a firmer bond than their common loyalty to the tradition of Yuri Andropov. One of the stranger features of Andropov's rise to power was how little time he had to consolidate his position in the key structures of the Soviet state. His job as head of the KGB from 1967 to 1982 was the kind of post which enabled him to talent-spot and recruit bright young men in the party and government who could be welded into a political alliance. Andropov did what he could, picking out Gorbachev, Aliev and Shevardnadze. But it was from within the central committee secretariat that it was possible to obtain the best overview of the problems emerging in the regions and in government, and the best access to the rising young men who would prove capable of resolving those crises. So Andropov looked at the alliances and interest groups that were coalescing around other Politburo figures, and staged a series of takeover bids. There were still men around who had been close to Khrushchev's old ally, the Leningrad party chieftain of the 1950s, Frol Kozlov. Mikhail Solomentsev, a candidate member of the Politburo for so long that he had become embittered, brought the old Kozlov group into Andropov's camp. Much more important were the young technocrats who had gathered around Andrei Kirilenko, who had been Brezhnev's chosen heir until arteriosclerosis made him an invalid in the late 1970s. Kirilenko was a Brezhnev loyalist who had been a member of the Dnepropetrovsk mafia, but in 1955 he was moved from Dnepropetrovsk to take over the party machine in the growing industrial centre of Sverdlovsk in the Urals.[17] He stayed there for almost eight years, winning a reputation for promoting able men quickly. Two of his Sverdlovsk protégés were Nikolai Ryzhkov, who has since become Gorbachev's premier, and Boris Yeltsin, whom Gorbachev appointed to run the Moscow party machine after sacking Viktor Grishin at the end of 1985. Kirilenko's responsibility for industry involved him in the building of the Fiat car factory at

Togliatti, in the Kuibyshev region of the Volga river. There he grew to admire another bright young technocrat, Vitaly Vorotnikov, who was then party secretary for industry in Kuibyshev. As Kirilenko's illness worsened in the 1970s, and his chances of succeeding Brezhnev evaporated, Andropov was able to win these men's allegiance, with his quiet advocacy of the need for economic reform, for a change of national mood from the growing laxity under Brezhnev, and for a firm campaign against corruption within the party.

The group of Andropov supporters that Gorbachev inherited, therefore, was a loose coalition, rather than a tight little band who had worked their way up together for a generation, as had Brezhnev's faction from Dnepropetrovsk. What united them was a conviction that the economy was in trouble, that the social cohesion of the country was starting to suffer, and that what was required was the smack of firm government. At the highest levels, this meant an end to corruption, to conspicuous privileges like Brezhnev's private stable of Western luxury cars, and to the vast estates reserved for the private hunting lodges of Brezhnev's cronies. In economic life, it meant insisting that factories met their delivery dates. The young technocrats who had worked in industry knew that the economy was working at about 70 per cent capacity because of the length of time machines stood idle, waiting for supplies to arrive. It meant cracking down on absenteeism from the workplace, stopping drunkenness on the factory floor, and giving the better workers some genuine incentive. At the end of the month, the idler and the drunk were receiving pretty much the same pay as the keen worker. The word that united these reformers was discipline, which was to become the keynote of Andropov's brief reign.

Andropov sent the police to scour the bars and the bathhouses in working hours and arrest those who could not justify their absence from work. He fired the corrupt old police chief, brought in a KGB man to whip the police force into shape, and authorised him to recruit 30,000 keen young communists from the army and the Komsomol to stiffen the police ranks. The anti-corruption squads were given an open mandate to investigate the party machines run by Brezhnev's supporters in the provinces. Solomentsev relinquished the job of premier of the Russian republic to Vorotnikov, and was sent to breathe new life into the people's control commissions, which were meant to function as a public watchdog over the administration. Solomentsov gave them a budget to hire accountants and lawyers who could do a better job of investigating, and encouraged them to probe as deeply as they liked into corruption and bureaucratic incompetence.

It was not simply Andropov's leadership, nor even the commitment to reform, which welded his group together, so much as a shared cast of mind. In the last years of Brezhnev, the level of public cynicism about the Soviet system had reached such a height that it seemed as if there were no more believers, that the enthusiasm to build a new world and the idealism of the old Bolsheviks had been imprisoned and betrayed by Stalin and finally put to contented sleep under Brezhnev. But the Andropov group remained believers. They had confidence in themselves, since each of them could point to a successful record of achievement in his own sphere, and they had confidence that the system could be made to work. This combination of faith, desire for reform and distaste for loose living and corruption had created a new, puritanical breed.

The puritanism was evident in their private lives. Andropov lived in the big Politburo block on Kutuzovsky Prospekt, but had only a small, one-bedroomed apartment. Ligachev was a teetotaller who believed in the sanctity of family life and refused to promote men who had been through a divorce.[18] Aliev and Shevardnadze had made their names by fighting corruption. As director of Uralmash, Ryzhkov had made a point of lunching in the canteen where the workers ate.[19] When Romanov was brought to the central committee from his Leningrad fief, Gorbachev went to Leningrad in person to stun the local party machine by recommending that he be replaced by Lev Zaikov, who held the lowly sixth place in the local hierarchy. But Zaikov was known as the only honest man in the city leadership; he was appointed, and three years later Gorbachev brought him into the Politburo.[20]

There is a tendency in the West to assume that reformers are liberals. In the context of Soviet affairs, this is an unwise assumption. Although Andropov's career in the central committee under Khrushchev showed him to be an anti-Stalinist, and a man with sophisticated tastes in the arts, neither he nor any of his supporters was a liberal in any sense that the West would comprehend. Indeed, the whole of their cultural background as Russians, and not just as communists, argues against such a likelihood.

Russia has always been an absolutism. The only governments

that have made the country function, let alone prosper, have been ruthless, driving and suspicious. From the days of Ivan the Terrible, the mad Tsar who finally broke the grip of the Mongols upon old Russia in the sixteenth century, a secret police has been the hallmark of the successful Russian state. In Ivan's day, it was called the Oprichnina, a black-garbed band of the Tsar's trusted henchmen. Part bodyguard, part foreshadow of the KGB, and part embryo of a professional bureaucracy, the Oprichnina's purge of the Russian nobility and gentry to assure Ivan's grip on power cost thousands of lives.[21] It was a minor purge by Stalin's standards, but the Tsars who followed Ivan built upon the model he had bequeathed them. In the nineteenth century, the Tsars came to depend increasingly on the Okhrana, the secret police which proved efficient enough to put its spies onto the Bolshevik central committee. The Okhrana outraged liberal opinion in the West much as the KGB does today.

The sheer physical size of the country has always been the main problem of the men who ruled from Moscow. Charles de Gaulle once wondered aloud how anyone could ever govern France, a country which produced over 300 cheeses. How much less possible to govern a country that takes eight days to cross by train, a country so huge that night never completely falls, a country that contains over a hundred nationalities, speaking over a hundred different tongues. The vast frozen tracts of Siberia, the dry deserts of Kazakhstan and the subtropical vineyards of Georgia were all conquered for the Russians by successive generations of absolute Tsars. Absolutism is as constant a factor in Russian history as Parliaments are in the history of England.

The absolutism is not necessarily aggressive. It began, and continued, as a prerequisite of national defence. The Tsars who are most revered in the Soviet canon are those who fought off invaders: Ivan the Terrible, who broke the Mongol yoke; Peter the Great, who fought off the Swedes; and Alexander, who withstood Napoleon's invasion and led his troops the long way back to Paris.

Hitler's invasion remains bright and terrible in the people's memory, so Stalin's ruthlessness has merged into the historical tradition of an absolutism that was justified in the cause of the nation's survival. The Russians know that the only way they have ever stopped invasions is under the merciless, implacable leadership of a single, centralised authority. This centralised absolutism has also been the bulwark against the other age-old Russian fear, of internal anarchy, whether in the form of peasant revolt, food riots, pogroms, or the rising of one or other of the minority nations that have been swept into the Russian fold once the invader withdrew, defeated.

This was the tradition that Mikhail Gorbachev inherited, the tradition in which Yuri Andropov had ruled the KGB. The menace to the nation came not only from the rich Western powers beyond the frontiers, but also from within. Yuri Andropov's great achievement as head of the KGB had been to contain the dissident movement. The other internal threats, from corruption and inefficiency, from waste and drink and idleness, were seen by the new puritans as enemies to be countered by the old absolutist methods.

In a speech delivered in December 1984, a speech which became his personal political manifesto, Mikhail Gorbachev told the Soviet people that the new industrial revolution they had to achieve would require the same national drive and the same political will that had marked the first five-year plans of the 1930s. There is hardly a Russian alive who has forgotten the awful price of the political commitment that Stalin imposed on that period. Gorbachev's words served not only as a warning that the soft days of Brezhnev were over. They also offered a promise that the new puritans, with their university degrees and their technocratic skills, would govern in the old, familiar and absolutist way.

3

The Economic Experiment

Professor Abel Aganbegyan is the most influential economist in the Soviet Union, and his Institute of Economics in the Siberian science city of Novosibirsk has been consistently the most exciting of the academic think-tanks which have been advocating economic reform. The leaking of his confidential report on the economy therefore caused something of a stir. He began by saying that the growth rate of the Soviet economy had begun to slow, while the American economy was not only booming but expanding particularly strongly in new technological areas like computers and automation. By contrast, whole sectors of the Soviet economy such as agriculture, services and retail trade were backward and showed few signs of improvement. The fundamental cause of the problem, he went on, was the staggering share of resources that the Soviet economy committed to defence, with something like a third of the entire workforce involved in the defence sector, and 'the extreme centralism and lack of democracy in economic matters'.[1]

Modern economies were simply too big and complex to be centrally planned in the style of the 1930s, Aganbegyan argued. But even to attempt to restructure the economy would require an end to official secrecy on economic affairs. 'We obtain many figures from American journals sooner than they are released by our Central Statistical Administration,' he noted. Moreover, it would need a massive amount of data processing power. 'The Central Statistical Administration does not have a single computer, and has no plans to acquire one,' he added.[2]

The planned economy could not work in the existing circumstances, and attempts to force it to do so built a whole series of distortions into Soviet life. It encouraged hoarding by factories and private consumers, because they could never be sure of obtaining future supplies. It encouraged the hoarding of labour,

38

as an insurance against being short of manpower to fulfil the plan for higher output in the future. Output measured simply by the quantity of production meant that quality was being forced out of the system, so consumers saved their money instead of spending it on shoddy goods, and encouraged the growth of a vast black market.

The point about Professor Aganbegyan's report is that it was written, and leaked to the Western press, over twenty years ago, in June 1965. His criticisms hold largely true today, except that the statisticians have several computers. And today, as in 1965, Aganbegyan remains in the forefront of the campaign for reform. Then, his patron was Alexei Kosygin, chairman of the council of ministers and the technocrat of the triumvirate of Brezhnev, Kosygin and Podgorny who replaced Nikita Khrushchev in 1964. Today, Aganbegyan's patron is Gorbachev himself, who summoned him from the Novosibirsk think-tank to Moscow, where he was installed as a personal adviser to Gorbachev and to the prime minister, Nikolai Ryzhkov.

Economic reform has a long and rather depressing history in the Soviet Union. In a sense, it began almost as soon as Stalin died, when, as prime minister, Georgi Malenkov put slightly more investment into consumer goods than into heavy industry. Khrushchev tried to decentralise industry and economic administration, and Kosygin tried a complex of measures to make managers more adventurous and the economy more flexible. Kosygin's three key reforms were to draft the plan targets not according to the number of goods produced, but according to the number that were actually sold, either to other factories or to the state or to private consumers. Second, to discourage the hoarding and waste of capital resources, he introduced a small annual charge for capital equipment provided by the state. This 'rent' on buildings and machinery would have to come out of each factory's 'profit', or the surplus it was thought to have made in receipts over expenditure. A proportion of this 'profit' could be retained by the factory, to use as the management wished, to pay incentive bonuses to the workers, to invest in holiday camps or sports facilities, or even to reinvest in the factory itself.[3]

The Kosygin reforms, which Aganbegyan had helped to draft, foundered on three separate rocks. The first was purely economic. In an economy where prices are fixed by the central planners at an arbitrary level which need have no relation to cost of production, the concept of 'profit' is meaningless. The manager had no control over his input costs, over how much he paid for electricity, for raw materials, for the machine tools his workers used. His 'profit', therefore, was an entirely notional figure, which depended on the prices the planners set. The only area of 'profit' over which he had some control was the bonuses the factory would be paid for meeting its plan targets.[4]

The second obstacle to the reforms was the deep suspicion and stubborn refusal to cooperate which they provoked within the bureaucracy, among party officials and civil servants in various ministries who saw their own authority being eroded by the new rights given to industrial management. They found it easy enough to be obstructive. A manager could not simply buy his raw materials on the open market; he required authorisation from the right ministries. A factory that was producing, for example, farm machinery would require design approvals from at least eight different ministries before it could begin production, and then its contracts with suppliers of raw materials, engine parts, tyres, compressors and so on would each require approval by all the ministries to which the suppliers reported.[5] This bureaucratic nightmare inhibited change and innovation. Even to improve the design of the farm machinery involved going through the whole tortuous approval process all over again. Better to carry on turning out the old product, even if it might be less efficient.

The third obstacle was the political implications of economic reform. Improving the efficiency of Soviet factories meant getting rid of surplus labour and firing idle or incompetent workers. In a state where the implicit social contract guarantees a job for every worker, this was dangerous. It was particularly dangerous in the wake of the riots in the Ukrainian city of Novocherkassk in 1962, when a nationwide increase in food prices was announced on the same day that the management of the Budenny locomotive works cut the piece-rates for their workers. The demonstrations grew into localised riots serious enough to require the intervention of KGB troops. At least seventy people were killed, and some dissident reports speak of many more deaths.[6]

There was a limit to the amount of discipline that could be imposed on the workers, and after de-Stalinisation and the steady improvement of living standards under Khrushchev, there was a limit to the degree of economic hardship that could be inflicted. The final blow to the Kosygin reforms was the brief and abortive emergence of a liberal communist regime in Czechoslovakia in 1967–68. The political reforms introduced by Dubček had followed a series of economic reforms that the Czechs had justified by reference to Kosygin's ideas. The Soviet tanks that rolled into Czechoslovakia crushed not only the Prague Spring but also the hopes of the Soviet economic reformers of the 1960s.

But some of the reformers' achievements survived. Industrial managers had acquired a taste for new responsibilities and opportunities, and some at least of the workers took advantage of the incentive payments for higher productivity. Some of the new methods of working began to spread through the economy. The most successful was known as the Shchukino method, after the chemical plant in Tula where it began in 1967. It was an attempt to increase individual productivity by offering the workforce a direct trade-off between pay and jobs. The factory was given a sharply increased production target that was fixed for five years, and a wage fund that was also frozen, which made it impossible to hire more staff. Then the management and workforce were told that they could share out the wage fund in any way they chose, and it was made clear to them that it was in their interest to sacrifice jobs. Over the first five years the average wage increased by 45 per cent and over 1300 jobs were shed, almost a third of the workforce. Over ten years, output rose by 170 per cent, and productivity by 240 per cent, and the share of wages as a proportion of production costs fell from 14 per cent to 5 per cent.[7]

These figures represent an increase in productivity that was slightly less than that being achieved in the British chemical industry over the same period. In the West, a fall in the share of labour costs in a capital-intensive industry like chemicals was commonplace. In the Soviet Union, it was revolutionary. The success of Shchukino led to a widening of the experiment in the ninth five-year plan after 1970 to a further 1000 enterprises, over a hundred of them in the chemical industry. The result was that 45,000 manual workers and over 10,000 skilled workers were made redundant. In the tenth five-year plan, over 11,000 enterprises were authorised to use the Shchukino method, and almost a million jobs were lost.[8]

The redundant workers were not, however, simply thrown onto the labour market. One of the reasons why the experiment worked at Shchukino was that the original management had established a retraining school at the plant where redundant workers could learn new skills, and the local party committee had cooperated by organising a form of labour exchange, where workers could find other jobs in other local industries. Similarly, at the Zil truck and auto works in Moscow, the introduction of automated equipment after 1985 meant that some 3000 workers were no longer required. The technical school that had been built up at the factory to retrain some workers in the use of new robots was then used to train others in different skills, and a branch of the Moscow engineering institute was opened at the factory where workers could do diploma and degree courses and upgrade their skills, while still receiving their pay from Zil.[9]

This was a humane and intelligent way of coping with the changes in workforce structure that automation and higher productivity made inevitable. But it was rarely organised as carefully as at Shchukino and Zil, where formal experiments had been publicly announced, and which were much in the eye of the Soviet media. Elsewhere, Soviet planners and engineers speak of redundant workers being subjected to hours of tedious political lectures by the local agitprop team from the party committee, and of skilled workers being re-employed as floor sweepers or just held in reserve for the 'storming' at the end of every month.[10] Storming was an inevitable consequence of a poor industrial distribution system. Delays in the delivery of spare parts or raw materials meant factories working slowly at the beginning of a month, and then going through a final week of intense overtime and accelerated production to meet monthly targets.

'We never use a screwdriver in the last week,' one production line worker at a Lithuanian television factory told me. 'We hammer the screws in. We slam solder on the connections, cannibalise parts from other TVs if we have run out of the right ones, use glue or hammers to fix switches that were never meant for that model. And all the time management is pressing us to work faster, to make the target so that we all get our bonuses.'[11]

The practice of storming was, in its own bizarre terms, a rational response by Soviet managers to an irrational situation. Their production targets and their prices were set for them by Gosplan and the ministries, and their supply lines were also outside their control. So their own authority was limited to the workforce and the work methods and pay distribution inside the factories. These constraints on management had been a key target of Professor Aganbegyan's confidential report of 1965. And while the other reforms that he and similarly minded economists had advocated sputtered and died, the need to widen managerial authority within industry became steadily more apparent.

There were three main reasons for this. The first was that the East German economy had been experimenting along these lines with considerable success. The second was that the ministries themselves were increasingly recruiting executives and ministers from the ranks of industrial management, who understood the nature of the constraints and wanted to remove them. Nikolai Ryzhkov and Vladimir Dolgikh are simply the two most prominent policymakers who have gone through the maze of trying to implement such policies in the factories. The third was that the structure of industry was itself changing, with industrial plants growing in size and becoming far more complex in their production processes.

The industry where the complexities of production were most advanced was that controlled by the ministry of instrument-making, automation equipment and control systems. In 1970, it was authorised to launch the Khozraschot experiment, which decreed that not only each factory but the industry itself had to become self-financing.[12] Hitherto, a manager could go through his industrial life without ever seeing a balance sheet. The money customers paid for his products went to the parent ministry, which also supplied investment funds and even payrolls. The self-financing system meant that the factory was paid direct, and was authorised to make its own investment decisions. In effect, the factory was given a bank account whose ups and downs ought to reflect the economic health of the enterprise.

By 1980, four more of the biggest industrial ministries had been transferred to the self-financing system: tractors and farm machinery, heavy and transport engineering, energy engineering, and electrotechnical. This accounted for half the industrial workforce. The principles of self-financing and management autonomy had also been adopted for the second great reform which was to get under way in the 1970s: the creation of territorial-production complexes (TPCs), the new industrial complexes that were established in the virgin taiga of Siberia.

The best known TPC is that at Bratsk–Ust'Ilimsk, north-west of Lake Baikal. It began with the huge Bratsk dam and the energy produced from its hydroelectric station. The energy was used to run a vast aluminium plant and to warm and light the new city that grew up in the area. Further north was a second dam, which powered a gigantic wood-processing factory, producing cellulose, paper and raw timber from the inexhaustible Siberian forest. The western Siberian oil and gas deposits were explored, drilled, exploited and then piped to the West by another TPC, which was responsible not only for the whole production process, but also for the construction of roads, towns, river ports and airfields. These TPCs were given vast investment budgets, and thereafter they were self-financing, and had to pay an annual charge on the state capital they were using.[13]

Their sheer size, and their responsibilities for construction, production and social as well as industrial development made the TPCs reminiscent of small nations. What they lacked was inhabitants. But they had the right to pay the usual Siberian bonuses, which could double and triple average pay. And the Soviet courts could also help. In Ust'-Ilimsk in 1985, one in five of the population had arrived in the city as a convict, sentenced to work in Siberia rather than go to prison. Convicted doctors and dentists, for example, were serving out their sentences by contributing their medical skills. (The most common crime of which they had been convicted was drunken driving.) They could bring their families with them, were assigned a small apartment and were free to visit the theatre and cinema and take part in the life of the town. But they were paid subsistence salaries, and convicts without skills were restricted to grim state hostels. According to local officials, rather more than half chose to stay on in Siberia after serving their terms. 'We are combining penal reform with economic reform,' claimed the local party secretary.[14]

These developments and reforms were taking place at a time of apparent quiescence among the academic economists and theoretical reformers. The debate that had got under way in *Pravda* in 1964–65 over Professor Liberman's advocacy of the profit motive for individual factories and over Abel Aganbegyan's call for decentralisation had not been silenced.[15] It had shifted its focus and its location. The increase in trained economists led to a growth in the number of academic journals, where the discussion continued. At first it was little noticed in the West because these journals were rarely read by Western correspondents in Moscow in the way that *Pravda*'s every line was scoured. But gradually academics and specialists in the West began to take note of Abel Aganbegyan's own magazine, *EKO*, and as the academic exchanges and international conferences blossomed in the detente years of the 1970s the ferment of Soviet economic debate started to attract attention.

The journal *Dengi i Kredit* was exploring the implications of the surge in savings and the limits of the Soviet financial system, and *Planovoye Khozaistvo* was looking at ways to reduce the inflexibilities of Gosplan. The economic journals of the individual republics were recounting the fates of localised experiments in the Baltic consumer goods industries and the success of Georgia's use of family private enterprise to keep once-impoverished mountain villages from depopulating. The journal of Moscow University's economics faculty was being edited by Professor Popov, whose thinking was uncannily close to that of the monetarist economists emerging around Mrs Thatcher in Britain and President Reagan in the USA. Indeed it was Popov's article in *Pravda*, on 27 December 1980, calling for wage cuts to increase incentives and a system of planned unemployment with a minimum wage of 80 roubles a month for the redundant that first alerted a wider audience in the West to the readiness of the new Soviet economists to think the unthinkable.[16]

The restraints on economic debate began to give way as it became increasingly plain that the economy was only sluggishly responding to the reforms that had been enacted so far, and that some of the reforms were having unexpected and undesirable effects. The growth in real wage rates that had followed the pay incentive and bonus system introduced by Kosygin in the 1960s had caused an explosion of savings-bank accounts and led to the vast, previously pent-up, demand that was fuelling the black markets. But industrial productivity was still failing to keep up to Western levels, and even the vaunted panacea of importing Western technology in the detente years was yielding only moderate results.

The Western suppliers themselves were staggered by the slowness of Soviet industry to absorb the new technology they were buying. A survey of twenty-six turnkey chemical plants supplied by Britain in the 1960s and 1970s found that the average time for negotiations, and installing and commissioning the plants was almost seven years, twice or three times as long as the process would have taken in the West. They found that Soviet manning levels of the plants were 50 to 70 per cent higher than in Britain, and that output was generally lower. A similar West German study found that Soviet productivity was about 70 per cent of Western levels. This still amounted to a significant improvement for Soviet industry. Slow as the installation time was, it was still twice as fast as that taken to instal Soviet plants. Also, the Western technology was staggeringly more efficient in energy use. Imported ammonia plants, for example, used only 5 per cent of the energy (and about 60 per cent of the workforce) of comparable Soviet plants. From 1971 to 1975, the costs of manufacturing ammonia in the Soviet Union fell by 8.5 per cent as the Western plants came on stream.[17]

This meant that the Soviet Union was paying Western prices for less than Western production, which was a gloomy thought for those who saw it as their duty to outperform the capitalist world. And the withering of detente in the later 1970s steadily narrowed the possibilities of resolving the failures of Soviet planning with Western machinery. Something more fundamental was needed, but the Brezhnev government could not bring itself to apply more than the usual piecemeal measures. In 1979, there was a series of economic decrees which drew on individual suggestions from the academic journals, but failed to apply them systematically.

The changes that were made, however, were significant. The decree on 'Strengthening the Economic Mechanism' tried to graft a system of measuring and rewarding quality onto the crude output targets so beloved of the planners, and tried to solve the chronic lateness of deliveries by making bonuses dependent on the fulfilment of contracts and delivery dates. These moves were promising, but the two reforms tended to cancel each other out. To meet delivery dates, factories would 'storm' their production targets even more vigorously than before, which meant cutting back on quality control.

The second reform of 1979 appeared initially to be rather more successful. It called for 'an extensive development of the brigade form of organising labour and incentives'. In theory, this should have given the workforce the right to form themselves into small groups, to elect their own foremen and to decide among themselves how the brigade's wage packet was to be distributed. Again in theory, this should have given every worker an incentive to perform well as an individual, so that his fellow brigade members would vote him higher pay, and to work well in cooperation with the rest of the unit, so that the collective pay packet would increase. At first, confident claims were made for the efficacy of the system, the shipbuilding industry being first to say that wages had risen by 12 per cent, and productivity had risen by over 20 per cent, while that the length of time equipment had been out of action or under repair had fallen sharply.[18]

Whatever the claims, the brigade system was not paying off. By 1982 over 60 per cent of industrial workers were nominally organised into a brigade system. But annual productivity growth rates for industry were still crawling along at less than 2 per cent a year. Craftsmen and veteran foremen did not want to cooperate with a system that undermined their traditional authority and cut the differentials between their pay and that of the rest of the workforce. They passed on their discontent to the trade unions and to management, and many of the brigades were organised in a purely symbolic way. Nor was it easy suddenly to transform the average Soviet industrial worker, drilled by years of scant personal responsibility, into a high-producing member of a self-managing team. And when the best workers grouped themselves together into such a team, the trade unions and management were left to solve the problems of the rest of the workforce – the elderly women on the collective farms whom no brigade wanted to carry, the drunks and unskilled on the shop floor. Furthermore, every Soviet manager knows full well that, once his workforce starts achieving great feats of productivity, his production targets will be raised for future years: better to keep to the comfortably low and attainable old targets. In a system where mediocre economic performance does not lead to bankruptcy, there is little incentive to shine.

It was frustration with the failure of piecemeal economic reform to make any fundamental impact that turned the reform-minded academic economists into revolutionaries in the 1980s. Popov called for redundancies as an economic mechanism; Volkonsky advocated 'the devolution of price-setting powers to the enterprises, who would negotiate prices and quantities with suppliers and customers; complete freedom for enterprises and production associations to choose their own suppliers and customers'.[19] Above all, there was the celebrated 'Novosibirsk paper', written by Dr Tatiana Zaslavskaya, a disciple of Aganbegyan from his Novosibirsk Institute. The leaking of her confidential report on the failures of the Soviet economy in 1983 recalled the leak of

Professor Aganbegyan's own paper back in 1965, at a similar time of official readiness to consider sweeping reform.[20]

Zaslavskaya's report was in no sense a samizdat. It was delivered to a top-level seminar attended by senior figures from the central committee, the Academy of Sciences, and from Gosplan. She began by repeating some of the broad criticisms contained in Aganbegyan's much earlier report, arguing that the underlying economic structure and control systems of the state had not changed since the 1930s, and were no longer compatible with the economy as it had evolved. 'The complexity of the economic structure has long since overstepped the threshold of its efficient regulation from a single centre,' she said.[21] Worse, the rigidities of the planning system were themselves a systemic cause of corruption, idleness and dishonesty among the population. The Soviet people were now too well educated and too well informed to be treated like mindless cogs in some huge and centrally planned machine. That system had worked for a generation of cowed and passive peasants fresh from the fields in the 1930s; it did not work for their grandchildren. She went on to attack 'the inhibition of market forces . . . the administrative limitations imposed on all kinds of formalised economic activity by the population in the spheres of production, service and distribution'. Dr Zaslavskaya did not specify what new mechanisms she would introduce to solve the problem. She did not need to; her prescription was implicit in her diagnosis: the Soviet economy needed more market forces and less planning.

The significance of her report lay not simply in the fact that it was written at all – similar analyses had been coming from the economic think-tanks and appearing in the academic journals for some years – but in the audience which attended her lecture. These were the people who had the power to initiate change – at the price of surrendering what they still saw as their own monopoly of economic control. She argued that:

> Any radical restructuring of the system of economic management will vitally affect the interests of many social groups, some of whom will hope for improvements in their status, whereas others will see it worsening. Attempts made by the higher organs of state power to improve production relations and bring them into greater correspondence with the new demands of the productive forces cannot be realised without conflict.

In terms of Marxist ideology, that statement is revolutionary. It calls for the rewriting of the second volume of *Das Kapital*. Marxist doctrine holds that, in a socialist state, in the absence of exploitation, there can be no contradiction between the forces of production and production relations. But, in terms of the realities of power and decision-making in the Soviet state, her statement was doubly revolutionary, because she went on to define exactly which groups in society would provoke the conflict. She described the middle-ranking bureaucrats in the ministries and the coordination offices who sat between the central planners and the manufacturing enterprise itself. Their numbers 'have sprouted like mushrooms in recent years', she noted, and went on to attack their ill-defined responsibilities and their 'comfortable offices and good salaries'. Their functions, their status and their jobs would be at risk from any reform which gave industrial management real authority. They would therefore fight reform.

The degree to which the economic reformers were winning the argument at the very top of the Soviet system became plain on 25 February 1986, when Mikhail Gorbachev made his formal report as general secretary to the twenty-seventh congress of the Communist Party. In the course of a long statement on the need for economic reform, he too declared his readiness to rethink the fundamentals of Marxist economics:[22]

> Life itself prompts us to take a new look at some theoretical ideas and conflicts. This refers to such major problems as the interaction of the productive forces and the relations of production, socialist ownership and its economic forms, commodity-money relations, the coordination of centralism with the autonomy of economic organisations, and so on. Practice has revealed the insolvency of the idea that under the conditions of socialism the conformity of production relations to the nature of the productive forces is ensured automatically, as it were. In real life, everything is more complicated.

Perhaps, as was claimed, Gorbachev wrote his own speech. But Zaslavskaya's Novosibirsk paper must have been close at hand when it was drafted. The similarity of phrase and language is uncanny. He went on to address the problem of bureaucratic opposition that she had identified:

> Every re-adjustment of the economic mechanism begins with a re-adjustment of thinking, with a rejection of old stereotypes of thought and actions, with a clear understanding of the new tasks. This refers

primarily to the activity of our economic personnel, to the functionaries of the central links of administration. Most of them have a clear
idea of the party's initiatives, and seek and find the best ways of
carrying them out . . . It is hard, however, to understand those who
take a wait and see policy, or those who do not actually do anything
or change anything. There will be no reconciliation with the stance
taken by functionaries of that kind. We will simply have to part ways
with them. All the more so do we have to part ways with those who
hope that everything will settle down and return to the old lines. That
will not happen, comrades!

There had been a gap of almost three years between the delivery
of Zaslavskaya's paper at Novosibirsk and its endorsement by
Mikhail Gorbachev in the party's most authoritative forum. Those
three years had begun with Andropov, as general secretary, launching the first wave of post-Brezhnev reforms, the attacks on
corruption and the scouring of the bars and public baths to round
up absentees from work. There had been intensive assessments of
the reforms that had long been under way in the East European
economies and in China, coordinated by Professor Oleg Bogomolov from his Moscow-based Institute of World Economic
Systems. There had been increasingly critical studies of the burden
of the massive state subsidies on basic foods and housing rents.
Research projects had begun into the feasibility of opening the
Soviet economy to the chill and bracing winds of international
competition through making the rouble an internationally
convertible currency. Backed by gold, oil and natural gas, the
argument ran, the rouble's international value should stabilise
fairly quickly.[23]

By the time Gorbachev came to power in 1985, the level of
intellectual debate among Soviet economists and planners was
more adventurous and outspoken than it had been since the
1920s. But the irony was that the new ideas, and their official
acceptance, had come ten years too late. Had Zaslavskaya's paper
been published in 1973, and endorsed by a general secretary in
1975, when the oil and gas revenues looked so promising and the
international climate seemed to offer some years of stable, or even
declining, defence expenditure, then the liberation of the Soviet
command economy might have been at hand. But Zaslavskaya's
paper was written at a time when the world price of oil was over
$30 a barrel. Gorbachev's echoing speech was delivered when the
price of oil had more than halved, to $14, causing a collapse of

Soviet hard-currency export earnings. At the same time, the armed forces were clamouring for higher budgets to match the West's technological lead in 'smart' weapons, and to keep pace with the American Star Wars project.

Ten years earlier, the Soviet economy could have afforded itself the luxury of an economic experiment along liberal, free-market lines. It could have afforded to make a few mistakes. By the time Gorbachev took control, the dilemma was cruel. Without reform, the Soviet economy could not hope to grow fast enough to keep pace with the raw energies of the renewed capitalist boom. Not only did Gorbachev accept the situation, but for the first time he spelled out its implications for a party faithful who had grown accustomed to cosy assurances that the collapse of capitalism was inevitable if not imminent. He told the party congress:[24]

> The present stage of the general crisis of capitalism does not lead to any absolute stagnation, and does not rule out the possible growth of its economy and the emergence of new scientific and technical trends. It permits capitalism to sustain its economic, military, political and strategic positions, and in some cases, even to achieve possible social revenge, the recovery of what had been lost before.

There was little room for manoeuvre. A reform which provoked popular unrest, through sudden increases in food prices, would alarm the army and the party and screw the lid back down for a generation. A reform which directly threatened the status of the party and the bureaucracy faced stubborn administrative resistance at best, and, at worst, the distant but still-distinct possibility of an internal party *putsch* of the kind which had toppled Khrushchev.

Gorbachev's solution, like that of many a skilful politician before him, was to spell out in detail the separate reforms he wanted to see, but to describe the whole package as something else altogether, as 'intensification'. But in the course of his address to the congress, he called for a series of changes in economic management which closely reflected the main arguments of the academic reformers:

> [Prices] must be made more flexible. Price levels must be linked not only to the costs of production, but also with the degree to which they meet the needs of society and consumer demand.[25]

> [Autonomy]: It is high time to put an end to the practice of ministries and departments exercising petty tutelage over industrial

enterprises . . . Enterprises and organisations should be given the right to sell to one another, independently, what they produce over and above the plan, raw and other materials and equipment which they do not use. They should also be given the legal right to make such sales to the population.[26]

[Agriculture]: Farms will be given the opportunity to use as they see fit all the produce harvested over and above the plan. In the case of fruit and vegetables they will also be able to use a considerable proportion of the planned produce as they see fit. They can sell it to the state, can sell it fresh or processed at the farm markets, or through the co-op trade outlets, or use it for other needs.[27]

[Wages]: It is essential that the government's wage policy should ensure that incomes strictly correspond to the quantity and quality of work done . . . It should be said quite emphatically that when equal payments are fixed for the work of a good employee and that of a negligent one this is a gross violation of our principles.[28]

[Bankruptcy]: It is important to carry out unswervingly the principle under which enterprises and associations are wholly responsible for operating without losses, while the state does not bear any responsibility for their debts . . . Increase of the social wealth, as well as losses, should affect the income level of each member of the collective.[29]

Gorbachev had begun the economic section of his speech with a call for 'revolutionary change'. He had paused for a long moment and stared aggressively at the 5000 party faithful who sat before him in the Palace of Congresses in the Kremlin. When he resumed, there was absolute silence in the vast hall. Then he said, 'There is no other way.'[30]

4

The Technology Revolution

In 1961, Nikita Khrushchev promised the Soviet people that, by the 1980s, they would be producing more industrial goods than the USA. This was dismissed at the time by Western observers as a grandiose and unrealistic prediction. The document in which Khrushchev spelled out his ambition, the third programme of the Communist Party, is today almost unobtainable in Moscow, and remains a source of embarrassment to his successors. Indeed, the fourth party programme, drawn up under the eye of Mikhail Gorbachev, represents an ideological retreat from Khrushchev's airy claim that, by the 1980s, the Soviet people would have completed the construction of socialism and would be living in Karl Marx's utopia of communism. The fourth programme sets the rather more modest target of 'perfecting socialism', and carefully offers no specific date for its achievement.

The curious thing is that Khrushchev's economic targets have been met. The Soviet Union produces 80 per cent more steel than the USA, 78 per cent more cement, 42 per cent more oil, 55 per cent more fertiliser, more than twice as much pig-iron and six times as much iron ore. It produces five times as many tractors, and almost twice as many metal-cutting lathes.[1]

In 1961, such products represented the sinews of industrial power and, had the world's economy stood still, the Soviet Union would be its industrial giant. The partial success of Khrushchev's plan points to the strengths and weaknesses of the centralised planned economy. The planners set their targets, and control the investment, the labour force and the education and transport and distribution system to see that their plans are carried out.

But the West is now living and working and producing in another kind of economy altogether, a post-industrial economy where the amount of steel, iron and cement produced is of less importance than the amount of plastic, the kilowatts of electricity and, above all, the number of microchips. Western economies were not planned centrally by an all-powerful state; they might not have grown so far and fast if they had been. It was the speed of reaction of individual entrepreneurs in the computer industry to the constant demands of a fashion-conscious market which fuelled the development of new products, which in turn inspired new industries. This did not happen by some accident or blessing of pure market forces. The move to the post-industrial economy was forced upon the profligate energy-users of the West by the OPEC price rises of 1973 and 1979. It was made possible because the West had developed a highly sophisticated and responsive infrastructure which could mediate and speed communications between consumers and producers. While Khrushchev's planners in Moscow had kept their eyes fixed firmly on manufacturing the hardware of industrial power, the West, almost without knowing what it was doing, had created the software that could act as midwife to the post-industrial economy.

The West had fostered an advertising industry which could not only convey the information about new products to the consumers but do so in an enticing and exciting way. The West's media were in large part funded by the advertising industry, and so the entire information network had a vested interest in promoting consumption. The system of personal finance, with the growth in credit and hire purchase, further fuelled the ability of the market to consume. Under the new conditions that followed the first OPEC price rise, what had seemed like a weakness of the Western economies – an advertising industry which spurred the production of, for example, new models of car that offered only differences of external design – became a source of strength. The industry could sell the concept of the energy-saving car and make low fuel consumption seem positively 'sexy', and all the more economic when it was run by a microchip inside the engine. The design industry responsible for the tail fins and the chrome bumpers and radiators which had contributed to the profligacy of the West's economies was able to adapt to safer and cheaper automated construction and new lightweight materials which sharply reduced the overall consumption of steel.

It is these soft economic skills of marketing and design and easy finance that the Soviet economy lacks. The planner and the producers rule and the consumer comes a very poor third, with few means of effectively communicating his dissatisfaction. As a result, across great swathes of the economy, the Soviet consumer has gone on strike, and leaves his money to pile up in the savings bank while he queues doggedly for those goods that are worth buying or that he cannot do without.

Like so much else in the Soviet Union, this can be perceived at the same time as both a problem and as an opportunity. This pent-up demand, representing as it does a potential consumer investment of massive proportions, could be harnessed intelligently, so long as the factories, the management skills and the political will are available. And they may be. Most Western analysts have long reckoned that there is one sector of the Soviet economy which functions on broadly similar lines to those which prevail in the advanced industrial countries of the West. The Soviet defence industry is thriving, in large part because the consumers have control. The consumers are, of course, the armed forces who will use the products.

In all the factories in the military-industrial sector, there is a quality-control section which is run by serving officers to monitor the output from the assembly lines, and to carry out random checks on the finished products. The military consumer is involved in the production process from the very beginning, defining the kind of weapons needed, drawing up the performance parameters, checking the prototypes, and then going back to the factory to demand changes and improvements and modifications as the field tests proceed. The Soviet military have a role in the industrial process which is in some ways more powerful than that of the Western consumer, because they can pre-empt raw materials and components, commandeer the best design skills and impose a rigorous industrial discipline on the factory floor.[2]

Brezhnev's determination to preside over a consumer boom and the generals' own need to find extra money for their arms budget led, in the 1970s, to an increasing diversion of the military-industrial complex into the civilian consumer goods market. The result has been that the defence industry now makes some of the best-regarded products on the civilian market. The best refrigerator that Russians can buy is the Biryuza model, which is produced by the factories of the strategic rocket forces. The best vacuum cleaner is the Raketa model, manufactured by the ministry of aviation, which also produces excellent children's prams.[3]

When Leonid Brezhnev told the twenty-fourth party congress

of 1971 that 42 per cent of the defence industry's output was for civilian use, he was widely mocked in the West. But he may not have been stretching the truth beyond recognition. The defence industries produce tractors, radios, stereo tape-decks, TV and video equipment, civilian airliners, ships and plastic goods ranging from children's toys to coat hangers and washing-up bowls. They manufacture about one third of all railway carriages, about 10 per cent of private automobiles, almost half of the civilian trucks, two thirds of the motorcycles, medical equipment and small electrical generators. They produce some of the best-quality colour-printed books in the country, employ teams of designers to turn out some of the better posters, and professional Soviet photographers swear by the films and camera lenses that come from the military factories.[4]

Soviet military hardware has been widely admired in the West. The Kalashnikov rifle has been the most efficient infantry combat weapon of the last thirty years. The Mi-24 Hind is the best combat helicopter of our time, and Western defence experts acknowledge that the metallurgic skills that have gone into the titanium armour-plate now used on Soviet combat helicopters and tanks is more advanced than anything available to NATO.[5]

The increasing integration of the Soviet defence and civilian industries is a central feature of Gorbachev's plans for economic reform. But it also plays havoc with Western intelligence guesstimates of Soviet military production. One of the standard Western methods to ascertain Soviet military output is to analyse satellite photographs and measure the floor space and production capacity of factories that are believed to be working for the defence sector. How much of that floor space may be turning out vacuum cleaners and washing machines is unknown. Furthermore, this partly civilian role of the Soviet defence industries casts doubt on the arguments of those American strategists who claim that Russia can be bankrupted by being forced into an arms race the economy cannot sustain.

Conversely, pressure on the arms industry may actually boost the Soviet economy. Soviet defence industries have the first claim on resources, investment and skilled manpower. Their traditions of quality control and the management skills which have been honed in these privileged factories can be passed on to the rest of the economy. The defence industries have had the lion's share of computer-controlled equipment, of automated assembly lines and of robotics, and they are now in a position to share these skills, and their experience, more widely.[6]

This would seem to be the logic behind a series of important administrative transfers that Mikhail Gorbachev authorised in his first year in office. Three new and relatively young deputy prime ministers were appointed to help the Politburo member in charge of economic reform, Nikolai Ryzhkov, to overhaul and modernise Soviet industry. They were Ivan Silaev, the fifty-five-year-old former minister of aviation; Lev Voronin, fifty-seven, whose previous job had been as head of the main administration department of the ministry of defence industries; and Yuri Maslyukov, forty-eight, former deputy minister of defence industries. The new super-ministry for machine tools was stiffened by a series of transfers and promotions from defence industrial management.

The capacity for technological transfer and the lending and teaching of advanced productive skills from defence to civilian industry has been a major contributor to economic growth in the West. The research and development role of the Pentagon in computing sciences, and in advanced materials such as the composites that were first used in military aircraft and in electronics and communications equipment, has played a significant role in changing the pattern and velocity of Western economic growth over the past two decades. Gorbachev has evidently decided to follow the Western model.

In Soviet political terms, Gorbachev delivered a very powerful message in March 1986 when he announced the promotion of Lev Zaikov to full Politburo membership. In July of the previous year, when he retired the former Leningrad party chieftain Grigory Romanov, Gorbachev had reduced the number of senior secretaries to two: only he and Yegor Ligachev were simultaneously full secretaries of the central committee and full Politburo members. But Lev Zaikov, the central committee secretary in charge of the defence industries, was raised to this elevated rank without ever having gone through the traditional stage of candidate membership. Nor did he have much knowledge of the party hierarchy. Zaikov's entire experience had been in the Leningrad arms industry, until he was plucked out by Gorbachev in 1983 to take over the Leningrad party machine.

Zaikov's promotion represented not only a public statement about the new responsibilities of the defence industries to the economy as a whole but also a distinct break with the Brezhnev tradition. Brezhnev had left the military-industrial complex in the capable hands of Marshal Dmitri Ustinov. But Ustinov had been promoted to be minister of defence, keeping his skills and the potential of his vast industrial base within the defence sector. Gorbachev's promotion of Zaikov, and the transfer of top defence managers into the civilian economy, signalled a dramatic shift of strategic emphasis.

Managers of this quality were not being assigned to improve the quality of Soviet television sets, appalling as they were. (In the month that Zaikov's elevation was announced, a survey in the newspaper *Socialist Industry* found that the average colour-television set had to be sent in twice for repair during its twelve-month guarantee period.[7]) Their task was to transform the means, rather than the ends, of the industrial base: to ensure that Soviet television sets of the future would be better designed, that the production lines would be reacting much faster to new designs, and that the scientists would be working more closely with the factories. It was a formidable challenge: to try to impose upon a centrally planned economy the same kind of industrial flexibility, speed of response and commitment to innovation that only the leading Western corporations had managed to achieve. It was, however, the policy that Gorbachev had begun to sketch out while Andropov was dying, and on which he had begun to campaign during the Chernenko interregnum.

Shortly before he left for his triumphant visit to Britain in December 1984, Gorbachev gave a speech to the All-Union Scientific and Practical Conference, a gathering of top managers, party officials involved in the economy, leading scientists and engineers. Had he been a Western politician, the speech could have been called his election manifesto. It spelled out the economic strategy he believed the nation must follow, and it was well received by an audience who knew better than anyone the shortcomings of the economy they managed.

This was the first of the Gorbachev specials, the kind of tough and critical but also visionary speech that was to become his hallmark. Unlike the usual smug accounts of success which had been the stock in trade of the party leadership since Brezhnev's day, he included some harsh facts:[8]

It often happens that the latest automatic production lines, robots and programmed machine tools are not effectively used because of insufficient skill on the part of workers, engineers and technicians.

He held out some carrots, offering 'more effective economic incentives for applying scientific achievements and technological inventions in practice', and suggesting that 'the spirit of competition in creative scientific work should be put to better use'. He promised to let industrial inventions carry the names of the individual inventors and vowed 'to carry out measures to enhance the role and prestige of the engineer'. He went on:[9]

> We have to achieve a breakthrough. Only an intensive and highly developed economy can ensure the strengthening of the country's position on the world scene and enable it to enter the next millennium in a manner befitting a great and prosperous country. . . . There is no alternative.

This was language reminiscent of a campaigning Western politician. To any British listener it carried echoes of Margaret Thatcher's own repeated slogan 'There is no alternative', and of Harold Wilson's clarion call of 1964, which won him the election, for the nation to commit itself to 'the white heat of the technological revolution'.

Perhaps the echoes were inevitable. There were considerable similarities between the Soviet and the British economies. Both were rather good at basic scientific research but woefully inefficient at putting it into practice on the factory floor. They tended to stick with the old traditions of heavy industry, and to be slow to adapt to the changing needs of the marketplace. They were bad at meeting delivery dates, had a reputation for poor quality and burdened their economies with disproportionately high defence budgets – although each produced high-quality military hardware. They were both fortunate in discovering large quantities of oil and natural gas in the 1960s and 1970s which for a time cushioned and disguised the failings of their industrial base. But they both needed radical industrial reform and, by a curious coincidence, they were each to experience an attempt to impose that reform from the top. Perhaps this explained why Mikhail Gorbachev, fresh from delivering his pioneering speech, got on so well with Margaret Thatcher when he met her at Chequers five days later.

One of the signs of success that Mrs Thatcher saw as justifying her own policies was the ability of the computing sector in the

British economy, or at least the ability of its importers and salesmen (and some of its own industries), to give Britain the world's highest penetration of home computers in 1985. There were more British homes with personal computers, and more British schoolchildren going through computer courses, than in any of the world's advanced economies. They may have been playing spaceship games, but the nation had taken great steps towards computer literacy. It was an achievement that Mikhail Gorbachev wanted to emulate.

When Gorbachev met Thatcher, the Soviet ministry of education had been set a target of installing one million microcomputers in Soviet schools by 1990. That target had been fixed by a special commission which Gorbachev had established in 1983, when Andropov had given him the job of drawing up the strategy for economic reform. Gorbachev had brought two top scientists onto the commission, Yevgeny Velikhov, a nuclear physicist, and Andrei Ershov, whose job was to devise the computer literacy programme that was introduced into the country's 60,000 secondary schools in September 1985.

This project was supposed to exemplify the advantage of the planned economy. A decision was made at the top to computerise the country, and within two years the national school curriculum had been transformed; five years after that, a new computer-literate generation should be graduating into Soviet universities and offices and factories. But it did not work out as planned. Before the school year started in September, the plan to instal a million micros by 1990 had been cut in half. Even the reduced plan to make 500,000 micros available looked highly optimistic.[10]

Moscow's school number 20, near the Belorossiya station, which I visited in March 1986, was one of the first to have the Soviet-made Elektronika 60 micros installed. The machines were little more than terminals, linked to the teacher's computer, which had its own disc drive. The teacher programmed the pupils' terminals from her own master computer, and there were programmes to learn English, to revise physics, to work out mathematical problems, and a programme to teach the students how to do their own programming. Like teenagers with computers everywhere, they were experimenting with inventing their own games, and writing their own programmes to play sea battles and galactic wars.[11] But they had to write down their programmes in longhand. There was no way their own limited 58 K terminals could store data, and although in theory an individual programme could be stored on the teacher's disc, the discs were in short supply. At the time of my visit she was using imported West German discs. The Soviet computer industry was still unable to mass-produce its own. Its first true micro, the Agat, which was modelled on the ten-year-old Apple One, never went into mass production because it had to rely on imported floppy discs, and the Soviet Union's COMECON partners in East Germany and Bulgaria were unable to guarantee an adequate supply. The Agat cost almost 4000 roubles, or $5200 at the official exchange rate, about ten times the cost of a comparable machine in the West.[12]

The backwardness of the Soviet computer industry is apparent throughout the economy. In one of the most modern factory complexes in the country, the Ust-Ilimsk timber and cellulose processing plant, the whole production operation is controlled by imported French and British computers.[13] At one of the country's leading research think-tanks, the Institute of Organic Chemistry at Riga on the Baltic coast, the computer room in entirely filled with Hewlett-Packard machines.[14] The failure of the Soviet computer industry to come up with their own technology for the schools programme meant that, in 1985, they imported 10,000 Yamaha micros from Japan.

There is no doubting the hunger of Soviet teenagers and their elders for home computers. On Moscow's Gorky Street, outside the Pioneer shop which sells electronic parts to young radio buffs, there is a thriving black market for circuit boards, chips and processors. Floppy discs that cost less than $5 in the West change hands for 60 to 80 roubles. Self-styled experts will offer to build a custom-made home computer for 1000 roubles, based on an 8-bit processor. A Polish-made copy of a basic Sinclair Spectrum, which is on sale in the West for less than £50 in the discount shops, can fetch up to 2000 roubles.[15]

When the official factories do produce their own hardware, the machines are backward. In the computer centre for the Lithuanian central economic planning board, the obsolete terminals each had tiny cooling fans built into the back of the casing, apparently because they still used vacuum-tube technology instead of transistors or printed circuits.[16] In the autumn of 1985, the specifics were finally agreed for a new Soviet micro, to be made by the ministry of defence industries. A 16-bit computer with PDP architecture, it was a virtual copy of the American Digital Equipment

Corporation machine – except that it was designed for use with a cassette rather than a disc memory.

Soviet science has been working intensively in the computer field since the late 1940s, when Professor Lebedev and his team at the Ukraine Academy of Sciences began designing the first Soviet machine. Dubbed the MESM when it was made in prototype in 1950, it was the basic building block for the big mainframes the Soviet Union started to manufacture in the 1960s. Two kinds of mainframes were produced, to fit the two kinds of computer centre which the planners had decided would meet the country's computing needs. There were the big regional centres, which were equipped with BESM 6 machines, capable of 600,000–800,000 OPS (operations per second), and there were slower machines for district computer centres, such as the BESM 4 and M 220, capable of 20,000–50,000 OPS.[17]

It was a classic illustration of the limitations of planned science. The planners had decided the proper function of computers and had told the scientists to produce the necessary hardware. But back in the 1950s, nobody knew the potential of computers, nor what kind of jobs they could be stretched to do, nor what kind of economy they could eventually help to create. The Soviet Union went into the 1970s with machines designed in the 1960s in accordance with the thinking of planners and politicians in the 1950s. It was a recipe for systemic obsolescence. In the course of the late 1960s and early 1970s, aware of the failure of their own production systems, the Russians bought British ITC and American IBM mainframes and made their own copies.

Soviet computer science faced other problems, probably unique to the Soviet Union. In the early 1950s, when the study of genetics was ravaged by the bizarre (but ideologically approved) theories of Lysenko, the whole field of cybernetics was simultaneously denounced as 'a pseudo-science serving the interest of bourgeois capitalism'. Until 1958, when the Academy of Sciences managed to get the party line reversed and set up its own approved Council on Cybernetics, it was a brave scientist who chose to work in the field.[18]

The second problem was more complex. The two most important institutions to back the idea of producing huge mainframe computers were the space-programme scientists, who needed number-crunching skills to calculate orbits, and Gosplan, the state planning board for the economy. The big mainframe seemed like the answer to the planners' dreams. Here, they believed, was a machine with the capacity to replicate the economy and allow them to simulate the effect of their schemes. (This delusion, it is fair to say, was shared by a number of Western finance ministries in the 1960s.)

The planners' enthusiasm stimulated research into and production of big mainframe computers (though at the expense of parallel development of micros). But it terrified Soviet industrial managers, who saw what little room for manoeuvre they had managed to win being eroded by the all-powerful Gosplan computers. The result was GIGO, which stands for garbage in, garbage out. Soviet managers were past masters at the art of massaging production figures to show that the letter of the plan had been fulfilled, even if its spirit had been thwarted. When Gosplan set a target for the production of a certain weight of nails, the factories turned out small numbers of very big nails, because it was easiest to meet the plan that way. When Gosplan caught on, and changed the plan so that a specific number of nails had to be manufactured, the factories began turning out vast quantities of tiny nails. The Gosplan computer failed to query the figures, while the Soviet economy suffered from a nail shortage.

In a sense, the coming of computers helped to fossilise some of the entrenched faults of the Soviet economy. Computers are efficient at processing figures, so the bias towards trying to manage the economy through crude statistics for output was intensified. But computers cannot measure the quality of goods produced, which was the kind of control the Soviet economy required. By the early 1980s, when computerisation had come to the stock-room and warehouse, Soviet planners were finally deluged with the hard data that proved the shortcomings of the system: the warehouses were filling fast with goods that nobody wanted to buy, but which had been counted by Gosplan as useful and which entitled the factories which made them to production bonuses for meeting their plans.[19]

In spite of all the problems and setbacks, by the mid-1980s the Soviet Union was becoming a computerised society. The ticketing system for Aeroflot, hotel bookings for Intourist, and telephone and telex bills were computerised. There was a computerised digital-reading system in the post offices and a national system of coded numbers for addresses which made the Soviet postal service at least as efficient as its British counterpart. There were computer games in amusement arcades, and clubs of young enthusiasts in Moscow who relished 'hacking' and drew up their own chess-playing programmes. The decision in 1986 to give exit visas to two Soviet Jews, Isai and Grigori Goldstein – who had been refused visas for fourteen years on the grounds that, as computer programmers, they knew state secrets – was a telling sign that computers were becoming part of society's furniture.

The credit goes to a handful of Soviet computer enthusiasts. Some of them were pure scientists, such as the Nobel Prize winner Leonid Kantorovich, a pioneer of the theories of linear programming. Others such as Academician Glushkov knew how to manoeuvre through the shoals of Soviet politics and had a rare skill for simultaneously simplifying and publicising the issues. Glushkov's 1960 prediction that within twenty years the entire Soviet labour force would be engaged in administering the plan with nobody left to man the factories helped convince the Politburo of the need to invest in computerisation.[20]

But it was all desperately slow. Gosplan itself only began to computerise its statistical centre in 1966, and the full specifications for the system were not approved until 1972. It only started full operation in 1977 and, by 1985, Gosplan had still not succeeded in putting together an integrated system which allowed them to construct a dynamic model of the economy.[21] And it was not until 1985 that the computer scientists finally won the argument to establish a super-ministry for computer sciences and break the fragmented old system which had different ministries producing different and incompatible models. The ministry for radio-communications produced a mainframe which used an entirely different language from the models produced by the ministry of instrument-building, and a new central authority was needed to cut through the old rivalries and vested interests – such as the one which gave the state committee for cinematography the monopoly of producing magnetic data tape.[22]

This establishment of a central authority or super-ministry was characteristic of the Gorbachev reforms – to the surprise of many Western observers who had seen him as a decentraliser, committed to increasing the autonomy of managements out in the factories. But this was to misunderstand the nature of the Gorbachev reforms, and of the Soviet system, which depends utterly upon the centralisation of control in the hands of the party leadership.

Gorbachev saw his role in almost military terms. As the

commanding general, he would lay down the broad strategy, while it was up to the junior officers who ran the individual branches and industrial enterprises of the economy to carry out that strategy with very much more tactical freedom than they had enjoyed in the past. The super-ministries that he established in the key areas of machine-building, agriculture and computers were like small general staffs. Indeed, when the six separate ministries of agriculture were merged into a new super-ministry, 20,000 staff cuts were made.[23] Gorbachev wanted to streamline that bureaucratic layer. The strategic decisions were to be made at the top, and the decisions about production, sales and workforces were to be made at the bottom, by industrial management. It was the job of the super-ministries to convey his strategy to industry, to pass on decisions and to coordinate their implementation.

Reforms of similar kinds had not worked in the past, in large part because they were frustrated by the party and ministerial bureaucracies who were jealous of their privileges and their roles. Gorbachev's answer was to cut the bureaucracy down to size; it was a bold step, and it depended heavily upon his belief that Soviet industrial management was waiting for the opportunity to stretch its wings, free of bureaucratic control. Certainly, such freedom was what top Soviet managers said they wanted, in discussions with the academic reformers of the Novosibirsk Economics Institute.[24] Whether they could take advantage of the new responsibilities was another matter.

Gorbachev's new deal for industry had two main thrusts, which he outlined as follows:[25]

[First]: Resolutely enlarging the framework of autonomy for industrial enterprises and associations, increasing their responsibility for attaining the best possible results. Towards this end, [we shall] transfer them to genuine cost-accounting, self-support and self-financing, and make the income levels of the workforce directly dependent on the efficiency of their work. [And second]: Enterprises and organisations should be given the right to sell to one another, independently, what they produce over and above the plan, raw and other materials they do not use, etc. They should also be given the legal right to make such sales direct to the public.

Had these reforms come out of the blue, they might well have suffered the same gloomy fate as so many other attempts at changing the intractable structure of the Soviet economy. But

Gorbachev was building on the foundation of the economic experiment, which had given management more power to set wages, to make their own investment decisions and to widen their product lines. Above all, he was, and is, counting on technology to bring the research laboratories closer to the workbench.

Western smugness about the technological backwardness of Soviet science is dangerously misplaced. There are entire sectors of Soviet excellence unrelated to the high-profile space programme or the defence industries. Apart from its outstanding capacities in pure theoretical mathematics, the Soviet Union excels in those areas where the research institutes have been integrated directly into the manufacturing process. Perhaps the best known example of this is the Paton welding institute in Kiev, which engages in contract research for specific projects such as the Siberian pipelines and the submersible oil rigs of the Caspian Sea. But the Soviet lead in power transmission, sending 1.5 million volts down a DC-transmission line, was developed at the science city of Novosibirsk, to solve the local problem of getting Siberian hydroelectric power to the factories of the west.[26]

Until the Chernobyl disaster, Soviet nuclear power engineering seemed on a par with the latest Western developments, its success in catching up helped by the long pause in Western commissioning of new nuclear power stations after the Three Mile Island controversy. The first of its fast-breeder stations has now been delivering 350 megawatts for twelve years on the shore of the Caspian Sea, and French nuclear scientists, who hold a clear technological lead in fast-breeders in the West, say that the Russians are equally far advanced.[27] Whatever the technical failures that led to the Chernobyl tragedy, the level of scientific skill and ingenuity that brought the rogue reactor under control was clearly of the very highest order.

The Soviet Union has long produced more scientists and engineers than any other country in the world. If Gorbachev can get them to work more closely with industry, the results could be dramatic. He complained to the party congress that over one third of the country's scientists and about half of its holders of doctorates were concentrated in the field of higher education – where they carried out only 10 per cent of all research projects:[28]

These university departments should draft and submit proposals for strengthening the links between university research and production . . .

college and university students must be drawn into research work and participation in applying research findings in production.

He went on to attack a number of ministries by name for failing to put into widespread manufacture the new products that the researchers had developed. He cited the ministry of petrochemical industries for failing to introduce new lubricants, the motor-vehicle ministry for failing to introduce a new low-friction bearing onto the assembly lines, the machine-tool ministry for foot-dragging over the development of new hydraulic motors:[29]

> This kind of attitude to new inventions is frequently based on the ambitions of separate groups of scientists, on departmental hostility to inventions made by others, and a lack of interest on the part of production managers in introducing them. Many institutes are still appendages of ministry staffs; not infrequently they support departmental interests and are bogged down in red tape and paperwork. We have already forcefully raised this question of bringing science closer to production . . . we must ascertain who is opposing this.

But if Gorbachev was unusual in his knowledge of and frankness about the failings of Soviet industry and research, the ability to define a problem does not guarantee its solution. And there is a further weakness in Soviet science which will be harder to overcome: the way that an almost paranoid obsession with security puts hermetic seals between whole sectors of research. Photocopying machines are still rare in the Soviet Union, because of fears that they could be used to reproduce 'subversive' literature. At top research institutes, the copying machine is kept under lock and key, and each sheet of paper copied must be logged in by a security guard. Printers for microcomputers are simply unobtainable and, until there is a fundamental change in the nature of the KGB's security policy, are likely to remain that way. The concept of a national database, available to home-computer users over a telephone and modem, which is now commonplace throughout the West, is quite alien to the Soviet system.

Professor Andrei Ershov, the man in charge of computerising Soviet schools, claimed in an interview with Western journalists that he saw 'no problem in sharing information of a social or cultural nature. Obviously, computerisation will cause some changes, just as tape cassettes have done. A society has to adapt to new technologies, even if it means changing the legal structure.' But, writing in *Pravda*, Professor Ershov had struck a rather different note. Computerisation, he wrote, 'must be carried out taking full account of our social system, its realities, and its cultural and social traditions'.[30]

Reading between the lines of his article, what Ershov meant was that state control over information, the state monopoly of technical facilities and the general spread of the state security network made it unlikely that a Western-style computerisation of society through its individual citizens would develop in the Soviet Union. But if it did not, how far would Gorbachev's reforms be able to go before they fell foul of the KGB? To modernise, the Soviet Union must change its regime of internal control. This state of affairs is ironic because, so far, the KGB has been one of the institutions keenest on economic reform – and upon computerising its own files. Perhaps the greatest unknown in Mikhail Gorbachev's plans is how far the system will let him set free the brains of the Soviet people.

5

Why the Time Is Right

The real surprise about the Soviet economy is how well it works, given its blithe disregard for most of the risks and incentives which the capitalist world regards as essential to economic development. The Soviet Union has built the world's second largest economy, and over the postwar period has grown faster than its main rival, the USA. Its industrial output has grown more than twice as fast, its agricultural output about 80 per cent faster, and its industrial productivity, which was running at 30 per cent of the American rate in 1950, is now at almost 60 per cent of that rate.[1]

While there is massive underemployment, there is no unemployment in the Western sense. There are food shortages, but there is no hunger. Housing is poor by Western standards, but cheap and steadily more adequate. Flawed as they are, the free systems of universal education and health care remain impressive achievements in a country as vast as the Soviet Union, which has faced total ruin twice within living memory. On the eve of the First World War, which was to bring famine, revolution, civil war and almost complete economic disruption, the Russian empire of the Tsars accounted for about 4 per cent of the world's industrial output. Today, after withstanding the second revolution of Stalin and the second economic devastation of the Nazi invasion, it produces over 20 per cent of world output.

In a number of key areas, its technology makes the Soviet Union a world leader. Its achievements in space are well known, and doubtless linked to the state's determination to keep abreast of American defence capacities, whatever burden this might impose on the rest of the economy. But some of its other technical successes are less familiar. Japanese steel technology depends in part upon buying in Soviet licences for the continuous casting process, for the evaporative cooling of blast furnaces, and for electro-slag remelting. British North Sea oil comes ashore in pipe-lines which depend upon Soviet welding technology. The country's own geography and climate, and its determination to conquer and exploit its more remote regions, have led to the development of nuclear-powered ice-breakers, arctic housing and the world's most powerful locomotives.

The failures of the Soviet economy, however, leap to the eye. The endless queues for food, the endemic shortages of consumer goods and the high proportion of people involved in manual labour are evident to every tourist. Soviet leaders no longer make any secret of the system's economic shortcomings, the sluggish growth in productivity, the cumbersome bureaucracy or the poor quality of goods. Mikhail Gorbachev rarely makes a speech without attacking bad workmanship, poor labour discipline, outdated management styles and the traditional profligacy of the Soviet economy.[2]

For the past sixty years, Soviet growth has depended on the almost inexhaustible supplies of raw materials to be found in the largest country on earth. Much of the growth in GNP over the last twenty years has resulted from the surge in oil and gas production, the opening up of the new Siberian coalfields and iron ore deposits, and on the vast reserves of labour that could be brought from the farms to the cities. But natural riches are proving harder and more expensive to find and to exploit. Falling birthrates among Russians (though not among the traditionally Muslim republics of central Asia) threaten labour shortages, unless the economy can start to produce more goods with a shrinking labour force.[3] Over the past fifteen years, the Soviet economy has been running faster and faster to stay in the same place, investing more and more to keep growing less quickly.

During the 1970s, the Soviet national income grew by 62 per cent – though surpassing the record of the USA or the EEC countries, this was the worst decade performance for the Soviet Union since the war years; and each extra 1 per cent of growth required an increase of 1.4 per cent in investment and 1.2 per cent in raw materials.[4] Moreover, the focal points of the Soviet economy were shifting inexorably to the nation's disadvantage. As the birthrates between the Muslim south and Russian north continued to diverge, and the geologists found ever more potential wealth in Siberia, it became plain that the Soviet Union was looking at a future with its people in the south, its factories in the west, its raw materials in the north and east, and thousands of miles between them. Soviet planners reckon that the cost of the cheap coal from the open-cast mines of Siberia doubles with every 1500 kilometres required to transport it.

Structural crises such as these forced the Western and Pacific-rim nations to adapt their own economies after the OPEC price shocks. It is far from clear whether a centrally planned economy like that of the Soviet Union can respond to such problems in the same speedy and creative way. Historically, the nation has reacted well to challenges of this kind, most notably the invasion of 1941, which left the bulk of its traditional food-growing areas, raw materials and almost half of its industry in enemy hands. The country was able to withstand the blow, fight back and recover because the process of industrial relocation had already begun under the first five-year plans of the 1930s. A second industrial region had been built in the Urals, a second coal production area developed in the Kuznetsk basin to the south of Tomsk, and a new coal and steel centre in Karaganda in Kazakhstan. The evacuation of 1523 entire factories from the path of the advancing Germans was one of the most remarkable feats of the war, and it dramatically accelerated the industrialisation of the far-flung provinces. Just over 700 of these factories were re-established in the Urals, another 350 across the Caspian Sea in Kazakhstan, and 200 more at the end of the Trans-Siberian railway in the Soviet far east.[5]

In the 1950s, the process received a further boost from Khrushchev's vastly ambitious virgin lands scheme.[6] This attempt to bring under the plough 40 million hectares of untilled pasture in the steppe lands east of the Volga river testified to the single great advantage of the socialist system. When the state announces a national priority, it can pour unlimited funds and manpower into a single mammoth project. The disadvantage is that the venture does not necessarily succeed. After initial success, the virgin lands project became an ecological disaster, as soil exhaustion and erosion cut the yields from the dry, thin topsoil. To this day, the European farming zone still accounts for about 75 per cent of Soviet agricultural output, with a bare 40 per cent of the farmland.[7] The virgin lands have scarcely justified the investment that was poured into them. But in another, unexpected way the virgin lands scheme succeeded. Up to 200,000 volunteers a year were persuaded by the Komsomol and national propaganda to go and open the uncultivated steppes. At least 300,000 of them stayed, and as they drifted away from the disappointing farmland they provided a ready-made workforce for the expanding mines and factories of the region. In the same way, the great campaigns to persuade young school-leavers to move to the heart of the Siberian taiga to build the huge Bratsk dam and power station at the end of the 1950s established an industrial nucleus hundreds of miles north-west of Lake Baikal.

The Soviet Union is no longer a tiny industrial state in the centre of old Russia surrounded by a huge non-Russian hinterland. But between the extensive industrial base of the Urals and the smaller regional bases of central Siberia, the Kuzbass and the Angara, or the industrial centre and textile plants of Kazakhstan are vast, barely populated areas across which raw materials and finished goods are hauled by massive freight trains and, in summer, barge trains on the rivers. The transport costs are punitive, and the folly of an administrative system which depends too much on decisions from Moscow and not enough on the self-generating potential of the individual regions has handicapped the economy. The pieces are on the chessboard, however; the challenge now is to coordinate them, to allow them to work together while growing separately.

In the much-maligned Brezhnev era, this process began. Again, like the great volunteer movements of the 1950s which settled the virgin lands and central Siberia, it was not exactly planned. But Brezhnev presided over four separate revolutions whose cumulative impact was to create comprehensive regional economies in these new industrial bases. These revolutions have provided the Gorbachev administration with the opportunity to let the economy grow in a different, more dynamic way; they have taken the Soviet Union to a springboard from which to transform itself into a 'post-industrial' society.

In 1965, the year after Khrushchev fell, Soviet geologists began to find the world's largest natural gas fields in the Tyumen province of western Siberia, in an area that straddled the Arctic Circle. The first was the 2 trillion cubic metre (TCM) field of Zapolyarnoe. The following year they found the 1.5 TCM field of Medvezhe and the biggest of all, the Urengoy field of 4 TCM. In 1969, came the 2.5 TCM Yamburg field.[8] At the time when these fields were first found, natural gas was being pumped at a rate of 130 billion cubic metres a year, providing about one fifth of the

Soviet Union's energy, almost all from the smaller and older fields in the northern Caucasus and the Urals. By 1985, gas was fulfilling over a third of Soviet energy needs, and pumping at a phenomenal rate of 600 billion cubic metres a year – more than half of it from the new Tyumen fields. This level of extraction can be maintained well into the next century, and new finds in eastern Siberia look like being double the size of the Tyumen fields. Soviet gas now makes up almost half of the world's known reserves.

The gas supplies were enough to satisfy not only Soviet needs. The energy bonanza was capable of providing the satellite states of Eastern Europe with their energy, and still leave enough over for export to Western Europe for hard currency. The luck of the Brezhnev years was that everything started to flow at once. The unexpected gas discoveries coincided with the planned increase in oil extraction, also from the huge western Siberian fields. From 150 million tons a year of crude oil in 1960, production leaped to 350 million tons in 1970, and to 600 million tons in 1980.[9]

Although these deposits had been found in the days of cheap energy, they were coming on stream after the first OPEC price rise of 1973, at a time of increasing panic in the West about future oil supplies. The Soviet Union was perfectly placed to fill the gap. Detente had eased the process of East–West trade, and Moscow's planners wanted to buy Western technology to improve their own petrochemical, fertiliser and auto industries. The foreign currency earnings from oil and gas, which thanks to OPEC were three times higher than had been anticipated, gave the Soviet Union access to Western technology on a massive scale. In the seven years after 1975, they imported $50 billion of machinery and technology from the West.[10]

The boom years of Soviet energy brought with them a series of changes in Soviet society whose impact had not really been assessed by the nation's leaders. First, it created a network of some 70 foreign trade organisations in Moscow, staffed by a new class of Soviet executives, multi-lingual, well travelled and accustomed to talking in the profit and loss language of their Western counterparts. Such people became increasingly familiar with Western lifestyles, and inevitably developed a taste for Western luxuries and the opportunity to enjoy them. At first this was done discreetly, but as the Brezhnev years wore on, with ever greater openness. More and more foreigners were given permits to live in Moscow. By the mid-1980s, there were thirty-six Western banks based in Moscow, and over a hundred big Western corporations and trading houses.[11]

The years of detente not only increased East–West trade, they also brought more and more Western exchange students, tourists and journalists to the Soviet Union. The first visible impact of this on Soviet lifestyles was the steady increase in the numbers of young Russians wearing that great Moscow status symbol of the 1970s, a pair of Western jeans. Western rock music quickly followed. It became an open secret among British exchange students at the Pushkin and Maurice Thorez institutes that their parsimonious grants could be extended by judicious sale of their jeans and records, their radio-tape recorders, and indeed almost anything that came with a Western label.

The energy bonanza also brought the era of the private motorist to the Soviet Union. When Khrushchev fell, the country was producing about 200,000 cars a year, mainly for official use. One of the first calls on the foreign currency earned by oil was the deal with the Fiat corporation to build a vast new car factory at the town of Togliatti, named after the veteran Italian communist leader. With the capacity to produce some 700,000 cars a year, the Togliatti plant turned out Soviet versions of Fiat saloons. The rather larger Volga saloon car, still the mainstay for official transport, is made in the industrial city of Gorki, and bears a close family resemblance to the German Opel cars on which it was originally based. The Moskvitch cars depend heavily on new assembly lines that have been built with help from the French Renault company. Since 1975, the Soviet Union has been turning out just over 1.3 million private cars a year. About a third of these go for export, so the private car passenger fleet consists of rather fewer than 12 million vehicles, or about one car for every seven households.[12]

Car ownership is not evenly spread across the country. The highest concentrations of private cars are to be found in the richest republics, the Baltic states and the Transcaucasian republics of Georgia and Armenia. In Moscow, where the figures are distorted by the high proportion of official cars, there is one car for every four households, which approaches British levels of car ownership in the later 1960s.

The coming of the private car is not simply a matter of numbers. It involves a social revolution in itself. In the West, the car is the second most expensive item that the average family will buy, after their house. In the Soviet Union, where house purchase is less common, buying a car is the biggest single financial outlay the average Soviet family will ever make. Car prices are kept artificially high on the home market, but still supplies do not begin to meet the growing demand. The cheapest car, the obsolete and questionably safe Zaparozhet, costs some 3500 roubles, or eighteen months of average earnings. It is understandably unpopular. The most common private car, the Fiat-based Zhiguli (known in the West as the Lada), costs just under 10,000 roubles, or four years of average earnings. There is a waiting list to buy a new Zhiguli which has come down from over two years at the end of the 1970s to less than a year in 1985. But the lucky new owner can still earn a quick 2500 roubles by selling his almost-new car immediately on the second-hand market.

On a large open space by Moscow's river port, just around the river bend from the Kremlin, is the city's second-hand car market, where the scale of the social revolution is visible. Antique Mercedes, almost-new Volvos and vast fleets of Russian-made cars are available, and what is meant to be a state facility to allow private buyers and sellers to come together has become something altogether different. Week after week, the same sellers offer different cars, and describe their dubious virtues with the professional skill of second-hand car salesmen the world over. In the course of the obligatory test-drive, buyer and seller bargain their way to a price which will be much higher than the official price registered with the nearby state sales office, which takes a 7 per cent tax on all second-hand transactions. It is, in effect, a free market, where the traditional instincts and skills of bargaining and haggling are being revived in a country that has spent sixty years discouraging them. There are secondary markets in spare parts, in tyres and imported Western accessories. The magic of the automobile brings teenage Muscovites buzzing round the market, and doubtless absorbing its mercantilist ethics. The thick wads of 50 and 100 rouble notes testify to the market's prosperity.

Motoring is an expensive business. Petrol costs 40 kopeks a litre, about £2 a gallon, which means that it costs a day's average pay to fill a Zhiguli's tank. Inevitably, a vast black market has emerged in siphoning off the petrol from official cars and trucks and selling it to the private motorist for half-price or less. The shortage of spare parts has spawned yet another black market, and means that almost every Soviet motorist keeps his windscreen wipers inside the car, and fits them only when it rains; easy to steal and hard to replace, the windscreen wipers are too valuable to be left outside the car. The shortage of service centres for cars has produced another growth industry, the private car mechanic, who works at evenings or weekends for double the pay he gets in the week. The really successful ones have jobs as *dvorniks*, or caretakers of apartment blocks, which leaves them enough free time to run full-scale private car servicing businesses from nearby lock-up garages. To do this seriously depends on access to spare parts, to tools and lubricants and motor oils, which are all difficult to obtain from the state shops. So the motorist who wants his car well cared for seeks out the best and most professional of the mechanics – which usually means those with the best black market connections or the most efficient route to the back door of the state spare parts warehouses.

To be a private motorist in the Soviet Union is to live permanently on the fringe of the black market. It also means incessant and expensive encounters with the GAI, the traffic police, who can stop and fine car owners on the spot for having a dirty car, for crossing a white line, or for any one of a host of minor traffic infringements. Slightly more serious breaches of the motoring rules result in having a hole punched in your driving licence – and three holes mean suspension. The consequence is an institutionalised system of petty bribery which induces most drivers to keep a 3 rouble note in their licence.

So the energy bonanza of the Brezhnev years led directly to the growth of the private car industry, which in turn opened an entirely new dimension to the black economy and the role of private enterprise. Petty corruption became commonplace, widely accepted by the public, and widely practised by officialdom. There was a steady and inevitable erosion of standards in private and public life, just at the time when increasing trade and contact with the West was stimulating new tastes and consumer desires, and widening knowledge about the luxuries available in the bourgeois economies over the border. It was a socially explosive mix, creating consumer demand while supplies remained strictly limited.

The process could not have gone so far and so fast but for the other revolution of the Brezhnev years: the dramatic increase in levels of pay. When Khrushchev fell in October 1964, the average monthly salary for all workers was just under 100 roubles – which itself was three times higher than it had been in 1940. When Brezhnev died in November 1982, the average monthly wage was 177.3 roubles. Industrial workers had seen their pay more than double, and the traditionally low-paid farmers had seen their wages triple under Brezhnev. Transport and construction workers did best out of the Brezhnev years, while scientists, teachers, health workers and office workers generally did worst – their salaries simply failed to keep pace with the growing incomes of the blue-collar working class. In the year before Brezhnev died, for example, the average monthly pay of coal miners was 298 roubles, while the average pay of librarians and museum employees was 112 roubles.[13]

This fall in relative incomes for what in the West would be called the professional and middle classes was a major contributory factor in the growing crisis of morale in the Soviet intelligentsia. It also helped to spread even more widely the burgeoning amount of moonlighting and freelance work. To earn extra money, teachers began giving more and more private tuition, and doctors and nurses became increasingly dependent on 'gifts' from their patients that years and custom made into a regular pattern of petty bribery.

The main reason for the faster growth of working-class salaries was a series of economic reforms, based on incentive payments, introduced by Brezhnev's technocrat prime minister, Alexei Kosygin. Intended to introduce the profit motive to the centrally planned economic system, it was not a great success. The incentive bonuses were payable to a factory if it fulfilled its plan – so, inevitably, managers and workers combined every year to massage the plan down to easily manageable levels. But they got their money, and the second part of the Kosygin reform, the boost to consumer goods, began at last to give them something on which to spend the extra money.

Although the quality of the goods was not high, the Soviet Union went through a consumer boom in the Brezhnev years. When Khrushchev fell, fewer than one household in four had a television set. At the time of Brezhnev's death, there was a television set in nine out of ten households, and almost a third of them were colour. The proportion of radios and motorcycles doubled, and the number of washing machines tripled, so that seven out of every ten homes had one by 1982. The biggest growth was in refrigerators, from one in every ten households in 1964 to nine in every ten in 1982. The refrigerator is a fitting symbol of the Brezhnev era, because those were the years that saw the transformation of the Soviet diet: a sharp reduction in the intake of bread and potatoes, and a steady increase in high-protein foods. Consumption of fish, butter and eggs doubled, and that of meat increased by just over 50 per cent. Consumption of milk and vegetables rose less sharply. The consumption of alcohol, however, rose most sharply of all, almost quadrupling during Brezhnev's time (much to the benefit of the state budget).[14]

By Soviet standards, the boom was unprecedented and comparable in scale to that enjoyed in Western Europe rather earlier in the postwar period. The Soviet boom had two distinctive features. First, it was spread remarkably evenly over the period, without the fits and starts of the credit squeezes and sudden recessions which mark the progress of Western economies. Second, and rather more important for the Soviet consumer, it was accompanied by a growth in personal savings that has no parallel in history. In 1960, the total deposits in the state savings bank was just under 11 billion roubles, or about 51 roubles per head. When Brezhnev died, the total deposits exceeded 200 billion roubles – not far short of 1000 roubles for every man, woman and child in the country.[15]

It is a staggering figure, and one which points to the incapacity of the Soviet consumer goods industry to meet popular demand, whether in cars or clothes or better foodstuffs. There was little benefit to be had from putting the money into a savings bank, which gave a standard rate of interest of 1.5 per cent, rising to 2.5 per cent for special accounts that were deposited over a longer term. The puny level of interest, even in a society that was not suffering from the inflation which raged in the West during the 1970s, gave savings the characteristic of a forced loan to the state.

Certainly, the savings bank had to concoct various tricks to keep the money coming into the system. There were lottery accounts, from which a handful of lucky savers could win the prize of a new car. There were lottery bond accounts, in which a saver paid 105 roubles to the bank, and was credited with only 100; the other 5 roubles went into a special lottery fund with prizes of up to 10,000 roubles: these became increasingly popular, as the growth of the black market meant that more and more people had large sums of money they could not honestly account for. To spend the money openly, on buying a country cottage or throwing riotous parties at restaurants, was to invite an anonymous letter to the authorities, who could ask embarrassing questions about the source of one's wealth. The result was that the lucky winner of a 10,000 rouble lottery prize could easily sell the winning ticket for a large bonus to someone who was happy to pay out 20,000 roubles for evidence that he had obtained half that amount legally.

This massive level of savings represents a national economic resource that is in its way comparable to the vast Tyumen oil and gas fields which helped launch the economic revolution of the Brezhnev years. It means that, for the first time, the country has a chance of financing its next burst of industrial growth from internal savings. The growth in capital investments over the next five-year plan will require 170 billion roubles, the highest figure in Soviet history, and a 45 per cent increase on the previous five years. It can be financed comfortably from the savings in the state banks. This gives the Gorbachev administration an unprecedented freedom of economic manoeuvre, since growth can be financed without imposing a heavy economic (and perhaps political) burden on the population.

The Soviet Union has undergone three major surges of industrialisation. The first was in the last thirty years of the Tsarist era, and was financed largely by French and British investment capital, and also by grain exports (in spite of regular famines). Tsarist Russia laid the basis for an industrial state in railways and in iron, steel and coal production, although much of the benefit was lost in the devastation of the revolution and civil war. Stalin's drive to industrialise in the 1930s was financed almost entirely on the backs of the Soviet peasantry, whose living standards were ground down to feed the burgeoning numbers of workers in the cities. The postwar industrial growth was also financed largely at the expense of living standards, with some help from exports of gold, furs and timber.

But in the 1970s there was no such squeeze on the standard of living to pay for industrial investment. Rather the reverse: a large proportion of the foreign currency earnings from oil and gas went to pay for grain imports to help improve the national diet. On the whole, the imported grain was not required to save the Soviet population from starvation but to provide fodder for the growing national herd of livestock and so meet the demand for increased meat consumption. The energy bonanza had convinced the Soviet leadership under Brezhnev that they could afford everything at once: a consumer boom, continued industrial growth and investment, Western technology and massive defence expenditure. They were in for a rude awakening.

In the mid-1970s, the energy boom began to go badly wrong. The first problem was the failure in 1973 to discover any major new oil field in western Siberia, the first year since 1965 that this had happened. The second sprang from too many years of overconfidence. During the 1950s, energy had accounted for about 40 per cent of the state's industrial investment. By 1975, it was taking up just 28 per cent, as Brezhnev's determination to maintain the consumer boom diverted ever more investment resources into agriculture. The third problem was that energy resources were located far from the factories and people which wanted to use them, and transport costs were proving unexpectedly expensive.

This third problem had not been ignored. The world's most ambitious nuclear energy programme was supposed to take care of the energy needs of the factories of European Russia. Indeed, by 1984, 60 per cent of the Ukraine's energy was coming from nuclear power.[16] But, in the Soviet Union as in the rest of the world, nuclear reactors proved easier to begin than to complete. By 1984, nuclear power was providing about 9 per cent of the country's electricity supply, against a planned 15 per cent. It had been assumed that any shortfall in nuclear energy could be made up from the traditional energy source of coal. By the late 1970s, however, it was plain that the Soviet coal industry was facing disaster. Too little money invested in new pits and progressive exhaustion of the old pits in the Don basin meant that, in 1980, the coal industry produced a staggering 74 million tons less than its target, a 10 per cent shortfall.[17] Low investment was not entirely to blame. In spite of the high miners' wages, there were serious problems in the workforce. In the big Siberian coal field of the Kuznetsk basin, absenteeism among miners was averaging eleven working days a year by 1980, sick leave was three times higher than the national average, and productivity in the Kuzbass was the lowest in the industry. If the workers were not producing, then neither was the management. In the decade from 1975 to 1985, coal production fell by 30 million tons a year, but the number of senior management jobs increased by 500.[18] The social problems and the lack of discipline that had marked the Brezhnev years were coming home to roost.

The Soviet Union's response to its own energy crisis was a crash investment programme. The five-year plan for 1981–85 was drawn up when Soviet planners had begun to realise the scale of the economic failure they faced. Economic growth rates had been declining throughout the 1970s, in part to pay for the consumer boom and in part because the erosion of labour discipline had led to a stagnation in productivity. The slowdown in growth meant that there was little extra money available. For the 1981–85 plan, the growth target for investment was, at 11.2 per cent, the lowest in Soviet history.

Of this 11.2 per cent, almost all of it, 85.6 per cent, was allocated to the energy industry alone, and most of that to the gas industry, which was told to achieve a 40 per cent increase in output over the following five years. Coal and oil were given much more modest targets (which in the event they proved unable to achieve). Gas was meant to provide 75 per cent of the total energy growth by 1985, and to replace oil as the Soviet Union's main foreign currency earner.

Meanwhile, outside Soviet borders, the Soviet army was bogged down in the Afghan guerilla war, the Polish economy was collapsing as the Solidarity movement posed an increasingly serious threat to communist rule in Eastern Europe, and President Reagan had been elected to the White House. Reagan could hardly have chosen a more crucial time to announce his sanctions on the export of Western technology to help build or equip the Soviet gas pipelines.

The energy crisis of Brezhnev's last years showed up the limitations of Soviet planning – the very thing of which Soviet economists had traditionally been most proud. The planners had been wrong in their estimates of the completion dates of nuclear power stations, wrong in their estimates of coal production, and wrong in the target dates they set for bringing the big new gas fields into production. But it is when one examines the detailed reasons for the failure of the gas industry to meet its targets that the wider limitations of the Soviet economy become plain. Gas travels by pipeline, and in the Urengoy fields near the Arctic Circle that means insulated pipeline. But Soviet factories are paid by quantity of output, rather than quality; for them to add their own insulation to the pipes would cut overall output, and therefore cut bonuses. So the factories are reluctant to provide the pipes required, and they have to be imported from Japan.[19]

Throughout the fat years of the energy boom, local engineers and party officials made their reputations by increasing output, not by thoughtful planning for the future; and the highest-value output came from the oil fields in south Tyumen, rather than the gas fields of the north. So when the crash programme to boost gas production was announced, the infrastructure was simply not available. Of the 4000 kilometres of all-weather roads laid in the region, only 150 kilometres were in the northern gas fields, and only ten kilometres in the Urengoy field. Only 15 per cent of the Tyumen construction department's 5500 transport vehicles were designed for the Arctic conditions of the northern fields. There was no housing prepared for the workers. In the town of Novou-rengoy, 18,000 of the 143,000 inhabitants were living in make-shift dormitories and railway carriages. The labour shortage meant that airlifts of skilled drillers from the Caspian Sea and Azerbaijan had to be arranged, flying in 11,000 workers twice a month.[20] No electricity power lines had been laid to the northern gas fields, so about 10 per cent of all the gas extracted was being used wastefully to run the compressors that pumped the gas down the pipelines. Lack of electricity also meant that the rig teams had to rely on old-fashioned, low-productivity diesel-powered rigs rather than advanced electric rig techniques – which *Pravda* estimated was 'losing' the programme fifty gas wells a year. The manufacture of the pipelines and the compressors was the responsibility of different ministries who failed to coordinate their work, and it was common for pipelines to be laid two years before the compressors were available to run them.

The situation seemed ripe for disaster, but the strength of the Soviet system lies in its capacity to respond to a problem when it has reached the proportions of a national crisis. In 1981, the Politburo's best young technocrat, Vladimir Dolgikh, was set the task of solving the gas problem and given full powers. His first step was to call a meeting of all the ministries and state committees and local authorities involved in the gas programme, to try and hammer out the problem of coordination. His second step was to persuade the Politburo to assign the whole gas programme the status of national defence, which gave it priority in factories, freight services and manpower allocations.

In some ways it resembled a military exercise. Moving the

millions of tons of equipment and thousands of men into the field of operations, in the brief time-windows permitted by the atrocious weather, and then keeping them supplied, was very similar to landing a military expeditionary force on enemy territory. The lack of roads and the huge pile-ups of equipment at river ports, while the thaw was awaited to free the barges, the high turnover of workers in the appalling conditions and the dependence on air support all gave the operation the characteristics of an economic version of the D-Day invasion.

Dolgikh took two key decisions which saved the day. The first was to concentrate all the equipment and the investment in one huge gas field, Urengoy itself. The second was to decree that all the six pipelines that were going to Western Europe, Eastern Europe and the various industrial zones of the Soviet Union should run through a single corridor.[21] This increased the mileage of pipeline required by about 15 per cent, but it simplified the construction and installation problems. The final stroke of fortune was that Soviet technologists were able to develop their own compressor stations to make up for the American General Electric compressors that President Reagan's sanctions had banned.

The crash enterprise succeeded. The target for 1985 gas production of 630 billion cubic metres, set in 1981, was more than fulfilled. On 10 December 1985, the minister for the power industry announced that gas production for the year so far was 642 BCMs. But the victory was won at considerable cost. Dolgikh's decision to concentrate on the Urengoy field meant that the same problems of under-investment and lack of infrastructure were already facing the teams that had begun work on exploiting the other big field, at Yamburg. There was also a growing crisis for the oil fields of southern Tyumen as transport, drilling rigs, pipelines and skilled management and manpower were diverted to the gas programme. The production target set for the oil industry in 1985 was 630 million tons. In fact, it produced only 597 million tons. Dolgikh had solved one problem, but had compounded two more.[22]

Once again, the Soviet energy programme brought about a social revolution. To attract workers to the desperate living conditions of the north Tyumen fields, the state had to offer unheard-of salaries. The drillers from Azerbaijan who earned the good pay of 300 roubles a month on the Caspian fields were offered 900 to work at Tyumen, and extra bonuses above that.

They were offered a free flight on Aeroflot to anywhere in the socialist bloc, and free holidays once they were there. They got three months vacation a year. The dependence on air support meant building air bases, landing fields and mechanical workshops beyond the Arctic Circle, where helicopter maintenance engineers were being paid over 1000 roubles a month. A year's work in Tyumen could buy a car. A three-year contract could buy a car and a dacha, and those who worked for the full five-year crash programme could return to European Russia or the warm south and buy themselves a cooperative flat in the city, a country cottage and car to commute back and forth.[23] The Tyumen gas programme put a final sleek layer on that Soviet middle class that had been building throughout the Brezhnev years.

6

The Party and the Twenty-seventh Party Congress

Talking of his capital city, Tsar Nicholas I once told a French visitor, 'St Petersburg may be Russian, but it is not Russia.' A similar paradox complicates the status of the modern Communist Party of the Soviet Union. The city that Peter the Great ordered to be built upon the swamps of the Neva estuary was an alien imposition upon old Russia. It was designed to modernise a backward land, to act not just as a window to the developed Western world but as a great door through which change could come. It became the seat of the Tsarist court, the repository of political power and even the industrial base. But it was never, finally, Russian. One of the first to realise this was Lenin; after the 1917 revolution, he shifted the capital back to old Moscow, the city Russians called 'the Mother', a city whose links of trade and culture have always been as much with Asia as with the West.

Yet, in some striking ways, Lenin's Communist Party is reminiscent of St Petersburg. The doctrine of communism was an alien imposition upon an ancient, conservative and deeply religious land. It preached industries and proletariats to a largely peasant country. As an ideology, its roots lay in the sufferings of the early English working class and the complexities of German philosophy. Communism was not simply a window to the West; it *was* the West, in all its furious commitment to change. And when, like Peter the Great's instant city, the Communist Party found itself placed at the head of all the Russias, it launched an era of social and economic transformation, imposed from above with a ruthlessness that even Tsar Peter himself never matched.

The Communist Party changed Russia, but in the process Russia changed the nature of the party. To this day, party authority is pervasive, but not complete. Almost all the people who govern the country and decide its priorities are communists, but the party as an institution does not run the country. For example, the Communist Party does not make the laws, although the laws are not drafted without party approval. The legislative body of the USSR is the Supreme Soviet, and about a third of its 1500 members are not party members. Throughout the country, in regional and local parliaments and town and rural councils (which are all confusingly called soviets) there are some 2.3 million elected deputies, and rather more than half of them are not party members.[1]

One way to think of the party's role is as follows. As in the West, the legislature, the judiciary and the executive are legally separate and independent. But in the Soviet Union these three pillars of the state are most accurately represented as three interlocking circles; and at each point where the circles touch and communicate, the party brings cohesion to what is theoretically separate. Such cohesion is maintained through the party's 19 million card-carrying members. The Supreme Soviet is dominated by party members, and so are the judiciary, the media and the armed forces. What unites those party members, and binds society together, is a common ideology – an ideology which provides a national ethic, defining what is and what is not legitimate in public and in much of private life, an ideology which sets national goals and provides mechanisms to see that they are achieved.

The role of the party in Soviet life is not a peculiarly Russian or even peculiarly communist invention. At various times, Western scholars have drawn parallels with the role of the Jesuits in the Catholic Church, with the functions and status of the gentry in Tudor England, and with the Indian civil service in the days of the British Raj. The critics of communism have suggested less flattering comparisons with freemasonry and with the Mafia.

The reason why each of these parallels is interesting, and not altogether misleading, is that the Communist Party is a far from static entity. It has been many things at many different times. In its infancy under Lenin it comprised a small, elite, conspiratorial band of committed revolutionaries. During the abortive revolution of 1905, its 8000 members became strike organisers. By October 1917, the party had over 300,000 members, who became at once the planners, the general staff and the cannon fodder of what is claimed as a revolution but might be more precisely described as a military coup.[2]

Having seized power, the communists then had to defend it against Russian counter-revolutionaries, and British, French, Polish, Japanese and American troops. They had to organise an army of their own, a railway network and a system of government that could feed and equip the new armies. They were an adaptable lot, the 500,000 or so old communists – which may explain why Stalin was so determined to wipe them out when he imposed his own crash programme of industrialisation and collectivisation of agriculture.

By 1933, Stalin had built a new mass party of 3.5 million members. Five years later, his purges had reduced membership to well under 2 million. But while prison vans, camouflaged in blue paint to look like bread delivery trucks, carried off the old Bolsheviks to their prisons and their mock trials, the hydroelectric dams and the steel works, the factories and the palatial Moscow metro were being built by the new generation of the party, men like young Nikita Khrushchev.[3]

It is hard to avoid a military analogy. The strict discipline of the party, and its idealism, meant that it could be deployed like a corps of elite troops. Aim them at an enemy stronghold, such as the moderately wealthy class of yeomen farmers, and they would topple it. Point them at some key terrain, such as nationwide electrification or exploiting Siberia, and they would take it, regardless of losses. Stalin loved to use military metaphors, and constantly spoke of sending his 'shock troops of labour' to open 'a new industrial front'.

With Hitler's invasion of 1941, party members were transformed into real soldiers. On the day war broke out, the party claimed 3.8 million members. By 1945, 3 million communists had died, but 5 million new members had joined, overwhelmingly from the armed forces.[4] These war veterans made up the bulk of the party that was rocked to its foundations when Nikita Khrushchev told the twentieth congress about half of the truth concerning Stalin's crimes. Khrushchev focused on the crimes against the party, and the enduring legacy of those days includes not just the brief intellectual and cultural thaw Khrushchev permitted but the establishment of party control over the secret police. Yuri Andropov, who directed the KGB throughout the 1970s, and the KGB's new chief Viktor Chebrikov were not career secret policemen but party professionals brought in to regulate the KGB in such a way that it could never run wild again.

This led to a new problem. In the thirty years since Khrushchev's attack on Stalin, the party has become a stable and rather
complacent body. Its top ranks are still packed with Brezhnev's
placemen, at best cautious old bureaucrats and at worst corrupt
and idle mismanagers. And in the lower reaches there is an
alarming proportion of cynical young careerists – 'people who
should not be allowed within gunshot range of the party ranks',
as *Kommunist*, the party's theoretical journal, put it.[5]

Yet it is on the party as an institution that Gorbachev must
rely to implement and administer his reforms – it is the only tool
at hand, and it is the machine that he knows. But, if those reforms
are to have a chance of success, the party too must change.
Gorbachev must inspire it, rejuvenate and convince it, and perhaps
on occasion threaten it, but all without reviving the dark old fears
and folk memories of Stalin's day.

To the West, the Communist Party of the Soviet Union is a
vast, mysterious and ominous body whose functions and role are
somehow both shadowy and menacing. To understand the part
it plays in the ordinary life of Soviet citizens, its influence and the
ways in which it is meant to be changing, we can do worse than
consider the case of the airport restaurant at Domodedovo, one
of the Moscow airports for internal flights.

Babka Gavrilova is an untidy, cheerful, middle-aged woman
who began work as a dishwasher. But as a party member, and a
keen volunteer for party duties, she was quickly promoted to be
administrator, or 'Metre'dotel' as the Russians quaintly call it, of
the airport's restaurant system. She did a good job. The coffee
tasted of coffee, the food was reasonable, there never seemed to
be any shortages, and the staff were friendly and courteous. As
an occasional customer, I gave the place high marks.

Just before the twenty-seventh Communist Party congress
opened in February 1986, Babka's trial ended. As well as administrator, she had become head of the small party organisation
among the restaurant staff, and the trial showed how she had
abused her limited powers. Anyone who wants to change jobs in
the Soviet Union has to obtain a character reference from his or
her job, signed by the manager, by the head of the party organisation, and by the trade union secretary. This meant that Babka
had the right to sign twice, and she charged 100 roubles in cash
for a good reference. If one of her staff faced the sack for persistent
absenteeism or drinking on duty, or as the result of a complaint

from the airport management, Babka could fix the problem for 200 roubles. Because the staff earned good money, and could take food home and even do a little discreet trading on the side, they wanted to keep their jobs – and each gave Babka between 5 and 10 roubles a month to do so. The local party organisation never received a single complaint about Babka, neither from customers nor from staff. They had her listed as a model communist, whose 'collective' always fulfilled its plan of the numbers of meals served, and who always brought a good turnout of 'volunteers' for the *subbotniks*, when people gather to donate a free day to labour in the name of Lenin's birthday, or a party congress. She was caught because somebody finally informed on her little network of corruption, and an entrapment scheme was arranged using marked banknotes.[6]

Day after day, the sad and sometimes shocking stories of corruption appear in the press, many of them far worse than that of Babka's puny rake-offs. There was the senior party official in Kazakhstan who built himself a private racecourse. There was a group in Uzbekistan who stopped work on a children's hospital and used the building materials to erect some private country homes.[7] There was the network of naval staff officers who requisitioned flats in coastal ports for fictitious officers on fictitious courses and inspection tours, and then rented them out on the black market.[8] And day after day, there are the anguished editorials in the party journals, such as this from *Kommunist*:[9]

> Every case of violation of party morality causes the party a great deal of moral and political damage. We ought to be shocked by the endless complacency of some party organisations and committees towards those who have committed criminal offences. The moral image of party members is a fundamental problem for the life of the party.

In spite of the growing Soviet fashion for opinion polls, there has so far been no published survey of what ordinary citizens think of the party, or of why so few of them bother to join it. The party's goal is that in every office, factory and collective farm, every tenth worker should be a member – a proportion that is meant to ensure a stiffening of the ranks and a direct channel of communication from central committee to shop and threshing floor, but which also means that very little organised corruption can take place without the knowledge and connivance of party members.

The obligations of membership need not be onerous. A monthly party meeting, two or three Saturdays a year of volunteer work, a few evenings of canvassing at election times, attendance at the occasional lecture: not a high price to pay for a party card that is always useful in one's career, and probably essential for the ambitious. In the arts and some sciences, in sports and some professions such as medicine, it is possible to rise far without a party card. But, on the whole, the higher the managerial or administrative rank, the greater the concentration of party members.

Of the 19 million members of the Communist Party, about one in a hundred is a full-time party worker, sustained by the profit made from the sales of *Pravda* and other party publications, and by the party dues, which take 3 per cent of the salary of those members earning above the average wage.[10] Not all party members earn even the average. For the past fifteen years, in response to alarm at the increasing dominance of intellectuals and professionals in the ranks, the policy has been to concentrate on recruitment from the traditional working class. Broadly speaking, 44 per cent of party members are workers, 44 per cent are white-collar workers, and about 12 per cent are farmers.[12] The statistics, however, are based on the job at the time of recruitment. Many a bureaucrat with soft white hands is listed as a worker thanks to a job he escaped from thirty years ago. The broad figures also conceal some curious imbalances in the membership. Attempts to increase the numbers of women have boosted their proportion from about one in five in 1960 to over one in four today. Jews contribute twice as many party members as their share of the population would suggest.[13] The traditionally Muslim republics of central Asia and the Baltic states have a significantly lower share of party members than the overall population. In the case of the Muslims, this may be explained by the high proportion of children in the population. For the Balts, it seems to reflect political disenchantment.

Party members are organised into just over 400,000 primary organisations across the country, party cells that are usually located in the workplace, be it factory, army unit, office or collective farm. The nature of the monthly meetings depends entirely on the enthusiasm, or the ambition, of the local party secretary and officials. 'We would sit there pretending to listen while somebody read aloud a *Pravda* editorial on American imperialism,' said Sergei, a young economist from Ryazan who says frankly that he joined the party because he thought it would help his career and prove that he was reliable enough to be allowed to travel abroad. 'Women would knit, and we all wanted to sit at the back and read books or write letters. I wrote all my love letters to my girlfriend in party meetings. Everybody thought I was making notes on the lectures.'

By contrast, on a greenhouse collective farm in the Arctic city of Murmansk, I met party members who were desperately keen, and who agonised over the composition of letters to the party journals and felt that the placing of each word in a *Pravda* editorial was a matter of enormous concern. For such cases – to check how assiduous their ideological studies have been – I have prepared a few questions based on the more obscure parts of *Das Kapital* and Lenin's writings: the Murmansk comrades passed with flying colours.

Then there was the simple, sturdy faith of Yuri Antonov, a tough old railway worker I met out in the wilds of Siberia. 'I live here because I love it, the hunting and the vastness of the land and the silence,' he told me one winter's night over some vodka. 'So I'm not a good party member. I don't study hard and don't spend too much time with people. But I'm a party member because it gives all the rest of my life some sense. It makes me part of history. You cannot live here in Siberia without loving it and wanting to make the land work for us all. Siberia is a great gift for the whole human race, and it is the party who have made us all unwrap that gift.'

Yuri is not the kind of hero worker who is delegated to attend party congresses or to become a deputy to the local soviet – not like the star milkman of Yakutsk, whose skill in persuading each of his cows to deliver 6000 litres of milk won him a hero's medal and a delegate's place. There was also the hero shepherd who won medals for producing 180 lambs from every hundred ewes each year and became a deputy and a delegate; then his fellow villagers explained how he would buy new lambs from other flocks each year to make what the press had called his 'miracle of the high pastures'.[14]

A party of 19 million, which is larger than the populations of most of the member states of the United Nations, will throw up the usual human quota of rogues and cheats. When human frailty is added to an economic system which suffers endemic shortages and deficits and a political system which gives party members a monopoly of power, then corruption is probably inevitable. But the corruption has become institutionalised in a bizarre way in recent years. It has become the catalyst of, or the excuse for, political change. Two members of the current Politburo – Eduard Shevardnadze and Geidar Aliev – owe their seats to the success of their anti-corruption drives in their home republics (see pages 143–44) and, like Yuri Andropov before him, Mikhail Gorbachev has no real need to overhaul the party hierarchy through Stalin-esque purges: the legal weapon of 'anti-corruption drives' does the job for him. Rising high in the party ranks remains a risky business. In Stalin's time, the penalty for transgression was a bullet in the back of the neck; today, it is a visit from the KGB's fraud squad.

There is nevertheless no shortage of ambitious young party officials who spend their military service volunteering to help the *zampolit* (the political officer) prepare his ideological lectures and their civilian life attending Komsomol meetings. One rising young official whom I know began by spending two months of his spare time visiting every flat of the apartment complex where he lived to obtain signatures on a petition for a gigantic 'glory to communism' neon slogan to be erected on the roof of the tower blocks. His 'spontaneous enthusiasm' paid off and he is now a full-time party official. His work since then has involved spending several months as part of a propaganda team going round factories to explain to the worried workers why the economic experiment will be good for them. The aspect of the experiment he was promoting fixed the factory's total wage bill for the next five years, while at the same time demanding higher production. The reform had the Thatcherite effect of giving the workers an incentive to reduce their numbers and thus leave the remainder a bigger share of the same cake. His main job was to reassure the redundant that there would be retraining and new jobs guaranteed – and his success has taken him into the ranks of the *Nomenklatura*.

The *Nomenklatura* is the key to understanding the way the Communist Party exercises control.[15] It is simply two lists. The first, the *osnovnaya*, is the list of jobs in key political and economic management positions throughout the country to which the party holds the monopoly of appointment. There are roughly 600,000 of these jobs and they represent the commanding heights of Soviet life. The second list is the *uchetnaya*, a catalogue of rather fewer than a million names of those who are judged suitable to fill a *Nomenklatura* vacancy as it occurs. It is a gigantic system of patronage, similar to the practice by which vicarage appointments in the Church of England used to be in the gift of the local aristocracy, and with obvious parallels to the network of political and civil service patronage controlled by a modern British prime minister or American president. Like the old-school-tie network, at an individual level it is based on personal loyalty and acquaintance. Brezhnev looked after the group of managers he had come to know when he ran the industrial city of Dnepropetrovsk, and Gorbachev is now promoting the people he grew to trust in his home region of Stavropol and Krasnodar.

One of the more interesting features of Gorbachev's career in Stavropol was the cautious way in which he began to erode the traditional power of the *Nomenklatura* system, by introducing the principle of elections. Not all the *Nomenklatura* lists are controlled from Moscow. The central committee of the party at the Moscow headquarters on Staraya Ploshadz has about 50,000 jobs in its list, which include the key posts in ministries, newspapers, television, the armed forces, key factories, and so on. The party committees of each of the fifteen republics around the country, such as the Ukraine or Georgia, control another 200,000 jobs or more. The district party offices then control something like another 300,000 posts, which extends the *Nomenklatura* system to such jobs as headmasters of special schools, middle management in factories, trade union officials and local municipal administrators.[16] The Gorbachev reform in Stavropol gave the local party committees at factory or office level the right to select, and if they so chose to elect, those who would go forward onto the *uchetnaya*, the list of those worthy for promotion. Previously, it had been the party district headquarters which had made the selection. This mild reform was a challenge to the influence of the headquarters officials, a breach in one of the main bulwarks of their power. But only a tiny breach. The party retains final control, and makes the appointment. But the workmates can at least choose the candidates.[17]

In other parts of the country, rather more ambitious experiments are under way. One began ten years ago in the Baltic city of Riga, where the big Kommutator industrial complex throws open all its middle management jobs for reappointment every two years, and the workers hold an open ballot for the posts.[18] In

Vladivostock, the important post of director of the container port was subjected to a new selection procedure. A commission of workers, party and Komsomol officials and port management held a secret ballot to choose one of the four candidates who had put themselves forward by writing personal manifestoes. Interestingly, the man they picked had not been considered earlier under the old procedure. 'Such a system avoids the rumours and conflicts and hurt feelings that can occur among the workforce,' *Sovyetskaya Rossiya* commented approvingly on the Vladivostock experiment. 'When people receive a job through open competition, they work harder, and their colleagues work harder too.'[19]

The new procedures have a great deal of official support. Gorbachev is known to approve, and in 1985 he appointed a head of the department of party work in the central committee in Moscow who thinks the same way, and is now in a position to promote the spread of the system. Before his appointment to this key post, Georgy Razumovsky had been first secretary of the Krasnodar district, where his experiments with extending the electoral principle had won Gorbachev's approval. These developments do not mean, however, that electoral democracy is about to break out across the Soviet Union; the electoral process is far too cautious for that, and Gorbachev probably lacks the power to enforce genuine change, even if he desired it.

Gorbachev's opportunity to bring about internal party reforms came within a year of his taking office, with the twenty-seventh congress of the Communist Party, which opened on 25 February 1986. This congress was vital to the new leader because, once its ten days of sessions and new elections were over, he had no more excuses. No longer could he blame the wasted years of Brezhnev for any shortcomings. The congress endorsed a new party programme, which set out the country's economic and political strategy into the next century. It agreed a new set of party rules, which defined the structure of party membership and the method of replacing top officials. And it elected a new central committee, the body which appoints the Politburo.

The last Soviet leader who had had a chance to transform these three elements of the party at once had been Khrushchev in the wake of his de-Stalinisation campaign. Each of the three is vital, but the most influential in the long term is the party programme, a curiously Soviet blend of political manifesto and Holy Writ.

The revolution itself fulfilled the first party programme, and Lenin's second programme called for industrialisation of the country. Over forty years and a world war later, Krushchev drew up the third programme, which is usually dismissed – in some ways unfairly – as a utopian document. One of its striking features is that it states explicitly the dilemma which confronts Gorbachev today. The grandiose economic plans that the 1961 programme embodied were devised in the light of Khrushchev's personal commitment to the idea of peaceful co-existence with the West. 'Complications in international relations and the resultant necessity to increase defence spending may hold up the fulfilment of plans for raising living standards,' the 1961 programme said. But it went on to stress that 'War and peace is the principal issue of the day; the main thing is to prevent thermonuclear war.'[20]

Gorbachev's fourth party programme, twenty-five years on, includes similar sentiments. In common with the West, the Kremlin remains locked in the grim and vicious spiral of the arms race; we are all certainly far worse off than we might have been, and perhaps even less safe than we were in Khrushchev's day. This is serious preoccupation for everybody, but it is a psychological disaster for devout communists, for the implacable rationality of their code insists that for every problem there is a solution, for every historical contradiction an ideologically correct way. One of the reasons why the men of the Kremlin deeply admire the USA is because they see it as a can-do society, which is what communism tells them theirs ought to be.

The history of the party is one of success, and the country is now led by a generation whose entire education was in the party's hands. Just as generations of British schoolboys were brought up on the thin red line, the Royal Navy and the empire on which the sun never set, young communists are brought up on the heroes of the revolution and of the drive to industrialisation. Most of the new rulers were approaching puberty as the Soviet state defeated Hitler and they grew up with war films that showed the party as the heart of the Red Army. Having talked to some of the older communists who survived Stalin's camps, I have found that a curious pride attaches to the tragedy of his purges. It was the party itself that bore the shock of his vindictiveness, they tell you, and the party under Khrushchev who admitted the crimes, rehabilitated the 5 million or so camp survivors and brought them home. It was the party which wrenched Stalin out of his place of honour in Lenin's mausoleum, which purged the secret police and which keeps the KGB on a tight leash.

There is a poem by Yevtushenko about an old Bolshevik who followed Lenin's call to electrify the vast country and then was arrested by Stalin, to be tortured and interrogated in the blinding glare of the lamps that his electricity pylons had created. After the camps, the old Bolshevik is released, and goes back to working on the power stations, still a believer.[21] The style of the poem recalls Kipling's hymns to the professionalism of engineers, to the men whose vision soared high above their own fate. And today's Soviet leadership, brought up to believe in the rightness of their ideas and in the inevitability of victory, are facing the same awful shock that Kipling's heroes and his avid readers met in the trenches of the First World War. Accustomed to success, to imposing their will on the frozen wastes of Siberia, they slowly learn that conviction and morale are not enough.

The new leaders are still trapped in the dilemmas that have always crippled governments: that one cannot provide both guns and butter, that the masses do not always heed the call, that the workers do not work as the leaders think they should, that the system which is supposed to create a new and noble form of humanity in Soviet men still churns out drunks and idlers, thieves and conmen. And the corruption reaches deep into the heart of the party itself. There are still many idealists in the party, and in private conversation they maintain that Gorbachev represents the party's last, best chance of building the decent, efficient society that is so keenly desired. 'It just needs a final push, somebody to get a grip on the system and shake it until it starts to work,' Professor Oleg Bogomolov told me during the party congress. As director of one of the main Moscow economic think-tanks, his job is to brief the central committee on the progress of economic reform in Eastern Europe and in China. 'Almost everything is in place. The railways are in place, and the oil and the gas and the energy. The factories are there, and the universities and the brains and the skills to build the robots. The housing is getting better and the investment is there – but the task now is to make it all fit together and work the way it is supposed to.'[22]

Exactly so. Only connect. The party has proved itself a brilliant organiser of the hard, objective skills of a modern economy, in building factories, pipelines, tanks and machines. It has yet to show the same ability to adapt to the soft skills, the subjective arts of design and marketing, of man management and fostering personal initiative. Above all, the party has yet to show how much truth there is in the slogan which appeared all over Moscow during the congress week: THE PARTY AND THE PEOPLE ARE ONE – THE PARTY'S PLAN IS THE PEOPLE'S PLAN.

The programme and the plan endorsed by the party congress spelled out Gorbachev's personal commitment to take the Soviet Union into a post-industrial economy, through automation, computers and a transformed service industry. But the people, the farmers and the industrial workforce and managers, have not so far proved themselves very efficient at running the old kind of industrial economy. The sheer scale of investment and the wealth of raw materials in the Soviet Union have brought a crude kind of success, thanks in large part to the way the party has set simple if ambitious production targets. The next goal is a complex one. It will mean shifting millions of workers from familiar old jobs to challenging new ones, and telling their managers to start taking risks without fear of retribution. It will mean telling the party that their job is no longer to help maintain a vast public orthodoxy, but to encourage creativity and help the innovators.

For over a year before the twenty-seventh congress began, Gorbachev had been telling the people that this new industrial revolution would have as dramatic an effect on Soviet life as the first industrialisation of the 1930s. And now, like Stalin, he is having to build a new party machine to see it through. To his credit, and in contrast to the course pursued by Stalin, the old guard is being thinned out through a system of retirements and decent pensions; he has reserved the purge weapon for those found guilty of corruption and, for once, it is being publicly applied. In the month that the congress finished, the trial opened of the most senior party official ever convicted and sentenced for bribery. Forty-five-year-old Vassily Vyshka, the former deputy prime minister of the small republic of Moldavia, had been taking bribes of up to 10,000 roubles to appoint people to jobs where they could earn even more money, such as head of a car sales depot or director of the food trade organisation. He was given the maximum sentence of fifteen years.[23] Then the deputy minister of foreign trade was arrested for taking bribes from Western businessmen. The death sentence was passed on two senior internal trade officials in Rostov. The rector of the Institute for International Affairs was publicly sacked for falsifying his war and academic record, and was investigated over allegations that some barely qualified students had managed to bribe their way into the institute. The newspapers were encouraged to probe cases of corruption, with or without assistance from the police. Soviet television began sending camera crews into factories without prior notice to ask managers probing questions about the cooking of the books. Customs officials were ordered to inspect the baggage of returning diplomats, even up to ambassadorial rank, and valuable items such as video recorders and stereo systems listed as 'private gifts' were to be deemed gifts to the state, and confiscated.

These events caused a considerable stir, and doubtless the salutary sentences acted as a deterrent to many. The real focus of the campaign, however, was not the party officials but the way in which they were perceived by the Soviet public. For the average citizen, party corruption meant the kind of petty graft that Babka Gavrilova had organised in the Moscow airport restaurant (see pages 88–89). The kind of organised corruption that was at work in Moldavia impinged upon them only at second hand. They knew they were paying more roubles to jump the queue for a new car, without necessarily realizing that the money was being squeezed from them to pay off a party official further up the line.

Public perception is the real issue. In spite of the increasing grip of the urban intelligentsia and the new educated elite upon access to the better schools and universities, the Soviet system remains open to the talented. A bright child from a collective farm in the Ukraine or a factory hand's children in some industrial city in the Urals can still hope to rise to the Kremlin, as Gorbachev did. But the sour legacy of the Brezhnev years has introduced a new question. Does a party career look like a way to public service, to fulfilling the idealism that is taught in schools? Or does it look like a guaranteed seat on a gravy train? How noble are the ambitions of the recent intakes of recruits into the party? How have they affected the character of the organisation on which Gorbachev relies to push through his reforms?

The party congress gave a partial answer to these questions. It changed the vital Rule 12, which previously had allowed party members who had done wrong to avoid police charges by being subjected instead to 'party discipline'. The rule had been passed in the Khrushchev years, to give party members some protection from the arbitrary arrests of Stalin's day. But it had degenerated. Members found drunk while driving could get away with a party 'reprimand', which would not even be entered in party records, as long as they had no further problems within six months. Some members had got away with far worse crimes, almost always involving corruption, by sheltering under the protection of 'party discipline'. The new rule stated that members had to face both party discipline and the police courts, and that a criminal conviction meant expulsion from the party.[24]

Other, perhaps more fundamental, changes in the rules were blocked. One of the main reasons for Khrushchev's downfall had been the new rulebook he introduced at the twenty-second party congress in 1961. Rule 25 stated that no party official should have more than three terms, or fifteen years, in office. Every party committee, from the central committee in Moscow itself down to the far-flung district committees, had to change one third of its members every five years. This was a very real threat to the full-time officials and their career prospects, and when Brezhnev toppled Khrushchev he amended this rule to pay only lip-service to 'the principle of systematic renewal of party bodies'.[25]

Before the most recent congress, a group of party reformers worked hard to restore Khrushchev's old rule, which they saw as the key to retiring that moribund generation of bureaucrats which Brezhnev had placed on committees round the country. A flood of letters to the party and national press suggested that there was considerable grassroots support for the rule, and the prominence given to those letters in *Pravda*, *Kommunist* and *Sovyetskaya Rossiya* in the weeks leading up to the congress suggested that the reform had top-level support. Indeed, the backing for the reformers was reliably said to be coming from Gorbachev himself.

When the new rules were finally published, it was clear that the reformers had lost the battle. Khrushchev's old Rule 25 was not restored. But there were three important changes, which meant that the reformers had won some skirmishes. In future, admission to party membership would take place at open meetings – that is, with non-party members present. A candidate's workmates and colleagues could be on hand to testify for or against his or her character. (The intention behind this was to involve the ordinary public more closely in the life of the party at grassroots level, and also to improve the quality of the party recruits.[26])

Second, the party hierarchy's control over the *Nomenklatura* was weakened, following the principle that Gorbachev had applied in Stavropol. The primary party organisations – that is, the factory- or office-based party cells – were given the right of 'participating directly in the implementation of the party's cadre policy' – or nominating the people to be considered for inclusion in the approved list of *Nomenklatura* candidates.[27]

Third, the right of individual party members to criticise their officials was established more firmly. Even more important, party officials were instructed 'systematically to inform party organisations of their work on the realisation of critical remarks and communists' suggestions in the interim between party congresses'. For the first time, the party had been given a mechanism to ensure that criticisms were not buried.[28]

These were useful, although modest, reforms, and they pointed to the limits of Gorbachev's power within the party. Not only were the reformers unable to sweep away Brezhnev's anodyne Rule 25 with its assurance of job security for party officials, they were also unable to sweep away the Brezhnev officials. If Gorbachev sought to transform the membership of the central committee, and it is widely believed that he did, then he failed.

The old men of Brezhnev's day retained their seats. Brezhnev's prime minister, Nikolai Tikhonov, and his old naval crony Admiral Gorshkov retained their seats, even while they had lost their jobs. The discredited veteran head of Gosplan, Nikolai Baibakov, retained his seat, to widespread astonishment. There was little injection of young blood; four out of every five members of the central committee were over fifty years old.[29] There were 125 new faces among the 307 members, as compared with 82 new names in Brezhnev's last central committee in 1981. But the new faces did not include Gorbachev's economic adviser, Professor Aganbegyan, nor his personal scientific consultant, Professor Yevgeny Velikhov, who had to be content with candidate (non-voting) status. Sixty per cent of Brezhnev's old central committee had been reinstated. The only significant change in the proportions of different professional groups among the membership was the decline of the military, from 41 to 30 seats, and the increase from 3 to 5 seats for the KGB. The single real sign of rejuvenation was the fact that only 172 members had the same job that they had filled five years earlier, whereas in Brezhnev's last central committee 231 had kept the same job for five years.[30]

Gorbachev had not failed. He had simply not been able to

proceed quite as fast as he and the reformers who identified with him had expected. It was as if a deal had been struck: the party hierarchy would go along with Gorbachev's economic reforms so long as he did not mount sweeping changes within their ranks. He could tighten the rules on party discipline, stamp on corruption, tinker with the rules of access to the *Nomenklatura*, but the fundamental structure had to be left intact – at least for the moment. During the congress, Gorbachev's most recent promotion to the Politburo, the new party chieftain of Moscow city, Boris Yeltsin, made a series of harsh attacks upon the structure of the central committee secretariat, the real centre of executive power. Another front had been opened in what will be a long battle to reform the party.[31]

No other Soviet leader has been able to consolidate his power in the Politburo as swiftly as Gorbachev has done. It took Stalin almost ten years to establish full control, and Khrushchev needed five years to build a position that never even amounted to full control. Brezhnev took five years firmly to establish his own position as first among equals within the Politburo. Gorbachev had brought his own men onto the Politburo within a month of taking office, and by the time the congress ended, there were only three full members of the Politburo apart from Gorbachev who had been in the job since Brezhnev's last party congress in 1981. Had any other Soviet leader achieved so much so soon, the world would have been hailing a Kremlin revolution. This may be still to come. But Gorbachev set such a cracking pace during his first year in office that even the appearance of a limit to his authority at the party congress came as a sobering surprise.

7

Foreign Policy: No More Need to Bluff

If there had been no Russian revolution in 1917, there would still have been Russian troops in Poland and Russian armies menacing the Afghan hills in the 1980s. In 1914, the whole of Poland remained a province of the Tsarist Russian empire, and Afghanistan marked the limit of Russian expansion in Asia. The troops of the British empire's Indian army and the Tsar's Asian divisions glowered at one another across the Khyber pass and alternated military missions in Kabul. There are continuities about Russian foreign policy and its concern for the security of frontiers that have little to do with communism or Soviet rule. They are based very much more on geopolitical realities, and upon the very nature of a Great Power.

The Russians have built one the world's great empires, yet psychologically they see themselves as the victims of other nations' imperialisms. Traditionally for Russia, war is something that other people inflict on them. Whereas for Britain and the USA war is something that takes place comfortably overseas, war to the Russians is invasion. Few people have been so regularly and so comprehensively invaded as the Russians. The heartland of the Russian state, the old medieval duchy of Moscow, began to flourish in the shadow of the Mongol invasion, an occupation which lasted for three centuries and which has left a deep and powerful folk memory which goes a long way towards explaining the delicacy of Sino-Soviet relations to this day.[1]

Before the Mongol invasion, the traditional centre of Russian power and culture had been the old Christian city of Kiev. The remoteness of Moscow, in the cold far north, spared it the worst of the Tartar depredations. But if it was far from the camps of the Mongol hordes, Moscow was conveniently placed to serve the traditional river trade route from Scandinavia down to the old Byzantine empire and the Levant. It prospered as a trading port, while the dukes fought and bribed and negotiated themselves slowly and steadily free of the Mongol yoke.[2]

With the Tartars on one flank, the embryonic state of Russia faced invasion from the Teutonic Knights to the west;[3] such attacks were to continue for centuries after the crusading order of the Teutonic Knights had stabilised into feudal state systems. There were invasions by the Lithuanian empire, which at its peak extended from the Baltic to the Black Sea. There were invasions from the Poles, whose armies occupied the Kremlin in the seventeenth century. Then came invasions by the Swedes, which were finally beaten off by Peter the Great in the eighteenth century. The nineteenth century saw the occupation of Moscow by Napoleon's *Grande Armée*, and the burning of the city. And the twentieth century has seen two massive invasions by the Germans, under the Kaiser and under Hitler, and a ruinous civil war after the revolution between Reds and the counter-revolutionary Whites who were supported by Polish, French, British, Japanese and American troops.[4]

There are deep and understandable reasons for Russian paranoia about invasion. War to the Russians means an enemy advancing into their homes, occupying their cities, behaving with terrible brutality and only being beaten back after heroic and catastrophic national efforts. At one time or another, the Russians have been invaded by each of their neighbours. Under Tsars and communists alike, this visceral fear of invasion has meant the establishment of a vast standing army, with the consequent tendency towards militarisation that comes with huge conscript armies and a large and permanent officer corps. The military has an influential voice in the government of all states; in the Soviet superpower, still haunted by age-old memories of invasion, the voice is disproportionately loud.

For the Soviet state, this paranoia springs not simply from folk memories, but from a constant and looming presence on their borders. The NATO alliance on the western flank stretches from Norway round to Turkey, and continues to the north, where Canada looms on the far side of the northern horizon, a bare seventeen minutes' missile time from Moscow. The Kremlin also fears a potential NATO-style alliance of Japan and South Korea and their American bases on the Soviet Union's eastern flank. The

Russians have felt encircled since the end of the Second World War. Their foreign policy is predicated on the need to break this encirclement, which became all the more menacing after the Sino-Soviet split opened a vulnerable new front with the teeming Chinese to the south. Growing American concern over the potential Soviet bases in Central America and the Caribbean suggests that this nervousness about unfriendly neighbours is not confined to the Russians. But for an American to understand Soviet fears of encirclement, he would have to imagine Soviet bases all along the Canadian and the Mexican borders.

The Soviet government has traditionally seen this encirclement as a direct consequence of ideology, of a capitalist system's determination to wipe out the socialist state. As Mikhail Gorbachev told the delegates at the twenty-seventh party congress in February 1986:

> Capitalism regarded the birth of socialism as an error of history which had to be corrected. It was to be corrected at any cost, by any means, irrespective of law or morality; by armed intervention, economic blockade, subversion, sanctions and punishments or refusal of any kind of cooperation.

If it were based on the first years after the revolution alone, when Winston Churchill talked of 'strangling the infant Bolshevism in its cradle',[5] there would be ample justification for Gorbachev's view. But since 1945 the main issue between the Soviet and Western power systems has been geopolitics rather than ideology. The NATO alliance came together in response to the menacing Soviet advance into central Europe. The American bases in Asia were established to halt what appeared to be another equally menacing advance into Korea, through China and into South-east Asia. In 1979, with the fall of the Shah of Iran and the Soviet military intervention in Afghanistan, the West saw a geopolitical threat, of Russia expanding to the warm-water ports of the Indian Ocean.[6]

That was not the perspective from Moscow, which maintains that, in each case, its actions were defensive. The occupation of Eastern Europe and the subsequent installation of communist governments followed logically enough from the Soviet determination to ensure that never again would Germany have the capacity to invade Russia. The only alternative that history has found to Soviet–American domination of Europe has been either

French or German supremacy; and each time France or Germany dominated the continent, the consequence was an invasion of Russia. The only guarantee against a revival of German aggression was the division of the country and armed occupation of Russia's share. But to occupy East Germany meant occupying Poland and Czechoslovakia too. It is striking that Moscow has been much more relaxed about signs of independence from those countries in the southern half of Eastern Europe, such as Romania and Yugoslavia, which govern neither the access to nor the borders of Eastern Germany. By contrast, signs of unrest and independence in Poland, Czechoslovakia or in East Germany itself have been met with invasion or intense pressure from Moscow.

In Asia, by contrast, Soviet support for its allies and client states has been limited, and on occasion grudging, at least until, in the 1970s, the Brezhnev government began to flex its muscles in the confidence of having achieved strategic parity with the USA. In the Korean war, it was China which gave all-out support to the North Koreans – rather than the Soviet Union, whose aid was limited to logistics and a 'volunteer' contingent of military advisers. During the Vietnam war, Soviet support was diplomatic and logistic, and was not allowed to interfere with the very much more important objective of building detente with the United States.

The Soviet military intervention in Afghanistan has been perceived in the West as the ultimate proof of Soviet aggression and determination to expand. This is not how it is seen in Moscow, where the invasion was planned as a brief incursion to sort out the chaos of a civil war between two rival factions of the Afghan Communist Party, each of whom was intent on pushing the revolution so far and so fast that they were force-feeding a resistance movement in a still largely illiterate and semi-feudal country.[7] Moscow did not envisage the long and costly guerilla war which followed, nor did it see the Afghan venture as a stepping stone to the Indian Ocean and the oil of the Gulf states.

By the end of the 1970s, Moscow was alarmed by the growing wave of Islamic fundamentalism that was lapping its own southern borders and threatening to bring political instability to the area's traditionally Muslim population. In 1940, the combined population of the six traditionally Muslim republics of Azerbaijan, Kazakhstan, Uzbekistan, Tadjikistan, Turkmenistan and Kirgizia was just 20 million. By 1985, it had leaped to 52 million, and the birth rate of the southern republics soared far ahead of that of the white Slavs of the north. On current demographic trends, by the year 2000, 40 per cent of conscripts to the Soviet army will be Muslims.[8] Through the 1970s, the Soviet Muslims of Azerbaijan and Turkmenia regularly tuned their radios to the popular Western and Arabic music that came from the Iranian transmitters just across the border. But in 1979, with the fall of the Shah, the broadcasts changed into strident propaganda from the Ayatollah. Soviet Muslims were betraying Islam and serving a godless state, went the message. At the same time, the members of the Tudeh, the Iranian Communist Party, were being hunted down like rats. By contrast, the Soviet Union had enjoyed rather good relations with the Shah, and indeed sent a senior delegation to his grandiose celebration of 2000 years of Persian empire at Persepolis in 1971.[9] Whatever anguish was felt in the West at the fall of the Shah was shared, to a surprising and largely unknown degree, in Moscow.

So events that have been perceived by the West as evidence of Soviet expansionism have been seen in Moscow as defensive precautions. Were it not for the peoples caught up in the path of these precautions, the difference might have been academic. But it is important to bear in mind the origins of Russian expansionism, which long predates the Soviet version. It is a complex and at times contradictory process. In the Caucasus, for example, the Tsarist state long resisted the appeals of the tiny Georgian and Armenian nations to expand in order to protect them against their even more menacing neighbours to the south. The alternative to Russian dominance has often been absorption by other states, and on occasion massacre and the threat of cultural extinction by the Turks and the Persians.[10]

Russian expansion into Siberia did not begin as a formal state policy. It was the Cossacks escaping from Tsarist rule who first surged through the Ural mountains and began the process of colonisation.[11] They were followed by freebooters, by Old Believers fleeing religious persecution and later by agents of greedy merchants and ambitious noblemen who wanted the wealth of the soft gold of Siberia's furs. The vast river systems, which remain in the 1980s the most important means of transport, carried these pioneers deep into the heart of the continent. The tributaries of the Irtush, the Ob and the Yenisei carried them far to the east, and long before Peter the Great assumed the throne, the bolder adventurers had crossed Lake Baikal and reached the distant Pacific coast.

At the time, the Russian state was still fighting desperately for permanent footholds on the shores of the Black and Caspian Seas. It was not until Catherine the Great had pushed back the Ottoman empire and secured the southern borders that the state could begin belatedly to impose even the framework of military and administrative control on far Siberia. After the defeat of Napoleon and the consequent stability of its European frontier, the Tsarist state began to move into central Asia, slowly and with much guerilla fighting absorbing the khanates of Bukhara and Samarkand, probing into the foothills of the Pamirs and nibbling at the Chinese border. If the British empire was acquired in a fit of absentmindedness, imposed by the need for securely held coaling stations to fuel the fleets and guard the sea routes to India, the Russian empire was acquired in spite of Moscow rather than on its orders – through the actions of ambitious local generals and zealous governors.[12] Just as the British could never understand why the rest of the world saw them as rampant and greedy imperialists, the Russians are aggrieved when the West accuses them of expansionism. The Russians look at the haphazard way in which the empire was acquired, while the West looks at the results on the map.

The West maintains that the inherent tendency of the old Russian empire to expand has been redoubled by the force of ideology, a faith in the manifest destiny of communism to embrace the world. Indeed, it was the fear of this ideological expansion in the Third World which eroded detente in the 1970s, as Angola, Mozambique and Ethiopia widened the Soviet orbit to include Africa, and the victorious North Vietnamese armies extended their grip throughout Indo-China.

In his speech to the twenty-seventh party congress, Mikhail Gorbachev sought to calm Western fears. He began, most unusually, by talking of Trotsky and the defeat of Trotsky's ambition for a revolutionary war to carry socialism into other countries. 'The views of the left communists and the Trotskyites were firmly rejected,' Gorbachev said. 'Today, too, we are convinced that pushing revolutions from outside is futile and inadmissible, and doubly so when done by military means.'[13]

The fact is that the spread of Soviet influence is hugely expensive, a great strain on the economy and highly unpopular with the Russian public, who regularly complain that their own food shortages are caused by the need to send supplies to Cuba, Vietnam and the African client states. This is untrue. Very little food finds its way abroad, even, for example, to Ethiopia during the famine. But the financial burden to the Soviet Union of its allies round the globe is enormous. Cuba alone is being subsidised to the tune of $3 billion a year, and Western intelligence estimates suggested that, in the 1970s, the cost to the Soviet Union of supplying subsidised oil to Eastern Europe had exceeded $20 billion. Non-military aid to Vietnam alone was approaching $2 billion a year in 1984, and the military cost, which included the expansion of the Cam Ranh Bay military base, was probably not far short of that figure.[14]

But whatever the expense, the Soviet Union has assumed the responsibilities of a global power; it has done so partly because the West has allowed it to. There is a pattern here. Whenever the West continues to support corrupt and brutal regimes which have no chance of maintaining public sympathy, then a domestic revolutionary movement inevitably develops. The longer the West supports the unpopular government against the revolutionaries, the greater the likelihood that the pro-Soviet faction will inherit the revolution. After Cuba, Yemen, South Vietnam, the Portuguese African colonies and Nicaragua, this is very nearly a universal rule. Islamic fundamentalism stopped the process in Iran, and the West's belated acknowledgement of what was happening may have saved the day in Haiti and the Philippines. Chile and South Africa wait in the wings.

The second reason for the extension of the Soviet Union's global reach has been the success of the Soviet navy in expanding its budget and its forces, in spite of the Politburo's decision to halt the production of ocean-going warships. In 1956, Admiral Sergei Gorshkov was appointed commander in chief of the navy, largely because he enthusiastically supported Nikita Khrushchev's view that the era of the surface warship had been finally closed by the submarine. Khrushchev had fired Gorshkov's predecessor, Admiral Kuznetsov, who had campaigned for an ocean-going fleet to challenge the NATO navies on the high seas. Khrushchev later said in his memoirs that he had agreed to retain four cruisers as a concession to naval commanders who 'thought they were beautiful and liked showing them off to foreigners'.[15]

Even before Khrushchev's fall, however, Gorshkov had won

enough political support to launch the new Kynda-class cruisers from the Zhdanov shipyards in Leningrad. When Khrushchev was replaced by Brezhnev, Gorshkov became the best-connected military man in Moscow. During the Second World War, the broadly undistinguished record of the Soviet navy had been partly relieved by the success of the Black Sea flotilla in coastal and riverine operations against the German flanks. The flotilla had been led by Admiral Gorshkov, and the political commissar on that front at the time was Leonid Brezhnev.[16] This personal link combined with the memory of the humiliation of the American naval blockade of Cuba during the 1962 missile crisis and the growth of the American Polaris nuclear submarine fleet to give the Soviet navy first call on the defence budget. By the time of Gorshkov's retirement in December 1985, the fleet comprised six brigades of naval infantry, 1659 naval aircraft, 380 submarines (81 carry missiles) and over 1400 surface ships.[17]

In an influential series of articles in *Moskoy Sbornik*, which attracted vocal but vain criticism from the then minister of defence Marshal Grechko, Gorshkov had argued that, as a Great Power, the Soviet Union needed an all-round navy that could project its influence around the world in peace as well as war.[18] He built heavy cruisers such as the 23,000-ton nuclear-powered *Kirov*, and the *Kiev* and *Moskva* aircraft carriers with their Yak-36 vertical take-off fighters. As he retired, a vast 60,000-ton aircraft carrier was being prepared for launch.[19]

But an ocean-going fleet requires a global network of bases, or at least friendly ports where the ships can rest, refuel and replenish. When Gorshkov took command of the navy, his ships were limited to Chinese and North Vietnamese ports and to the traditional Russian waters of the Baltic, the Black Sea and the Arctic Ocean. By the time of his retirement, the Soviet navy had one of the world's biggest bases at Cam Ranh Bay in Vietnam, more modest bases at the neck of the Red Sea in Aden, Socotra Island and in Ethiopia, base facilities in Cuba, Libya, Syria, the Seychelles and Guinea. It maintained an average fleet of twenty ships in the South China Sea, twenty-five in the Indian Ocean, four off West Africa and in the Caribbean, and up to forty warships in the Mediterranean.[20]

These fleets, alarming as they appear to their NATO rivals, have proved remarkably ineffective at projecting Soviet power ashore. They played even less part in the Grenada crisis of 1983 than the much weaker Soviet navy had ventured twenty years earlier during the Cuban missile crisis. They made no move to do anything but observe the US fleet operations off the Lebanon, including the USS *New Jersey*'s bombardment of the shore. They stayed well clear of the British operations to recover the Falkland Islands in 1982, and were reduced to cooperating with the French and British in evacuating their own Soviet nationals from Aden during the Marxist civil war which erupted there at the beginning of 1986. Admiral Gorshkov had built the world's second most powerful navy, but was careful never to use it in action. Even the operations in support of the Marxist government of Angola in 1975–76 were restricted to convoy duties.

Nor did the Soviet Mediterranean fleet act even as a deterrent in March and April 1986 when the US Sixth Fleet bombed and rocketed Libyan targets. During the first strikes, when the US fleet was asserting its freedom to sail in the Gulf of Sirte, which Libya was claiming as its own territorial waters, the flagship of the Soviet Mediterranean fleet was moored off the Libyan capital of Tripoli while the American carrier-based jets blasted Libyan SAM-5 sites. Soviet troops had installed those very sites, maintained the equipment there and trained the Libyans in its use. Western intelligence reports claimed that Soviet personnel had been on the sites when the Americans hit them. But neither then nor during the second strikes in April against targets in the cities of Benghazi and Tripoli did the Soviet fleet seek to intervene. At the beginning of 1986, the usual Soviet fleet of some thirty vessels had been reinforced with two capital ships, the cruiser *Slava* and the guided-missile cruiser *Grozny*, but they were withdrawn to the Black Sea before the US carriers began their movements. For all the expense lavished on building the Soviet navy, it played no operational role when one of Moscow's closest friends in the Arab world was being bombarded.[21]

Short of risking a shooting war with the Americans, however, there was little the Soviet fleet could have done during the Libyan crisis. The Soviet navy's one overwhelming job in war is to stop reinforcements and munitions coming across the Atlantic to the NATO European ports. It must do what neither the Kaiser nor Hitler's U-boats were capable of in two earlier world wars: enforce a submarine blockade of the Atlantic shipping routes. There is so far little sign that the navy plans to go to the expense of building a balanced surface fleet that can challenge the USA and the NATO allies for command of the seas. Even if the Russians chose to do so, or if they could afford it, the geography is against them. The great land masses that separate the Soviet northern fleet from the Pacific, and separate both from the Black Sea and Mediterranean fleets, mean that each of the regional fleets can be outnumbered and defeated in turn. Even to deploy onto the high seas, the northern fleet must run the gauntlet of NATO airbases in Britain and Norway as well as NATO ships and submarines. The strategic purpose behind the expansion of the Soviet navy seems almost modest: to maintain some kind of surface naval capacity for wars where there is little prospect of a superpower confrontation, to be able to give at least a degree of naval support to distant allies, and to keep in being a fleet which, while it is not big enough to challenge for maritime supremacy, nevertheless has the power in particular locations to give its American counterpart pause for thought.

The cost of expanding the surface navy seems disproportionate to these very modest strategic benefits; and at the end of 1985, it began to appear that the new Soviet leadership was doubtful of the wisdom of proceeding with Gorshkov's grandiose plans for future growth. In the very month that his first genuine aircraft carrier was launched, a 65,000-ton ship with a through-deck that looked capable of accommodating enough aircraft to match an American carrier, Gorshkov was retired. More to the point, he was not replaced by his deputy, Admiral Nikolai Smirnov, but by a submarine expert, Admiral Vladimir Chernavin, the captain of one of the first of Soviet nuclear subs. The implication of this appointment was that, henceforth, submarines were to be the focus of Soviet naval strategy.[22]

This change of direction carries a further implication for the future of Soviet foreign policy. For if the Soviet Union is not going to pour roubles into an expansion of its ocean-going fleet, and build the sort of 90,000-ton aircraft carriers that give the USA command of the seas, then Moscow's global reach will remain limited. The growth of the Soviet navy in the 1970s was seen in the West as part of an overall strategy of Soviet expansionism. A slackening in growth could therefore portend a less vigorous foreign policy – or, at least, one less heavily based on military capabilities. As Mikhail Gorbachev's individual style of dealing with international relations became more apparent, more and

111

more evidence began to emerge that he was looking for a new course, at once less costly and more stable.

In July 1985, barely four months after Gorbachev took office, the world's veteran diplomat was finally relieved of his post, just two weeks before his seventy-sixth birthday. Andrei Gromyko had been a dominant figure in Soviet foreign policy since his appointment as ambassador to the USA in 1943. He had been the Soviet representative at the meetings which created the United Nations, and was one of the last surviving participants of the Yalta summit between Stalin, Roosevelt and Churchill which had shaped the postwar world. He had been foreign minister since 1957, and in spite of his lack of any experience in the central committee secretariat, he had achieved a unique authority within the Soviet system. A Politburo member since 1973, he had been one of Gorbachev's key supporters when the succession to Chernenko was decided, and had made the speech nominating Gorbachev as general secretary to the full central committee.[23]

Gromyko was promoted, or kicked upstairs, to the post of titular head of state, and one of his last duties as foreign minister was to give his successor Eduard Shevardnadze, the plain-living former security chief from Georgia, a detailed briefing on the state of international relations and the main lines of Soviet policy. It was, by all accounts, a remarkably self-congratulatory report.[24]

Gromyko began by saying that, until the beginning of 1970, his job as foreign minister had been based very largely on bluff. American superiority in strategic weapons had dominated the bulk of his career. That superiority had been masked from the world by the occasional, enormously costly success, such as exploding a Soviet atom bomb, putting the first Sputnik and the first man into space, and carrying out the world's biggest nuclear test explosion of some 50 megatons. But the Soviet Union's strategic weakness had been cruelly exposed in 1962, during the Cuban missile crisis. It had been his duty, Gromyko continued, to defend Soviet interests and Soviet allies and the national liberation movements in spite of this inferiority.

Some defeats were beyond his control. Khrushchev had alienated the Chinese, which had exposed the Soviet Union to an even greater threat of encirclement. The lack of any effective naval presence had meant watching impotently while the Indonesians massacred their entire Communist Party of 500,000 members in 1965. But after 1970, when the Soviet defence industries had finally produced enough hardware to give the country strategic parity with the Americans, Gromyko had been able to take advantage of the favourable circumstances which developed. There had been the economic crisis which gripped the West after OPEC price rise of 1973–74, which made Western economies desperate to find new export markets in the Soviet Union and provide the technology that the Soviet Union had been unable to develop alone. The psychological mood of isolationism and defeatism which gripped the USA in the wake of their defeat in Vietnam had allowed the Soviet Union to extend its influence far beyond the boundaries of the Eurasian landmass.

In 1970, the virtually besieged island of Cuba stood alone, Gromyko went on. But now there were Soviet bases and friends in the South China Sea, in the Mediterranean, in the Red Sea and in Angola. The Vietnamese allies dominated the whole of Indo-China, and the anti-imperialist forces were now entrenched in Nicaragua. The Arab world was reasonably well disposed to the Russians, in spite of the Afghan problem. Relations with China were improving rapidly. Trade was expanding, and regular diplomatic exchanges were taking place. Western Europe was beginning to look quite promising, after the Mitterand visit to Moscow in 1984 and the Gorbachev visit to London in December of that year. The European peace movement had been disappointing in its attempts to stop or even much delay the installation of American Cruise and Pershing missiles, but at least Gromyko's talks with the American Secretary of State George Shultz in January 1985 had got the two superpowers talking again. There was even the possibility of a meeting between President Reagan and Mikhail Gorbachev later in the year. The Soviet foreign policy machine was well trained and efficient. There was a network of think-tanks and research institutes specialising in each region of the world, capable of training new diplomats and providing detailed expertise. The Institute for the Study of the US and Canada had won international credibility, and had at last given the Soviet Union a respected voice in the Western media. Gromyko could also commend to his successor the work of the Africa Institute, which happened to be run by his son, Anatoly. All in all, Shevardnadze was inheriting an enviable position.

Shevardnadze listened respectfully, but was privately perplexed by the complacency. On one point, he firmly agreed with

Gromyko: the strategic inferiority of the Soviet nuclear forces in the 1950s and 1960s had imposed desperate constraints on its diplomacy. But both Shevardnadze and Gorbachev felt that a similar period of inferiority now loomed, unless the economy could be drastically reformed, and unless some way could be found of stopping the American Star Wars programme.

Nor was Mikhail Gorbachev much impressed with the foreign policy machine he had inherited. He found it slow to react, clumsy and long-winded. Although his experience of international diplomacy was recent, he felt confident that he could impose his own priorities upon the policy. He had been on two successful foreign trips, to Canada in 1983 and to London in 1984. He had no fears of the Western media, and felt able to meet and debate with Western statesmen on their own terms. For the past two years, Gorbachev had been chairman of the Foreign Affairs Commission of the Supreme Soviet, which had given him access to the diplomats and the documents and self-confidence in his own negotiating skills. But it had also confirmed him in his fears that all was not well with Soviet foreign policy.

The first sign of Gorbachev's determination to run things his way came immediately after Chernenko's funeral, when the world's leaders had gathered, ostensibly to pay their respects to the departed general secretary, but in fact to sound out the new one. In the absence of a network of royal families, the informal international summits which had once taken place at royal weddings now gathered around funerals. Vice President Bush and Secretary of State George Shultz, Prime Minister Thatcher and President Mitterand, India's Rajiv Gandhi and Pakistan's President Zia stood in line in the Kremlin's St George's Hall to shake Gorbachev's hand, and to wait for the private session with the new Soviet leader. When the moment came, they were struck by his self-confidence, his readiness to interrupt and overrule the veteran Gromyko, his lack of need for the briefing papers Gromyko had prepared. Gromyko had maintained a firm grip on such top-level briefings in the past, giving Brezhnev and Chernenko written texts to read aloud before discussion began. At these first meetings, and during subsequent negotiations, Gorbachev relied on notes scribbled in his own hand. From the start he assumed personal control over foreign policy.[25]

Gorbachev did not move precipitantly, but within a year of taking office he had transformed the three pillars of the foreign policy machine. He had retired Alexandrov-Agentov, the veteran diplomatic aide to the general secretary's office whom he had inherited from Brezhnev. He had replaced Gromyko, and he had begun to reorganise the foreign departments of the central committee. The fundamental weakness of Soviet diplomacy, he judged, was that Gromyko's personal expertise and experience had allowed him to run the foreign ministry on Sverdlovsk Square as if it were a personal fief. All other ministries of the Soviet government were shadowed and guided, and in the last resort controlled, by a comparable department of the central committee secretariat, which guaranteed party control. The central committee's international department had been unchanged since Stalin's day. It was even run by one of Stalin's appointees, eighty-year-old Boris Ponomarev, who had been in charge of relations with foreign Communist Parties since the days of the Cominform in 1946. There was the separate international information department, which had been the vehicle for Leonid Zamyatin as the official foreign affairs spokesman. But even this function was being steadily eroded by the ever-expanding foreign ministry and its own new spokesman, Vladimir Lomeiko, a fluent German-speaker who had worked as a journalist in Bonn, had co-authored an important book on foreign policy with Gromyko's son, and who embodied the cool professionalism and smooth style of the new generation of diplomats trained by Gromyko.[26]

Gorbachev had no objections to the style, nor to the evident success of Lomeiko with the Western media, but he wanted more coordination in his foreign policy machine, and he wanted its structure modernised. He was appalled when Shevardnadze told him that its internal departments were little changed since Tsarist days. The British empire, for example, was still treated as a geographic unit, with the old dominions of Australia and Canada still handled by one department, the second European desk.

However, structural reforms, although essential, were too slow for Gorbachev. He wanted action at once. Indeed, even before becoming general secretary, he had been the first senior Politburo official to call for a renewed dialogue with the Americans. This speech in Smolensk in June 1984 was delivered as Chernenko's long summer 'vacation' began and Gorbachev was chairing Politburo meetings and fulfilling the role of acting general secretary.[27] In fact, Chernenko was recuperating from a new attack of the lung illness that was to kill him the following year. Gorbachev used the time well. When Chernenko returned to the Kremlin at the beginning of September from his long convalescence at Mineralnye Vodi, in Gorbachev's old power base of Stavropol, he was presented with two decisions that had been agreed between Gorbachev and the defence minister, Marshal Dmitri Ustinov. The first was that the chief of staff, Marshal Nikolai Ogarkov, should be transferred out of the post which made him Ustinov's automatic heir; and the second that Gromyko should take advantage of the UN General Assembly meetings late in September to reopen talks with the Americans. Significantly, Gorbachev's main rival for the succession, the old Leningrad party chieftain Grigory Romanov, was on an extended visit to Ethiopia.[28]

Gorbachev then travelled to Sofia to try to soothe the emerging problems in Warsaw Pact relations. The Soviet decision to install SS–20 missiles had been no more popular in Eastern Europe than it had in the West. In October 1983, the East German government signalled their own concern by authorising the publication in the official party newspaper *Neues Deutschland* of a letter from the Lutheran churches of Dresden which said:[29]

> We are filled with horror that at the very time we condemn the deployment of nuclear missiles in Western Europe we should be taking similar countermeasures on our own soil, and that our children will have to live as neighbours with nuclear missiles.

The following month, the East German leader Erich Honecker told his own Communist Party that the deployment of SS–20s 'will not gain acclamation in our country' and called for a new East–West dialogue.[30] Honecker's plea was echoed in Hungary, Romania and even Bulgaria. And Gorbachev's trip to Bulgaria, which saw him promise to work to establish a nuclear-free zone in the Balkans, exposed him to the growing sense of unease among the Warsaw Pact allies. Gorbachev did the job the Politburo had sent him to do: dissuading the Bulgarian leader Todor Zhivkov from taking up an invitation to direct talks with the West Germans in Bonn. But Gorbachev realised that the Warsaw Pact was facing the kind of crisis of faith which could not be resolved by tank divisions. The evident concern of the loyal party leaders of Eastern Europe was itself proof that something was very wrong with the diplomacy of Andrei Gromyko.

Gorbachev suspected that Gromyko was obsessed by relations with the USA, the country on whose affairs he had specialised

116

since the 1930s. Perhaps because of his origins in Stavropol, just across the Caucasus mountains from Turkey and Iran, he himself was fascinated by Asia, and appalled at the diplomatic troubles Moscow faced there. In the Middle East, largely because of Gromyko's breaking of diplomatic relations with Israel in 1967, the Soviet Union had been played out of the game. Its only friends in the region were Syria, an endless sink for Soviet arms, and the highly unstable Libya led by Muammar Gadafy. All Moscow's support for the Palestine Liberation Organisation had done little to advance its cause, and the Arab world was now rent by a new war on the Soviet Union's own possibly inflammable borders. The Iran–Iraq war was being fought very largely with Soviet weapons, and across the border in Afghanistan Russian boys were still dying six years after the army had promised a short, sharp operation to sort out the civil war between two factions of the Afghan Communist Party. Relations with China were not as bad as they had been, but remained stalled at the barely polite level of diplomatic exchanges, and Vietnam's problems in Kampuchea continued to poison Soviet attempts at profitable trade relations with the booming countries of the Pacific rim, which ought to prove a more reliable source of Russia's hi-tech needs than the USA. Japan was moving ever faster into the Western military camp, and something that looked dangerously like a Pacific NATO was building on the Soviet Union's eastern flank.[31]

In his first days in office, Gorbachev made it clear to the Chinese that he wanted a serious improvement in relations, and for the first time in over twenty years Peking and Moscow began to address one another as 'Comrade'. He invited Rajiv Gandhi to Moscow to cement what he saw as the Soviet Union's healthiest friendship. Shevardnadze arranged to visit Tokyo – a trip Gromyko had never made; and in the spring of 1986 prepared a South-east Asian tour, which, instead of the traditional calls in Hanoi and Vientiane, was scheduled to include the ASEAN countries of Thailand and Indonesia.

Gorbachev also participated in a flurry of European diplomacy. Italy's Premier Craxi was welcomed to Moscow, not to be browbeaten over Euromissiles but to be told that it was time for formal economic links between the EEC and Eastern Europe's COMECON. Willy Brandt was invited to five hours of Kremlin talks that focused on the need to build a special relationship with Europe's social democrats. The Soviet leader arranged to visit

Paris in October, a rehearsal for the summit with Reagan the following month. Concern with the world beyond the superpower relationship became the hallmark of Gorbachev's foreign policy. In his first interview as leader, in *Pravda*, he stressed that the Soviet Union did not see the world 'solely through the prism of our relations with the US, important as that is'.[32]

The new thinking owed a great deal to Alexander Yakovlev, who was swiftly emerging as one of Gorbachev's chosen aides. The two men had met during Gorbachev's trip to Canada, where Yakovlev was ambassador, having been posted abroad almost in disgrace. Yakovlev had been a rising young star of the central committee, acting head of the propaganda department, when he had written a long literary review which attacked the then fashionable cult of Russian nationalism. He criticised Solzhenitsyn, not for his dissidence, but for his almost mystical Russian chauvinism. This made Yakovlev some powerful enemies, and he was quickly sent abroad, where he built on a familiarity with the North Americans that had begun during his time as an exchange student at New York's Columbia University in the 1950s. A hard-liner on relations with the USA, and author of a series of studies on 'the ideology of American imperialism', he felt that the key development of the post-OPEC capitalist world was its growing fragmentation into different power centres. He saw Japan and Western Europe and, in the future, Brazil as increasingly effective rivals to the USA, complicating the nature of the capitalist world and increasing its economic resilience, while at the same time offering alternatives to an astute Soviet diplomacy.[33]

Gorbachev's Canadian tour was a personal triumph, thanks largely to Yakovlev's choice of appointments and meetings where his leader's informal style could be seen to best advantage. Gorbachev was impressed by Yakovlev's thinking on the new world of capitalism, and on his return to Moscow arranged for Yakovlev to be summoned home to run the main foreign policy training school and think-tank. Later recruited as one of Gorbachev's speechwriters, he was responsible for the section in Gorbachev's personal manifesto of December 1984 which prophesied 'a gradual but ever clearer loss of America's earlier economic and political hegemony'. Yakovlev was then included in Gorbachev's personal staff on his trips to Britain and the Geneva summit. In summer 1985 he was made head of the propaganda department of the central committee, and immediately after the party congress in March 1986 promoted to a full secretaryship.[34]

Yakovlev was joined in this elevated rank by Anatoly Dobrynin, for twenty three years ambassador in Washington, through the Cuban missile crisis, through detente – when he and Henry Kissinger had provided the celebrated 'back channel' for secret diplomacy – and through the new chill of the Reagan years. Urbane, intelligent and well informed on American life, he was brought back to Moscow to fill a role similar to that of Kissinger when he had been President Nixon's national security adviser: not the executor of foreign policy, but its architect and strategist. His location inside the central committee apparat had, for Gorbachev, two clear merits. It re-established party control over the broad lines of foreign policy, marking a firm end to the Gromyko period; and it concentrated the formulation of foreign policy inside Gorbachev's personal cabinet, allowing him to think on his feet, with Dobrynin there to give instant briefings on fast-moving world events or the sudden twists of an American foreign policy that seemed to unfold through a series of White House press leaks. Gromyko's ponderous style of diplomacy owed a great deal to the fact that his experts were physically removed from the Kremlin, in the foreign ministry in Smolensk Square. With Dobrynin running the central committee's international department, Foreign Minister Shevardnadze concentrated on reorganisation inside his ministry and on effecting an anti-corruption drive in a diplomatic service which had for years used its access to foreign travel and goods to become sleek, lax and a source of envy to less well-placed officials. There were police investigations and arrests in the embassy in Japan, transfers and demotions for obvious beneficiaries of nepotism, and a change in organisational structure that at last acknowledged that the British empire's day was over. Australian and New Zealand affairs were moved to a new Pacific department, Canada was moved to the North America desk, and Britain itself moved into a genuine European department. And Gromyko's long favouritism for his clutch of American experts was cut back, with the veterans of the foreign ministry's European desks being promoted to key ambassadorships in Paris, Bonn and even Washington itself.[35]

The key change taking place in the content of Soviet foreign policy was less immediately noticeable than the change in its style. Gorbachev was the first Soviet leader of an age to understand television and its uses, and he exploited the medium to involve the Soviet public in world affairs in a quite unprecedented way. He gave live television conferences to the foreign press, fielding hostile questions on human rights and political prisoners, and screened them on Soviet television. He spoke best without a prepared text, occasionally glancing at notes, sounding relaxed and sincere. The contrast with the poor public performances of Brezhnev and Chernenko could not have been more glaring.

Powerful as the Gorbachev presentation proved to be – and it came as a serious surprise to the Americans at the Geneva summit – its effect would have faded swiftly had there not been some substance in his approach to the most serious issue of foreign policy. While Yakovlev was right to point out that there was a world beyond Washington, relations with the USA would perforce continue to be the main priority for any Soviet leader.

Here again, Gorbachev was not impressed by the state in which Gromyko had left US–Soviet relations. The two superpowers were talking again at Geneva, but only within the straitjacket that Gromyko had tightened around their agenda. There are three main types of nuclear weaponry, and one of them does not yet have physical existence – President Reagan's Strategic Defence Initiative, which the Russians prefer to call Star Wars. The other two exist in abundance. There are strategic missiles, based in underground silos or in submarines, the weapons that can erase whole cities; and there are the medium-range missiles, often known as Euromissiles from the sites where they are deployed in most profusion, even though the Soviet SS–20s are also to be found in the Far East, aimed at Chinese and possibly Japanese targets. At his talks with the Americans in Geneva in January 1985, before Gorbachev came to office, Gromyko said that each of these three categories should be discussed 'in their interrelationship'.[36] He then insisted that this meant that there could be no progress in one of the three fields without simultaneous progress in the others; or that, even if the two sides agreed to cut Euromissiles and strategic missiles, without an American commitment to stop Star Wars the cuts would not be made. This was the kind of diplomatic and syntactic complication that Gromyko relished. Gorbachev found it hard to understand. As soon as Gromyko stepped down from the foreign ministry, Moscow signalled that it was ready for an entirely separate deal on Euromissiles. The log-jam had broken.

Gorbachev believed it was important to create a momentum of detente before trying to confront something as close to the American president's heart as Star Wars. His personal scientific adviser, Academician Yevgeny Velikhov, had told him that the Star Wars technology was desperately dangerous and destabilising, but that its chances of working as a defence system were slim, and that it would not go into production for at least a decade in the future. There was time to restore good relations with the Americans before Star Wars became an immediate threat, and any arms control agreement could give the Soviet economy a much needed respite from the voracious demands of the military men.

Gorbachev's personal experience of diplomatic affairs had convinced him that the decision to walk out of the Geneva disarmament talks in October 1982 had been a serious mistake. It had undermined, at a crucial time, the pressure that had been building from peace movements in NATO to stop the installation of Cruise and Pershing missiles. It had left the Soviet Union isolated and apparently intransigent. It was now important to seize the moral high ground, and in his first six months in office Gorbachev announced that he was ready for an agreement to remove both Soviet and American missiles in Europe irrespective of Star Wars. He gave an interview to *Time* magazine to signal that there was even some room for manoeuvre on the distinction between research (permissible) and deployment (impermissible) of Star Wars technology.[37] In a gesture aimed directly at Japanese as well as NATO opinion, Gorbachev declared a unilateral Soviet moratorium on nuclear tests, to begin on the fortieth anniversary of the dropping of the first atomic bomb on Hiroshima.

The Russian leader later told a visiting group of American Congressmen that this nuclear moratorium had been 'a personal risk', a decision taken against the advice of his generals. Whether or not this was true, he was making more conciliatory gestures towards the West in the months leading up to the summit than Moscow had offered for years. 'We did everything we could to lay the ground for a mutual understanding, to improve the political climate,' he explained at his Geneva press conference. Although the summit saw no substantive agreements, it was another personal triumph for Gorbachev, who demonstrated that the Americans no longer had a monopoly on showmanship with which to dominate the media. President Reagan's affability and his Hollywood experience had accustomed him to television successes; but in Gorbachev the Soviet Union was at last able to field a media superstar of its own.[38] The Gorbachev campaign continued after the summit. On New Year's Eve, in a message to the Moscow diplomatic corps, he spoke positively of the prospects for agreements emerging from the talks on conventional arms reductions in Vienna and from the separate negotiations on confidence-building measures in Stockholm.[39]

On 15 January 1986 Gorbachev launched the main offensive: an ambitious and detailed programme for universal nuclear disarmament by the year 2000. Utopian in tone and ambition, its presentation was hard-headed enough. Bowing to French and British concerns for their own small but important nuclear forces, he stressed that they too had to be brought into the process of phased disarmament, and that these two European powers should be able to deploy their own nuclear weapons for as long as the two superpowers maintained theirs. The previous Gromyko line had infuriated the Western European powers because it had lumped in their 'independent' warheads with the overall NATO totals. Gorbachev set forth a three-stage process of nuclear disarmament, of which each stage would involve major reductions. Inevitably, the proposals were conditional on an American agreement to abandon Star Wars – but Gorbachev was offering a very much grander price for such an agreement than Gromyko had ever done.[40]

The American reply, delivered on the eve of the party congress, gave a cautious welcome to the Gorbachev proposals, and called for an early and less ambitious agreement on reductions in medium-range missiles. Gorbachev, clearly irritated by the timing of the reply, which seemed designed to distract attention from his keynote congress speech, said that he found it 'hard to detect any serious readiness by the US administration to get down to solving the cardinal problems involved in eliminating the nuclear threat'.[41] He urged swift progress to agreeing a nuclear-test ban, and to eliminating medium-range missiles in Europe, in advance of the second summit planned to be held in the USA later in 1986. 'But there is no sense in empty talks,' he went on: a sentiment which dominated Western reports of his speech, and which seemed to cloud the whole prospect of further summits.

American diplomats in Moscow were not downcast. They had expected, indeed predicted, such a response. They were, however, very much more excited by an earlier part of Gorbachev's six-hour speech which, they suspected, amounted to a fundamental change in the ideology governing superpower relations. It had come in the first section of the speech, entitled 'The contemporary world: its main tendencies and contradictions', the section which would provide the ideological backbone for future commentaries on international affairs, and the basic text for party ideologists in their lectures and articles for years to come:[42]

> The course of history, of social progress, requires ever more insistently that there should be constructive and creative interaction between states and peoples on the scale of the entire world . . . Such interaction is essential in order to prevent nuclear catastrophe, in order that civilisation should survive . . . [and] that other worldwide problems that are growing more acute should also be resolved jointly in the interests of all concerned . . . The prevailing dialectics of present-day development consist of a combination of competition between the two systems [capitalist and socialist] and a growing tendency towards interdependence of the countries of the world community. This is precisely the way, through the struggle of opposites, through arduous effort, groping in the dark as it were, that the controversial but interdependent and in many ways integral world is taking shape.

No such text had appeared in the draft of the party programme, published the previous year. These were Gorbachev's personal additions – and the same words found their way into the full party programme as agreed by the congress. Second, the concept of an interdependent, let alone 'in many ways integral world', was without precedent in a party document of this importance. Its inclusion seemed to imply that Gorbachev was looking towards a world with less confrontation and very much more cooperation; and that, in spite of his ritual phrases about the ideological struggle between socialism and imperialism, he believed that the two systems had not only to learn to live together but to work together as well. This was taking Lenin's concept of 'peaceful co-existence' rather further than Lenin had intended. But then the entire Gorbachev speech was peppered with ideological novelties. What impressed the American Kremlinologists in the State Department was that a world founded on a Soviet acceptance of 'interdependence' could prove to be a world in which detente might be made to work.

8

The Armed Forces: the Struggle for Cash

The Soviet army began to change on Christmas Eve 1979, when it went into Afghanistan. For almost thirty-five years it had been a peacetime army, endlessly training in garrisons and camps, its upper ranks monopolised by steadily ageing men who had made their names and won their medals fighting Hitler. The army's only flurries into anything like active service were the interventions against the East Europeans; and, apart from the brutal street fighting in Budapest in 1956 to crush the Hungarian rising, their activities resembled police actions rather than military operations. Ambitious young officers would compete to be sent as military advisers to one of the brushfire wars that sporadically erupted in Angola and Ethiopia. But as two whole generations of Soviet teenagers were conscripted into the army, drilled and trained and bored and bullied, military skills slowly rusted from disuse.

The old veterans of the Second World War clung tenaciously to their positions. When Defence Minister Marshal Dmitri Ustinov died in December 1984, at the age of seventy-six, he was succeeded by Marshal Sergei Sokolov, seventy-three. The head of the navy, Admiral Gorshkov, was a venerable seventy-five. General Yepishev, the head of the political directorate and the man who kept the armed forces ideologically sound, was seventy-seven. The commander of the ground forces, Marshal Vassily Petrov, was sixty-eight. When he was promoted to be deputy minister of defence, he was replaced by the sixty-seven-year-old General Yevgeny Ivanovsky.

These men were in command of armed forces totalling almost 6 million; if servicemen's wives and dependants were included, they were responsible for the population of a small nation. They also had something close to control over a vast sector of the Soviet

124

economy. The best Western estimates reckon that about 12 per cent of the Soviet Union's GNP is spent on defence, and defence has first call on the best factories, the best raw materials and the best research institutes in the country.[1]

The defence supremos were in control of vast greenhouse farms in the Arctic Circle, where the northern fleet was proud of growing its own fresh vegetables.[2] They commanded huge bases overseas, at Cam Ranh Bay in Vietnam, on Socotra Island at the mouth of the Red Sea, in Ethiopia, Angola and Cuba, where Soviet influence had steadily extended during the long years of superpower peace and endless Third World wars. They ran a large civil defence programme, and a cadet force scheme that was designed to give every Soviet teenager 140 hours of military training while still at school.[3] They ran their own diplomatic service, a special command which turned out officers who were authorised to mingle with Western military attachés at home and abroad.[4] They trained pilots and soldiers from all over the world, sent specialists to Indian factories to show the workers how to build Soviet-style warplanes and produced their own multilingual salesmen who kept the Soviet Union just behind the USA in the world's arms sales league. They had their own publishing house, their own daily national newspaper, their own film studios and their own worldwide intelligence service. They had their own luxurious villas and rest homes on the shores of the Black Sea, where they could relax and reminisce about the days of real soldiering against the German Panzers.

Like generals in any country, these men were a vital and privileged part of the national establishment, and convinced that they were the custodians of the national honour. But in the Soviet Union, the officer corps could not remain isolated from politics. The worst ordeal of the Soviet armed forces was not the war, desperate and uniquely bloody as it had been, especially on the eastern front. That was, after all, war – and armies were trained and prepared for that. But, before the war, they had been the casualties of another kind of bloodbath altogether.

Stalin's purges had devastated the upper ranks of the Soviet forces. By 1940, three out of five marshals, all three of the commanders of army groups, all twelve commanders of armies, and sixty out of sixty-seven corps commanders had been arrested, and most of them shot out of hand. The commanders of the Black Sea and Pacific fleets fell victim, and so did most of their ship commanders. Two thirds of all the divisional and regimental commanders suffered the same fate.[5] It was a beheaded army that faced the German invasion of 1941, led by swiftly promoted officers who had to learn the art of command while under fire, and reeling back in rout and defeat.

After the war, the army developed an unwritten law that such a purge of their ranks must never be allowed to happen again. When the head of Stalin's secret police, Lavrenti Beria, looked like succeeding the old dictator with the help of his own private army, the generals made common cause with the rest of the Politburo to stop Beria by arresting him in the Kremlin, and deploying tanks in Moscow's streets as a precaution. In 1957, when Khrushchev looked like being toppled by the old Stalinists on the praesidium, it was Marshal Zhukov who arranged the airlift into Moscow of the full central committee, who were able to give Khrushchev a vote of confidence.[6]

The army did not want to run the country, nor even necessarily to be closely involved in its government. They wanted a veto power over any government or secret police that looked like getting out of hand again, and they wanted their budgets and their economic priorities to be guaranteed. Broadly speaking, they succeeded, because their priorities were shared by the party leadership. Inevitably, there were arguments and trade-offs. Alarmed that the army might be getting too powerful, Khrushchev retired Marshal Zhukov within a year of the airlift by which Zhukov had saved his leader's skin.

Khrushchev then began a dramatic reduction in the army ranks, arguing that, in the age of missiles and nuclear warheads, rockets were of more value than simple riflemen. The army grumbled, but under their new minister of defence, Marshal Malinovsky, an old comrade-in-arms of Khrushchev from the Ukraine battles, they acquiesced. Khrushchev's own war record had brought him an influential group of friends in the officer corps whom he promoted to key positions, such as his new chief of the general staff, Marshal Grechko, another fellow veteran of the Ukraine front.[7]

If there were fewer troops to command, there were new budgets for the strategic rocket forces, new aircraft and new warships. In the course of 1960–61, some 1.2 million men were demobilised, including 250,000 officers, and there was little provision made for them in civilian life. Khrushchev justified the cuts on the grounds of a growing detente with the Americans, but the detente proved short-lasting, and the military men had further grounds for complaint with the humiliation of the Cuban missile crisis of 1962. When Suslov and Brezhnev organised their palace coup against Khrushchev in 1964, the military were happy to back them; the price of their support was the expansion of their weapons budgets and a new burst of recruitment that took the army from 150 divisions when Khrushchev fell to 180 at the time of Brezhnev's death.[8]

Admiral Gorshkov obtained the funds to build an ocean-going fleet of surface ships, and to match the American lead in submarine-launched ballistic missiles. The strategic rocket forces were given the production facilities and the budgets to develop intercontinental ballistic missiles that could balance, and eventually outnumber, the American Minutemen missiles. The air defence troops were kept busy building the surface-to-air anti-aircraft missiles which were to give the Israeli air force a rude surprise in the Yom Kippur war of 1973.

Official Soviet figures of defence spending are of little value, and although CIA and US Defense Department estimates should be treated with caution, they and the independently calculated NATO figures agree that the Soviet defence budget began to grow at a steady 5–6 per cent a year (in constant prices) from 1965 onwards. By the early 1970s, the rocket forces had achieved strategic parity with the USA, while maintaining what NATO was convinced was a significant superiority in conventional forces in Europe.

In the mid-1970s, however, the problems of slowing growth which were afflicting the whole Soviet economy began to concern the army. The death of Marshal Grechko in 1976 became a watershed. In the army's view, he should have been succeeded by the chief of staff, Marshal Kulikov, a tough armoured commander from the hard school of the Second World War tank battles. But Brezhnev chose to appoint instead the first civilian defence minister since Trotsky. Dmitri Ustinov was perhaps the one civilian the armed forces could genuinely welcome. As the commissar for armaments during the war, he had worked closely with the army and performed feats of organisation to supply them with the weapons they needed. After the war, he continued to run the defence industries and brought together the budgets, the researchers and the facilities to produce the nuclear weapons and the rockets that a superpower now required.[9]

Brezhnev appointed Ustinov because he needed to rein back the growth in defence spending. Strategic parity had been achieved, detente with the Americans was at its peak and Brezhnev thought that at last there was a chance of keeping the arms budget under control, perhaps even of reducing it. In spite of the oil and gas bonanza, the Soviet economy was under strain. When describing the new five-year plan up to 1981 to the central committee in October 1976, Brezhnev told them of the record 170 billion roubles being invested in agriculture, and added, 'I tell you frankly, comrades, it was not easy to find it. We had to curtail the requirements of other branches of the economy.'[10] The money had been found from a shrinking investment budget. The plan for the first five years of the 1970s had called for, and almost achieved, a 41 per cent growth in all investment. But, for the following five years, investment growth was cut to 26 per cent; and for the first five years of the 1980s, it was cut again, to a mere 14 per cent, the lowest figure in Soviet history.[11] Ustinov was responsible. Although American Defense Department and CIA estimates continued to claim for the next decade that Soviet military spending was still climbing at the old rates, they eventually acknowledged in 1984 that they had been wrong, and that Ustinov had kept defence budget growth down to 2 per cent a year after 1976.[12]

Ustinov also tamed the military in another way. He transferred the hawkish Marshal Kulikov from the chief of staff's job in Moscow to be commander of the Warsaw Pact armies. When Kulikov accepted the job, it was a promotion. But Ustinov then juggled the precedence of the various ranks to make Kulikov subordinate to the new chief of staff, Marshal Nikolai Ogarkov. At the same time, Kulikov was brought under firmer civilian control in his Warsaw Pact empire, as a permanent commission of the Warsaw Pact foreign ministers was established, with a full-time secretariat, and Kulikov was instructed to report to the commission, as well as to the high command in Moscow.[13]

For Kulikov, and his fellow tank generals who had been accustomed to running the army, the most galling feature of Ustinov's reforms was the new chief of staff, Marshal Ogarkov. An intellectual soldier from the engineering branch of the army, Ogarkov had been for years the butt of the tankmen. It was they who circulated the story of Ogarkov's military incompetence, saying that he had lost the bulk of his platoon in peacetime, while clearing an enemy minefield after the war.[14] As chief of staff, Ogarkov pushed through a new command and communications structure which had the effect of increasing Moscow's operational control over the various army groups. At the same time, he tried to increase the scope for initiative by lower-ranking officers. Kulikov and his generals felt they were being squeezed from above and below.

Ogarkov, as the top Soviet officer in the SALT negotiations on strategic arms limitation, had a reputation as a detente general. It is not easy to see why. Until well after his appointment as chief of staff, his published views accorded exactly with the official Soviet military doctrine that the army should be geared to fighting and surviving a nuclear war, and being in good enough shape to win the peace. In 1979, he published in Vol. 7 of the Soviet military encyclopedia an article on 'Military Strategy' which was entirely orthodox. He maintained that victory in a nuclear war remained 'an objective possibility'.[15] Two years later, in a lengthy article in *Kommunist*, the party's leading theoretical journal, he wrote of the operational requirements of a nuclear war, and the need for provision to be made for the unprecedented losses in supplies, equipment and trained troops that a nuclear war would bring. This was a barely disguised call for bigger military budgets.[16] Ogarkov's article began a discreet but vitally important debate at the top of the Soviet war machine. It had appeared in late July 1981. In November, Marshal Ustinov published a seminal article in *Pravda* (again, significantly, a party rather than a military publication) which rejected the idea that Soviet military doctrine accepted 'a possibility of surviving or even winning a nuclear war'. Ustinov insisted that the Soviet armed forces had been given 'everything they need to administer a timely and appropriate rebuff to any aggressor'.[17]

In the course of 1982, as Brezhnev was visibly dying and Andropov already launching his own campaign for the succession, the dispute between Ustinov and his chief of staff became more open. They each published a pamphlet on Soviet military strategy. Ogarkov's *Always Ready to Defend the Fatherland* appeared in January, arguing that it was the duty of the ministry of defence to prepare for the eventuality that the West might launch a nuclear war. (Indeed, statements coming from President Reagan's administration at the time made Ogarkov's proposition entirely defensible.) The soldiers had to be provided with the equipment, in the form of theatre nuclear weapons, which 'would give them the increased ability to achieve their war aims'. Moreover, the objective of the Soviet armed forces should be victory. The Soviet Union should set itself 'decisive political and strategic aims'.[18]

Three months later, Ustinov published his own pamphlet, *Serving the Country*, which was a classic text in defence of detente. 'To count on victory in the arms race and in nuclear war is madness,' he stated. In direct rebuff to Ogarkov's call for theatre nuclear weapons, Ustinov went on, 'There can simply be no such thing as a limited nuclear war.' It would inevitably become a worldwide conflict. Ustinov was speaking not simply for himself. His pamphlet and his subsequent articles in *Pravda* made a point of quoting Leonid Brezhnev's comment that 'Only someone who has decided to commit suicide can start a nuclear war in the hope of winning it.'[19]

Ustinov was also speaking for the man who was about to succeed Brezhnev, Yuri Andropov. In Andropov's first formal statement on foreign policy, delivered the month after he was elected general secretary, he was uncompromising:[20]

> Our position on this issue is clear. A nuclear war, whether big or small, whether limited or total, must not be allowed to break out. No task is more important today. One has to be blind to the realities of our time not to see that, wherever and however a nuclear whirlwind arises, it will inevitably go out of control and cause a worldwide catastrophe.

Faced by these authoritative statements from Andropov and Ustinov, Ogarkov recanted. In March 1983, he condemned American strategists who were musing about the possibility of limited nuclear war, and said that those who pinned their hopes on theatre nuclear weapons were guilty of 'dangerous folly'. He came out in full support of Andropov's arms control proposals.[21]

This entire dispute was about more than the rather arcane theology of nuclear strategy. It was about military budgets, and the generals' increasing distress at the tight controls that Ustinov was imposing. Having at least made his peace on the issue of nuclear weapons, Ogarkov then returned to the fight, but this time chose another part of the battlefield. On 9 May 1983, in the armed forces newspaper *Krasnaya Zvezda*, he called for higher military spending on 'smart' conventional weapons.[22]

In the course of Israel's occupation of southern Lebanon in

1982, there had been a series of air battles over the Beka'a valley in which the Syrians, equipped with the latest in Soviet anti-aircraft technology, had been humiliated. The Syrians lost seventy aircraft, and the bulk of their anti-aircraft missile batteries and radar posts. The Israelis were almost unharmed, thanks to their dramatic lead in the technology of modern warfare. They had 'smart' bombs that could be guided direct to their targets and even ride down the Syrian radar beams. They had pilotless drone aircraft that could force the Syrians to switch on their radars, and allow the Israelis to monitor the Syrian frequencies and devise how to block them.

Marshal Ogarkov's article in *Krasnaya Zvezda* reflected the alarm of the whole Soviet military. Conventional weapons were becoming so efficient, and also so destructive, he argued, that a global war which excluded the use of nuclear weapons was now a very real possibility. Ogarkov's real concern was for what the NATO lead in 'smart' technology might do to the Soviet plans for the European battlefield, which called for a series of rolling attacks on the NATO positions. The first wave would fight until exhaustion, and then be followed by a second wave, and then a third, until the NATO defences cracked under the strain. NATO's 'smart' weapons gave them the capability to hit those second and third waves, known as the follow-on forces, with unerring accuracy, when they were still far from the battlefront. Cruise missiles with conventional rather than nuclear warheads could hit the command centres and the key bottlenecks such as rail junctions and bridges. 'Smart' technology could give NATO the command of the air, and almost guarantee its anti-tank helicopters and missile-armed infantrymen a hit with every shot. Vast as the Soviet tank armies were, they were hardly prepared for the losses this kind of technology could impose.

Ogarkov's article said that future Soviet military spending should be concentrated, not on more nuclear weapons and warheads, but on building up conventional arms and, above all, bringing technology up to date. His concern for the technical lag was evident, but in the context of the low economic growth rates and the debates under way in the Politburo about state budgets, the real thrust of his argument was aimed at increasing defence spending.

This was the cause of his surprise dismissal as chief of staff in September 1984. The Politburo was not prepared to give the marshals the blank cheque they wanted. And, in the summer of 1984, Ustinov had fallen seriously ill. If he died, Ogarkov would be his natural successor as minister of defence. This was seen as dangerous by the leading group in the Politburo, which was effectively dominated by the Andropov loyalists behind Mikhail Gorbachev. With Ogarkov as defence minister, and Grigory Romanov in charge of the defence industries and ready to buy the army's support in exchange for a promise of higher budgets, Gorbachev's own chance of the succession could be at risk. Ogarkov was transferred to the western theatre command, and replaced by his deputy, Marshal Sergei Akhromeyev, whose most recent public statement had been that he 'did not see the possibility of winning a nuclear war', and who endorsed the party's doctrine that the Soviet Union wanted not strategic superiority but parity.[23] Parity, the Politburo believed, was cheaper.

When Marshal Ustinov died in December 1984, he was replaced by a conventional armoured corps veteran, Marshal Sergei Sokolov. Aged seventy-three, Sokolov was clearly an interim appointment, whose purpose was to keep the generals quiet while the Politburo haggled over the succession to the dying Chernenko and the nagging economic crisis. The army welcomed his appointment: as former first deputy minister of defence, his promotion meant that formal respect had been paid to rank, and Sokolov was one of them, a professional soldier of the old school, although there was to be some grumbling at the speed with which his two sons were promoted to generals. But the army was concerned that, with Ustinov's death, they had lost their voice on the Politburo, and Ustinov was not replaced. For the first time in a generation, the armed forces had no representative on the Soviet Union's highest body. Even when Mikhail Gorbachev brought Marshal Sokolov into the Politburo in April 1985, it was only as a candidate member.

To sweeten Sokolov's appointment, and placate the armed forces, the Politburo found some extra money for defence in the 1986 budget. It was announced to the Supreme Soviet as a 12 per cent increase, which sent a suitably uncompromising message to the USA on the eve of the Geneva talks about talks.[24] In fact, it was nothing of the kind. The official Soviet defence budget, as approved by the Supreme Soviet, had been stable at 17,100 million roubles for the period 1981–84. But that was less than Britain was spending on its defence budget. The Soviet defence bill, at least the official version, does not include the cost of research, development and manufacture of weapons and missiles. It does not include the armed forces' fuel bills, nor the cost of military construction, pensions, support for servicemen's families, nor the bills for running overseas bases, which are listed under the foreign aid accounts. The real cost of the Soviet defence forces, including civil defence and school cadet training is between 150 and 200 billion dollars, and it is not easy to be more precise.[25]

While the generals had received a little extra money, it was plain that their generation was losing its control. A combination of car and air crashes and simple old age carried off a considerable proportion of the high command in the months after Marshal Ustinov's death. The entire air staff of the Carpathian military district died in a plane crash on 3 May 1985, swiftly followed by the death of General Babayev, sixty-three, the pioneer of jet combat flying and head of the Leningrad military district. Marshal Moskalenko, the man who had arrested Beria at gunpoint in the Kremlin, died in the summer, followed by the former wartime flying ace, General Gulayev. Marshal Pkryshkin, another wartime ace, died later in the year. It was a year of military funerals and lyings-in-state. And when Mikhail Gorbachev came to power in March, it was a time of rapid retirements and promotions of younger men. In Chernenko's last weeks, the old generation mounted a quick shuffle to promote Marshal Petrov, sixty-nine, to first deputy minister of defence, and replace him as commander in chief of ground forces with the sixty-eight-year-old General Ivanovsky. Two months after taking office, Gorbachev retired Marshal Tolubko, seventy-two, from his post as head of strategic rocket forces, and replaced him with General Maksimov, sixty-one. A month later, the veteran head of the main political directorate General Yepishev, seventy-seven, was retired, and replaced by fifty-eight-year-old General Lizichev. In December came Gorbachev's most startling change. The father of the Soviet navy, Admiral Gorshkov, was retired and replaced by Admiral Vladimir Chernavin, fifty-eight,[26] one of the first commanders of the Soviet nuclear submarines, who had no great faith in the capacity of the expensive surface ships to survive in a modern naval war. [27]

But the greatest generational change in the Soviet armed forces was not taking place in Moscow. When Marshal Ustinov died, the war in Afghanistan had been grinding on for five hard years.

For the Kremlin's policymakers, the most important single feature of the long and nagging conflict was that the Soviet army thoroughly enjoyed it. This does not reflect the attitude of poor Private Ivan Ivanov living on his nerves while escorting a convoy up a mine-strewn mountain road and waiting to be ambushed; but his ambitious young lieutenant and his company and battalion commanders were well aware that their future promotion would depend on the combat experience, and perhaps on the medal they might earn in the Afghan hills.

Promotion is slow in the peacetime Soviet officer corps, and the casualties of battle lead to vacancies. Each war creates its own tactical problems, and the men who solve them in the field know that their own careers will benefit. The helicopter forces, for example, have come of age during the Afghan conflict. The helicopters themselves, whose numbers have doubled to over 4000, have been repeatedly modified in the light of battle experience. New baffles have been fitted to exhausts to cut down the heat emissions that attract infra-red missiles. A computer study of the bullet-holes on downed aircraft has led to the redesign of the armour.[28] Professional military journals bubble with articles about the new mobility and tactics the combat helicopters require. Their authors go into complex detail about the way battalion officers should set up their own ambushes of enemy helicopters, placing their anti-aircraft missiles in such a way that the enemy is steered onto the waiting multiple cannon of the anti-aircraft tanks.[29] The art of a helicopter ambush was something the Soviet army learned from the enemy in Afghanistan.

It is the need for first-hand combat experience, rather than any fears about political reliability of the troops, that accounts for the speed with which army units are rotated through the Afghan theatre. Professional officers and NCOs find out what battle does to radio communications, how the efficiency of casualty evacuations affects the morale of the soldiers; they discover, in a way that they never can from training exercises, which units are good and which are shaky. The officers learn to coordinate their artillery and air strikes with infantry and armoured troop movements, in the knowledge that any mistake will result in the deaths of their own men; and they are field-testing their equipment, to see which items can withstand the strain of battle.

The American army gained similar benefits in Vietnam, in spite of the price they paid. Young officers in the US army schemed to 'get their ticket punched', knowing that their future careers would depend on their Vietnam combat record. The Americans went to Vietnam fighting in much the same style as they had in the Second World War and Korea, with air strikes and artillery bombardments from prepared fire bases and set-piece offensives. By the time they left, they had learned painfully how to fight a modern war, albeit of a specialised kind; and they had developed a vast nucleus of combat-hardened officers and NCOs who could do it.

The Russians are now rather gratefully going through the same process, and paying a very much smaller price for it. They have 115,000 troops in Afghanistan, in contrast to the 600,000 deployed by the Americans in Vietnam. They do not have the eyes of the world's media upon them, let alone those of their own. There are no nightly bloodbaths of kith and kin on Soviet television screens, no angry demonstrations in the streets or at Moscow University, and no mass burning of draft cards and call-up papers. The war has never been popular in the Soviet Union, but neither has it ever become a focus for mass discontent. Well-connected parents have schemed to get their sons an academic deferment, or a posting to some safe staff job, and there have been occasional reports and denunciations in the press of draft evaders, and even harsher attacks on those city authorities who have not given preferential treatment to disabled veterans.

After the first years of relative silence in the Soviet media spawned a host of word-of-mouth rumours of steep casualties and Afghan atrocities, the Soviet press and television are now careful to present the war in a positive light. It is portrayed as an opportunity for advancement, for finding yourself as a man, for fulfilling your socialist duty by bringing civilisation to a backward and almost feudal land. There are now official campaigns to give priority for housing, education and better jobs to the Afghan veterans. Mobile exhibitions of sketches of Afghan life tour the provincial cities. Some of the leading Soviet authors are sent to Afghanistan on army tours to write about the war in the same kind of upbeat, morale-boosting way in which the British and American media covered the Second World War – except that, in the Soviet media, there are no defeats: civilian casualties are inflicted only by the rebels and the bandits, who are armed to the teeth by the capitalist-imperialist puppet-masters.

Bestselling novelist Julian Simyonov went to Afghanistan and sent back reports of the dollar bills and pornographic photos found on the bodies of the dead guerillas, of the mines camouflaged as children's toys, and the dedication of the Soviet army doctors in treating the civilian casualties.[30] *Literaturnaya Gazeta* sent Alexander Prokhanov to the battle zones, and published his realistic but lyrical account of the war:[31]

> The commanders, turning grey with age at the temples, have come under fire for the first time here in the Afghan mountains. For the first time, they saw their own soldiers being wounded. And for the first time they are sending their troops not on some training exercise but against the bunkers and the weapons of the enemy. And these commanders with their grey hair and their university degrees have finally become real soldiers here in the Hindu Kush.

The Soviet media also reports the promotions of the men who have done well in the war. There was Albert Slyusar of the paratroops, who won a Hero of the Soviet Union medal in the Panjshir valley and is now promoted to major-general and in charge of the commando training school at Ryazan. There is Colonel Yuri Kuznetsov, another winner of the Hero medal from the paratroops, who has now been promoted to command the elite Panfilov motorised infantry division. Viktor Kot headed a squadron of fighter-bombers, leading and coordinating air strikes around Herat, and has now been promoted to deputy commander of aviation in the far eastern military district.[32]

These men represent the new military generation which is hammering at the doors of the general staff in Moscow and waiting for the 1945 veterans to retire so that they can take over the Soviet armed forces. Many of them are of Gorbachev's own age, but they will face the same bureaucratic battles with the Politburo and central committee as their seniors, as they argue for increased defence budgets to buy the 'smart' weapons Marshal Ogarkov demanded and the technology to match the American plans for Star Wars.

The air force wants new planes and new radar systems that can locate and catch the American Stealth bombers, and new laser-guided bombs and missiles for their air strikes. The navy wants a new generation of silent-running submarines, to enable them to evade the advanced Western sonar-detection systems, and sophisticated electronics systems to decoy the NATO ship-seeking missiles. The army wants laser-guided missiles for its infantrymen, a computer-controlled satellite communications system to transmit battlefield orders, and a new light tank with composite armour. Above all, the army seeks a greater say in the state education system to ensure that the growing proportion of its recruits who come from the traditionally Muslim republics of the south should be able to speak Russian. There are still whole battalions of conscripts whose knowledge of the language is limited to the basic words of command.

All the services are clamouring for the budgets and equipment to confront the threat of Star Wars. The strategic rocket forces are convinced that, with enough extra missiles and decoy warheads, they can swamp the American defences. The navy claims that its new submarines with sea-skimming Cruise missiles carrying nuclear warheads will be able to duck under the American defence canopy. The air force argues that its new supersonic Tupolev bomber, codenamed Blackjack by NATO, will be able to deliver stand-off bombs and air-launched Cruise missiles that can evade the Star Wars lasers. And doubtless the army planners are devising anti-Star Wars projects of their own, as the entire Soviet armed forces compete for their share of what promises to be the biggest research bonanza the Soviet economy has ever had to finance.

They cannot all be satisfied; the state simply does not have the money. The indications are that the new Soviet leadership has already started to make the hard choices which will impose strict limits on military spending. The appointment of Admiral Chernavin was a sign that future navy resources will be concentrated under water, rather than on a growing surface fleet – which, while visibly prestigious, would be desperately vulnerable. Gorbachev's new priority of detente on his eastern front with China and Japan could lead to reductions in forces on the Chinese border; and in February 1986 the Soviet leader spoke publicly of his desire to start withdrawing troops from 'the bleeding wound' of Afghanistan.[33] Above all, he wants to avoid the need for a new arms race in space, because its costs in funds, research and productive resources will derail his plans to modernise the civilian economy.

Soviet tradition and the overwhelming importance of national defence means that, if he must, Gorbachev will cut back civil investment to maintain parity with the Americans – but even that will involve continuing budgetary battles with the armed forces as they pick and choose between the services and the military projects on offer. Whether Gorbachev succeeds in reaching an agreement with the Americans to limit Star Wars or not, he and the armed forces are set on a collision course over the defence budget. The arguments that cost Marshal Ogarkov his job will rage on for the rest of Mikhail Gorbachev's term as general secretary.

9

Soft Repression: the Future of the KGB

At the beginning of 1986, only seven of the fifteen separate republics that make up the Soviet Union had the republican KGB
director on their individual politburos. By the end of February,
the local KGB chief had been elected to every one. This was a
dramatic extension of the overseeing by the KGB of the daily
administration of the entire country. It almost symbolised the
KGB's triumphant recovery from its humbling at the hands of a
vengeful party machine over thirty years earlier.[1]

The KGB, or Committee for State Security, was established in
1954 after the death of Stalin and the fall of Lavrenti Beria, the
secret police chief who sought to succeed him in the position of
supreme power. Beria's attempt to secure power, backed by the
private army and massive secret police machine that were
combined in his ministry of internal affairs, was frustrated by a
tactical alliance between the party and the army. Beria's fall was
swiftly followed by the dismantling of his security empire. The
secret police were downgraded from the status of having their
own ministry, and became a state committee, responsible both to
the Council of Ministers and to the Politburo.[2]

For army and party alike, this was both an act of revenge and
a defensive precaution. In the manic years of Stalin's purges in
the 1930s, the first target had been the party hierarchy itself.
More than half the delegates to the seventeenth party congress of
1934 were to be arrested over the following five years. Of the
139 men elected to the party's central committee in 1934, 98
were arrested as enemies of the people and shot. These are the
party's own figures, reported to the twentieth congress by Nikita
Khrushchev in 1956. 'This was the result of the abuse of power
by Stalin, who began to use mass terror against the party cadres,'

139

Khrushchev told the congress. The second victim of the purges had been the officer corps, which lost 90 per cent of its generals, 80 per cent of its colonels, all 11 vice commissars for war, and 75 out of 80 members of the supreme military council.[3]

The alliance of army and party against the secret police in 1954 sought to ensure that the new, tamed KGB would never again be capable of holding such power. It was a difficult matter of administrative balance. On the one hand, the Soviet Union required an efficient intelligence service overseas and a counter-espionage system at home. On the other, it needed a large and powerful secret police for internal surveillance and control. Khrushchev's solution was characteristically complex and cunning. He took responsibility for the prison camps from the KGB and transferred it to the ministry of public order. The KGB was stripped of the right to hold its own trials, and could make arrests only with the permission of a public prosecutor. It did not have the right to arrest party members at all, but only to present a dossier to an offender's party committee. One whole layer of secret police administration, the district level, was abolished altogether.[4]

Khrushchev's reforms also inserted party loyalists in key positions throughout the KGB hierarchy and, in particular, recruited them from the Komsomol, whose members were too young to have been implicated in the crimes of the past. His first choice to run the KGB was a personal friend, General Ivan Serov, but Serov's involvement in the brutal deportations of the Crimean Tartars virtually forced his dismissal in the heady liberalising mood which followed the twentieth party congress. He was succeeded by, in turn, Alexander Shelepin and Vladimir Semich-astny, each of them a former head of the Komsomol with no experience in security.[5]

As the dissident movement grew in the 1960s, this lack of experience became an embarrassment. Encouraged by Khrushchev's thaw, and by his revelations of Stalin's crimes, an entire generation of writers, artists and intellectuals started to explore the vague new limits of cultural and political freedom. After Khrushchev's fall in 1964, Brezhnev began to tighten those boundaries once more, as symbolised in the trial of the dissident writers Sinyavsky and Daniel. But Khrushchev's liberalisation had been profound. The only charge which could be brought against the two writers was 'spreading anti-Soviet propaganda', under Article 70 of the criminal code. The resulting trial developed into an international tragic farce. To secure a conviction, the authorities had to dispose of the defence lawyer and to claim that statements put into the mouths of characters in the defendants' books were the genuine and subversive opinions of the authors themselves.[6]

Over sixty members of the Moscow Union of Writers protested at the precedent of putting a satirical work on trial, and the international outcry helped to encourage the growth of intellectual dissidence throughout the country. Khrushchev's constraints on the KGB had left it too clumsy to cope. There was a further humiliation for the KGB when Stalin's daughter, Svetlana Allilu-yeva, defected to the West. A furious Leonid Brezhnev fired Vladimir Semichastny as head of the KGB, and brought in Yuri Andropov, armed with a catch-all new law in Article 190–191, which made it an offence to publish 'false information which slanders the Soviet state'. With astonishing courage, those Soviet critics who continued to publish the *Chronicle of Public Events* were able to take advantage even of this new law by making a point of publishing strictly accurate information.[7]

Yuri Andropov was faced with a desperately difficult task. He had to rebuild the KGB as an efficient internal police force without in the process creating a Frankenstein monster that could devour the party and, at the same time, without alienating that fragile but curiously potent new force, Soviet public opinion. Within a year of taking over at the Dzerzhinsky Square headquarters of the KGB, he was faced with the new challenge of internal opposition to the Soviet military occupation of Czechoslovakia. There were demonstrations in Red Square, a surge in the output of samizdat literature, and increasing international attention focused on the dissidents' fate.[8]

It was not simply yearnings for cultural and political freedom that fuelled this wave of dissent, but also a growing sense of disgust with Soviet life as it was developing under Leonid Brezhnev. The disgust was shared by Andropov himself, and by many in the KGB and in the lower ranks of the party. The inefficiency of the economy was chronic, and cases of corruption in high places were legendary. As a result, what the West came to call the dissident movement was not restricted to a radical fringe of society. Dissidence merged imperceptibly into a wide-spread constituency for reform that included army generals, top scientists and key figures in the judicial hierarchy. There was a very real danger that the Soviet system under Brezhnev would lose the allegiance of its entire intelligentsia.

A man of ruthless intelligence, Yuri Andropov devised a strategy which succeeded slowly in isolating the real dissidents from the reformers. The key to his success was his realisation that there was no such thing as a dissident movement: there were instead a whole series of quite separate currents of criticism which only appeared to have merged into one. There were national minorities who sought more rights for their national culture and language, and on occasion, as in Georgia, Andropov was prepared to compromise. There were people who simply wanted to leave the country – and, true to his policy of divide and rule, Andropov ensured that those with the best-organised support system and political lobby in the West were given exit visas. The decision to allow 230,000 Jews to leave the Soviet Union in the 1970s not only eased the wheels of detente with the USA but enabled Andropov to portray them as unpatriotic, thereby making it that much more difficult for other Soviet nationalities to claim common cause with the 'privileged' Jews.[9]

Through a combination of exit visas, selective deportation of key figures such as Solzhenitsyn and the callous use of mental hospital prisons for the more dangerous, Andropov was able to contain the dissidence. Remarkably, he did so without resort to the mass purges of a Stalin or the Tsars.

But the most audacious feature of Andropov's strategy was the way in which he tamed the widespread hunger for reform by presenting himself as its hope, if not its spokesman. He did this by transforming the image of the KGB. The first step was borrowed from the West, where the craze for spy fiction and James Bond films persuaded Andropov to mount a similar campaign at home. He created annual KGB prizes for literary works, films and television serials which showed the defenders of the Soviet people in a valiant light. The movement began with a series of novels and films about the work of Soviet secret agents fighting the enemy that the entire country could agree to hate: Nazi Germany. Deputy head of the KGB General Tsvigun (who was also Brezhnev's brother-in-law) published thrillers about his own days in SMERSH, the counter-espionage organisation which hunted down German spies and their Russian collaborators.[10] Author Julian Simyonov created the fictional hero of Shtirlitz, a Soviet agent at Hitler's headquarters. Simyonov's two television series, *Seven Days in May* and *TASS is Authorised to State . . .* , had most of the nation glued to their sets. There were even complaints in the press that Aeroflot flights were being delayed because the crews wanted to watch the programmes.

Andropov's second way of popularising the KGB was to deploy it as an anti-corruption force. During the 1960s, corruption had reached deep into the heart of the party. And in those southern republics with a tradition of bazaar trading and tight-knit family clans, corruption had become an institution. In the traditionally Muslim republic of Azerbaijan, tucked between the Iranian border and the Caspian Sea, literally anything could be bought, from university places to official jobs. An appointment as a public prosecutor (who could earn bribes for not bringing criminal charges) cost 30,000 roubles. To be a local police chief cost 50,000, and promotion to first secretaryship of the district party committee was a cool 200,000 roubles.[11]

In 1969 Geidar Aliev (known locally as Geidar-Ali Ali-Zadeh), the head of the KGB in Azerbaijan, presented Andropov with a full and detailed report on corruption in that republic. Andropov put the report before the Politburo; the Azerbaijan party leadership was sacked, and Aliev was put in charge. His purge entered legend. The entire praesidium was fired, and with them all the party first secretaries, the minister of the interior and his deputies, and the bulk of the senior policemen.

In the neighbouring republic of Georgia, Stalin's homeland, corruption was equally widespread, but its character was subtly different. Whereas in Azerbaijan the main object of bribery was to gain the power and privileges that could go with public and party office, in Georgia the aim was to find space to allow profitable private enterprise to flourish. The top Georgian tycoon was Otari Lazishvili, who ran a chain of underground factories turning out high-quality clothing. He paid good wages, ran a highly efficient distribution network, and acquired all his raw materials and machinery from the state. His success depended on paying bribes, and also on ensuring official support and protection – both were provided by the party boss of the republic, Vassily Mzhavanadze, whose ostentatious lifestyle, seven country villas and bacchanalian parties were the talk, and in a curious way the pride, of Georgia. The nineteen years that Mzhavanadze ran Georgia are known locally as the Victorian era, after his wife

Victoria, who had a great fondness for diamonds. She was given a particularly large diamond by Otari Lazishvili – which later was to find its way to Brezhnev's own family.[12]

There was one member of the Georgian communist elite who spurned the corruption: the police general and minister of the interior Eduard Shevardnadze, who stunned his neighbours by rejecting the lavish house that could have gone with his job and living in a standard apartment block. A history graduate who started full-time party work in the Komsomol from the age of twenty-four, Shevardnadze was something of a puritan, but he came from an influential political family. His elder brother was a first secretary in the Georgian capital of Tblisi.[13]

Encouraged by Aliev's success in Azerbaijan, and with Andropov's backing, Shevardnadze steadily gathered a dossier on Mzhavanadze and his cronies. It was a delicate matter, because all these people had friends in high places throughout the Soviet Union. When Lazishvili was finally arrested, it was in the offices of his friend, the chief prosecutor for the Soviet Union, Roman Rudenko. When Victoria Mzhavanadze was threatened with arrest, she fled to her sister, who was married to Petr Shelest, the party chief of the Ukraine.[14]

The occasion for the toppling of Mzhavanadze was a series of raids by Shevardnadze's police on underground factories manufacturing firearms near the coastal resort of Sochi. According to Georgian sources, Shevardnadze was so unsure of his own police force that he brought in KGB officers from Moscow to help with the investigations. News of the raids was published in the Georgian press, and even Brezhnev's friendship was not enough to save Mzhavanadze from disgrace. Eduard Shevardnadze succeeded him as party chief in Georgia and proceeded with a thorough purge of two thirds of the party secretaries, a score of central committee members and ministers, and a series of mayors and officials in the trading departments.[15]

Their pioneering role in the KGB's anti-corruption drive took both Geidar Aliev and Eduard Shevardnadze into the Politburo as candidate members. They were not popular in their home republics. Indeed, Shevardnadze was forced to travel in a bullet-proof car, and was the intended victim of a bomb explosion outside party headquarters in Tblisi. But among the potentially dissident intelligentsia of Moscow and Leningrad, and among those disgusted by the endemic corruption of the Brezhnev era, they and Andropov became, if not popular, then at least symbols of the system's capacity for reform.

During the 1970s, Western visitors and correspondents began to notice an increasing number of small photographs of Stalin appearing in buses and trucks, and to hear more and more Russian workers grumbling about the need for another *vozhd*, another tough leader who could clean the place up. Less noticeable, because more discreet, was the appearance inside the homes of intellectuals and officials of large framed portraits of Andropov himself. He had become a symbol of reform. There was nothing in the least liberal, however, about the kind of reform he represented; it was uncompromising, puritanical, and even austere. Almost alone among the Politburo, he insisted that his student daughter travel to her institute by public transport rather than by official car. Stories began to circulate among Moscow's intellectuals that reassured them that Andropov was one of them. Yuri Lyubimov, the director of Moscow's Taganka theatre, told of being summoned to see the head of the KGB to be thanked, as a father, for dissuading Andropov's son from trying to embark on a career as an actor. From then on, it was said, the Taganka's adventurous plays received discreet official backing.[16]

If Andropov's campaign to deploy the KGB as a national clean-up squad had begun as a way of demonstrating that the system had the capacity to reform itself, it imperceptibly developed into something else: a political challenge to the Brezhnev system. By the end of the 1970s, Andropov had become, if not the official opposition, then the government-in-waiting. It is possible that he helped the process along. Western radio broadcasts talking of official corruption and investigations into Brezhnev's family went mysteriously unjammed, doubtless with Andropov's authorisation. Accounts of corruption and scandals about Brezhnev's daughter were deliberately leaked to Western journalists in Moscow.

As an institution, the KGB had passed out of Brezhnev's control – despite the fact that the Soviet leader had carefully positioned two of his own loyalists just below Andropov as deputy chairmen of the organisation. The first was his brother-in-law General Tsvigun, the spy-thriller writer and, until 1967, the KGB chief in that deeply corrupt southern republic of Azerbaijan which Geidar Aliev had scoured clean. But, in January 1982, General Tsvigun was found dead. The official version was suicide in his office;

rumour had it that he was murdered in a KGB safe flat. In either event, he was no longer in any position to help Brezhnev. The other deputy chairman was Viktor Chebrikov, who was a member of the celebrated Dnepropetrovsk mafia (see page 29). Chebrikov had studied at the metallurgical institute in Dnepropetrovsk, and made his party career there until 1967, when he was suddenly moved to Moscow as head of the KGB personnel office. Appointed as a Brezhnev man, he must have impressed Andropov mightily, or switched allegiance with excellent timing, for he was Andropov's own choice for the KGB succession.[17]

Chebrikov has not had an easy time. Although Andropov was able to contain the dissidence of the 1970s, and divert some of its energies towards a faith in reform, there were many who simply withdrew their allegiance from the state and retreated into private life, ignoring politics and public affairs altogether. There were others whose opposition to the Soviet system and all that it stood for was more active. In the 1930s in Western Europe and North America, there was a similar generation which rejected a capitalist system that produced the Great Depression and seemed unwilling or unable to stop fascism, and they devoted their youthful idealism to the Soviet Union. Philby, Burgess, Maclean and Blunt were four of the most valuable spies ever recruited by Soviet intelligence.

It is not easy to imagine the students of Harvard or Cambridge universities in the 1970s being quite so ready to devote their lives to the cause of Moscow. Thoroughly discredited by Stalin, whatever idealism the Soviet Union could still inspire was constantly being battered by proofs of economic inefficiency and bad harvests, by Solzhenitsyn's books and by his deportation. On the other hand, to a generation of students at Moscow State University, the West must have appeared a rather more attractive proposition. The 1970s was a decade when Western intelligence services could hope to take revenge for the damage done to them by the Cambridge undergraduates of the 1930s. The temptation to recruit young dissidents, steer them into an official Soviet career and await results must have been overwhelming.

In February 1986, Viktor Chebrikov told the twenty-seventh congress in Moscow of a major spy swoop by the KGB:[18]

A number of agents of imperialist intelligence services have been uncovered in the government apparatus. These are renegades who sold important official secrets. They have been found in various ministries and departments, and have received strict but just punishments in accordance with the law ... The West spreads lies about human rights violations to spread anti-Soviet aspirations among such renegades.

Chebrikov's nightmare had come true. Eight months before the congress he had published a long article in *Kommunist* in which he had explored this very possibility:[19]

> The class enemy increases the scale of his attacks, trying to spread the subversion into all forms of our social life, politics and the law, philosophy and morality, science, the arts and religion. Ideological diversionists try to make use of the continued vitality of old customs and morals, traditions and old habits. They cheekily speculate on the problems we experience in our development, on our unsolved tasks and shortcomings, and give them a distorted interpretation. Only some ideologically immature individuals get hooked by the bourgeois disinformation and lies, and believe the cunning fairy-tales about the alleged advantages of the bourgeois way of life. Sometimes such people start to spread the imperialist slanders. We should not underestimate the fact that foreign agents sometimes find people who fall under their influence and step onto the path of anti-Soviet activities. We see our major task as preventing such incidents.

This unusually public concern by the head of the KGB helps explain the recent readiness of the Soviet authorities to welcome home their defectors. The first to return was Oleg Bitov, foreign editor of the cultural magazine *Literaturnaya Gazeta*, who had apparently defected to Britain in 1983. He had signed some lucrative book contracts, published highly critical articles on the Soviet Union in the conservative press and seemed to be genuinely disgusted by the society he had fled. But the following year he reappeared in Moscow, claiming that he had been drugged, kidnapped and brainwashed by British intelligence, and had awaited only his chance to escape back to the Soviet Union. He gave a bizarre press conference which did little to convince his fellow Soviet journalists, let alone the Western correspondents, and then resumed his journalistic career on his old magazine.[20]

In November 1984, a rather more prominent prodigal returned home, after seventeen years in the West: Stalin's daughter Svetlana; with her came her non-Russian-speaking daughter. Then came two young soldiers who had 'defected' after being captured by the Afghan resistance and settled briefly in the West. Then in the summer of 1985 came a KGB officer, Vladimir Yurchenko, who had been hailed by American intelligence as one of their most important defectors ever.

Yurchenko reappeared in Moscow telling a very similar tale to that of Bitov, except for the astonishing claim that he had escaped from his CIA captors while being given lunch at a pleasant French restaurant in Washington. While the Western intelligence services racked their brains to establish whether he had been a genuine defector or a deliberate plant, the message being received by the Soviet public was that mistakes could now be officially forgiven. One could defect but still be welcomed home again.[21] That dark memory of the terrible fate meted out to the Red Army prisoners of war who were shipped home from Germany direct to Stalin's labour camps (Solzhenitsyn was one of them) could remain safely buried. The state could now show mercy, and even kindness. Stalin's daughter was allowed to live in her father's old homeland of Georgia, assigned a large and pleasant flat that had once belonged to a senior party official, and given a pension of 300 roubles a month and a car with a driver. Her daughter was admitted to a prestigious special language school, and one of Georgia's prizewinning artists, Herakli Ochiauri, was engaged as her private art tutor.[22]

This new attitude of welcome was in part a reflection of the very real changes that had taken place in the KGB under Andropov, but it may also have been a sign of something close to panic. The KGB's reputation may stand high in the Western imagination, but as an intelligence agency it has been subject to an embarrassing number of humiliations in recent years. Its basic job is to gather intelligence on political events before they happen – and it does not seem to be very good at it. The KGB seemed thoroughly unprepared for the revolution which toppled the Shah of Iran on the Soviet Union's southern border, and stood by impotently while the Khomeini regime efficiently dispatched the Tudeh Iranian Communist Party virtually in its entirety. It has proved no more effective at infiltrating and neutralising the Afghan resistance; and it was evidently taken by complete surprise at the sudden surge in support for the Solidarity movement in Poland. In 1986, it failed to foresee the debilitating civil war between the Marxist factions of its Arab satellite of Aden. The KGB's rather naive faith in the political weight of the peace movements in Western Europe proved unfounded and, above all, its internal morale has been badly battered by a series of important defections.

The French were delivered file upon file of KGB internal reports on the not very impressive record of KGB attempts to steal Western technological secrets. The British welcomed with open arms the head of the KGB in London, who had also run the KGB networks in Scandinavia and, most important of all, had worked in the 'illegals' department in Moscow Centre. Illegals are the deep-penetration agents, the ones hardest to trace and capable, like Kim Philby, of doing maximum damage. This defector, Oleg Gordievsky, gave British intelligence information which led to the expulsion of thirty-one Soviet diplomats, journalists and trade officials in September 1985.[23]

These are not the signs of an efficient, nor even of a very happy, intelligence service. Moreover, Viktor Chebrikov's public fretting about the skills of Western intelligence agents at recruiting his disaffected citizens suggests that he does not have complete confidence in his counter-espionage departments. The reason for this crisis in the KGB's intelligence function may well spring from the fact that an increasing proportion of its resources and its brighter, more ambitious officers have been deployed in the organisation's new anti-corruption role.

Traditionally in the Soviet Union, anti-corruption work has been carried out by the civilian police, by a special department for the protection of state property, OBKSS, and by a specialist fraud squad in the procurators' department. In the course of the 1970s, and ostensibly because of increasing foreign involvement in corruption, the KGB were brought into the process. In a celebrated caviare scandal, when the expensive delicacy was being packed in tins labelled 'Herring' and secretly exported to the West, it was a KGB operation to trace the foreign bank accounts and arrest the officials responsible. The deputy minister of fisheries was sentenced to death.[24]

The example of Geidar Aliev in Azerbaijan had given Andropov the excuse to encourage KGB officials around the country to investigate corruption wherever they suspected it might be found. Once Andropov became general secretary, he moved against the head of the civilian police, General Nikolai Shchelekov. Shchelekov was stripped of his post, then of his military rank and central committee status, and died before being brought to trial.[25] He had lived well and lavishly; and under his leadership, the behaviour of the Soviet police had become a national scandal. Schelekov was replaced by the man who had briefly succeeded Andropov himself as KGB chief, General Vitaly Fedorchuk.

One of Fedorchuk's first moves was to draft 35,000 young communists from factories and the army Komsomol into the police service in an attempt to clean it up.[26] He also assigned responsibility for corruption inquiries to the KGB. But the effect of almost two decades of Brezhnev government had been virtually to institutionalise corruption throughout party and official life. During Mikhail Gorbachev's first year in office, not a month went by without a major corruption scandal being reported in the Soviet press. There was the Kirgiz official who built himself a private racecourse, the police involvement in the meat sales racket of Saratov, the sales of university entrance places in Georgia, the dismissal of virtually the entire politburo of Uzbekistan. The correspondence columns of the newspapers kept printing angry letters that called for a mass purge to clean up the party.[27]

In Stalin's day, a purge meant the prison camps and a bullet in the back of the neck. In the Gorbachev era, it was a visit from the KGB fraud squad. But some of the results were similar. An old, tired and potentially troublesome layer of party officials was removed, and the organisation that removed them, the KGB itself, rose in prestige and institutional weight. Given its lack of outstanding success in international espionage, the KGB must have felt considerable relief that its image was being so resoundingly redeemed at home. The signs of its growing political weight became unmistakable: in the elevation of the local KGB chief to each republican politburo and, above all, in the elections to Gorbachev's new central committee in 1986, when the KGB doubled its representation on the party's ruling forum.

'Viktor Chebrikov is now the third most powerful man in the country, immediately after Gorbachev and Ligachev,' the old Marxist-dissident historian Roy Medvedev told me, the day after the central committee elections.[28] This was the culmination of Khrushchev's policy of keeping the KGB under strict party control. Having been led since 1957 by a stream of loyal and watchful party officials, rather than by career intelligence officers, the KGB had not simply remained the party's faithful watchdog, bloodhound and wolf pack; it had also nuzzled its way into the party hierarchy. From having party apparatchiks grafted onto its top ranks, the KGB was now inserting its own men into the upper echelons of the party.

But by 1986 it was a different kind of KGB from the one which Beria had made into an instrument capable of a political coup. First, it had a very much higher calibre of officials, better educated and, according to the testimonies of many dissidents who have brushed with them, rather more aware of at least the forms of 'socialist legality'. Second, there was a huge contrast in immediate operational experience. Beria's machine had been trained in the hard schools of the purges and Gulags, and in the merciless conditions of war; a man like General Tsvigun had spent four wartime years in the killer squads of SMERSH. By the mid-1980s, there were very few KGB officers left with anything but peacetime experience.

During the period of their greatest internal challenge, in containing the wave of dissidence in the 1960s and 1970s, the KGB had had, in Yuri Andropov, a leader of real intelligence who imposed upon them the doctrine of minimum force. The original Cheka of Felix Dzerzhinsky in the years after the revolution had been trained to administer and execute the Terror. In the 1920s and early 1930s, the secret police had been fighting guerillas in the southern Soviet Union and seizing grain from peasants at gunpoint. Then they launched the purges. There was little attempt to analyse, in any professional sense, the nature of what they had been told was a threat to state security: in the old days, they simply liquidated it.

Under Andropov, the KGB learned to think first, and only then to act, and to do so with discrimination. Andropov had analysed the dissident 'movement', and seen that its unity was more apparent than real. There were several dissident movements among the Jews alone: those who wanted to leave, those who wanted to oppose any vestiges of official anti-semitism and discrimination, those who wanted to follow their own religion while remaining inside the Soviet Union, and those whose literary yearnings and cultural discontents made them part of the wider intellectual malaise that gripped the country as Khrushchev's thaw failed to blossom into spring. For each of these groups, Andropov devised a different response, ranging from mass emigration, which reached the level of 1000 people a week in 1979, to selective persecution in mental hospitals, prison camps, forced labour colonies, and the like. At the peak of Andropov's repression, in the mid-1970s, Amnesty International published the result of their own exhaustive investigation into 'Prisoners of Conscience in the USSR; their treatment and conditions'. They examined the estimates of Soviet dissidents, from Edward Kuznetsov's figure of 2000 prisoners to Andrei Sakharov's reckoning of 'between 2000 and 10,000'. Amnesty researchers interviewed former prisoners, assessed the CIA's satellite photographs, and succeeded in badgering rather more out of the Soviet judicial bureaucracy than other Western researchers had managed. Amnesty noted the difficulty of distinguishing between political prisoners and those convicted of 'religious offences', and concluded, 'There are at least 10,000 political and religious prisoners in the USSR today.'[29]

This is a grim and disheartening figure, representing a great ocean of human misery. But it does not begin to compare with the millions who went to the Gulags in Stalin's two last terrible decades. Nor does it compare with the last heavy spasm of Tsarist repression, the 1100 executions carried out by Stolypin's field courts-martial in the wake of the abortive revolution of 1905.[30] By the standards of Tsarist or communist Russia, Andropov's repression was mild; and, judged in its own terms, it was a success. The dissidents, even the religious and national movements, found no great resounding echo in the mass of the Soviet population. In the cases of individual priests in Lithuania, or on a matter as intrinsic as the apparent attempts to tamper with the status of the national language in Georgia in 1976, one could discern stirrings through the whole body politic of a republic, but never of the Soviet Union as a whole. Nor did the dissidents succeed in colonising what once seemed like the fertile ground of the intelligentsia. The fundamental loyalty of the intellectuals to the nation, and even to the system, was obvious to a generation of Western correspondents who watched individual artists, writers and scholars transfer their sympathy from the dissidents in the 1970s to Andropov's and Gorbachev's hopes of reform in the 1980s.

What are the implications of the KGB's increasing political weight? The dangers inherent in an overmighty secret police are stamped on the thinking of every party member who lived through the Stalin era. At fifty-five, Mikhail Gorbachev is still the youngest member of the Politburo he leads, and Stalin died when he was a university student. His personal knowledge of the dark side of Stalinism is limited to the wave of anti-semitism that swept through the country in Stalin's last months, after the monstrous allegations of the 'doctors' plot' – that a number of leading (and mainly Jewish) surgeons had planned to poison the leadership. The sobering aspect to Gorbachev's relative youth is his very lack of personal experience of a secret police running out of control.

Yet Gorbachev, and Andropov before him, may have had little choice but to turn to this most dangerous of weapons. After Brezhnev's death, they knew that the only way to reform the country was to reform the party itself, to dismantle the networks of corruption that had oozed their way through the system, to find a key that would unlock the layers of privilege and placement that had frozen so much of the party and ministerial bureaucracy. The only tool to hand was the KGB.

Gorbachev has taken matters further. To use the KGB to root out corruption is one thing, but to appoint KGB officials into key posts in the rest of the government machine is quite another. The new head of the enormously influential state television and radio service, Alexander Aksyonov, began his career as a KGB officer. In the central committee and in the republics, the profile of the KGB edges steadily higher. There is a risk involved in this, and Gorbachev is evidently gambling on his own conviction that the organisation is no longer the ruthless and voracious machine of suppression that the secret police became in Stalin's time.

Shortly after Andropov died, a film to commemorate his life was commissioned. Finally screened in Soviet cinemas in the summer of 1985, just after Gorbachev had come to power, it was remarkable for the intimacy of its insights into the family life and country dacha and rather stilted love poetry of the man who had led the KGB and gone on to rule his country. Rarest of all was the sequence of Andropov saying farewell to his KGB top executives in his panelled office at Dzerzhinsky Square, and of his speech to a passing-out parade of a new batch of KGB trainees. 'You must always remember the rule passed on to us by Dzerzhinsky himself, the founder of our service, that a Chekist must have clean hands, and a warm heart,' Andropov told them.[31]

Mikhail Gorbachev is depending on a belief that the KGB has indeed been reformed and tamed by Yuri Andropov, and that the service which perverted psychiatry to make mental hospitals into a system of punishment for dissidents in the 1970s is now a worthy recruiting ground for officials to help the new leader reform and administer the country. Trust in the KGB is far from being a hopeless gamble, but it remains a constant risk.

10

Changing Soviet Lifestyles

About a hundred yards from the back door of Moscow's Bolshoi theatre runs a short street called Stolyshniki, the alley of the tablecloth-makers. Its eighteenth-century church and small palace give it a certain faded grandeur, but it has a new attraction for Muscovites. It is the showcase and the launching pad for the life's work of a short, cheerful and untidy engineer called Anatoly Kapivsky, who is almost single-handedly making the Soviet capital a more pleasant place to live.

About ten years ago, the corner of Stolyshniki Street was famous for a rough and rowdy basement beer hall known as 'Yama' – the Pit. Like most such bars in Moscow, it was usually grubby, the chest-high tables awash with spilled beer and scraps of food, and the floor layered with fish bones, shrimp shells and the cardboard tubes from the coarse *papyrosi* cigarette stubs. The smell was powerful, the yeastiness of the beer and the old reek of oily fish combining with the press of bodies and the tobacco smoke to produce a peculiarly Russian aroma. There are Russian exiles in the West who are still nostalgic for the smell of the Yama on a Friday night in winter.

One evening in 1974, the young engineer Anatoly Kapivsky called in for a drink after work, and began looking at the place with a professional eye. He had given up his early dreams of a military future as a tank officer and made a career in what he thought would be the growth industry of automated food and drink machines. He had been installing the new automated beer dispensers in bars around Moscow, and he was increasingly unhappy with their effect. The old barmaids and waiters had gone, and the staff now sat in little cubicles dispensing cheese and ham sandwiches through hatches, or changing rouble notes for the 20-kopek pieces that would fit into the beer-dispensing machines. The new automated glass-washers did not clean the glasses properly, and Anatoly's vision of clean, efficient and gleamingly modern automated bars was turning rapidly sour. The character had gone, and the conviviality with it. There were more fights, and a surliness about the bars and their customers that he suspected came from the grim anonymity and functional decor.

'I began to get to know the bureaucracy very well,' he recalls now.[1] 'I went to the city council, to the district council, to the food and drink administration, to the department of trade, and finally persuaded every office that mattered that it was worth trying an experiment with the Yama. We redecorated the place in the style of the bars of Tsarist days. It is plain enough, off-white walls, but with some of the old Russian colours on the woodwork and some stained glass and better lighting. I could not do anything about the automated beer dispensers, but what we could do with decorations and furnishings alone we did. We tried to make it cosy and friendly.'

Within a year, the turnover at the Yama had increased fourfold. It became a trendy place for a drink before and after a Bolshoi performance. The police approved, because the number of fights and brawls had dropped sharply; and, remarkably for the Moscow bar, the occasional woman would brave the all-male preserve.

The success of the Yama gave Anatoly the lever he needed to extend the experiment. While installing and servicing the automated beer dispensers all over the city, he had become steadily more fascinated with the old buildings. He had met architects who recognised his interest and confessed their own unhappiness at the way that old churches and the old buildings of Moscow's suburbs were being steadily demolished to make space for the modern systems-built apartment and office blocks which they had to design but which they loathed.

The time was ripe for a conservation movement. Powerful interests were becoming involved. Intourist, the organisation which was planning to earn more and more foreign currency by bringing in five million Western tourists a year, knew that the churches and buildings of old Moscow were among the things they wanted to see. Some of the best Soviet novelists began writing letters and campaigning for a more thoughtful, even respectful, attitude towards the past and its buildings. Valentin Rasputin in Siberia attacked the mindless way that development was sweeping aside the old wooden town centres of Irkutsk and Tomsk. In Moscow, there was Yuri Bondarev, who seemed never to write a book that did not contain some lyrical urban memories of the city's left bank, the riverside suburb where he had grown up.

Conservation gradually became a fashionable national hobby. Politically, too, the time was ripe. In its first fifty years of power, the Communist Party had been consumed by the passion to build, to sweep away the past and to impose the new. The party believed in new cities, wide new thoroughfares, urban planning on a heroic scale. Stalin had even demolished the old cathedral on the Moscow riverbank, planning to erect a vast new palace for the Supreme Soviet with a giant statue of Lenin on its roof, towering above the puny symbols of Tsarist days, the golden domes of the Kremlin. For all of Stalin's ruthless determination, his engineers could never make the foundations stable enough to build on the marshy riverbank. Eventually, they gave up and built a giant open-air swimming pool instead.[2]

Khrushchev continued this almost messianic mission of the early communists to rebuild the capital anew. He bulldozed away whole swathes of the Arbat, the residential heart of old Moscow, with its quiet courtyards and romantic alleyways and buildings with a curiously French flavour – curiously, given that they were all rebuilt after the great fire that finally drove Napoleon and the French invaders from the city in 1812. In their place, he built the soulless modern artery of Kalinin Prospekt, lined with dull grey tower blocks. It was under Khrushchev that plans were drawn up to build the biggest hotel in the world, the 6000-room Rossiya, at the corner where Red Square runs down to the river. The plans blithely assumed the demolition of three tiny but delightful churches of the sixteenth and seventeenth centuries that had nestled there since the area was known as Kitaigorod, or China-town, the ghetto to which the old Tsars had consigned the useful but dangerous foreign traders.

Within a year of Khrushchev's fall, a national conservation movement had been born, a voluntary organisation but with backing from a number of key party officials. Perhaps the most important of these was Mikhail Suslov, the man who had built and orchestrated the palace coup which toppled Khrushchev, and the guardian of the party's ideological purity. Suslov was sympathetic to the growing mood of Russian nationalism which began to flourish in the 1960s.

The nationalist movement had many roots. In part, it was a

reaction against the excesses of Stalin, the man from Georgia. More important was the steady growth of political tensions with China, whose countless millions were thought to be gazing hungrily at the barely populated Siberian lands. The arrival of more and more Third World students at Moscow's Lumumba University provoked the occasional ugly racist incident, and the traditionally Muslim deep south of the Soviet empire in Kazakhstan and Uzbekistan was integrating more deeply, and more visibly, into Soviet life. Nationalism took some curious and unpleasant forms, such as anti-semitism, or politically alarming directions, such as the revival of interest in the Orthodox religion. Some of its key figures, including the novelist Solzhenitsyn, were open dissidents. Others, such as Suslov himself or the ambitious young party officials who ran the Molodaya Gvardia publishing house, were convinced communists.

Perhaps the healthiest effect of this mood was to spread public interest in prerevolutionary Russia, and in its physical remains in churches and buildings and whole quarters of old Moscow. A department of architectural history was established, and the popular magazines began to publish more and more articles on the life and buildings of old Russia. The inexorable march of the bulldozer was not stopped, but it was slowed, and turned to new directions, towards the city outskirts. The three churches by the giant Rossiya hotel were saved, and thenceforth anyone who wanted to campaign to preserve an old building could be confident of getting at least an official hearing, if not support.

Without this change in public attitude, Anatoly Kapivsky could not have proceeded to the next stage of his plan. Just up Stolyshniki Street from the Yama beer hall was an old palace that had been the headquarters of the French cavalry commander, Marshal Murat, during the French occupation of 1812. It was run down and crumbling. Some of its rooms were empty, and others used as municipal offices. Attached to its courtyard was a church that had been made into a cramped tailors' workshop. The ancient stables were used to store the brooms, crowbars and spades that cleared snow in winter, and there was a gatehouse facing onto the street. Anatoly persuaded the city council to let him restore the gatehouse and convert its basements into a new kind of restaurant. He had been to the old Baltic port of Riga and to the Lithuanian capital of Vilnius on holidays, and had been enchanted by the care the Baltic states took of their old buildings and the charm of their bars and restaurants.

'You just had to walk into a place like that and you knew that this was a café where the customer was important, where he was respected, and where the staff took pride in doing a good job,' he recalls. 'It felt so very different from our Moscow bars. I showed photographs of some of these Vilnius cafés to the officials in Moscow, and they agreed to let me try. But then another department said I could not do it, because there were sewers down there and underground springs and the job would prove impossible. I had to go ahead on my own, using friends and volunteers.'

The embittered young architects Anatoly had met and some of the happy regulars of the Yama bar who had friends who were builders and plumbers were able to do the job that the city construction officials had said was impossible. It took them two years to clear out the basements, to repair the old sewers and build new drains for the spring, and by this time the city council was helping with funds, tools and workmen. Some Moscow journalists became interested after Anatoly found some old wooden printing blocks down there from a nineteenth-century cultural newspaper that had been published on the site, and they began to give his efforts some publicity.

Today, after your wait in the permanent queue, you pass under a beaten copper portico, through a heavy medieval door and down the steps to a basement brasserie that would do credit to any city in the West. There is a series of small, almost intimate dining rooms, candlelit and darkly furnished. There are antique wooden water wheels, and a blonde young girl from Latvia croons soft folk songs to an acoustic guitar. There is a circular coffee room, its walls lined with the old wooden printing blocks and some of the pages from the newspaper that was printed here a century ago; it has become an unofficial meeting place for Moscow's younger journalists.

'I wanted somewhere that anybody could afford to use, not just the rich or privileged. I was a student once, and remember how hard it was to take a girl to a decent place on a student grant. So for a standard price of 5 roubles a head [about £4.70] you get a plate of zakuski, with some smoked fish, a little red caviare, pickles and bread, followed by a dish of meat and raisins and potatoes, stewed in an earthenware pot. Drinks or coffee are extra, but the prices are not too high, and we get a pleasant mix of customers. There are always some students, usually journalists and writers and people from the Bolshoi, which is not too far away, and some of my old friends who are architects and some of the lads from the Yama who want to see what we have done here,' beams Anatoly, as he looks proudly around at his achievement.

In his office are the plans for the next stage, the restoration of Marshal Murat's old headquarters, the small palace that is being transformed to include more restaurants, a café, a bookshop and an area for a small exhibition about the history of the quarter – from its time as the street where artisans embroidered tablecloths, to the French occupation, to the period of the newspaper and the local theatres that the journalists of Tsarist days had described.

In the next side street is the site of the old Moscow Arts theatre, where Stanislavsky first staged Chekhov's play *The Seagull*; the haunting art-deco bas-relief of a seagull still dominates the theatre's façade above the scaffolding and rubble of its restoration. The rebuilding of Stanislavsky's theatre is a popular affair; anyone can join in. In Moscow's evening paper, *Vechernaya Moskva*, they publish each week a list of the historic sites where volunteers may turn up the following weekend and help with the work. Unskilled hands are welcome to cart away rubble, to sweep up after the builders or to make tea. There are usually three sites to choose from each weekend, and skilled engineers or architects are made particularly welcome by the coordinator, who is always a full-time worker for the national volunteer society for restoring cultural works, the body set up after Khrushchev's fall.

When I went along to volunteer to clear rubble from the Moscow Arts theatre site, my fellow workers ranged from school-children to grandmothers. We were all given a quick lecture on the history of the place, why it was felt important enough to be restored, and shown the plans for its eventual transformation. It will remain a theatre, and internally it is being restored to how it was in Chekhov's day, but the area behind the stage will be tripled in size, a revolving stage installed and vast flies to hang and store the different stage sets. After the formal opening, there will be tickets reserved for the first few weeks of the new theatre for those who helped to restore it.

It was a fellow volunteer for the theatre restoration who first introduced me to Anatoly Kapivsky and his Stolyshniki restaurant and his plans to revolutionise the nature of leisure time in Moscow. Perhaps the most remarkable feature of his work is the determination and diplomacy needed to negotiate his way through the profusion of overlapping bureaucracies that administers this city of over 8 million people. He is the first to stress that he could not have begun without friends and support, and the Anatoly method is now spreading throughout the city, as his disciples apply his methods to saving the simple red brick church on Serpu-khovsky Val and making it into a neighbourhood restaurant, or restoring the Kirovsky tearoom to its Tsarist grandeur.

As well as acquiring the permissions and the support to restore such places, Anatoly and his followers must then deal with the even grimmer bureaucracy that has made Soviet public catering so poor for so long. For Anatoly to gain permission to serve his standard meals at a standard price required diplomatic skills that make a superpower summit look simple. His food supplies come from a city department which works on the principle that restaurants should serve whatever food they happen to be given. The quality of the food, or its variety, or any specialities that the restaurant may want to offer, are not the business of the supply warehouses. It is their job to fulfil the plan they have been given, to supply so many restaurants, factory canteens and public cafe-terias with so many thousand kilos of meat, bread, eggs, and so on. It is a state of affairs that invites poor quality and careless service at most restaurants, and which leads to corruption even among those who take enough pride in their work to want to serve something better. For a manager to ensure that steak, pork chops or decent veal appear on the menu, or that there is a choice of wines on offer, or adequate quantities of delicacies such as crab or caviar, means his developing special relationships with a series of officials in the supply departments.[3] This can involve open bribery, or it can mean keeping open house for the officials and their families and friends; either way, the restaurant manager has to recoup his investment in obtaining better supplies. But restaurant prices are fixed by the relevant municipal department, so this becomes a desperately complex business of preparing 120 meals from a food supply designed for 100, and using the profit from the extra twenty to look after your suppliers and your better waiters – while not forgetting the drivers on whom you rely to deliver the goods on time.

At last the Soviet system has found a better way. It began, like so many of the economic experiments, in the small, inventive republic of Georgia, tucked down in the Caucasus between the Black and the Caspian Seas. Just outside the old Georgian capital of Mxheta, an ancient Christian city which had the honour of being comprehensively sacked by Tamburlaine the Great, is an excellent modern restaurant which specialises in the local cuisine. The Marani is imaginatively designed and pleasantly furnished, with an open fire for cooler weather, and it is very nearly a private enterprise. It is run by a collective, whose members give up 40 per cent of their profits to the state and use the rest to pay their own bonuses or to reinvest in the business. They have effectively contracted out of the state supply system; they buy their meat and fish at the local free market, and grow their own fruit and vegetables at the small farm which the collective also runs. Their prices are higher than in the state eating places, and a lavish lunch for four with wine can cost about £30.[4] The quality is excellent and the staff are well paid. The waiters earn a basic 200 roubles (£185) a month, a fraction above the national average, but their tips and share of the profit double their salaries. The chef reckons to take home about 500 roubles a month, and the manager about the same. There are now family collectives in Georgia running restaurants that are almost indistinguishable from private family businesses. So far, such places are few, but they are now receiving official encouragement, and Mikhail Gorbachev has promised to increase their number as part of his determination to overcome the failings which bedevil the whole service sector.[5]

In another example of this development, television repair workshops in Estonia have become self-employed collectives, and the incomes of the workers depend entirely on their productivity and on the quality of the work, since there is now competition between the various collectives.[6] At last the Soviet consumer is beginning to know the luxury of real choice – and more and more frequently he or she has the money, and the taste, to exercise that choice, to dine out and require a reasonable level of service, pleasant food and attractive surroundings. Until now, such standards were rarely found. But the same could have been said of large swathes of Britain and the USA in the 1950s and 1960s. When we mock Soviet lifestyles and restaurants, we forget how recent has been the transformation of living standards in the West. The problem in the Soviet Union has been that, while people have increasingly acquired the means, the shortages of goods and services have led them to find ways through and around the system to fulfil their wants. This unfulfilled consumer demand has been the dominant cause of the growth of corruption, and those who take the risks to meet it have become the Soviet Union's new rich.

Larissa Vasilyevna is a trained hairdresser with a natural gift for her trade and a healthy commercial instinct. In the state shop where she worked, she looked after the hair of some women who worked as extras at the Moscow film studios. She did a good job, better than the professionals at the Mosfilm beauty salon, and actresses began to patronise her. To make sure that she could do their hair whenever required, they would give her small gifts of Western shampoos and conditioners, and pass on to her Western fashion magazines which showed the latest hairstyles. Then her old customers started to offer large tips to have a 'Western' hair wash and style, and Larissa rescued an old hairdryer that was being thrown out and set herself up in business in her home in the evenings. Through word of mouth, she then attracted regular customers from the Bolshoi ballet chorus, who were happy to pay her in theatre tickets.

Bolshoi tickets are valuable. The teacher who gave Larissa's son private tuition to get him into one of the special foreign language schools was happy to be paid in tickets. Larissa was able to barter more tickets for imported Italian shoes, for Western lingerie and clothes. She still had enough money left over to start dining out at Moscow's big restaurants, to buy antiques at the state *kommissioni* shops, where second-hand goods are sold by the state on a 7 per cent commission, and to hire a moonlighting carpenter to fit out one room of her flat as a plush hairdressing salon. So far, she had not really broken the law, whose main concerns about private enterprise are that there should be no employees who can be 'exploited' by a small capitalist and that no state goods or services should leak into the private sector. Then Larissa gave up her job at the state salon and began working full-time from home. But her time was being wasted taking appointments, cleaning up after each customer and having to handle one client at a time. So she became a real capitalist and hired a friend, a young mother who could bring her baby to the flat, give shampoos and do the cleaning while Larissa increased her own productivity.

'I have gone as far as I can,' she told me once, when explaining her problems as a '*biznizmin*'. 'Now I'd like to take on two or three young girls I know, train them as they work, and start a proper salon providing a full beauty-care service, with advice on cosmetics, and do facial treatments, manicures and perhaps these whirlpool baths I see in Western magazines. I am always having to turn away people who want to come to me. But if I go on, I could be in trouble with the police and the tax people.'[7]

She had bought a Zhiguli saloon car, which cost 13,000 roubles when almost new – she had had to pay a hefty sum over the list price to avoid the waiting list. Her clothes were good, and the furniture in her modest flat was expensive, with two of the small but ornate nineteenth-century gilt tables that sell for thousands of roubles in the antique shops. She and her engineer husband and son all lived well, unconcerned at paying up to 20 roubles a kilo for tomatoes at the free markets in winter.

'I have heard about this idea of the new collectives, but if I tried to start one of those I would have to look around for proper premises, and then I would have to go to the state suppliers for all my equipment,' Larissa went on. 'And if I expanded the business, I could never get enough of the Western cosmetics and shampoos that my customers pay for. I don't think that legalising my business through a collective would make much sense.'

Larissa already has more money than she can spend, and certainly more than she could honestly account for if she were to flaunt her prosperity. She would like to buy a dacha outside Moscow, a small country cottage. They are advertised for sale in the weekly small-ads supplement of the Moscow evening paper. Within an hour's drive of Moscow, a two-bedroomed cottage, with an earth privy in the garden, would cost at least 25,000 roubles. Larissa can afford that, but she cannot afford a police inquiry into the source of her funds – which a new law of Gorbachev's 1986 reform programme requires for any purchase worth more than 10,000 roubles. So she will wait until it is her husband's turn to be assigned a small patch of land through the institute where he works, and they can then build a dacha of their own.

Rather, they can hire builders to do it for them, either a team rounded up by the moonlighting carpenter who fitted out Larissa's salon or made up of '*shabashniki*', the freelance builders who work for cash and have their own shady ways of obtaining materials. There are no official figures of their numbers, but Soviet press reports, which are often quite favourable, claim that, in the

Kurgan area alone, the *shabashniki* are responsible for 70 million roubles' worth of construction.[8] There are barely a million people in this south Urals region; if these figures are representative of the whole Soviet Union, then the *shabashniki* are doing something like 20,000 million roubles' worth of work a year. Minister of the Interior Vitaly Fedorchuk told *Literaturnaya Gazeta* in 1984 that the *shabashniki* accounted for half of all construction work in some rural areas.[9] They are used on major state projects, such as the Urengoy pipeline, and on state and collective farms which do not want to wait for the state construction organisation. Their usual payment is a quarter of the estimated value of the completed building, which Soviet press commentaries reckon to be fair. There are cases on record of state bank officials coming out to inspect the finished product and making formal estimates of the price to be paid. The *shabashniki* can get bonuses of up to 40 per cent for completing a job ahead of time; they often take oaths of sobriety and work sixteen-hour days when the bonus is good.

Useful as they are, the *shabashniki* live in a shadowy world of semi-legality. In May 1985, *Izvestia* published a long and sympathetic story about a group of *shabashniki* who had contracted to build a road for a collective farm in Armenia. The farm needed the road to take its beets to the refinery in the rainy season. The *shabashniki* were not asking an exorbitant sum, but they and the farm chairman were charged with 'engaging in private enterprise under cover of collective farm activity' and given long prison terms. The investigators from the procurator's office were within the law to bring charges, just as the local party committee which had first blown the whistle on the road builders were within their rights to call in the procurator – except that, usually, party committees and procurator have more sense than to show too much zeal in such matters, particularly when the project makes financial sense. Stopping the road meant that the farm's beet crop continued to spoil, as it had for years. *Izvestia* commented:[10]

> We keep talking more and more of the need for economic initiative, but where are the criteria to judge whether initiative is good or bad . . . Why is it that in practice the framework of the law is so tight that initiative and law-breaking are one and the same?

This is the dilemma that confronts people such as Larissa and the self-employed car mechanics who keep the bulk of Soviet private cars on the roads. State service stations are few, ill equipped and inefficient; private motorists can wait up to a year for an appointment. Easier, although more expensive, to go *na lyeva* (on the left): the universal Soviet phrase for something not quite legal.

It is almost impossible to live in the Soviet Union without becoming involved in the black economy. The man who services your refrigerator and the man who instals your telephone will expect a bottle of vodka for his trouble. To get theatre tickets for a hit show you will either have to go *na lyeva* or have some *blat*, or influence, with the box office. To get a table in a decent restaurant will usually require a small bribe to the doorman or some *blat* with the management. Your doctor will expect small gifts or even cash to give you a speedy appointment; and, once you are in hospital, the standard rate for getting the ward attendants to clean round your bed or bring a bedpan is a rouble a day. When the doctor has prescribed some drugs, it is up to the patient or the patient's family to obtain them. Anything more than the most commonplace medicine is unlikely to be had from the pharmacies, but you will usually find a helpful black marketeer outside the shop who will obtain what you want, for a price.

This behaviour is not necessarily a criminal matter. There are people who make a living out of queuing to buy, quite legally, rare goods. The black market comes in when such people then resell at a profit. The latest example of this kind of free enterprise to hit Moscow are the vodka sellers. To buy a small bottle of vodka will cost you 7 roubles and, since the campaign against alcoholism closed so many of the wine shops, an average wait of three hours. But for 9 roubles you can buy a bottle from someone who waits in line for a living. The practice is widespread. On the day that publishing houses issue the lists of books they will bring out that year, the professional book buyers begin to wait outside the bookshops to get their orders in early. Books are cheap in the Soviet Union if you can find them in the shops, but the prices climb steeply once you go *na lyeva*. A translation of a Western bestseller such as Hailey's *Airport* will be less than 4 roubles in the shop, but 25 roubles if you buy it later. Rare Russian books like a volume of Akhmatova's poetry will go for up to 100 roubles – the price of a pair of imported Western jeans.

During and after the Second World War, Britain experienced a similar black market in goods and foodstuffs that were rationed and, as in the Soviet Union, there was broad public acceptance of the practice. The difference in the Soviet Union today lies in the curious nature of money as a commodity. The high level of subsidies on basic foods, rent and transport means that a large proportion of the average pay packet is disposable income. The average Moscow dweller pays less than 10 roubles a month in rent, including heating, out of an average salary of 185 roubles a month. (Since the average salary includes the rather lower basic pay of collective farmers, the average urban salary is significantly higher than this; and given that more than half of adult women are in full-time employment, the average household income is higher again.)

Meat subsidies cost the state over 20,000 million roubles a year, and with meat at 2 roubles a kilo (though admittedly of poor quality) in the shops, shortages amount to an enforced rationing system which is probably essential to helping the state balance its budget. A rouble will buy 5 kilos of bread, or 10 kilos of potatoes, or 6 kilos of cabbage, or 3 litres of milk.[11] The total cost of food subsidies is over 55,000 million roubles a year, or 182 roubles per head of the population – the equivalent to an extra month's salary.[12] Subsidies on housing and public transport probably cost the same again, and holidays are subsidised by the trade unions and factories. Local phone calls are free. The basics of life are cheap, so the luxuries are disproportionately expensive.

The success of the Soviet system in boosting people's real incomes exposes the more cruelly its failure to provide the consumer goods on which the money could be spent. The black market is an inevitable result of this state of affairs, and in some ways a healthy one. To a degree, the state has legitimised the process by authorising the free markets in which the collective farmers may sell the produce from their private plots. On Moscow's Tsvetnoi Boulevard, just beside the old circus, is the Tsentralni Rinok, the central market, where tomatoes, fresh salads and vegetables can be had even in winter. At 8 roubles for a cucumber or up to 50 roubles for a whole suckling pig, the prices are staggeringly high, although they drop sharply in springtime and summer.[13] Such markets exist in each of Moscow's boroughs, and their profits are so steep that they have brought crime in their wake. Protection rackets abound, and during the anti-corruption drive of 1985 half the officials who controlled the Moscow markets were under police investigation. Innocent farmers who came up to Moscow without knowing the ropes found themselves in hospital, beaten up by the regulars for trying to occupy one of the better-placed stalls, reserved by custom and cash for the professionals who have become millionaires from the system.[14]

Few aspects of a society are more illuminating about the way that society works than the nature of its criminal activity. Early on an April morning in 1985, when the housekeeper of a block of flats in the Volga city of Saratov looked into the back of a parked saloon car, she began to unravel one of the most appalling yet revealing crimes of recent Soviet life. In the back of the almost new car was the partially dismembered body of an ex-convict called Akchurin. In a grisly irony, Akchurin, a butcher by trade, had been killed with a meat cleaver.[15]

Akchurin had worked in the meat department of the local Saratov free market, where peasants are allowed to sell their own livestock at much higher prices than those in the state shops. As an ex-convict, under Soviet regulations he should never have got the job, which involved handling public money. In fact, Akchurin had bribed the local police and the manager of the meat department, a professional butcher called Anisimov, who had been in the job for twelve years. In that time, Anisimov had become a rouble millionaire. He had doctored the market scales with an ingenious system of magnets, so that when meat was checked in to the market, the scales recorded only about 90 per cent of its real weight. He then sold the extra meat at the full market price and pocketed the profit. It was a simple system, but one that required a wide network of corruption to maintain.

The local police station was located within the market, and its officers had to be paid. There were local party officials to be taken care of, as well as the administrative staff of the market. But for over ten years the Anisimov system ran like clockwork. When large consignments of state meat were delivered to the market, Anisimov could skim off as many as three hundred carcasses for private sale. The scheme could have worked indefinitely, except for Anisimov's mistake in hiring the ex-convict Akchurin as part of his gang. Once installed, Akchurin began to take over the operation from Anisimov. Strong enough to cow the other market workers, and having bought the loyalty of the police, Akchurin was determined to drive Anisimov into retirement. When a million-rouble consignment of state meat came into the market, he skimmed off 150,000 roubles for himself, and Anisimov got none. The ex-convict began to live well. He built himself a two-storey mansion on the Volga riverbank, bought three cars and took his mistress to lavish holidays on the Black Sea.

But Akchurin had underestimated Anisimov, who decided that the only way to regain control of the operation was to murder the ex-convict. Unable to do it himself, he hired a contract killer, a man whose ostensible job was that of a factory mechanic but whose record was that of a professional criminal. His name was Slovesnov, and he agreed to kill Akchurin for 10,000 roubles in cash. But the killing had to be special, with a message attached to it: a meat axe was used to ensure that those in the know were aware that this was a professional butcher's butchery.

'Such crimes give us the opportunity for moral evaluation,' claimed the newspaper *Sovietskaya Rossiya* in its account of the trial, which saw the contract killer sentenced to death and Anisimov to fifteen years' imprisonment. They also give a rare insight into the nature of organised crime in the Soviet Union. It was inconceivable, as *Sovietskaya Rossiya* commented, that such a rake-off of meat and money could have gone undetected for so long, or that the Anisimov system could have functioned, without the cooperation of police and other senior officials. Similarly, the case that resulted in a decision by the procurator's office in April 1986 to carry out the first death sentence on a woman convicted of corruption again demonstrated that organised crime in the Soviet Union is not something that takes place in defiance of the system but by working through and with it.

Berta Borodkina was in charge of catering services at the Black Sea resort town of Gelendjik. She ran the local restaurants, arranged the food supplies, and became a rouble millionaire in the process. Perhaps not quite a millionaire. When the death sentence was carried out, the state confiscated all her property, whose worth amounted to 986,383 roubles. The state was able to prove that she had taken 530,000 roubles in bribes, mainly from the cooks and restaurant managers whom she appointed. The going rate for bribes was 500 roubles a month in cash, rising to 3000 roubles a month during the four months of the summer season. During the trial, the prosecution read out a secret contract she had signed with one of the restaurant managers which committed the manager to a steady increase in bribes paid over five years. In return for the bribes, the cooks and managers kept the jobs which allowed them to get rich by selling food on the black market, and received guaranteed shipments even of foods in short supply, such as caviare, crab and best-quality meat and wines. In order to obtain these supplies, Berta was herself paying bribes to two top officials at the Moscow ministry which dealt with health resorts. She was also paying the head of the police fraud squad, and the head of the regional construction department, who would build extensions to the Gelendjik restaurants and provide new and luxurious building materials and decorations.[16]

A woman of considerable organisational skills, Berta had helped in the previous ten years to transform the once sleepy town of Gelendjik into a bustling and increasingly popular tourist resort. Its restaurants were known to be expensive but good. Luxury foods were always available and, for those Russians with the money, it was a fashionable place to visit. But for those who went to Gelendjik in the usual way, staying at the trade union sanatoria and rest homes, the food was much worse, because these were the mass-catering establishments whose supplies were being pillaged to pay for the corruption and the higher quality at the top end of the scale. Berta was shot, and her partners in the police and the ministries were imprisoned, according to the report of her trial in the journal *Literaturnaya Rossiya*.

Reports such as this became commonplace in the Soviet media in the years after Brezhnev's death, as the campaign against corruption intensified. But to attack corruption was to treat the symptoms rather than the cause of the illness: that a growing sector of the Soviet population was getting too rich for the society's own good. By the mid-1980s, in every faculty of Moscow University there were students who had cars of their own or who been given cooperative flats by their doting parents. A cooperative flat is a privately owned apartment in all but name. Prospective purchasers band together to put down 30 per cent of the cost price of an apartment block and pay the rest back to the state over twenty years at a very low rate of interest. Each flat is then the property of an individual owner and it can be passed on to other family members. In Moscow, about one flat in eight is now 'owned' in this way. The rich kids of Moscow, who start in life with the advantages of a flat, a car and perhaps even a country dacha, contrast sharply with the majority of their fellow students who find it hard enough to get by on their state grants, and even harder to get a flat of their own to begin married life.

In his speech to the party congress in 1986, Gorbachev promised to introduce an inheritance tax, a measure clearly aimed to quiet growing public concern about the sleek new rich.[17] But there has so far been no sign of draft legislation, and Moscow lawyers believe that any such law would face a long delay, because the taxation of inherited wealth runs directly counter to the main thrust of the Gorbachev economic reform, which is to persuade people to work harder by giving them cash incentives for higher productivity. This conflict between the state's need to tax and the economy's need for incentives is a problem that affects all types of government. But, in the Soviet Union, Marxist ideology makes it particularly acute.

So far, the state's response to the emergence of a Soviet new rich has been to attack, through official propaganda and through the police, those who make their money from unearned incomes or corruption. But there are many ways of becoming legally rich in the Soviet Union. In cash terms, perhaps the most privileged people of all are the composers of popular music. While the performing musicians receive a mere 15 roubles a concert, every time a song is played, in a live concert or on the radio, the composer earns a fee. The best known, such as Raymond Pauwels, earn over 15,000 roubles a month in royalties, and even a moderately successful composer can earn 1000 roubles a month, about five times more than the average wage.[18] Some writers, too, earn fabulous amounts – so much so that the state savings bank has opened special accounts for them from which they can draw unlimited sums, on the assumption that, however much they spend, bestselling authors will not exhaust the credit built up from their royalties. Authors, composers and artists who also have foreign currency earnings from overseas sales, such as pop star Alla Pugacheva, can legally acquire the ultimate status symbol of a Western car. The red-headed Alla drives a black Mercedes. The author of children's books, the voice behind many Soviet cartoons and the star of Soviet television's Sherlock Holmes series, Vassily Livanov, drives a Volvo estate. Vassily's father was a famous film actor who also worked with Stanislavsky, and Vassily lives in the old family flat just off Moscow's Gorky Street, which is itself almost a museum of Soviet theatre. He spends most of his time out at the riverside dacha where his neighbours are the Kapitsa family, whose father was the great man of Soviet science, and the family of the handsome young Russian who married Christina Onassis.[19]

Artistic success is well rewarded in the Soviet Union, and nowadays is not restricted to those who toe the state line. Cultural policy is still strictly controlled by the party, but it is no longer bound in a straitjacket. The group of young modern artists whose 1974 exhibition in a Moscow park was infamously broken up by bulldozers have now been given a kind of official licence to hold an annual show in the basement of the trade union hall of the ministry of culture workers; in April 1986, 85,000 people bought tickets to attend it. Sadly, the collection was not impressive. Artistic themes and style appear little changed over the past twelve years; they are still derivative of Western art a generation ago, and still dependent on religious themes for a shock value that is steadily decreasing.[20]

The more adventurous young Soviet artists mock this group of ageing rebels as 'foreign currency painters', for a very large proportion of their sales go to the endlessly self-renewing ranks of Western diplomats and businessmen in Moscow who see the paintings as politically daring. The Soviet art scene is now a great deal wider and more eclectic, and far more difficult to categorise. Again, the growing size of the market is important. The state art salons can no longer begin to meet the public demand for art. Outside most of the salons hanging officially approved painters, whether members of the union of artists or members of approved amateur clubs, stand unauthorised painters selling their own work, usually garish acrylic landscapes of old-fashioned Orthodox churches against a vast sky. And there are more and more unofficial art galleries suddenly appearing in the parks. The big expanse of open country in southern Moscow, known simply as Bitza Park, has played host to such a weekend gallery winter and summer for the past two years. In winter, the customers and the curious arrive through the snow on skis, to browse among the hippies selling the hand-carved Buddhas and the painters showing their heads of Christ, mock icons, landscapes and still lifes.[21]

In spring I recognised some of those Buddha-selling hippies at the Art Days festival in the old Hanseatic League city of Riga, in Soviet Latvia. They were among the audience in the Allegro café when Art Troitsky from Moscow and Seriozha Kuryakhin from Leningrad came together to stage a bizarre experimental concert of electronic music and light show. Troitsky is famous in Riga, where he introduces the only rock video programme on Soviet television, an immensely popular show called *Video Ritmi*. Just before the concert began, Siim Annuss, a brilliant young graphic artist from the Estonian capital of Tallin, had come down to stage a '*performanz*' (for which he is celebrated), a kind of cross-cultural happening that may make Westerners nostalgic for the sixties but still seems fresh and daringly strange to a Soviet audience.[22] It began with the solid thudding of drums, followed by the plaintive song of the microchip, as eerie electronic music set the mood for Siim's entry. Barefoot, and wearing a long white cotton shift to which daffodils were pinned in a strange pattern, he paraded solemnly around the café audience, while a haunting song told of the legend of a king who left footsteps on his lands, some black and some gold, and the fate of each city was told in the colour of the footprints he left. Then a mass of voices roared out the chorus over and over again: 'The king has come to Riga.' Siim placed one bare foot on a tray of gold paint, the other in a tray of black, and stepped delicately on the sheets of white paper that trailed between the tables. Only then did I realise that each sheet was already signed, dated and numbered, with a frame for each footprint neatly drawn on it: an item of *performanz* art that was to be given to each member of the audience.

The café was packed. I recognised not only the Moscow hippies but some of the artistic types from Soviet television who had come up from Moscow for the concert and some of the Leningrad underground artists. The women looked stunning, in clothes and hats of their own design, black face-veils hanging from vast millinery confections, dark purple lipsticks. There were men in wing collars and outlandish home-made ties, and girls in the fantastical home-knitted robes of clashing colours that is Riga high fashion. Forget the anti-alcohol laws; under every table teacups were being filled from bottles. The place was lit by the flashes of comic strips and weird abstract paintings that were beamed randomly through film slides.

From the moment I had left the station and walked through the pedestrian underpass, the kind of grim grey complex of tunnels where people are processed like peas, the place had not felt like the Soviet Union of Western imagination. There was a crowd watching a young man spray-painting graffiti on the wall, and another crowd laughing at some comic paintings of public bath-house scenes packed with grotesque nudes. Along the tunnels were placed odd sculptures of raw wood and brick and scrapyard junk.

Another young artist with ink-black hands and a print roller was helping children impress their own designs.

In the great square by the old cathedral, dancers in black leotards were dancing austerely in the rain to eerie electronic sounds punctuated on the hour by church bells. Gaily coloured flags hung across the square and along one side street; the walls of the old buildings had become a gallery of modern art. Down another street, a tangle of strangely painted plaster mannequins pointed erotically at a mass of disembodied arms that showed the way to a sculpture exhibition in the gardens of the old presidential palace. In public buildings around the city there were numerous exhibitions of the kind of modern art one never expects to see in the Soviet Union, displayed in wayward and experimental mockery of the traditional socialist realism that Soviet officialdom promotes.

In this context, however, officialdom means Moscow. The people who run art in Latvia are Latvians. The woman responsible for nurturing in the city one of the boldest and most impressive artistic traditions in the country, and for making art fun and publicly available, is Djemma Skulme.[23] As chairman of the union of artists, she defends and promotes the new and the unorthodox because she and her husband have spent most of their lives being dangerously ahead of official fashion. In 1984, the Riga art festival featured a single daring exhibition in St Peter's church under the single theme of 'Environment'. There were wrecked cars with grass growing where the engines used to be, a chandelier with statues of burning humans instead of candles, and a triple portrayal of the last supper. The first of the three huge tables in this latter exhibit embodied purity, with classic white statues of Jesus and the disciples. That was then. The second table showed the drunks, the vomit and pollution after the supper had ended. This was now. The third table was empty and posed the simple question: What next? The conservatives in the Riga art world complained to Moscow, whose ministry of culture sent down a team of assessors who closed the exhibition. It is indicative of changing times that, two years later, the Riga festival had recovered as boldly as it had, and that the Environment exhibition, all of its exhibits having been carefully stored, was being reopened.

Then there was the fuss about the rock concert *Cyrano de Bergerac*, written and performed by the enormously talented young Martin Brauns.[24] It contained some lines critical of censorship and of mindless patriotism. There were attempts to ban its production. But Brauns himself was the musical director of the national theatre; the lyrics for his opera had been written by the leading Latvian poet Janis Peters, who is also chairman of the Latvian writers' union. The point is that, in Latvia at least, yesterday's artistic rebels are today's establishment – and they have neither tamed their own styles nor lost faith with the thrusting new generation that is emerging.

Clearly, there are still restrictions on artistic freedom, and the grim old hand of the worst and most closed-minded traditions of Soviet cultural orthodoxy has not lost its grip. The artists of Riga and of much of the rest of the Soviet Union remain deprived of international contact, of Western art magazines and shows, of familiarity with the ideas and experiments of other countries. They crave travel. They are starved of books and journals. But the boundaries have been widened much, much further than most Westerners might expect. This is partly because Latvia and the other Baltic republics enjoy closer links with the West than most of the Soviet Union. In Estonia, they can receive (and understand) Finnish television, which is beamed to them from just sixty miles away across the Gulf of Finland. Lithuania and Latvia each year play host to thousands of Lithuanian expatriates who emigrated to the West before and during the Second World War, and who are encouraged to return on holidays, to spend their foreign currency and rediscover their roots. Furthermore, the artists, perhaps more than most other Soviet groups, have been able to take advantage of the sheer size and diversity of the world's biggest multinational state. The fertility of Riga, for example, is nourished by personal links between its artists and those of Georgia and Armenia, by the closeness of Leningrad and Moscow, by its citizens' occasional trips to the Islamic regions of Kazakhstan and Uzbekistan, and by the strangely powerful primitive arts of the old Siberian tribes. What Russians are unable to receive from the West is, to a degree, compensated for by the sheer variety of the cultural traditions incorporated within the Soviet Union.[25]

Yet, inevitably and healthily, there remains a thirst for more, for a cultural reintegration into the life and art and consciousness of the rest of the world against which the Soviet border has proved such a rigorous barrier for so long. This is not a phenomenon restricted to the European parts of the country. The Soviet Union is unique in its equal proximity to – and one could almost say its geographic definition by – the three great cultural traditions of the human race. To the west is old Europe, to the south is Islam, and to the east the Orient. There are inspirations, challenges and ancient nationalist hankerings that make each tradition as attractive to various sections of the Soviet people as it seems politically threatening to the Kremlin. But the changing pattern of Soviet lifestyles, the people's increasing prosperity, the options that are starting to come with that modest wealth, and the divisions of class and social expectation that the new rich represent, are each of them fundamental and far-reaching transformations which have occurred very largely in spite of the Kremlin. The country went through a social revolution while Brezhnev slept. The wide-awake new leadership has to live with the consequences – and might just have the wisdom to enjoy them.

11

The Women's Lot

On 8 March every year, celebrated by the Soviets as International Women's Day, the ladies of the Kremlin throw a discreetly lavish tea party for the wives of the Moscow diplomatic corps. The buffet table of the state guest house in the Lenin hills groans with caviare and lobsters, smoked sturgeon and the finest delicacies from the Kremlin commissariat. A full orchestra plays light classical music as the ladies circulate in their elegant dresses and ballgowns, drinking tea and soft drinks and nibbling at the food. Then the wife of the general secretary of the Communist Party begins the dancing with the senior diplomatic wife, and the ladies dance together to the waltzes, and gather into rings for the communal dances the Russians love.

The ladies' tea party in March 1985 was unusual for two reasons. The first was that New Zealand had appointed a woman ambassador, the tall and statuesque Alison Stokes, and protocol required that she lead the dance for the diplomats. The second was that rumours were flooding through Moscow that Konstantin Chernenko, visibly ill since the moment of his accession, had collapsed and been rushed to hospital. But there was no sign from the Kremlin wives of a leadership crisis. Mrs Chernenko pleaded tiredness and sat out the dancing, so there was no chance of asking her any discreetly concerned questions about her husband's health. Mrs Gromyko shared her husband's reputation for discretion. Raisa Gorbachev – 'dripping with jewels', as one ambassadorial wife described her – looked slightly bored and disdainful of the entire proceedings. The party was not a success.[1]

The following year, with Raisa Gorbachev evidently in charge, there was none of the rather forced dancing in pairs. And there was a new woman in attendance, Alexandra Biryukova, the first woman to have been admitted into the top ranks of Soviet power for twenty-five years. She had been made one of the eleven full secretaries of the party's central committee secretariat only two days earlier. After the twelve full members and seven candidate members of the Politburo, the central committee secretaries are the most influential people in the country. Not since Ekaterina Furtseva had been voted off the praesidium in 1961, after a four-year term, had a woman risen so high.[2]

Women have consistently been far better represented in public bodies such as the Supreme Soviet and the district and city soviets then they are in most Western parliaments. A third of the 1500 members of the Supreme Soviet are women, and women also make up slightly more than half of the 2.3 million deputies to all the local soviets around the country.[3] One of the earliest real achievements of the Soviet revolution was to give women full legal equality with men. They enjoy full rights to vote, to stand for public office, to have an education and to follow a career. Whereas in the West, barely 60 per cent of women of working age have a job, over 85 per cent of Soviet women work; indeed, they make up a slight majority of the entire labour force.[4]

But, as in the West, legal equality does not mean equality in practice. The higher the rank in politics or industry, the fewer the number of women. Women make up a quarter of the membership of the Communist Party, but hold only about one in twenty of senior posts such as regional first secretaryships or membership of the central committee. Although women dominate the medical and teaching professions, they tend to fill the junior, subordinate positions. Almost 70 per cent of Soviet doctors are women, and 73 per cent of teachers; but these professions have seen a sharp fall in pay and status.[5] Although more than four out of five primary school teachers are women, more than two thirds of all head teachers are men, and the average pay of a primary teacher is less than 150 roubles a month, well below the average industrial wage. In medicine, women doctors dominate general practice, manning the polyclinics where they have an average of thirty patients a day to see and treat, while the senior posts that provide time for research and writing articles for the medical journals are dominated by men.[6]

In the factories, women tend to work in light industry, where the pay is traditionally lower than it is in the heavy industries of coal, iron and steel. Soviet economic journals tend to assume that a wife's earnings will be about two thirds those of her husband. But there are some of the heavier jobs that have become, by relatively recent tradition, women's work. The sight of bands of tough, squat, ageing women, heavily wrapped against the cold, chipping away at the ice of Soviet streets has become characteristic of modern Russia. Like so much else, it was a result of the war. In 1940, the year of the last census before Hitler's invasion, there were 93 million men and 101 million women in the country. The first full postwar census of 1959 showed that the male population had increased by barely 1 million, whereas the female population had increased by 14 million. Over 15 million men died in the war; the impact of the casualties on the Soviet labour force was devastating, and was felt well into the 1980s.[7]

Even in the late 1930s, women made up about a third of the labour force, but the war forced them to take over the jobs of the conscripted males in heavy industry, in munitions plants and in public services. Many of them stayed, and women construction workers, painters, decorators, street cleaners and bus drivers are now commonplace. The expanding service sector and the retail-trade network have been staffed overwhelmingly by women, and so has the growing clerical sector. In the 1970s, some two thirds of the female workforce could be classified as engaged in manual labour, whether on the farms, serving behind a shop counter, or clearing ice from the winter streets.[8]

In common with other members of their sex everywhere, Russian women often face the double burden of running the home and family as well as doing their own jobs. The endless queues in Soviet shops make this a much greater trial than it is in the West. Although most Soviet homes now have washing machines, they are crude by Western standards, many of them needing to be filled with water and drained by hand. Soviet men are at least as chauvinist as their Western counterparts, equally reluctant to do their share of household chores and minding the children. The number of kindergarten and nursery places for pre-school children has almost quadrupled in the last twenty-five years, from 4.4 million in 1960 to over 16 million today;[9] but they are still too few, and the standards in many of them are so low that mothers prefer to make private arrangements, or to rely on *babushkas*, the legendary Russian grandmothers.

The combination of work, domestic chores, the difficulty of shopping and the problems of arranging childcare means that the average Soviet woman spends her life rushing. She gets up early to prepare breakfast, takes her child to the daycare centre, goes to work, shops in her lunch hour and even in work hours, travels back to pick up the child, to prepare an evening meal, to clean the flat. And everything seems to demand more effort than it does in the West. The public transport systems are more crowded, the gaps between stations longer, the food supplies in the shops more problematic, the vacuum cleaners less efficient, the refrigerators smaller, the freezers rare, and convenience foods even rarer. You can now buy frozen TV dinners in Moscow supermarkets, but they are uninviting. There are a handful of pizza parlours in Moscow, but the queues are long, and sometimes they run out of cheese, and sometimes they run out of tomato paste.

Perhaps the hardest part of being a woman in the Soviet Union, however, concerns almost everything to do with sex. It begins with the housing problem, the small flats and the lack of privacy. Young lovers have to exercise considerable ingenuity to find a place to be alone. Those with the money can book an overnight cabin on a riverboat cruise or take the 'soft class' on a night train with its two-bunk compartments. In summer there is the open air, but a superhuman degree of passion is required to make love outdoors in a Russian winter. Most students live either with their parents or in an *obshesitiye*, a hostel with little privacy and ubiquitous monitors. Hotels mean document checks, so most lovers try to borrow a friend's flat.

Then there is the problem of contraception. Soviet condoms come in two kinds: the military variety that are so thick they could be used as galoshes, and the domestic brand that are so thin that they are holed either before use or during lovemaking. There is a lively black market in East German and Hungarian contraceptive pills, but growing concern about their effects on health. And, except for the well connected, the supply of the pills is too irregular to be relied on. Soviet gynaecologists insist to Western interviewers that there are five sizes of diaphragm available, but few Russian women would claim to have found more than two sizes – too big or too small.[10] Spermicide creams are simply not to be found, which dramatically reduces the effectiveness of the diaphragm. IUDs are available for women who have already had children, but Soviet men complain that their shape, or the thickness of the nylon cord which allows them to be removed, makes sex uncomfortable. Western condoms are therefore in great demand in the Soviet Union, and even influential

179

Russian friends and officials are not shy about asking Westerners if they have any to spare.

The tragic result of all this is that the standard method of birth control in the Soviet Union is abortion. Moscow gynaecologists have said, even on the record to Western journalists, that there are two abortions for every live birth.[11] I have yet to meet a Soviet woman who has not had one abortion, and most who are prepared to talk about it will admit to having had several. And they shudder as they recount the awful, assembly-line atmosphere and lack of anaesthetics of the abortion clinics.

'The only experience worse than an abortion is having a baby in a Soviet hospital,' one young mother, a literary critic married to a magazine journalist, once told me. 'The fathers are not allowed into the maternity ward. Unless you pay a bribe there will be no anaesthetic, and if you do not pay a rouble a day to the ward attendant you have to clean the space round your own bed and she will not bring you a bedpan. Even if you have stitches, there is nothing but the rough lavatory paper, and if you give birth on Friday night or on Saturday, you will not see your baby again until the Monday morning.'[12]

The Soviet health authorities have largely discontinued the publication of official statistics on mortality, but for the last period when figures were available, 1971–74, the deaths of infants under one year old increased sharply from 22.9 to 27.9 per 1000 live births. According to Russian mothers, the conditions inside the maternity hospitals are partly to blame.[13]

One of the worst features of the Soviet system's attitude towards women, because of the constant humiliation it involves, is the lack of provision for feminine hygiene. Apparently, the Soviet Union does not manufacture tampons. (The standard solution is to use cotton wool – and, on occasion, there are shortages of cotton wool, just as there are shortages of everything else.) This is a fundamental disregard for the dignity and comfort of women, but it is part of a pattern. The Soviet Union has barely begun to produce attractive clothes for women. It produces perfumes, but few popular cosmetics. Its lingerie for women is functional and crudely old-fashioned, and the shoes and boots clumpy and ill made. In the circumstances, it is remarkable how stylishly the women dress, particularly the young. In part, this is made possible by the limited availability of Western imports, particularly Finnish clothes; the supply of Soviet oil and gas to Western Europe is slowly increasing the imports of French, Italian and German clothes and cosmetics. Indeed, Pierre Cardin signed an agreement to open a Moscow store in the spring of 1986. But a mere rumour that a consignment of Polish bras, or Hungarian sweaters, or Yugoslav shoes has arrived is enough to summon the queues.

Inevitably, the black market provides a solution. Western tampons are available, as are Western condoms, cosmetics and a growing range of clothing. American jeans are widespread, and so are women's tights, T-shirts and jogging shoes. But jeans and a pair of training shoes will cost 200 roubles on the black market, a month's average salary.

There are legal ways of dressing well. The Soviet Union is one of the last bastions of the bespoke tailor, the small atelier who will produce made-to-measure suits, dresses, blouses or women's hats. The customer provides the material and the design is discussed. Like so much else in the country, it is a transaction which can go badly wrong, without the right personal connection. Anywhere in the world, the relationship between a woman and her dressmaker is important and deeply personal. In the Soviet Union it is crucial, because it is not easy to replace a piece of material once the atelier has cut or sewn it badly. 'If I have to choose between wearing my last pair of good tights for my lover and giving them to my dressmaker, my dressmaker wins every time,' one Soviet actress told me. Small gifts of perfume, and flowers on the appropriate occasions of Women's Day, May Day, 7 November and birthdays are customary.[14]

Then there is Dom Modi, the house of fashion directed by Slava Zaitsev, the man they like to present as the Pierre Cardin of Moscow. He holds fashion parades with blaring disco music and light shows, charges fabulous prices and seeks to convince the women of the diplomatic corps that there is a touch of elegance and chic about the Soviet capital. His clothes are stylish, often based on a traditional Russian or Slavic design set off with a Western flair. But they are also disappointing, the finest silks usually sewn with a cotton thread, and the finish of buttonholes or zips letting down the overall image of luxury. To a cynic, Slava Zaitsev's house of fashion on Prospekt Mira is another Potemkin, another example of tokenism that serves to conceal the short-comings of the system as a whole.[15] But it is also a symbol of social change. There is a large and evidently growing number of fashionable women in Moscow, with the money and the taste and the burning desire to dress well. Few of them buy from Zaitsev, but they go to his shows, note his designs, and get their own versions made up by a trusted local atelier. Slowly, the state clothing factories are trying to follow the trend, producing a wider variety of styles, just as the official women's magazines such as *Robotnitsa*, with its monthly circulation of over 17 million (and published by *Pravda*), are running fashion pages and hints on cosmetics. Moreover, the basic shape of the Soviet woman is changing. A steadily improving diet, with more protein and less starch, has seen the average height of Soviet women grow by 2.8 inches in the last thirty years.[16] The average weight seems to have dropped sharply too – although that is a subjective judgement. The official encouragement of sports and the stress on physical exercise in schools have probably played their part. The ideal shape of woman in Soviet art has undergone a dramatic transformation in the past generation; you seldom see these days those classically buxom peasant wenches of socialist realism, with their enormous haunches and milkchurn bosoms.

The Kremlin ladies of today provide a dramatic contrast to the Politburo wives of even five years ago. The wives of Khrushchev, Brezhnev, Andropov and their generation were short, stolid and dumpy, reminiscent of the classic Russian *babushka*, built like tanks with severe hairstyles. They were seldom seen on Soviet television or in the press; when they were, they were instant reminders of the grim past of famines and life on bread and potatoes, of women conscripted into factories and fields, of work and struggle and childbearing. They were the image of tough old Mother Russia, where a woman's lot was endlessly to endure.

In comparison, Raisa Gorbachev, like the wives of the other newer Politburo men, is an intellectual in her own right, a university graduate, and a stylish dresser. On her visit to London in 1984, she went shopping for jewellery with a credit card.[17] In Paris, she did not look out of place in Yves St Laurent's showrooms. At the Geneva summit, she capably handled a human rights demonstration at the university and two media-intensive tea parties with Nancy Reagan, and more than held her own on the fashion front. For the first time, Soviet television devoted programmes specifically to the wife of their nation's leader, as if intent on ramming home their pride in having not only a leader who could perform stylishly on the world stage but a whole first family. The Red Square appearances of Raisa, daughter Irina and granddaughter Oksana on May Day and at the November parades have already become part of a tradition, prominently featured on Soviet television. Additionally, the usual Soviet sources have been careful to leak the news that Raisa enjoys an unprecedented degree of political influence. When the decision was taken to allow Stalin's daughter Svetlana Alliluyeva and her daughter Olga to return to the West, British diplomats were told that Raisa had had a hand in it.[18] Certainly, Soviet dramatists and theatre producers are convinced that the easing of cultural controls has been due in part to the new first lady and her personal interest in literature and the arts.

It was shortly after Soviet television news had focused on Mrs Gorbachev's role at the Geneva summit that the first letters began to appear in the Soviet press asking why there were so few women in the top echelons of the party.[19] One even made the point that, in Lenin's day, women such as Alexandra Kollontai, Elena Stasova and Nadezhda Krupskaya had been political figures in their own right. It was as though the Soviet public were being prepared not only for a much higher profile for the wife of the man in the Kremlin but also for a greater role for women in Soviet life. If so, the first step was cautious indeed, with the elevation of Alexandra Biryukova, the top woman in the Soviet trade union movement, to a central committee secretary's post. The portfolio she was given included women's affairs, but ranged far wider, including trade union and social issues.

Biryukova was a classic apparatchik, a prim and severe woman with no known interests outside her own family, her career and the party. Trained as an engineer, she was an administrator who had risen through the trade union structure in the textile industry.[20] She and the cosmonaut Valentina Tereshkova, who had until then been the most prominent woman in Soviet public life, seemed to have come from the same coldly orthodox mould. They dressed in plain suits, wore strict hairstyles and relentlessly businesslike expressions: women who were determined to blend into the customary forms of a man's world. Tereshkova had started work at a tyre factory at the age of sixteen, and had obtained the qualifications to become the first woman in space by studying in her spare time, acquiring a correspondence course diploma from a technical school, and joining a parachuting club to occupy what little leisure remained to her. The self-control and dedication that she had put into her teenage and young career was carried on into middle age, when she became the Brezhnev system's token woman, chairman of the Soviet women's committee and a kind of ambassador-at-large at international conferences.[21]

The contrast between Tereshkova and Raisa Gorbachev is, in its way, as glaring as the contrast between Raisa and the old generation of Kremlin wives. They are entirely different types of woman, although they have each built their own careers, and each has climbed the ranks of Soviet privilege. The contrast is not just in their dress and their personal styles, in the way that Raisa smiles naturally and often while Tereshkova hardly smiles at all. It is the impression that Raisa gives of having a mind of her own, and being determined to use it, while Tereshkova has never dropped the slightest hint of having an opinion that diverges by one iota from what *Pravda* tells her to think. Perhaps this explains why Raisa arouses so much personal curiosity among Soviet women. They seem to warm to her as they have not done previously to influential women. If they are looking for a role model, then Raisa is doubtless a great deal more attractive and genuinely interesting than the leading lady comrades the system has produced in the past. But the real change is to be found not simply in the first lady, but in the position of Soviet women as a whole.

For all their burdens and frustrations, women in the Soviet Union are also enjoying the fruits of the long, slow social revolution that has come with forty years of peace. They are increasingly well educated; in 1985, 84 per cent of them had had a complete secondary education and nearly 3 million were at universities and colleges. They have a growing curiosity about the world outside the Soviet Union, not only for its cosmetics and its consumer goods, but for its ideas about women. There is no organised feminist movement in the country, but there have been stirrings.

In 1979, the first issue appeared of a samizdat journal called *Zhenschina i Rossiya* (*Almanac: Woman and Russia*). Ten copies were typed by a group of Leningrad feminists, circulated among friends, recopied and, in the way of samizdats, spread more widely until Western correspondents read it and wrote stories about it which were beamed back to the Soviet Union by Western radio stations; then more and more Soviet people began trying to borrow copies. As is usual in such cases, a summons to the KGB office in Leningrad was sent to the editor and founder of the journal, Tatyana Mamonova. On Human Rights Day, 19 December 1979, Tatyana was formally warned that, if a second issue appeared, she would be arrested. The name of the journal changed to *Rossianka* (*Russian Woman*), a second issue did appear, and the handful of copies typed out laboriously by hand spread far beyond Leningrad and Moscow. Then came a third issue, and four of the 'ringleaders', as the KGB called them, were sent into exile.[22]

The KGB's reaction was to be expected, but that of the 'second culture', the underground artistic, free-thinking and dissident circles, was not so predictable. Feminism receives a grim enough response from liberal-minded men in the West. The Soviet attitude was considerably more hostile, since the underground circles were not even prepared to handle the idea of a militant feminism. The *Almanac* accused them of being sexist, dominated by men and male values, attacked their art and attitudes in print, and condemned some of them as rapists.[23] In return, the editors of the *Almanac* were attacked as Russian nationalists, on the flimsy evidence of the journal's title. Then the arguments began to widen. Some of the original *Almanac* editors formed a separate group called Maria, which tried to express feminism through and within the Russian Orthodox church.[24]

The awakening interest in feminist ideas did not stop with the exile of Tatyana Mamonova and her friends; they continued to publish the *Almanac* from Paris, and copies managed to find their way inside the Soviet Union. Soviet feminism has far earlier roots than *Almanac*. In the first heady days after the 1917 revolution, the Bolshevik and pioneering feminist Alexandra Kollontai advocated free love and the reduction of the formalities of marriage and divorce to a matter of simple registration. Since that time, feminist ideas have never disappeared from the official Soviet media, and the wryly humorous story of the pressures on a modern woman 'A Week like any Other', by Natalya Baranskaya in *Novy Mir*, deserves to become a classic of women's writing.[25] But, so far, there has been little sign that the women's movement in the Soviet Union has gone much beyond stirrings and the occasional samizdat publication. An explanation for this has been put forward by one of the *Almanac* writers, Alla Sariban:[26]

The crux of the matter is this: Soviet women, in some inner part of their beings, frequently without being aware of it, have a distinct tendency to make common cause with the Soviet system and to identify with it . . . The average Soviet woman does not have the time, the strength or the inner psychological reserves to think of anything other than the immediate, the close at hand, and the day to day.

There is another factor. The status of Soviet women is changing, the quality of their lives and of their housing and the services available to them is improving. Not fast enough, doubtless, but dramatically by comparison with their mothers' generation – and that is the only comparison they can easily make. It should not be difficult for a centrally planned economy to start mass-producing tampons and decent, effective sanitary towels, and it should be simple enough to produce contraceptive sheaths that neither break nor remove the pleasure from love-making. The system has already, with lumbering slowness, responded sufficiently to start manufacturing disposable nappies for babies, which, Moscow mothers claim, have revolutionised their lives.

Perhaps the most popular single act of the Gorbachev administration from the women's point of view has been the strict new campaign against alcohol abuse. Women always bore the brunt of Soviet drunkenness. They were the ones who saw the housekeeping money pillaged for a bottle of vodka, who were beaten by drunken husbands. One of the saddest sights of my first winter in Moscow was of a mother and children trying to haul a drunken father from the snow, heaving him over the drifts alongside the pavements.

In material terms, as regards the quality of daily life, women stand to be the greatest beneficiaries of the Gorbachev reforms, if his administration can add a little sensitivity to its grand modernising purpose. But they are also the key to the process. The service and the retail sectors are overwhelmingly staffed by women. Their streamlining and improvement depend on women's cooperation, and since women appreciate better than men the deficiencies of Soviet shops, they have the incentive to cooperate. Moreover, it is the women, to a large degree, who run the private plots on which so much of the Soviet food supply relies, just as it is the women who staff the lower ranks of the bureaucracy which Gorbachev has identified as one of the leading candidates for reform.

Maybe the least noticed section of Gorbachev's personal manifesto of reform, in his speech to the twenty-seventh party congress, was the open bid he made for women's support. He promised that, within five years, there would be a place at a pre-school nursery or kindergarten for every child. He announced that paid leave for new mothers would be extended until the children were eighteen months old, and that the number of paid days off for mothers to care for sick children would be increased. He increased child allowances for low-income families, and announced that there was a plan 'to extend the practice of letting women work a shorter day or week, or to work at home':[27]

> Why not reintroduce women's councils within the workplace, or residentially, integrating them in a single system with the Soviet women's committee at its head. Women's councils could help to resolve a wide range of social problems arising in the life of our society.

Evident here, it was assumed, was the influential hand of Raisa Gorbachev, who had been one of the first Soviet academics to draw attention in the course of her research to difficulties faced specifically by women. Her studies of rural life in Stavropol had stressed that one of the greatest problems on the collective farms was the low status and position of women. She described a divisive system on the farms which saw the men receive the mechanical training to run the tractors and the machinery while women were increasingly left with the heavy physical labour. She wrote of the powerful rural traditions which kept women locked in their old roles, and of the sharp disparity between urban and rural incomes, amenities and lifestyles. It was not a feminist document; as a formal thesis for a doctorate, it could not possibly have been presented in that way. But it was an acute observation of the limitations of the agricultural system her husband was helping to administer, and of the central place of women within it.[28] It had been a long time since an intelligent and reform-minded woman had been in a position to influence Soviet policy at the top, and to point out that it was not enough to carry on uttering the tired old platitudes about the Soviet achievement in giving women equal rights and opportunities. In Gorbachev's speech to the party congress, the signs were that the most powerful Soviet man was at last prepared to listen.

12

The Sons of the Elite

Of the current members of the Politburo and secretaries of the central committee, only Vladimir Dolgikh, a candidate Politburo member, comes from a privileged family background. His father was a senior official in the ministry of internal affairs.[1] The rest are the sons of peasants, workers, local officials like Gorbachev's grandfather, who was chairman of a collective farm. Their own rise to power from modest or even humble origins points to the peculiar way in which the Soviet Union recruits its political leadership. Until now, not even the almost universal criterion of a good education has been required. Mikhail Gorbachev is the first Soviet leader since Lenin to have enjoyed a conventional university training.

There are historical reasons for this, and most of them are to do with the revolution itself, and with Stalin, who beheaded the old revolutionary leadership. The revolution disposed of the ruling class of the Tsars, which was not only a hereditary aristocracy but also an aristocracy of bureaucratic rank. A civil servant who reached a senior grade in the Tsarist bureaucracy was automatically elevated to the ranks of the nobility. Indeed, the success of Lenin's father as an inspector of schools in the ministry of education led to his ennoblement.[2] When Lenin applied to enter university, his rank was listed as 'son of a nobleman'. So in sweeping away the Tsarist nobility, the Bolshevik state evicted, in addition to the dukes and the landowners, the upper ranks of its civil service. But the administration of the state had to continue, and a new bureaucracy had to be appointed; its members were obliged to learn their jobs as they did them, and to pick up what education they could from night schools, correspondence courses and the party's own college system.

The only groups of the Tsarist elite left relatively unscathed by the revolution were the professional soldiers and the cultural intelligentsia; they lost their homes and estates and many of their treasures but, on the whole, they kept their lives, so long as they were loyal to the new regime. Indeed, Trotsky's success in recruiting the Tsarist officer corps to train and lead the Bolshevik Red Army was a key factor in ensuring the state's survival.[3] And many of the actors, artists and musicians who had formed the cultural elite under the Tsars were sympathetic enough to the cause of revolution to stay and prosper under Bolshevism, particularly during the 1920s, when the infant Soviet Union went through a cultural flowering and dynamism that has few parallels. Stanislavsky and Meyerhold in the theatres, Eisenstein in film, Shostakovich and later Prokofiev in music, Kandinsky and Chagall in art, Blok and Yesenin and Mayakovsky in poetry, and indeed Mayakovsky in almost everything, made it a heady and hugely creative period.

Stalin stopped all that. He purged the officer corps, the intelligentsia, the old Bolsheviks who had led the revolution, and a large proportion of the party officials who had been recruited since. Having lost its Russian and Tsarist elite in 1917–21, the country lost its Bolshevik and much of its Soviet elite in the 1930s. This was a double blow from which the social system has only recently begun to recover. The relative stability of Soviet society since the end of the Second World War has resulted in the emergence of a class system, as senior officials ensure that their offspring receive the advantages of a good education, and graduate smoothly into the elite in their turn. Soviet laws on inheritance are not punitive. Private property, whether a country cottage or a privately owned 'cooperative' apartment in the city, cars or antiques or cash can be left to one's heirs. Consequently, a curious new class is developing in the Soviet Union.[4] It is tempting, but misleading, to see it as a middle class, neither enjoying the state-provided privileges of the political elite, nor sharing the comparative lack of consumer goods and comforts suffered by the newly urbanised workers. But its members are a middle class only by virtue of their possessions. They are not a profit-making or entrepreneurial bourgeoisie; such a section of society exists in the Soviet Union, but it is rooted in the family groups of farmers from the sunny south who profit from the endless hunger of moneyed Muscovites for the fruits and vegetables that can be bought at the free markets. They should perhaps best be described as a professional class, with conventional Western tastes in acquiring consumer goods and possessions. They have been the beneficiaries of the explosion in education and in academic institutes. They have degrees, and they teach, research and administer. They have benefited also from the new industries and professions that have emerged during the long stability of the postwar years. They work in television, or in the ever-expanding sectors of publishing and journalism. They are lawyers, whose growing status, income and role in Soviet life is one of the more remarkable features of the social revolution that has been under way since Stalin's death. They have learned foreign languages and work in the highly prized jobs that permit foreign travel, in diplomacy or in foreign trade, in administering the huge organised sports sector, or in culture.

The Russian language has no precise words to describe this social class, except the rather loose form 'intelligentsia'. The term is justified to the extent that this class is very much better read, and tends to be more culturally aware and curious, than its counterpart in the West. This may simply reflect the high quality of Soviet education, which seems to have spread a knowledge and a love of literature, foreign as well as Russian, remarkably widely through the population. It may also reflect the continued and deeply offensive constraints upon cultural life generally.

It remains dangerous and physically almost impossible to try to publish outside the permitted state system of the writers' union and the established journals. In 1980, a group of young writers openly petitioned the Moscow cultural authorities and the central committee for permission to establish a new literary club to be called Belles Lettres, and to publish an occasional collection of their writings, uncensored. Within hours they had been detained by the police, their apartments searched, their manuscripts, address books and even their typewriters confiscated.[5]

Some of the outstanding works of Soviet literature, such as Boris Pasternak's *Doctor Zhivago*, remain banned, or virtually impossible to obtain, except in the hard-currency stores reserved for foreigners. The poems of Marina Tsvetaeva or Anna Akhmatova, or Bulgakov's superb novel *The Master and Margerita*, or copies of Vladimir Vysotsky's poems, come into this distinguished, but effectively rationed, category. The inevitable result is a large, lucrative black market. There is little logic in this. Privately, the senior men at Soviet publishing houses say that they want to publish new editions of these books, but know that they would never get permission from the cultural authorities in the central committee. They shrink from the responsibility of trying, because they remember the suddenness with which official policy can change, and the way in which distinguished careers can be broken. And the officials in the central committee have memories of their own, of how the publication of Solzhenitsyn's novel of life in Stalin's Gulag *One Day in the Life of Ivan Denisovich* in *Novy Mir* magazine helped to radicalise a generation.

Apart from that heady decade of the 1920s, censorship has been a constant feature of Russian literary life under Tsar and commissar alike. The censor has thus become a kind of political barometer, whose decisions over what to permit and what to ban indicate the alarms and the moods of the leadership. Khrushchev loosened the controls during his de-Stalinisation campaign and then tightened them again when that seemed like a cheap way to win back support from the hardliners. Brezhnev screwed the controls down very tightly indeed with the trials of Daniel and Sinyavsky, and in the 1970s the close identification between writers and open dissidence led to the persecutions of Solzhenitsyn, Kopolev, Aksyonov and others.

The system was never rigid, perhaps because the human beings who ran it were themselves unsure where the boundaries should be. KGB head Yuri Andropov's curious indulgence towards Yuri Lyubimov, director of Moscow's Taganka theatre, gave Lyubimov licence to produce such bold and innovative drama as *House on the Embankment*, a study in guilt and moral choice based on an informer during Stalin's terror.[6] But while this play was permitted, and the novel by Yuri Trifonov on which it was based had been published in 1976, there were strict crackdowns in other areas. The group around Vasili Aksyonov, who tried to publish the experimental literary magazine *Metropol* in 1979, were threatened with expulsion from the writers' union, which would mean effective unemployment and inability to publish new work. Aksyonov was driven into exile, and his colleagues given solemn warnings.[7]

Yet the very harshness of the literary suppression under Brezhnev was a testimony not only to the strength of Soviet writing but also to the quality and size of the new audience that had emerged and was prepared to take considerable risks to read it. Khrushchev's thaw had far-reaching social implications. Literary critics, novelists and poets who had been writing for the private drawers of their desks were emboldened into print; and the same readers who had devoured *Ivan Denisovich* were hungry for *First Circle* and *Cancer Ward*, even when the price of reading a samizdat was to spend night after night typing another copy to send along the endless grapevine. What had startled the KGB in the 1960s was not the authors and the books themselves so much as the enormous response they provoked in an underground audience. And that audience was beyond the KGB's control. It was too big and, oddly enough, it was one of the prime achievements of the Soviet state. Its education policies and the endless journals and books of 'approved' literature that the state presses pumped out had whetted a public appetite for more.

It was not easy for the censors to define the line of control, and the growth in samizdat publishing meant that the line was no longer holding. Perhaps the most remarkable cultural phenomenon of the Brezhnev years was the poet–actor–balladeer Vladimir Vysotsky. His songs of prison and the low-life, of drinking and political disillusion, became known across the whole country. But very few of them, or of his poems, were ever officially published. They spread by word of mouth, by samizdat, but above all by tape cassette, a new technology of publishing that seemed beyond the authorities' control. Recorded at Moscow parties when Vysotsky sang in a crowded room, the tapes were copied and re-copied. I have heard them in Siberian hunting villages, in mining towns, in Muslim homes down by the Iranian border, and sung in chorus by young conscripts in the back of an army truck. Vysotsky's funeral in Moscow during the 1980 Olympic Games was a remarkable social and cultural event. The authorities had tried to block news of the entire affair. Just as in life they had never allowed him to sing on television, had refused him the sonorous title of 'people's artist' which is bestowed like so much confetti on less controversial figures, so at first they tried to ignore it altogether. There was no announcement of his death, no obituaries in the press, and his family were told they could bury him only in some provincial cemetery far from Moscow. Then a black-bordered portrait of Vysotsky appeared at the Taganka theatre, where his *Hamlet* had become one of the classic modern productions of Soviet drama, and the news spread across the city. Vysotsky's Hamlet had been part of the trouble. He portrayed the Danish prince as an honest, if hesitant, young man, fighting hopelessly against an evil rule and the deadening grip of an entire society weighed down by corruption and hypocrisy. The message for a contemporary Soviet audience was explicit.

In an earlier time, the state could, and probably would, have crushed Vysotsky. But perhaps because of Andropov's patronage of the Taganka, or an increasingly self-confident public mood, or even because of the nature of the changes under way in the Soviet leadership, they tried less to control the Vysotsky phenomenon than to contain it. But Vysotsky had too many powerful admirers. One of his friends telephoned Brezhnev's daughter Galina, and asked her to intercede over Vysotsky's burial ground. She managed to secure him a plot in Moscow's Vagankovskoye cemetery, where the poet Yesenin is also buried. The theatre itself announced a memorial commemoration on the morning of the burial, and tens of thousands of Russians defied the massive police presence for the Olympics to gather at the theatre and then at the cemetery. At the theatre, the party's cultural commissar for Moscow, Vitali Anturov, spoke of Vysotsky's acting skills, ignored his songs and poems, and tried to appropriate his memory in the name of official culture. It was Lyubimov, the theatre director, who then rose to tell the truth about Vysotsky's appeal, to explain why the surrounding squares and streets were packed with silent, weeping Russians: 'He was our bard, the keeper of the nation's spirit, of our pain and all our joys.'[8]

Vysotsky remains the most powerful cultural figure of the modern Soviet Union, with a much wider, because so much more human, appeal than Solzhenitsyn. Belatedly, the state has acknowledged this. On the fifth anniversary of his death, I followed Bella Akhmadulina, Russia's finest living poetess, and Vysotsky's mother and half the cultural elite of the city into the cemetery to put flowers on his grave. It has become a national shrine, open to all, constantly heaped with flowers and small candles that burn day and night in tiny jars. The writers' union, whose apparatchiks for years blocked the publication of his poems, has now been forced to establish a formal commission on Vysotsky's literary heritage, collecting his manuscripts and letters, planning a museum, and finally giving him the honour his art deserved.[9] The commission is chaired by the poet Robert Rozhdestvensky, and it also contains some of the band of writers like Bella Akhmadulina who tried with Vysotsky to publish their uncensored work in *Metropol*; in fact, it is made up of people who were seen twenty years ago as the dangerous young of Soviet cultural life, on the fringes of dissidence – they were the champions of the unorthodox, and friends of those forced into exile.

Among them are Bulent Okudzhava, a balladeer whose style and songs pointed the way to Vysotsky's work; Oleg Yefremov, now director of the prestigious Moscow Arts theatre; and Andrei Dementyev, the poet who edits one of the best and most adventurous of the official magazines, *Yunost*.

The rebellious generation has now at last become a part, and perhaps the key part, of the Soviet cultural establishment. This should not surprise us. Artistic fashions change in this way throughout the world. Yesterday's angry young man becomes tomorrow's grand old man of letters. But this transformation has not happened before in the Soviet Union. To give honour to the poets who were once dubbed dangerous by the party is an act, still, of some courage. It is symbolic not only of change, but also of that quintessential product of the long stability of the last forty years, the growth of the Soviet literary and cultural audience.

To capitalise on that growth, a further ingredient was needed: editors of personal courage, prepared to follow in the tradition established by Alexander Tvardovsky, who edited *Novy Mir* in the two periods of Khrushchev's thaw, and tended and cherished the new and controversial generation of his day. In 1985, Tvardovsky's chair at *Novy Mir* was occupied by a remarkable man, Vladimir Karpov, whose patriotism and personal courage could never be in dispute. He wore the coveted medal of a Hero of the Soviet Union, won during the war for his forays behind German lines, bringing back prisoners for interrogation. (The Russians call these German prisoners *yaziki*, or tongues.[10]) But Karpov himself was a veteran of Stalin's prison camps, who had won his medal from the ranks of a penal battalion. In 1940, while in his last year at officer training school, he had incautiously muttered to a fellow cadet that all they ever heard these days was the name Stalin: whatever had happened to Lenin? He was arrested the next day and sent on the long trail to Siberia that was taken by so many millions. After the German invasion in 1941, Karpov began petitioning from the camp for permission to be sent to the front. In the desperate winter of 1942, he was transferred to a penal regiment, and began his long, slow climb back into the Soviet establishment. By 1985, he was a member of the Supreme Soviet, and sat on the foreign affairs commission that Gorbachev had chaired. He had been part of the official delegation to India for Indira Gandhi's funeral, and accompanied Vladimir Scherbitsky on his tour of the USA in March, the tour that was inter-

rupted by Chernenko's death. Later that summer, a thick manuscript arrived on Karpov's desk at *Novy Mir* from Yevgeny Yevtushenko, the controversial and mercurial poet who had been in
and out of official favour for thirty years.

The manuscript, entitled *Fuku*, was a strange mixture of essay,
poem, memoir and polemic. It contained moving passages about
Yevtushenko's handicapped son, and some bold, discursive
poetry. But it was political dynamite. There were long passages
on forbidden topics, on Soviet neo-Nazis who sported swastikas
on Hitler's birthday, and on Beria, Stalin's notorious police chief,
and his odious habit of picking up teenage girls and bullying them
into sex. Yevtushenko wrote about the Gulags in Kolyma, and of
a truck driver he had once met who hailed from Kolyma and
who, like so many other Soviet blue-collar workers, kept a portrait
of Stalin in his cab. He wrote about the row he had, and he
wrote disapprovingly of the assassination of Trotsky. In short, he
deliberately jabbed at a whole series of political nerves.[11]

Karpov knew at once that it was important, and that he must
publish. He also knew it would not be easy. But he went through
the motions, submitting the text to the censorship board of Glavlit
in the usual way. Instant rejection. Karpov then called a full
meeting of the editorial board of *Novy Mir*, made them all read
the manuscript, and, with a stenographer sitting ostentatiously at
the table, asked each of them to vote – whether or not to publish.
They were unanimous for publication. Armed with this collective
decision, Karpov went to see Mikhail Gorbachev, his erstwhile
colleague on the foreign affairs commission. The new general
secretary skimmed the text and said he saw no problems but that
the new head of ideology, Yegor Ligachev, had better check it
too. Ligachev read it with care, and gave Karpov a handwritten
note saying that the central committee of the party had no objections. Karpov happily took the note to Glavlit, and *Fuku* was
published in the September issue of the magazine: the first concrete
indication of the advent of a new literary thaw. Six months later,
Karpov had been elected to the central committee.

Vladimir Karpov is one of hundreds of thousands of Stalin's
victims who have been rehabilitated and brought back into the
mainstream of Soviet life. In common with all of them, he is
unable to forget the Stalin period and what it did to him as an
individual, to the country, and to the army, which paid such a
desperate price for Stalin's purges and strategic errors in the first

years of the war. Karpov's own novel *Field Commander* is based on the life of another of Stalin's victims, one of the Red Army's finest fighting generals.[12]

Karpov's effort for Yevtushenko was significantly different from the long and valiant campaign that Alexander Tvardovsky had waged in support of Solzhenitsyn in the 1960s. Tvardovsky and Solzhenitsyn were both in their ways men of Stalin's era, shaped by a nightmare that Karpov had also shared. But Yevtushenko was from another generation altogether, a child of Khrushchev's de-Stalinisation – as indeed was Mikhail Gorbachev.

Yevtushenko and Karpov had, however, both sat in the hall at the third congress of the writers' union in 1967 when the grand old man of Soviet letters Mikhail Sholokhov, author of *Quiet Flows the Don*, had risen to lend his name to the renewed hard line under Brezhnev. Sholokhov had attacked the prominent author of the first post-Stalin thaw, Ilya Ehrenburg, for setting a bad example to the young. He had then attacked the young writers: 'They have on their conscience a certain defiance, a rejection of generally accepted norms of behaviour.' And he attacked those such as Solzhenitsyn for their campaign for press and literary freedom because 'It is in the bizarre company of the CIA, the rabid White Guards, the US senators and the defector Svetlana Alliluyeva [Stalin's daughter, who had fled to the West that year] that our zealots of freedom find themselves.'[13] But Sholokhov, with all the weight of his Nobel Prize behind him, had another point to make. There are things, he said, 'to make one stop and think – the average age of the delegates to this congress is almost sixty, and that makes rather a sad impression'. He gave some statistics. At the first Soviet writers' congress in 1934, 71 per cent of the delegates had been under forty. Now it was a gathering of old men. Only 12 per cent of those delegates who heard him were under forty. And that was before the flower of modern Soviet letters were harried into exile. The devilishly clever system of controlling the arts that Stalin and Zhdanov had devised back in the 1930s, permitting authors to work and publish only within the straitjacket of the party-controlled writers' union, was losing its grip on the new generation of Soviet literature.

It is a potent witness to the persistent health of Russian writing that fine authors continued to emerge and, increasingly, to publish novels and poems that went up to, and on occasion beyond, the limits that the old straitjacket had tried to impose. Even while

Solzhenitsyn and Kopelev were being exiled, a new school of rural writers was emerging. On the shores of Lake Baikal was Valentin Rasputin, chronicling the slow death of the old and decent simplicities of peasant life under Soviet power. Yuri Bondarev, who had made his name writing war novels, suddenly chose a new course, exploring the links between the artists in exile and those who had stayed.[14] The elderly woman mathematician who wrote under the pen-name of I. Grekova had lost her teaching job at a military academy for publishing a novel about the tensions and backbiting in a top-secret military research establishment. But she continued to write and publish; indeed, her grim play of women sharing a collective flat in Moscow at the end of the war, *Ship of Widows*, became the hit of the 1985 season at the Mossoviet theatre in Moscow.[15] There was Ghingiz Aikhmatov, the writer from the old Asian republic of Kirgizia, who sat on the board of *Novy Mir* and backed Karpov's campaign to publish *Fuku*. There was Fazil Iskander, who had been one of the group who tried to publish their uncensored work in *Metropol*.

The Soviet literary and cultural world was not only healthy, it was fashionable, thrilling and deeply attractive to the children of the political elite. They too formed a part of that growing Soviet audience who were moving away from politics and economics and turning instead, as previous Russian generations had done before them, to the arts. The special relationship between the Taganka theatre's Yuri Lyubimov and the KGB's Yuri Andropov sprang from an audition at the Taganka attended by Andropov's son Igor, who wanted to become an actor. Without knowing the identity of the young hopeful, Lyubimov gently warned him off, telling him of the hardships of an actor's life and the need for an almost inhuman dedication. He had then been summoned to the Lubianka by Andropov, who thanked him. But Andropov's daughter Irina, who had also been dissuaded by Lyubimov's fatherly advice, married a Taganka actor, Alexander Filipov.[16]

In the event, Andropov should not have been so grateful. His daughter's marriage soon ended in divorce, and his son was never happy in the diplomatic career his father then chose for him. Igor was given the privilege of foreign travel, authorised to work and study in the USA to write a thesis on the history of the American labour movement before joining the diplomatic service. He proved a singularly ineffective ambassador in Greece before being recalled in 1985. Moscow rumour had it that he had fallen victim of the bottle, a fate that was to afflict so many of the gilded young of the *Nomenklatura*. Brezhnev's son Yuri spent ten pleasant years in Sweden, representing the ministry of foreign trade, a post he interspersed with big-game hunting trips in East Africa and other game hunting in Paris, where he won a brief notoriety for tipping a topless dancer at the Crazy Horse with a hundred-dollar bill. As so often, he was drunk at the time.[17]

Yuri's sister Galina was the focus of much of the scandal of the last years of her father's rule. Her husband was the deputy minister of the interior, and one of her lovers was the celebrated Boris the Gypsy, a well-known crooner and one of the stars of what became known in the 1970s as the 'Highlife-isti'. Galina too hung around the fringes of cultural life, most of it at the circus, but with the occasional foray into the theatre, ballet and literary worlds. In the West, she would have been a rich groupie. In Moscow, she was a living refutation of the ideals Soviet society was supposed to stand for.

In Brezhnev's last years, the privileges of the children of the powerful became a public scandal, a major cause of the disgust that grew between governors and governed. There was Galina herself, with her taste for diamonds; and Igor Shchelekov, wastrel son of the corrupt old police chief, who drove to classes at the elite diplomats' training school in his own Mercedes limousine.[18] This sort of behaviour had been a recurrent feature of the top levels of Soviet life since the almost legendary drinking bouts and lavish parties of Stalin's son, Vassily. After Stalin's death, Vassily's drunken driving and cavalier attitude to public funds secured him an eight-year prison sentence.[19] But in the Brezhnev era, the kind of controls on the gilded young that had put Vassily in prison were no longer enforced – at least until Yuri Andropov began to use anti-corruption as a weapon to chip away at the power base of Leonid Brezhnev and his entrenched allies. The lavish dacha and lifestyle of the son of Politburo member Viktor Grishin had aroused no more than gossip – until Grishin made his tentative foray to stop the Gorbachev succession after Chernenko died. The KGB chief Viktor Chebrikov said pointedly in a Politburo meeting that a man who could not control his own son was hardly fit to control the destinies of the Soviet state.[20]

The striking feature of the privileged children of the Soviet leadership, however, is their reluctance to follow in their parents' footsteps and seek to climb the ranks of party power. Even those who go into public life, or into the party hierarchy of the *Nomen-klatura*, do not choose the kind of career pattern which leads to the central committee or the Politburo. The jobs they choose are those which allow them to continue to live in comfort, with access to Western luxuries and, if possible, a life abroad. Brezhnev's son Yuri went into the desirable ministry of foreign trade, as did Kosygin's son-in-law, Dzhermen Gvishiani. Andropov's son joined the foreign ministry, as did Gromyko's son Anatoly, who served at both the London and Washington embassies before returning to Moscow to run the Africa Institute, a foreign affairs research base and think-tank. Mikoyan's son Sergo became editor of *Latin America*, a job which was in the central committee's own *Nomenklatura*, and guaranteed regular trips abroad; his son joined the foreign ministry and was assigned to the Washington embassy.[21] The requirements for such posts are a facility in the English language and a diploma from MGIMO, the Moscow State Institute for International Affairs, Moscow's equivalent of a specialised foreign affairs school at Oxford or Harvard. The career pattern of an ambitious young political apparatchik would be rather different. He would choose to start at the Bauman Physics Institute in Moscow, or perhaps the Paton Institute of Welding in Kiev, and combine assiduous work in the ranks of the Komsomol and the party with acquiring top engineering qualifications. He would then pursue the technocratic route to the top, proving his political reliability by party work and perhaps by an application to study at the Higher Party School in Moscow. Or he would follow in the steps of Mikhail Gorbachev, and take a law degree at Moscow State University, ensure that he became a member of the Komsomol committee, and work to get a job in the party hierarchy of his home region.

That so few sons of the recent and current party leadership are following these well-established trails is revealing. A political career remains full of risks and, except to those committed to the pursuit of power, not a particularly attractive life – not, at least, to be compared with the life of a diplomat or foreign trade official or star journalist with a licence to travel, to buy foreign clothes and luxuries, and even to live abroad. So, in spite of the privileges which are available to the leadership, and the advantages they can pass on to their children, there is little sign that the Soviet system is producing a hereditary political elite. The senior ranks of the party are constantly replenished by new blood, and much of that new blood has no family influence which would allow them to pull strings. A party career remains open to the talents.

At the same time, the fact that the children of the elite are making their careers elsewhere, in journalism and diplomacy, academic think-tanks and the vast culture industry, has contributed to the creation of a much wider and more resilient upper class than would otherwise have been the case. The children of power can continue to enjoy privileged and pleasant lifestyles without risking the vicissitudes of the political arena; and the bright young apparatchiks from outside the magic circle can still make their way to the top. This, it should be noted, is in keeping with the traditional way in which class systems have developed in Russia. Peter the Great established his post-feudal society on similar lines, allowing the traditional aristocracy to keep their lands and privileges while opening the ranks of the nobility to the bright civil servants who actually ran the state.

It is a model that can promote great social stability, as the bright spirits from the mass of the population are attracted into careers that match their talents, or at least their ambitions, and the children of the privileged do not fear dispossession. Such a system maintained British stability for centuries, and it gave Tsarist Russia the resilience to withstand enormous economic and political strains before finally buckling under the military defeats of the First World War. Much more flawed than the social structure which has been emerging in the Soviet Union during the past forty years of peace, the Tsarist regime meant that the hereditary aristocracy and landowning classes did not need to work at all; indeed, the very boredom and social uselessness it generated, so perfectly chronicled in the plays of Chekhov, made the system less and less worthy of their allegiance. In the Soviet Union, the children of power have, with the exception of the occasional Galina Brezhnev, real jobs and responsibilities. Even Galina was nominally a journalist for the Novosti press agency.

Both of these social groups – the rising apparatchiks and the children of the apparatchiks in power – have entrées to the key privileges of Soviet life. They can get their children into the better schools, where English or other languages are taught throughout the curriculum. They have access to the better hospitals, and to the special pharmacies where there are no shortages of Soviet drugs and where even Western pharmaceutical products are available. They can obtain Western or Hungarian contraceptives. The best restaurants in Moscow are not at the big public hotels, but in the headquarters of the writers' union, the film-makers' club and the journalists' union, and in the central committee building. The writers' union dining hall occupies the marvellous panelled hall that Tolstoy chose as the setting for the masonic rituals in *War and Peace*. The union of journalists have taken over a grand eighteenth-century palace near the old Arbat. The think-tanks and research centres, such as Georgy Arbatov's celebrated Institute for the Study of the US and Canada, or Anatoly Gromyko's Africa Institute, are pleasantly located in grand prerevolutionary mansions of the diplomatic quarter of old Moscow.[22]

But, although they share privilege, these two groups live in a state of potential tension, if only because of their entirely different approaches to the cultural world of the Soviet intelligentsia. For the hard-line party official, culture is a force to be drilled into the service of the Soviet state. For the children of the elite, it is something to be enjoyed, in which to participate, and something which by definition must spill over the boundaries the politicians would set for it. This contradiction lay at the roots of the cultural rows of the 1960s, just as those cultural debates laid the basis for the dissident movements of the 1970s.

In spite of the KGB's earlier success in containing the dissident movements, the debate has now re-opened. The appearance of Yevtushenko's *Fuku* in *Novy Mir* was one sign; another was his speech to the Russian federation writers' union in December 1985, which took as its basis a series of statements by Mikhail Gorbachev on the need for *glasnost*, or openness.[23] 'But articles that call rhetorically for openness are not the same thing as openness itself,' Yevtushenko said to loud applause, in words which were drastically sanitised before extracts of the speech were published in *Literaturnaya Gazeta*, the weekly organ of the writers' union. He talked of the need to tell the truth about Soviet history, to print in full the suppressed or bowdlerised classics of the past, of the failures of the Soviet economy to do away with queues, and of privileges. 'It is morally impermissible that there should be any kind of restricted distribution of food and consumer goods, including the existence of special identity cards which bestow upon the holder the right to make purchases in the special shops in this hall, cards which every congress delegate – me included – keeps in his pocket,' he went on. Then he talked of the rationing system in force in many Soviet towns for meat and butter. The contrast, he argued, was ethically unjustifiable.[24]

This was a new angle of attack with potentially far-reaching consequences. For years in the Soviet Union, it has simply not been done to raise the question of the privileges of the elite. The kind of privileges that Yevtushenko mentioned – the special shops in the hall of the writers' congress where imported Western clothing, books, rare foods and wines were available – represented part, and only a part, of the unwritten deal that the party leadership had with its intelligentsia. The deal allowed the cultural stars and the intellectuals to share some of their leaders' privileges. Not only did the writers' union offer one of the best clubs and restaurants in the city, not only were special food shops available, but Soviet writers and artists and composers were the beneficiaries of a royalty system which allowed them, quite legally, to become some of the richest people in the country. If they sold books or music abroad, they had access to foreign currency stores. And even if they were not making the huge sums that came with a Soviet bestseller, they could still obtain dachas in the writers' union colony of Peredelkino. The quid pro quo was that the intellectuals gave broad support to the party.

Yevtushenko's speech publicly called this deal into question. Matters might have stopped there but for the fact that the question of party privileges was then publicly raised in the august columns of *Pravda*. In a long article which reviewed the tens of thousands of letters from readers about the forthcoming party congress, the party's own official newspaper singled out a letter from one comrade N. Nikolaev from Kazan, a party member since 1940:[25]

> We can no longer close our eyes to the fact that party, soviet, trade union, management and even Komsomol officials sometimes deepen existing social inequalities through their use of special canteens, special shops, and special hospitals. . .
> Let the bosses go and stand in queues with everybody else at the ordinary shops. And then perhaps at last we'll see the end of those queues which depress us all so much.

Nothing like this had been seen in the Soviet press before. Indeed, there were people serving prison sentences for having written in samizdat what was now being published in *Pravda* with official support. It proved a controversial experience for the newspaper's editor, Viktor Afanyasev, who was to be reprimanded by Gorbachev's deputy, Yegor Ligachev, later in the month.[26] Afanyasev insisted that the reprimand was not for raising the question of privileges, but for another letter in the same article which had warned the party leadership that 'between the central committee and the working class there lies a thick, viscous and inert layer of bureaucracy, people who call themselves communists but who should have handed in their party cards long ago.'[27]

Even at the twenty-seventh party congress, the issue was not resolved. Politburo member Geidar Aliev gave an unprecedented press conference to field questions about his salary, his lifestyle and the privileges of the party elite. His salary was similar to that of a manager of a large industrial enterprise, he said, his lifestyle pleasant but not luxurious. There were no privileges for top party officials – or, if there were, they were no different from the special holiday homes and sanatoria that trade unions provided to their workers, and anyway they were justified by the fact that party officials worked up to eighteen hours a day. The whole question of privileges was still being discussed, Aliev went on. It was a muddled and unconvincing performance, confirming little save the relevance and controversy of the debate that Yevtushenko and comrade Nikolaev had launched.[28]

But the very fact that the debate had been opened, and that the nature of the unwritten deal between party and intelligentsia had been explored, symbolised the way in which old rules were changing. In the week of the writers' congress at which Yevtushenko delivered his speech, the Moscow Arts theatre was performing *Silver Wedding*, a play about the private lives of party officials, and their cautious, self-serving loyalties, their betrayals, and their privileges. Yefremov, the theatre director, was a personal friend of Gorbachev, who had telephoned him from the Kremlin shortly after taking power to promise, 'As soon as I have sorted out this mess here, we have to do something to help culture.'[29] At the same time, another play was running, called *Dictatorship of Conscience*, which referred openly to the corruption and criminal activities of the former Politburo member and party chieftain of Uzbekistan, Sharaf Rashidov, and his love of luxuries that could have put a Tsar to shame.

A month after the twenty-seventh congress ended, there was a conference of Russian composers in Moscow at which the party came in for a new kind of attack at the hands of the musical elite. Playing the same serious gadfly role that Yevtushenko had assumed at the writers' congress, the composer Rodion Schedrin began by attacking 'the artistic eyewash and anachronism of the galas and ceremonial concerts by which we mark important social events'. The problem, he went on, was that thoroughly incompetent people were in charge of artistic affairs. The Bolshoi was in trouble because its artistic decisions about how many singers to use and how big an orchestra to deploy were being taken by accountants and administrators who knew nothing about music: 'The situation is explained by the fact that there are practically no competent professionals in the ministry of culture.' He proceeded to attack the deputy minister Ivanov by name, as a man who 'does not respond to musicians' appeals, does not support their initiatives, but now and then issues contradictory decrees – he ought to be replaced by a competent musician'.[30]

Spring 1986 saw some dramatic extensions of this sense of cultural independence by the intellectuals themselves. In May, the union of film-makers brought off a procedural coup in their elections, voting out the old generation of party hacks and tamed cinematographers. They elected as new first secretary Elem Klimov, whose own films had in the past fallen victims to the censors. His film of the last years of Tsarism, *Agonia*, with its sympathetic portrait of Tsar Nicholas, had languished on the shelf for years before being released, to win prizes at European festivals. Klimov's first act was to set up a new commission to review all cases of Soviet films banned in the past twenty years. And, strikingly, Klimov had been nominated for the post by the new head of cultural affairs in the central committee, Alexander Yakovlev, a man very close to Gorbachev.[31]

In June, the writers' union held their own conference, and elected as their first secretary a veteran of Stalin's Gulag, the respected editor of *Novy Mir*, Vladimir Karpov. They also elected to their ruling praesidium a whole range of unorthodox writers who had not even been approved to attend the congress as delegates by the old regime of the writers' union, including Bella Akhmadulina and Bulent Okudzhava. It was a heady week for Soviet writers, when the delegates were told that the reign of Glavlit, the state censorship board with its 10,000 bureaucrats, was to be brought to an end. Censorship henceforth was to be limited to state and military secrets, to pornography, racism and 'war propaganda'. The first fruit of the new system, Yevtushenko said immediately after the congress, would be a new commission to honour the life and work of Boris Pasternak, and to publish all his works, including the long-banned novel *Doctor Zhivago*.[32]

Mikhail Gorbachev came to power with the reputation of being the first intellectual to run the Kremlin since Lenin. He was an educated man, a concert- and theatre-goer, with a wife who still taught at university and was known for her passion for literature. In his first year of office, the intellectuals had staked out important new ground. At the writers' union, Yevtushenko had asserted the author's right to raise topical and controversial questions. At the composers' congress, Schedrin had claimed the right of the musicians to run their own affairs, without the incompetent interference of party officials. In the theatres, the playwrights and directors were seizing the right to put party life on stage. This amounted to a different kind of challenge from that presented by the intelligentsia during the Khrushchev thaws, and it was a challenge rooted in the self-confidence of the cultural elite – which, in turn, stemmed from the social changes that had come with the forty years of peace, with mass education, with the growth of the Soviet intellectual audience. Yet, even though Gorbachev was himself almost an archetype of this social change, and of the new cultural constituency that had emerged within the Soviet Union, he was also a product of the party apparat. Herein lay the real measure of the Soviet Union's postwar social revolution. After Stalin's purges, the party's cultural policies had been drawn up by men who were neither intellectual nor culturally aware. Men like Zhdanov not only felt no hesitation in asserting party control over creative artists and writers, they never even felt there could or should be a choice. When Khrushchev reacted angrily to an abstract art exhibition at the Manege, asking if all the artists were homosexuals and telling them that donkeys could paint better with their tails, he was the living exemplar of the kind of party leadership that Stalin had left, a half-educated peasant bewildered by a confrontation with something he could not understand.[33] But the party now has leaders with intellectual pretensions of their own, who know that there is not only a cultural and political but also a moral choice involved in the way they respond to the new challenge the intelligentsia is presenting.

Between them, the revolution, the civil war and Stalin did a ruthlessly effective job of wiping out the old Russian ruling class and its intellectual elite. But now, in a new and Soviet form, they are back, and they are increasingly speaking the same language.

13

The Return of History

Joseph Stalin was born in the Georgian town of Gori, which stands in the shadow of an old hill fortress which guarded the fertile valley for centuries against the repeated invasion of Turk, Tartar and Persian. Gori contains the Soviet Union's only museum to the old dictator which still survives after the de-Stalinisation campaigns of 1956–64. A giant statue to the man soars above the party headquarters in the main square, overshadowing the long paved avenue which leads to the modest house where he was born, the son of a cobbler. The cottage is now enclosed and protected by a large marble building which bears a disconcerting resemblance to a Greek temple. Behind that is the Stalin museum, all colonnades, gardens and curlicued rooflines. It needs only a proper belltower to be the image of the old Spanish Catholic missions in California.

Once inside the museum, the visitor is confronted by a sweeping marble staircase, dominated on the half-landing by a large white statue. Past this classical Stalin, and on up the staircase and into the galleries: Stalin the schoolboy poet, Stalin the young revolutionary with his code-name Koba, Stalin in Siberian exile, Stalin's escapes from the relaxed Tsarist gaols, Stalin as Lenin's right-hand man. The famous photograph of Lenin speaking at the Finland Station is prominently displayed, with Trotsky airbrushed out from his place at the side of the wooden podium. There is a room full of the bizarre presents sent to Stalin on his seventieth birthday, his portrait in sand, wood, porcelain and mosaic; and there is a room devoted to his time as war leader. His purges, his crimes, his suspicions and persecutions have no place in this museum.

There are some low stairs into the last hall of all. It is dark, the walls lined in black velvet, and at first the only light seems to be that which picks out a portrait in oils of the man on his deathbed. Walk forward a little further and to the right appears a large pit, carpeted from floor to ceiling in dark purple. In the centre of this shrine stands a white pedestal, topped by the death mask, which gleams a brilliant gold. The entire pit is fenced off by a row of thin white pillars, and those in the centre are broken off to allow the visitor to peer in. The effect is solemn and uncanny, like a broken cage from which the beast has escaped.

For the brief year that Konstantin Chernenko was in power, the beast was very nearly free. The war veterans of Volgograd had petitioned for their city to revert to its heroic wartime name of Stalingrad.[1] The dictator's old henchman Molotov, still alive and working on his memoirs in Moscow, was re-admitted into the ranks of the Communist Party. Stalin's daughter Svetlana was welcomed back from her seventeen years of exile in the West. Marshal Zhukov's war memoirs had been reissued, in time for the massive celebrations of the fortieth anniversary of victory in the world war, with the passages critical of Stalin tastefully edited. In the films, newsreels and television programmes about the war, the dictator's face was prominent. The stage was being set for his rehabilitation.

And why not? Stalin was a great historical figure, the man who shaped the modern Soviet state, who wrenched the peasantry from their smallholdings and dragooned them into vast collective farms. He pushed them into the cities to man the new factories that his crash programme of industrialisation had built. He educated their children, and built a system strong and resilient enough to withstand the assault of Hitler's *Wehrmacht*. He expanded the frontiers of Russian empire beyond the wildest dreams of the greediest Tsars. His achievement was colossal.

But so was the price that his people paid. The famines that attended the collectivisation of the peasantry killed 7 million, probably more. In the six years of the purges after 1935, 18,840,000 people were arrested. Of these, 7 million were shot in prison. The rest were sent to the camps, where an unknown number died. Stalin's purge of the Red Army, his decimation of the trained officer corps and his lack of preparedness for Hitler's invasion made the awesome price of victory all the heavier. The Soviet Union lost 20 million in the war, and there is no way of knowing how many fell to German bullets, and how many to Russian. Penal battalions were sent to clear minefields by marching through them. Prisoners of war who had been captured largely because of Stalin's incompetence in the first years of the war were liberated from the German camps and sent back to be incarcerated once again in Stalin's camps. In the last years of his life, there were more purges.[2]

The victims of Stalin far outnumber those of Hitler. But the loss cannot be counted in statistics alone. Stalin's victims were not only an unimaginably huge mass of individual people; they were whole classes. The hardest-working and most self-reliant of the peasantry were a threat, so they were exterminated. The old Bolsheviks who had helped bring about the revolution were a potential alternative government; they were liquidated. The officer corps could mount an effective challenge; they were wiped out. The old cultural elite, the thinking and the writing and the dreaming classes, were sifted, arrested, terrorised and killed. The idealists – those who had gone to Spain to fight against fascism, and had come into dangerous contact with an international left that was not yet fully drilled in Stalin's ways – were shot on their return.[3] The soldiers taken prisoner, who might have been infected by their constrained sight of a world beyond the Soviet borders, were imprisoned and worked and starved to death.[4] An entire generation of the cleverest, the bravest, the most creative, the most able and even the most devoted was swept and scrubbed away.

Almost as chilling as the exterminations was the silence. The only sound was the clamour of lies told at the staged trials of the most dangerous men of all, those who had helped Lenin make the revolution and who remained loyal enough to its ideals to make false confessions in the name of protecting the revolution. The killings went unheard. The arrested were removed in prison vans painted to resemble bread-delivery trucks. The trains that carried them off to the camps and the mines were sealed. Victims simply disappeared, their names erased from the books, and their faces from photographs. Future historians were condemned to live the same lie, as the documents were shredded and rewritten. History itself had to be drilled into the service of Stalin.

The truth came out, all the same. And it was Russians who extracted it. Khrushchev began the process, with his secret speech to the twentieth party congress in 1956. In 1961, at the twenty-second congress, he revealed yet more of the price Stalin had made the country pay for his achievements, and Stalin's embalmed corpse was removed from its place of honour beside Lenin in the

Red Square mausoleum. Statues were removed from around the country, save in Georgia, where Stalin's fellow-countrymen drew up rotas to stand guard each night over the memorials to their country's most famous son. A curious loyalty: Stalin's purges were particularly hard on his fellow-countrymen.

Russian historians, brave and honest and driven men like Roy Medvedev, Anton Antonov-Ovseyenko and Alexander Solzhenitsyn, gathered what documents were still available, interviewed those who knew and who could speak, collected letters, memoirs and evidence from around the country.[5] Their work had to be published abroad – with the tragic result that the rest of the world today knows far more about Stalinism than the people who suffered it. In the two decades that followed Khrushchev's fall, when Brezhnev tried to screw back the lid of the Pandora's box that his predecessor had opened, Stalin slowly became once again a kind of folk hero. He was the *vozhd*, the boss, the man who kept the streets swept clean in winter and made people work hard. He was the war leader who drove the Germans back to Berlin. His portrait began to reappear on the windscreens of trucks and buses, a working-class hero. In the Georgian capital of Tblisi, underground studios had continued to print photograph calendars of the year graced with portrait after portrait of the old dictator; they are hung prominently in the basement wine bars, as well as in private homes, and in the 1970s and 1980s they began to appear more and more widely in the rest of Russia.

This was an inevitable, and not necessarily dismaying, reaction to the conspiracy of silence that had built up around the whole question of Stalin. There were spasmodic attempts in the 1960s to rehabilitate him, to restore him to his former place of honour in the Soviet canon. The most serious official attempt came at the twenty-third party congress, in 1966. It was the time when Solzhenitsyn's manuscripts had been confiscated, Daniel and Sinyavsky arrested, and the KGB chief Semichastny was urging the need to arrest 'a thousand intellectuals' in Moscow. The intellectuals felt that they had enough support to fight back. A prominent journalist, Ernst Henry, collected over a hundred signatures of leading scientists such as Pyotr Kapitsa and Andrei Sakharov, Bolshoi stars such as Maya Plisetskaya, and retired ambassadors such as Ivan Maisky, and sent a letter to the central committee urging no rehabilitation of Stalin. The signatories were assured that they had powerful friends and backers, conspicuous among them Yuri Andropov, a full secretary of the central committee and the man who was to become the head of the KGB the following year.[6]

There was, in effect, a stalemate. There would be no more public examination of Stalin's crimes, but nor would he, or by implication his methods, be restored to acceptability. The consequent silence itself helped to foster the groundswell of nostalgia for the old brute. This was probably the lesser of two evils. It would have been worse to rehabilitate Stalin, but what happened was almost as bad: the Soviet people continued to be denied access to their own history. There was, and remains to this day, a hole where the nation's memory ought to be.

With the Khrushchev succession the hole grew wider. Khrushchev's greatest achievement was to begin the essential process of freeing the country from the grip of Stalinism, to admit the crimes and the mistakes and allow people to think and talk with increasing openness about the times through which they had lived and suffered. His boldness in challenging the party's position, in telling the truth about the price that had been paid for victory in war and industrial progress, will doubtless be recognised by future generations of Soviet historians. It was, perhaps, the first time since Lenin's day that the Soviet public had been treated like adults who deserved to know their own history. But precisely because this was the central achievement of the Khrushchev years, far more than the Sputniks and cosmonauts, the chaotic agrarian reforms and administrative upheavals, to talk about Khrushchev was to talk about Stalin. The silence grew to swallow him too.

In April 1986, the Soviet Union celebrated the twenty-fifth anniversary of Yuri Gagarin's flight into space. In honour of the occasion, some Western journalists were allowed into the usually closed area north-west of Moscow which secretes the space mission control centre, and Zvyezdi Gorodok (Star City), the base and training and residential centre for Soviet cosmonauts. In the museum there, among the old space capsules and displays of space food and documents, is a large photograph of Yuri Gagarin in the Red Square parade after his return to earth. He is saluting. But the man he is saluting, Nikita Khrushchev, has been cropped from the picture.[7]

Khrushchev is remembered, however. On the twentieth anniversary of his fall, I visited the cemetery where he lies buried, within the walls of the old Novodevichy convent, on the Moscow riverbank. There is no Red Square tomb for Khrushchev. But the Novodevichy is a far lovelier place to lie, in the shadow of the golden domes and spires that have seen so much of Russia's history since the building was first constructed as one of the great fortress-monasteries to guard the city in the days when the Mongols were still feared. Boris Godunov was proclaimed Tsar within the convent walls. Peter the Great incarcerated his sister here and hanged her supporters from a gibbet outside the window of her cell. Gogol is buried in its grounds, along with Mikhail Bulgakov, Chekhov, Mayakovsky and Scriabin. Nikita Khrushchev is in fine company. His grave on plot 20/19 was covered in flowers. Old men who owed their freedom to his decision to open Stalin's camps came to lay their tributes, bow their heads in silence, and then walk solemnly away. The headstone is striking. A bronze head of the man, resembling a gleaming round cannonball, is supported by two interlocking and jagged pillars, one black, the other white. It was designed by the sculptor Ernst Neizvestny, whose unorthodox and abstract work Khrushchev had denounced as 'dogshit' during the famous row at the Manege exhibition hall in 1961. When Khrushchev died, his son Sergei and Mikoyan's son went to the sculptor's studio. Neizvestny was already suffering the political attacks that were to lead to his exile. They asked him to design the gravestone and then explained that Khrushchev had written the request into his will. The old man never lost his capacity to surprise.[8]

With all its historical associations, the convent is a fitting burial ground for the leader who did so much to restore to the Russian people an awareness of their history. All nations need such an awareness. Even Stalin had known its power. In the desperate autumn days of 1941, when the German tanks were racing towards Moscow and Stalin had been neither seen nor heard from since the invasion began, he suddenly gave a radio broadcast, to rally the people to the defence of the homeland. Not to the cradle of socialism, but to the *rodina*, the motherland. He did not greet them as *tovarishi*, comrades, but in the old religious phrase, brothers and sisters. In the crucible of war, he reached an accommodation with the Orthodox church, in whose seminaries he had been trained as a boy, and won its support in the defence of what could be called once more 'Holy Mother Russia'.

Perhaps the most famous Russian poem of the war was written during the terrible retreat of the first autumn, by a young soldier called Konstantin Simonov. Most Russians to this day know the first lines by heart:[9]

> Do you remember, Alyosha
> The Smolensk roads
> Where the dank rains fell unending.

It was a poem not only of war and defiance but of discovery. Simonov was a city boy and, like so many who had grown up in the 1930s, he saw the future in terms of the Stalinist vision of endless factories and cities, wide roads and a countryside of collective farms so big that the places where the farmers lived had become small industrialised cities in their own right. What he discovered in the battles around Smolensk was that Russia was, at heart, a land made up of all the villages he had passed through and fought in. The poem goes on:[10]

> In the end, I think you know that our motherland
> Is not the city of my carefree boyhood.
> It is the villages where our ancestors lived before us
> With plain wood crosses on their Russian graves.

The war began the process of preserving the national memory, and, in what has developed into perhaps the dominant literary movement of the last twenty years, the writers then set this great Russian nostalgic hunger into print. Vassily Belov has become the unofficial historian of the old Russian village and its peasants' instinctive sense of community and closeness to the hallowed earth.[11] One of Russia's bestselling authors is Vassily Shukshin, whose *Kralina Krasnaya* (*Red Berry*) is about a Russian village lad who gets caught up in a gang of city criminals, goes to jail, and comes out resolved to start anew, with the help of a simple peasant girl. But the grip of the city is too strong, and the gang sucks him back in. The story ends with the boy's death:[12]

> There he lay, a Russian peasant on his native steppe . . . his home not far away . . . he lay with his cheek flat against the earth, as though listening for sounds that only he could hear.

Valentin Rasputin, one of the finest of contemporary Russian novelists, has written in *Farewell to Matyora* of the destruction of an old village, an old peasant community, in the inexorably rising waters of the dam that will power the turbines of the Bratsk hydroelectric plant.[13] Rasputin has gone further, becoming a key figure in the public campaign to preserve the hearts of the old Siberian towns, the wooden buildings and narrow streets of old Irkutsk and Tomsk. His part in the mass protests against the pollution of Siberia's Lake Baikal is again rooted in the sense of fidelity to the old Russian earth, to the need to preserve the purity of its history and traditions and of the soil itself.

In many ways, as Stalin knew, the history of Russia is the history of the Orthodox church. It was the church's monasteries which preserved the nation's culture during the Mongol invasions, and when the Tsars proved too weak and the nobility too venal to protect the land, the great monasteries with the high walls and well-stocked granaries were the fortresses and bastions of resistance. The church is very nearly as old as the Russian nation, which began to take shape around the river trade routes which spawned the rich city of Kiev. In the year 988 AD, Vladimir I, Grand Prince of Kiev, had all his subjects forcibly baptised into Christianity in the waters of the River Dnieper, and the old pagan idols toppled. Vladimir himself had been baptised for his marriage to the sister of the Byzantine emperor, and the Byzantium connection brought the Eastern Orthodox rite to Russia. Byzantium claimed to be the second Rome, and Tsarist Russian historians have claimed that, after the fall of Byzantium to the expanding Islamic empire in 1485, this marriage entitled Russia to be seen as the third Rome, the heir to the Christian tradition of the Holy City and centre of Christendom.

The year 1988 will see the millennial anniversary of this mass baptism, the establishment of Christianity in Russia. In preparation for what is planned as a vast international celebration, the Soviet state has granted a series of important concessions to the Orthodox church. A working and worshipping monastery is to be set up in Moscow for the first time since the 1920s. The Danilovsky monastery dates back to medieval times, but since the revolution it has been in turn a base for the Iskra electrical factory and a home for juvenile delinquents. But in 1985, at a moving religious ceremony which had all the building workers crossing themselves and joining in the hymns they still knew by heart, the foundations of the new monastery building were blessed by the Metropolitan Alexei of Tallin. For the first time since the days of Peter the Great, Moscow is to become the base of the Orthodox church. The Danilovsky monastery will be the official residence of the patriarch, who has hitherto been based in the vast monas-

tery of Zagorsk, about a hundred miles from Moscow. The Holy
Synod, founded by Peter the Great as the church's ruling body,
and based by him in St Petersburg, will also move to the monastery, along with the church's administrative headquarters. A hotel
is being built in the grounds for the church's foreign guests, along
with conference halls, restaurants and libraries, while the old
churches and walls of the monastery are being restored to their
former grandeur. The money for this building and restoration was
raised by the church itself. The state's contribution was simply
the granting of permission and the provision of the land.[14]

For a socialist state, with an ideology committed to atheism,
and concerned about the revival of religious interest among the
young, the granting of that permission was an important
concession. It points to the political benefit that the state believes
will come from having a religious showcase in the centre of
Moscow – and one, moreover, that will be the temporary home
of the world's religious leaders when they attend the anniversary
celebrations in 1988. It points also to the success of the Orthodox
church leaders in reaching an accommodation with the state. The
fact that the church has survived seventy years of communism is
an achievement. That the church now prospers is remarkable. The
question is to what extent the church has compromised itself, its
teaching and its flock in the process of reaching that
accommodation.

At the outbreak of the Second World War there were only four
Orthodox bishops still free in the country. There was no patriarch,
for no church council had been permitted that might elect one.
Until the Stalin constitution of 1936, the clergy were not even
permitted ration cards, while still being subject to ruinous
taxation. Their physical survival depended on the generosity of
their impoverished congregations. The monasteries had been effectively closed, churches were being demolished, and tens of thousands of the clergy were arrested and sent to the camps. On the
day after the German invasion, the Metropolitan Sergei, who was
acting as the unofficial head of the church, made a dramatic
appeal for the defence of the homeland; he is said to have acted
spontaneously. This religious patriotism worked. A church council
was permitted; Sergei was elected patriarch in 1943; and a theological college was opened in Moscow the following year. Sergei
died soon afterwards, but another council was convened to elect

a new patriarch. Even after the liberation of the Ukraine and Belorussia, the monasteries which the Germans had re-founded, or encouraged, were allowed to remain open.[15]

The church's patriotic support had been useful in wartime. But after 1945 the church had to find another means of ingratiating itself with the state. A complete support for Soviet foreign policy proved to be the basis of the concordat which has lasted, although at times barely, until the present day. In 1949 the Orthodox church joined the World Peace Council, in 1958 the Christian Peace Conference, and in 1961 the World Council of Churches, and has worked tirelessly in these bodies to support what it terms the Soviet Union's 'peace policy'.

After Stalin's death, the Soviet state under Khrushchev did not keep its side of the unwritten bargain. Khrushchev's years saw the closure of almost two thirds of the Orthodox churches, seven out of ten theological schools, and the vast majority of the monasteries. Churches were bulldozed aside irrespective of their architecture or antiquity, and the campaign grew so intense that it backfired, provoking a wave of indignation among architects, historians and those intellectuals who claimed that the nation's cultural heritage was being destroyed. Their concern was reinforced by the Russian nationalists, many of them in powerful positions, including members of the central committee. They saw no contradiction between being successful communists and passionate Slavophiles, and they saw church buildings as the embodiment of the nation's traditions.

In the Brezhnev period, the church began to recover; by 1985, it had even secured something very close to property rights over the lands on which the churches stood. All land in the Soviet Union is owned by the state, but the new leases the state was prepared to grant gave the church very powerful titles to property, and full control over church documents, archives, valuables and relics. It was also given the right to open more churches in rural areas; in the mid-1980s, in addition to the new Danilovsky monastery in Moscow, there were eighteen other monasteries and nunneries in the country, eighteen theological schools, and a total of some twenty thousand functioning churches.[16]

In return, the Orthodox church redoubled its support for Soviet foreign policy, publishing a long and formal statement from the Holy Synod, which stressed 'our believers' full acceptance and support of the peace policy of our motherland, which is seeking a lasting and just peace for all nations'. This was a reiteration of the traditional foreign policy support. But now the church added that the Soviet system:[17]

> creates real conditions for Christians and other religious and non-religious people to cooperate for the good of their society. We are deeply satisfied that our believers have successfully combined their religious life with their public and human responsibility.

The Holy Synod statement then went further still to give the Soviet system what sounded like a full-scale endorsement: 'Man is the focus of all the concerns in our society,' it began, in an almost verbatim quote from Gorbachev's address to the party congress:[18]

> It is the respect for the dignity of man regardless of his social status, education, sex, religion, nationality or race that determines the internal unity of socialist society, in which there are no antagonistic sections of the population.

Yet, in spite of this religious ratification of the Soviet state's self-image, the state exercises considerable ingenuity in keeping the church short of recruits. The big festival of the Orthodox religious year is Easter, and the church services at the midnight leading into Easter Sunday are always the most crowded. Worshippers and the simply curious alike cram into and around the churches, and the sense of joy that runs through them as they cry 'Christ is risen' is electrifying. The ceremony is a passionate affirmation of the continued power and health of religion. The state, accordingly, has taken countermeasures, particularly directed at the young. On Easter Saturday 1985, Soviet television screened a long rock–pop spectacular featuring the country's leading superstar, Alla Pugacheva, complete with the kind of dancing, light shows and international showbiz gloss that had been ideological anathema not long before. For Easter Saturday 1986, the state authorised the biggest live rock concert of Russian bands that young Soviet people had ever seen. In each case the object was transparent: to seduce the young away from the Easter services. It is impossible to say, however, to what extent the growing interest of young Russians in the church springs from curiosity, from a more national interest in the history and cultural tradition the churches represent as buildings and as symbols, or from a genuine religious revival.

The revivalist movement has been marked not only among the Russians with their Orthodox traditions but among the Muslims of Soviet Central Asia. There are no reliable Soviet statistics for the number of Muslims in the country, but the census figures list over 35 million people with the mother tongue of a traditionally Muslim group. The same broad state policy is applied to their faith: toleration, in return for loyalty to the state and support in the Soviet 'peace policy'. Mosques are kept open, and restored with state help, and Muslim leaders are encouraged to go on the Haj pilgrimage to Mecca and to maintain contact with their fellow-Muslims in the Arab world. This has provided a useful lever of support to Soviet Middle Eastern policy, which backs the Arab cause against Israeli 'Zionism', and in 1985 Soviet Muslims helped pave the way for the opening of diplomatic relations with the traditionally pro-Western Arab states of Oman and the United Arab Emirates. But there is an unofficial Islam flourishing outside state control, with underground preachers and Koran schools which are occasionally mentioned and condemned in the Soviet press. Their presence has become the more alarming with Soviet troops fighting the Muslim resistance in Afghanistan and the Iran–Iraq war raging just south of the Soviet borders. Teheran radio constantly beams Islamic propaganda to the Soviet Muslims and, just as Russian youngsters have a lively black market in Western pop music on home-made tape cassettes, so young Muslims in Baku and Samarkand can obtain Arab music and, more dangerously, sermons on tape.

In Baku itself, capital of the Azerbaijan republic on the Iranian border, the last three years have seen party conferences on the need to intensify atheist education, and the opening of new ideology centres aimed at spreading anti-religious propaganda. The local KGB chief General Zia Yusuf Zade has publicly denounced the effect of 'the sectarian underground and reactionary clergy on certain representatives of the intelligentsia and young people'.[19] The Baku newspaper *Kommunist* boasted in 1985 of the 3761 atheist propaganda groups now at work in Azerbaijan, of the 6911 propaganda collectives and the 32,250 instructors specially trained in anti-religious propaganda – all of which seems somewhat excessive for a population of barely 7 million.[20]

Just outside Baku, the old oil capital of the Soviet Union, in a wasteland peppered with rusted derricks that still leaks fire from the oil-sodden grounds, there is a carefully restored temple of the fire worshippers, the Indian Zoroastrians who saw the oil fires burning magically from the earth and came to worship. The temple symbolises the way the Soviet state would like religion to be: safely dead, a tourist attraction and a museum, rather than a shrine.

But the old religions and the national traditions that blend and identify with them simply refuse to die. And, in a curious way, the Soviet state has provided them with a life-support system. The education service conducts its lessons in forty-five languages and, although all children study Russian at school, the minority nations are generally taught in their mother tongues. The policy seems to be to make Russian the common second language for that full half of the Soviet population who are not Russians by nationality. The programme has had mixed results. Every second citizen of Belorussia is fluent in Russian, but only one Uzbek in seven is bilingual.[21]

The state clamps down hard on any political manifestation of nationalism among the minority peoples, and there was a severe anti-nationalist campaign in the Ukraine throughout Andropov's time as head of the KGB, from 1967 through the 1970s. But, in each republic, one television channel broadcasts in the local language, and newspapers and magazines are published in over a hundred different tongues. Four fifths of the 1900 million books published each year are in Russian; only 14 per cent of them are in minority languages – considerably less than their share of the population would warrant. Nonetheless, authors writing in languages spoken by only a few thousand people are published and given state backing and without this support whole language groups of many of the remote Siberian tribes would by now have been lost for ever.[22]

The pattern that emerges in Soviet language and nationality policy is broadly similar to that which has evolved for religion. A faith or a language that remains under state control is protected, and even cautiously encouraged. National traditions which present no political challenge may also flourish. Thus, folk dancing as a people's art form is lavishly financed and subsidised by international tours and conferences. The Lithuanians are encouraged to build potential Disneylands, to restore their old villages and inhabit them, and to transform them into working and living museums of the way peasant life used to be. The

Georgians fill a whole mountainside near Tblisi with examples of every kind of house built by the different tribal groups, from semi-cave to pleasant villa. Meanwhile, however, whole nations such as the Crimean Tartars continue to suffer discrimination. Deported from the Crimea by Stalin for their alleged wartime support of the German invader, the Tartars were later rehabilitated, but they are still forbidden as a people from resettling their old homes and lands. General Grigorenko, a war hero who took up their cause and campaigned for it, was consigned to a psychiatric hospital for his pains.[23]

Soviet policy on nationalities has been a mess almost since the ink was dry on Lenin's Decree of Nationalities. Composed in the headily idealistic days which followed the 1917 revolution, the decree made membership of the Soviet Union virtually voluntary for the minority nations. Then Stalin was appointed commissar for nationalities and he began to interpret that decree with the ruthless singlemindedness he later imposed on the entire country. Indeed, in 1922, Lenin himself condemned the 'Great Russian chauvinism' Stalin had brought to his work in the Caucasus.[24]

Sixty years later, within a month of his succeeding Brezhnev, Yuri Andropov made a historic speech on the anniversary of the six Soviet republics coming together to form the Soviet Union:[25]

> National distinctions will exist for a long time to come, much longer than class distinctions. We must remember that there are good and bad and outdated elements in the cultural heritage, traditions and customs of each nation . . . the natural pride in the gains achieved should not degenerate in ethnic arrogance or conceit. Yet such negative phenomena still occur, and it would be wrong to attribute them solely to the traces of the past. Among other factors, they are sometimes fostered by the mistakes we make in our work.

This was audacious, coming from the man who had run the KGB during the crackdown in the Ukraine, and who had denied the Crimean Tartars their homeland. But it was a significant admission, and he went on to advise 'great tact in selecting and assigning personnel', and to call for a state education policy committed to a multinational ethic. The problem for the teachers and the administrators who drew up the national curricula was that so many of the topics they had to teach were composed of potential political dynamite. Part of the debate centred on how to teach the history of the Soviet Union without exploring exactly what 'the cult of personality' meant for many of the Soviet nations. This anodyne phrase was the catch-all concept used to condemn Stalin's crimes. Its effect, however, was to sanitise them. The classic example of this sanitisation came in February 1986, when Mikhail Gorbachev gave an interview to the French Communist Party newspaper *L'Humanité*. He was asked whether the vestiges of Stalinism had been overcome, and his reply was grimly, depressingly orthodox:[26]

> Stalinism is a concept made up by opponents of communism and used on a large scale to smear the Soviet Union and socialism as a whole. Thirty years have passed since the question of overcoming Stalin's personality cult was raised at the twentieth party congress. To tell the truth, these decisions did not come easily to our party. It was a test of party principle and of loyalty to Leninism. I think that we have withstood that test with honour, and drawn proper conclusions from the past.

This was a profoundly inadequate answer for a Western European Communist Party that was seeing its supporters desert in their droves. Stalinism was not a concept invented by anti-communists. It was a long and murderous nightmare through which whole nations and whole classes of the Soviet people had passed. It was not simply a cult of one man's personality, which makes it sound more like a lapse of taste than a regime of mass murder. It was a crucible in which the country was reshaped, for good and ill, the kind of climacteric by which nations are defined. Just as the French have returned again and again to the events and the meaning of their revolution of 1789 and its subsequent Terror, as the Americans have with painful honesty come to explore their own history of slavery, the British to analyse their own experience of empire, and the Germans to explore the guilts and horrors of Hitler, to expiate and begin to exorcise, so the Soviet Union must at some point unleash its own historians upon the time of Stalin.

The continued refusal of the Soviet state to confront that past, to assess the scale of the purges and to count their cost, has devalued for most foreign observers the very real achievements of Stalin's time. More than that, it has tarnished their cause. Khrushchev complained in his memoirs that he had been dissuaded from publishing proof of Stalin's personal responsibility for the murder of Kirov, which launched the purges, because of the pleas of Togliatti, the Italian communist leader who saw his party membership start to erode after Khrushchev's secret speech of 1956.[27] But the real impact of Stalinism was felt much later, when the Italian Communist Party under Berlinguer reshaped and redefined itself in the 1970s as an openly anti-Stalinist body.

It is a matter not simply of denying Stalin, but of the hole in the national memory that simply will not close, the sense of loss that will not go away. It has resurged in the novels about the old ways of the Russian peasantry, in poems, in theatre and cinemas, and in ordinary Soviet lives around the country. The Soviet Union is too sophisticated, too well educated, and no longer so intimidated as to let the party fence round that deliberate, gaping void in the nation's sense and appreciation of its identity.

The poet Yevtushenko, so often criticised as a party hack, and sneered at as a privileged bard at the Kremlin court, has always held to one great rock of integrity. He despised Stalin's crimes, and has fought the secrecy which tried to conceal them. He has used all his considerable political skills to publish his objections, to find the kind of arguments that might convince the party to investigate and reveal that truth it has so long refused to face. In April 1986, as if in response to Gorbachev's grim interview, he persuaded the editors of *Sovyetskaya Kultura* to open a new section, 'Personal Opinion', and to give him first opportunity to fill it. He returned to the theme of honesty in history that he had raised at the writers' congress:[28]

> Our socialism is in itself a living text book, from which we can tear neither the heroic pages of our victories nor the tragic pages of our losses and our mistakes. If we do, neither we, nor the generations that follow us, will ever be able to use this book, nor to learn from it.
>
> Now that our state has matured and become strong, there are few grounds to fear our frankness, our own critical expressions of our views. Such an openness is a sign of our maturity as a nation, our strength as a people. And the cover-up is a sign of weakness, public silence is a hidden form of anarchy. Nothing can harm us more than endless, obedient votes, when those dutifully raised hands do not follow the call of our hearts. It is simply inertia, the kind of non-vote that will lead to the sabotage, deliberate or not, of the very decisions we just 'voted' for.

It was a brave article that Yevtushenko wrote, and it provoked discussion in Moscow and admiration among the Soviet intelligentsia who knew how to read this sort of coded language. But for anyone unfamiliar with the codes, who did not know that he

221

was talking about Stalin, it read like so many bland truisms. That is the measure of the problem that still confronts the Soviet leadership: how to advance into the future while living a lie about the past; and how to recognise the scale of the problem, when even a favoured poet, a skilled and licensed controversialist, must define it so obliquely.

Between the thirty-year-old Mikhail Gorbachev who voted at the twenty-second party congress in 1961 to take Stalin's corpse from the Lenin mausoleum and the fifty-four-year-old Soviet leader who discounted 'Stalinism' as a Western invention there lay a triumphant career, but in that period there had also grown a dangerous caution. Gorbachev's first year in power was remarkable for the frankness with which he spoke of the problems of the present, and the failures of the immediate, Brezhnev-ruled past. But there were other truths to tell, of Khrushchev's time, and of Stalin's; and without the readiness to tell them, Gorbachev's hopes of a brave new Soviet future will be built on so much spiritual sand.

14

Chernobyl

The disaster at the Chernobyl nuclear power station was not only the first real test of the changes Mikhail Gorbachev is trying to introduce in the Soviet system; it was also a microcosm of the world of difficulties he confronts. Faced with the unexpected, the Soviet system reverted to type and, as if by automatic reflex, reacted with all the worst old instincts of secrecy and defensiveness.

The Gorbachev regime inherited Chernobyl, and the long-standing policy of expansion of nuclear power that made it so potentially dangerous. The geography of Soviet energy supply and demand had been a major factor in the siting of the Chernobyl atomic energy complex. With the raw materials of oil and gas in Siberia's east and north, but the bulk of the factories in the European west, the choice was simple: either to pay the high extra cost of transporting energy to the European factories by pipeline, or to build nuclear power stations on the spot.

Once it had been decided to expand nuclear power, the severity of the Russian winter was taken into account. The winter cold has encouraged Soviet municipalities to use the waste heat from conventional power stations to warm nearby buildings and apartment houses.[1] It is a rational energy-saving policy, at least where conventional stations are concerned. But it led to the alarming decision to site nuclear power stations near the cities. On the outskirts of Leningrad is an RBMK nuclear power station, almost identical to the ones at Chernobyl. There are four more outside the city of Smolensk, and another four near the Lithuanian capital of Vilnius.

The father of Soviet nuclear energy is Professor Nikolai Dollezhal, who designed and built the first experimental 5000-kilowatt reactor in 1954.[2] The basic designs which he developed in the 1950s are still, with modifications for size and new construction materials, the key building blocks for the 58 nuclear stations built in the last twenty years. In 1977, Professor Dollezhal began to campaign, in the discreet way of the Soviet system, against the dangers of nuclear power. He wrote a series of articles in the Soviet scientific press about the problems of transporting and disposing of nuclear waste, and of the need to site power stations in the wilderness of Siberia, rather than near densely populated cities. He and his disciples were able to cite the lesson of the American nuclear accident at Three Mile Island as an awful warning of what could go wrong. But their campaign had little effect.

He was not able to use the example, widely known among Soviet scientists and in the West, of the nuclear disaster that had taken place at Kyshtym, in the southern Urals' hills, in the winter of 1957–8. Barely 100 miles north of the industrial city of Chelyabinsk, Kyshtym was believed by Western intelligence to be one of the main production centres for plutonium for the Soviet military programme. Something, and it is still not clear what, went terribly wrong. In 1976, the exiled Soviet dissident scientist Zhores Medvedev claimed that radioactive waste had exploded after being carelessly stored and allowed to overheat.[3] American scientists at the Los Alamos laboratories agreed that a nuclear wasteland had developed around Kyshtym, but at first suggested the cause was accumulated fall-out from the Novaya Zyemla weapons testing ground in the Arctic, and finally concluded that there had been a series of nuclear leakages, rather than the single, volcano-like eruption that Medvedev had described. But there was agreement on the effects of the disaster. Some thirty small towns in the region simply disappeared from Soviet maps. A river system was diverted through miles of canals to avoid the contaminated valley, and subsequent Soviet exiles who have driven through the area have reported signs instructing motorists to drive as fast as possible for the next twenty miles, and on no account to stop or leave the car. It is now used only as a training ground for Soviet troops being taught the precautions of warfare in a nuclear age, and wearing their protective suits.

Whatever the dangers, the economic planners resolved to increase the Soviet Union's reliance on nuclear energy. Two months before the Chernobyl disaster, Prime Minister Nikolai Ryzhkov told the twenty-seventh party congress of the economic guidelines for the country up to the year 2000, and stressed that in the next five years alone, the output of nuclear power stations would double.[4] By 1991, more than 20 per cent of the country's power would be nuclear-generated. By the year 2000, nuclear energy would provide up to half all electrical power output. The increasing costs of exploiting the ever more remote oil and gas fields of Siberia left the planners little choice. But Chernobyl was to show that the costs of nuclear power cannot be measured simply by commercial calculations.

The crisis began on Friday, 25 April 1986, at reactor No. 4 in the vast nuclear power station complex on the low plain where the Pripjat river joins the main waterway of the Dnieper, which debouches into the great inland lake the locals call the Sea of Kiev. Kiev itself, a city of 3 million people lies less than a hundred miles to the south. The first two reactors on the site had been ordered in 1971, and began commercial operation in 1978. A third reactor was ordered in 1975 and began delivering power to the grid in 1982. The fourth reactor, the one which exploded, was also ordered in 1975, but only went commercial, after a series of construction delays, in 1984. In 1981, two more reactors were ordered at the Chernobyl site, due to come on stream in 1990.[5] Delays and faults in their construction, and a scandal about the poor quality of cement being delivered to the construction site, had already been publicised in an unusually outspoken and critical article in *Literaturnaya Ukraina* just a month before the accident. 'The construction is not fit for assembly, and never will be,' the newspaper claimed. 'Equipment, machines and mechanisms started to wear out and shortages of basic mechanical devices and instruments took place. Problems have multiplied and become overgrown with a massive quantity of unknowns.'[6]

On the afternoon of 25 April, just before a weekend when the local factories' demand for electricity could be expected to decline, the almost-new fourth reactor – which had been in operation for just over a year – was being stood down for what Soviet officials insist was routine maintenance. It depends what is meant by 'routine'. The Chernobyl reactors were designed to produce 1000 megawatts of power, and there is a programme to upgrade them to produce 2400 megawatts. The schedule for the upgrading programme has never been made public, and there has so far been no official announcement that it has begun. But there are reasons to suggest that Chernobyl No. 4 was being prepared for a dramatic increase in its generating capacity.

The RBMK reactor, or Reaktor Bolshoi Mosnosti Kipyasii, is one of the two dominant models of nuclear reactor on which the expansion of the Soviet nuclear power industry is based. The second is the VVER, a pressurised water reactor, which has the disadvantage that one third of its fuel rods need to be replaced each year, and the reactor must be shut down for the rods to be reloaded. This means the reactors are shut down for at least a month each year.[7] The VVER is the main export model, with 64 reactors built or ordered in Eastern Europe. Since one advantage of the RBMK is that it does not require a shutdown for reloading the fuel rods, it is not clear why the relatively new Chernobyl reactor was being shut down at all.

The VVER is the main export model because it does not produce plutonium. The RBMK does.[8] Plutonium is not its main product, but an inevitable by-product of a fairly crude reactor system. The sources of weapons-grade plutonium for Soviet military programmes are a very tightly guarded secret, but the plutonium from the RBMK reactors could be requisitioned if the Soviet military is embarking on a crash programme of building new nuclear warheads. US intelligence sources suspect that this is indeed the case. Faced with the prospect, however distant, of the American SDI programme – 'Star Wars' – Soviet military planners have reckoned that their best short-term response is to fire many more missiles and decoys and swamp the Star Wars defences. More missiles require more warheads, and more warheads require more plutonium. The evidence is purely circumstantial, but there is a possibility that the Chernobyl reactor exploded in the course of a special shutdown that was designed to extract plutonium for warheads.

The long process of the shutdown began on the Friday and, almost immediately, something began to go wrong. The volume of radio traffic from Chernobyl and Kiev to Moscow monitored by Western electronic intelligence listening posts rose sharply on the Friday.[9] According to Russian scientists familiar with the events at Chernobyl, only a minimum staff was still on duty in the control room when the explosion occurred. They claim that this explains why only two men died in the initial explosion, which took place at 1.23 a.m. on Saturday morning, 26 April.[10]

At the time of writing, there has been no authoritative Soviet explanation of the explosion. In his account to the Soviet public on television three weeks after the disaster, Mikhail Gorbachev said only that there was a sudden surge of power produced from the reactor, a release of hydrogen and an explosion which damaged the reactor roof and control room, and started a series of fires.[11] According to the first Western expert to visit the scene, Dr Morris Rosen of the Vienna-based International Atomic Energy Agency (IAEA), the reactor was operating at only 7 per cent capacity when the explosion came, and 'the process of chain reaction automatically stopped'.[12]

Immediately there was chaos. The explosion in the reactor also blew in part of the control room and the first two fatalities were control-room personnel, one from falling debris and the other from terrible burns. When the local fire brigade arrived, within thirty minutes of the alarm, they numbered only twenty-eight men, under the command of Leonid Telyatnikov.[13] They had been given some training in how to cope with a radiation emergency but initially had no specialised protective suits. Their first priority was to get the flames, already leaping up to 200 feet into the air, under control. They could not begin to quench the fire inside the reactor itself, where the graphite core was burning. But there were five other conventional fires they could fight, and the priority was the one that threatened the turbine room, with the terrifying prospect that it might reach the oil storage reservoir, and the neighbouring third reactor. Indeed, the roof of the building housing the third reactor briefly caught fire, but the firemen were able to extinguish the blaze. Throughout the long springtime night, with their boots sinking into the melting asphalt of the road outside the reactor, the firemen fought the blaze, while the radiation counters they had been hurriedly issued climbed off the top of the scale.

By 5 a.m., when dawn was beginning to break, over fifty fire-fighting teams had arrived from Kiev and other nearby towns.[14] Most of their efforts were spent on stopping the fires reaching the third reactor block. Some clambered on to the roof to fight the fires in the reactor building, and received lethal doses of radiation. Medical staff who arrived in the ambulance to take away the injured were also exposed to lethal doses. All of the firemen were to be taken to hospital, and almost all of those who had been inside the power station when the reactor exploded. A woman security guard who left her post at the station entrance to help the ambulance crews also received a lethal dose.[15]

But if there were heroes on the spot, there were also those

whose nerve broke under the impact of the worst disaster in the history of nuclear power. Several simply fled, including the plant's deputy director, R. Solavyov, and several shift managers and senior foremen fled so far that six weeks after the disaster they were still posted as 'on the run'.[16] But outside the plant, life went on almost as normal. Satellite photographs taken over the next two days showed barges sailing serenely down the Pripjat river as the smoke from the reactor drifted slowly north, and the satellites even picked out football teams playing almost within sight of Chernobyl. Officials from Kiev who arrived at the scene on Saturday found wedding parties proceeding in the nearby settlement of Pripjat, some two miles from the plant, and in the small city of Chernobyl itself, just eleven miles from the reactor.[17] One of the first tasks of the special police contingents drafted into the zone was to halt all traffic coming into the nearby Yanov train station, to supervise unloading of goods and the reloading of passengers and to move them out from the danger zone.[18]

In Moscow, the ministry of power and the Institute of Atomic Energy were informed that an accident had occurred. The KGB headquarters were perhaps the first to be informed, since security at the power stations is among their manifold duties. What is still unclear is exactly what Moscow was told over the first weekend. At least three powerful men were assigned to emergency duties on the Saturday morning. Major-General Gennady Berdov of the MVD militia, the deputy minister of the interior of the Ukraine, was assigned to take charge of the Chernobyl region and arrived shortly before lunch.[19] Within a week, his general's uniform was to be burnt because of the radiation it had picked up. In Moscow, Air Force Major-General Nikolai Antoshchkin was ordered on the Saturday to fly down to Chernobyl and assemble a specialised team of helicopters to smother the reactor with sand. 'No other method can work,' he was told, according to an interview he gave to the military newspaper, *Krasnaya Zvezda*.[20]

This interview is the first real evidence that at least some officials in Moscow knew of the seriousness of the situation during that first, confused weekend. But the third powerful man sent down to Chernobyl on the Saturday, Academician Valery Legasov, deputy director of the renowned Kurchatov Institute of Atomic Energy, later told *Pravda*, 'We got the information about the disaster immediately. But it contained many strange and contradictory things. Believe me, it was impossible to comprehend exactly what had happened, and to realise the scale of the accident. For example, the information we had spoke of radiation, but one of the dead had succumbed not to radiation but to chemical burns.'[21]

On the Saturday morning, the Council of Ministers (which is the government and cabinet, rather than a party body like the Politburo) had established an emergency commission to deal with the disaster, and assigned Deputy Prime Minister Boris Scherbina to run it. Even while the members of the commission were being summoned and briefed, the first team of scientific experts, including Legasov, were on their way south.

'I won't try to hide it from you. I did not realise that the scale of the disaster was as great as it proved to be. And it was only when we approached the town of Pripjat and saw the red glow in the sky that I began to appreciate the character of what had happened there. It was impossible to evaluate what was happening while sitting in Moscow,' Legasov later told *Pravda*.[22]

It is important to establish exactly what Moscow knew of the accident on the Saturday and Sunday, because the Soviet authorities have tried to deflect international criticism of their long silence with the argument that they wanted to release only authoritative information. In his first press conference after the accident, on 6 May, Boris Scherbina began the process of shifting blame on to local officials.

'There were many unknown features and a very complex situation,' he said. 'The first information we obtained was not correct. On the ground, local experts and officials did not have a true assessment of the event.'[23]

This line was later widely repeated. And on 15 June, announcing the dismissal of the Chernobyl power station director Viktor Bryukhanov and other senior management figures, *Pravda* quoted Ukraine party officials who said they had been fired 'Because they could not give an evaluation of what was happening nor take the proper measures to organise the work of damage limitations.'[24]

Scherbina himself arrived at Pripjat on the Sunday morning, and immediately set in train the evacuation of the town, and of an area drawn arbitrarily on the map, with a radius of ten kilometres from the burning reactor. The evacuation began at 2 p.m. on the Sunday, with the help of buses requisitioned from Kiev. Some 40,000 people were moved out in the space of two hours, in a convoy that stretched for eight miles along the road. It did not include all the inhabitants of Pripjat. Six weeks later, two old ladies of eighty-five and seventy-two were finally found after hiding from police searches and refusing to obey loudspeaker appeals to leave. They had lived on canned food and oatmeal porridge, simply reluctant to be parted from their homes.[25]

But the next morning, almost 700 miles to the north, at the Swedish nuclear power station at Forsmark, abnormal levels of radiation were first detected at 9 a.m. The plant's 600 workers were evacuated and checked with geiger counters, and their clothing was found to be contaminated. Outside the plant, the grass and surrounding air were showing radiation levels four times higher than normal.[26] By midday, with similar reports coming from other parts of Sweden and Finland, an analysis of wind drift made it plain that the radiation was coming from the Soviet Union. Throughout the Monday afternoon, Swedish diplomats in Moscow badgered officials of the Soviet foreign ministry and Moscow's Institute for Atomic Energy for an explanation. They were met with bland denials. That evening there was a cocktail party at the Swedish embassy; Ambassador Torsten Orn pressed Soviet diplomats for some information, and finally made it clear that Sweden was going to file an official radiation alert with the IAEA in Vienna, whether Moscow made a statement or not.[27]

At this time, 7 p.m. on Monday, a full 65 hours after the explosion, Soviet foreign ministry press officers were still categorically denying that anything had happened, and indeed were telling Western correspondents that the leak came from somewhere in Sweden. They later explained that they had not been informed. But Russian journalists certainly knew of the disaster on Sunday. Valentin Falin, head of the Novosti press agency, confirmed that he had heard on the Sunday, and acknowledged to Western journalists that the news should have been made public then.[28]

Finally, at 9 p.m., in the course of the television evening news, and long after the usual fragments of film of combine harvesters and information about a new heavy truck being produced, a terse announcement was read. It said only: 'An accident has taken place at the Chernobyl power station, and one of the reactors was damaged. Measures are being taken to eliminate the consequences of the accident. Those affected by it are being given assistance. A government commission has been set up.'[29]

That was all. One hour later, after urgent requests from Sweden for more information on possible danger to Swedish nationals, Lars Nilsson, second-in-command at the Swedish embassy, telephoned Yevgeny Rymko, deputy chief of the Soviet foreign ministry department that handles northern Europe. Rymko referred him to the communiqué issued on television and said, 'I have no other information to give.'[30] In Vienna Dr Hans Blix, director of the IAEA, heard of the increased radiation in Sweden and waited in vain for any official word from Moscow. Finally he asked his deputy, Soviet scientist Leonid Konstantinov, to make his own enquiries, and on Monday evening Konstantinov telephoned him to confirm the Chernobyl accident.[31]

This is the essential background to Mikhail Gorbachev's subsequent statement: 'As soon as we received reliable initial information, it was made available to Soviet people and sent through diplomatic channels to the governments of other countries.'[32]

But the gap of almost three full days between the accident and the formal Soviet statement was a public relations disaster that badly damaged the progressive and dynamic international image that Gorbachev had been at such pains to construct. The delay was seen as evidence of the old Kremlin instinct to secrecy, and it was widely suggested that without the Swedish warnings, the Kremlin might not have chosen to release any information at all.

There were a number of complex reasons for Moscow's delay. The first was that the man who had been most prominent in the new campaign of *glasnost*, or openness – at least in international matters – was the director of information at the foreign ministry, Vladimir Lomeiko, and he was in New York for a conference. One of the few official voices with the seniority to argue for an earlier statement was simply not in Moscow. The second was the genuine fear of causing a panic among the Soviet public. The third was the contradictory nature of the information coming from local officials in Kiev and at Chernobyl, and the bewildering mix of radiation readings being made in the area.

In a sense, the Soviet government was lucky. The sheer power of the initial explosion, and the enormous heat of the flames, had sent the first, intense burst of radiation high into the air. According to the IAEA experts, they were told by the Soviet authorities that the radiation peak on the night of the explosion was 36 milli-roentgens per hour.[33] By the Saturday afternoon, the readings were down to 15 milli-roentgens per hour, but they surged again on Sunday, 27 April, and surged yet again to the highest ground readings of all on Tuesday, 29 April.[34] But the spread of radiation was bizarre. Up to ten miles from the spewing reactor there were pockets giving off intense readings, from highly irradiated particles of graphite which had been in the reactor core. In the following month, more such hot spots were found up to a hundred miles north of the reactor, leading to further evacuations. But the worst concentration of radiation, from the first explosion, did not land all over Chernobyl. It was being carried as a great plume northwards by the winds. The radiation that was to cause alarm and destruction of food across northern and western Europe over the next two weeks was highly diluted. Had it landed in concentrated form around Chernobyl, the casualty list would have been far, far longer than it was.

The almost random distribution of the intense radiation came as a considerable surprise to Soviet and Western scientists alike. The American doctor Robert Gale, who flew to Moscow to help treat the victims, pointed out that even the people inside the reactor control room had got strange doses.[35] Radiation doctors are accustomed to thinking in terms of the dose as measured on the body's centre-line. But, as Dr Gale pointed out, he was treating people who had an intense dose to one foot, or a high dose on one side of the body and almost nothing on the other. There were people with limbs that had received a massive dose which proved to be lethal, even though all vital organs seemed untouched. Medical science had much to learn from the first real field test of radiation since the bombs on Hiroshima and Nagasaki in 1945.

While the scientists were still trying to assess how much radiation had been leaked and how widespread was the contaminated zone, the priority at Chernobyl was to seal off the great hole the explosion had torn in the reactor. Major-General Antoshchkin's helicopters were the only solution, but for the first few days their work was slow, and Boris Scherbina complained it was 'like hitting an elephant with shotgun pellets'. It was not until 2 May, six days after the explosion, that their work-rate had speeded up sufficiently to win some grudging praise from Scherbina. By 10 May, the helicopters had dropped 5000 tons of sand, lead and boron on to the reactor, steadily sealing off the radiation.[36]

But the very weight of the smothering material contributed to another, more desperate problem. From the beginning of the Chernobyl disaster, the great, unspoken fear among Soviet experts had been that the reactor itself might melt down uncontrollably. Their relief had been enormous when the first patients from the reactor had been examined and found to have no trace of neutron flux, which would have indicated that a chain reaction was still taking place. The chain reaction had stopped automatically when the reactor exploded, one key part of the designed-in safety features that worked.

Meltdown is a vague word, too loosely used during the Chernobyl crisis, but the worst case of a meltdown had already been avoided when the chain reaction stopped. The new fear was of something rather different: the glowing-hot reactor core burning its way through the floor of the power station and into the earth. And every extra ton of the vital shielding the helicopters were dropping was helping to press the reactor core down through its floor. Below that floor lay the water table, ominously close to the surface. At the very least, the sinking reactor would contaminate the ground water of the Dnieper valley, with awesome consequences for the vital granary of the Ukraine, for the city of Kiev and, eventually, for the Black Sea itself.

But even before that happened, the likelihood was that the reactor would instantly vaporise any pockets of water it reached, creating a kind of steam bomb, able to explode the reactor and its 5000-ton burden of irradiated sand. They would be blasted into the air in a cloud of radiation that would have made the first plume seem like so much air-freshener.

There was no single solution to this threat. A series of remedial measures had to be taken simultaneously. The first priority was to cool the reactor, because the insulation effect of the sand had started to increase the core temperature, which could eventually have made the core go critical again. The cooling was done through a complex system of tubes feeding liquid nitrogen, which were pushed into place by radio-controlled robots, at least three of them supplied from West Germany.[37]

Beneath the reactor, teams of miners were boring a series of tunnels. There were tunnels to pump out the ground water, and tunnels driven directly underneath the reactor to pump in cement and molten lead. The lead was intended to stop radiation seeping into the water table, and the cement was a giant barrier to slow, and eventually stop the sinking reactor. At the same time, huge screens of lead were being pushed into place around the sides of the reactor above ground level. Again, remote-controlled vehicles were used, but satellite photographs identified what seemed to be military armoured vehicles, taking advantage of their protection against radiation designed for use in the event of a nuclear war.

Between the stricken reactor and the river Pripjat, teams of bulldozers built a vast high dyke, to prevent a sudden rainstorm washing the contamination on the ground into the river that fed Kiev's water supply. Near Kiev itself, deep wells were sunk into artesian water, to guarantee pure water should the rivers be contaminated.[38] And unknown to the Soviet public, supplies began to arrive from the West: anti-radiation suits from Britain, drugs and medicines from fifteen countries, decontaminants and a special ground-sealing film from Sweden.

Among the thousands of troops, police, nuclear physicists and officials drafted in to manage the crisis, some groups stand out. Perhaps the most heroic were the teams of nuclear technicians who spent the first drastic days in the control rooms of the other three functioning reactors on the site. They had to be closed down, but they had to be constantly monitored during the shutdown and, even then, men had to stay inside the control rooms, working brief rota shifts and dressed in protective suits, until they had accumulated the maximum permitted dose of 25 rems, five times the level allowed to British nuclear power station workers in the course of a year.[39] Then there were the first teams of miners sinking the vital tunnels, who were allowed to work in fifteen-minute shifts before being withdrawn and checked.

It is doubtless invidious to single out individuals, but the work of Boris Scherbina and of Mikhail Gorbachev's personal scientific adviser, Professor Yevgeny Velikhov, was of central importance. Scherbina was the country's most experienced trouble-shooter, the party secretary of the Tyumen region who had managed the crash programmes to develop first the oil and then the gas reserves of western Siberia. He was also the man assigned to build the pipelines to Western Europe after President Reagan's embargo on Western technology, and he had been rewarded with the rank of a deputy chairman of the Council of Ministers. A thrusting technocrat of the 'Can-do' school of management, he was a natural choice to head the emergency commission into Chernobyl.[40] It was he who organised the first efforts to contain the damage, and authorised the first evacuation of some 40,000 people on the Sunday immediately after the explosion. The entire medical services of the Ukraine were mobilised to screen all the

Chernobyl

evacuees, and 18,000 people spent two or more days in hospital being checked. In the event, only 299 were confirmed to be suffering from radiation sickness.[41]

Described by his friends as 'the kind of man who leads from the front, who pushes aside the officials and insists on seeing things for himself', Scherbina was reported to have received an alarmingly high dose of radiation during his first few days at Chernobyl, sufficient with his exhaustion to put him into hospital by the middle of May.

Scherbina's job was to make the preliminary assessment of the scale of the problem and start assembling the men and the machinery and the organisation that he would need to contain it. He seems to have run across some difficulties in doing so. With the air-drop of lead and sand on to the reactor under way, the military decontamination teams beginning their work and the miners and construction teams being assembled, the logistic problem was at least being defined. But then, just before May Day, it seems that Scherbina flew back to Moscow to say that he needed more political support. That is the most obvious explanation for the sudden visit of Prime Minister Nikolai Ryzhkov and ideology chief Yegor Ligachev to the stricken region on 2 May. It was a fairly mysterious trip. It was never made clear how close they came to Chernobyl, nor what they saw and decided. The official communiqué said only that they instructed that 'additional measures be taken'.[42] During their visit, the evacuation zone was suddenly increased from a ten-kilometre to a thirty-kilometre radius around the point, and the population of the small city of Chernobyl itself began to be evacuated, a process that was to take five days.[43]

And with the visit of Ryzhkov and Ligachev, Professor Yevgeny Velikhov suddenly began to appear as a spokesman in the Soviet press and on television. It is a remarkable illustration of how well the Soviet system can keep its secrets that nobody outside the ruling group really knows who was responsible for what at this stage of the operation. But it seems that Scherbina's demand for more political muscle on the spot, to ensure greater support from the military, and from the party and government hierarchies in the Ukraine and Belorussia, was provoked by new fears that the reactor itself was going out of control. According to Scherbina's statement at his press conference on 6 May the radiation levels peaked on 27 April, when the bulk of the population of Pripjat was evacuated. But essential workers stayed on. 'Two days later, when the situation was more dangerous, all of the workers were evacuated,' he said, which suggests that it was the new crisis on 29 April which led him to go to Moscow.[44]

The new crisis was the fear of meltdown. The heat of the reactor and the still burning graphite fires had buckled the steel supports inside the concrete of the reactor building. The reactor was physically sinking and shifting, and giving off surges of radiation that seemed like secondary explosions. This was entirely new ground for the scientists. Nobody had ever had to cope with a rogue reactor like this before. And the eyes of the world were on the Soviet Union. Britain had insisted that its seventy students in Kiev and the thirty in Minsk be evacuated from the danger zone, and they flew from Moscow on 1 May, to be checked with geiger counters in Moscow and in London. Their doses were high, but not dangerous. Satellites were now peering almost constantly at Chernobyl, and in Western Europe the EEC was debating how to ban food imports from the radiated lands of Eastern Europe. In Tokyo, the leaders of the Western world were gathering for a scheduled summit, a meeting that was overshadowed by their and their electors' concern for the fallout from Chernobyl.

That concern was being fuelled by an irresponsible Western press. On the Tuesday immediately after the accident, just before the Soviet government issued a statement on TASS which acknowledged that two people had died, the UPI news agency in Moscow put out a story quoting a woman in Kiev who was attached to a local hospital saying that 2000 people had died. The story, although cautiously phrased and described as 'an unconfirmed report', was instantly seized upon by Western media starved of news, and expecting the worst.[45] It could not possibly have been true. Radiation does not kill that fast. The only way 2000 people could have died in the four days since the accident would be through the kind of explosion that Western seismic stations could have recorded. The Soviet authorities were rightly outraged by what they saw as irresponsible slander. And the *New York Post*'s indefensible front-page splash headline 'MASS GRAVE', claiming that 15,000 corpses had been bulldozed into a nuclear waste pit, allowed Moscow to mount a counter-offensive against what Gorbachev was to condemn as 'malicious mountains of lies'. The Soviet system was paying the price not only for its secrecy over Chernobyl, but for the accumulated hostility and suspicions of generations. A society that had lied for days about the fate of the Korean airliner shot down in 1983, that had still not faced the truth about Stalin's gross slaughters, was not going to be easily believed or trusted over Chernobyl.

The world was not only watching, it was actively involved. Under intense international and diplomatic pressure, the Soviet authorities had invited a team of experts from the IAEA, led by the director, Dr Hans Blix, to visit Chernobyl and be given a series of briefings by Soviet nuclear engineers. A team of three doctors from the US and Israel, backed up by other medical specialists in London and elsewhere, were at work in Moscow on thirty-five more seriously affected patients. Chernobyl had always been an international problem as much as a Soviet disaster, and at last Moscow was ready publicly to tap the resources of the international community.

It was at this stage that Professor Velikhov became visibly involved at Chernobyl. One of the country's top scientists, he had also shown a distinct flair for public relations, and had become an official and highly public campaigner against the American SDI project. Ironically, he had also been named by the US Department of Defense as the main co-ordinator of the secret Soviet Star Wars programme. He was certainly a personal friend of the Gorbachev family, a vice-president of the Academy of Scientists and one of the youngest men ever to be appointed to a professor's chair at Moscow University. He did not even bother to join the party until he had been a professor for three years. He also held the top-security post of director of the Institute of Atomic Physics at Troitsk, where he worked on high-power lasers and the plasma process for nuclear fusion.[46]

Velikhov himself, in a series of press conferences and television interviews, spelt out what he described as 'the danger of catastrophe' that a melt-through of the reactor into the ground water would involve. But Velikhov's first clear statement that it was touch and go whether the technicians would be able to stop the process came only on 11 May, twelve clear days after the Western European diplomats had been formally summoned to the foreign ministry to be assured that there was no danger to their students and nationals living in Kiev. Velikhov's technical explanations, in the words of one European ambassador, 'meant that we had been told a series of bare-faced lies about the situation'.[47]

There was a palpable tension in Moscow throughout this entire period between those who wanted to continue with the traditional policy of cover-up and those who were promoting the new trend towards *glasnost*. Velikhov was clearly in the second category, but the sheer weight of institutional secrecy continued to horrify public opinion in the West. A small group of Western correspondents were allowed into Kiev and to visit one of the evacuation centres, but were in effect given little more than bland assurances that everything was under control.[48] The IAEA experts, who were taken in a helicopter to within half a mile of the still smoking reactor on 8 May, stressed repeatedly at a Moscow press conference that they were relying on the figures supplied to them by the Soviet authorities.[49] Their statement that the reactor was being brought under control stood in stark and embarrassing contrast to Professor Velikhov's interview with *Pravda* on 13 May, which described the desperate battle the technicians had been waging even as the IAEA experts had been at Chernobyl.

'The reactor is damaged,' Velikhov had begun. 'Its heart is the white-hot core. It is as though in suspension. The reactor is covered on top with a layer of sand, lead, boron and clay, and this is an additional load on the structure. Down below, in a special reservoir, there might be water. How would the white-hot core of the reactor behave? Would we manage to keep it intact or would it go down into the earth? No one in the world has ever been in such a complex position. It was essential to estimate the situation very accurately, and not to make a single error.'[50]

Bringing the reactor finally under control was an outstanding feat of scientific ingenuity and engineering skill from which the world's nuclear power industry will learn for decades to come. When it came to the test, whatever secrecy the system imposed and whatever prevarications its officials mouthed, the Soviet state machine did an awesome job of containing the world's worst nuclear accident. And it did so in a characteristic way, a reminder of how it had reacted to the strain of world war a generation earlier. After the initial disaster and confusion, the false optimism and the refusal to face, let alone admit, the truth, the vast resources of the state were lumberingly mobilised into effective action. Slowly, the right men were put in the right jobs, the helicopters and the construction workers and the medics put to work and the series of emergencies was managed and mastered.

It was a series of emergencies because Chernobyl was not simply a matter of containing the rogue reactor. There were three successive waves of evacuation to be planned, a massive food-screening operation to be mounted across most of European Russia and a large medical effort to be organised. The evacuations were a classic illustration of the Soviet system at work, desperately slow but ultimately effective. The first evacuation of the 40,000 people in Pripjat and the immediate vicinity of the reactor took place thirty-six hours after the explosion, when most Western experts claim it should have begun within eight hours. The second phase, after six days, was far too long delayed. The 52,000 people from Chernobyl city and the rest of the thirty-kilometre zone were exposed for a dangerously long time, and many of them seem to have accounted for the steady increase in the casualty figures. On 6 May, Boris Scherbina claimed that 214 people were in hospital with radiation sickness and, of these, eighteen were serious.[51] (Within the month, twenty-five people had died, so at least seven were very much sicker than Scherbina knew.) Eight days later, Gorbachev told the nation on television that 299 were in hospital. An earlier evacuation of the thirty-kilometre zone might have reduced the casualties.

The third evacuation wave was never publicly announced. It emerged only on 4 June in an interview given to *Pravda* by Alexander Petrov, the deputy premier of Belorussia.[52] He described how the first two evacuation zones had been drawn on the map with a pair of compasses, and how these perfect circles bore little relation to the levels of radiation on the ground. The radiation had fallen in uneven patterns, and there were 'hot spots' spreading up to a hundred miles to the north of the reactor, in the Gomel region of Belorussia. A further 60,000 children had been evacuated, with their mothers and schoolteachers, to holiday camps across the country, from the Baltic to the Crimea.

Although earlier official statements had claimed that food grown outside the thirty-kilometre zone was safe, Alexander Petrov also revealed that people throughout the Gomel oblast, an area the size of southern England, had been warned not to touch the food from their private plots. All food was being bought in centrally, and then checked with geiger counters before a decision was made to bury it or release it for processing. The farmers were being reimbursed with tinned food.

There were further indications that the evacuation programme had been even more widespread. A group of Western journalists visiting a car plant at Togliatti, far to the east of Moscow, found that the local sanitarium had been prepared to receive evacuees from the city of Gomel.[53] But however widespread the programme, the shortage of facilities meant that many people had to be left in place. *Izvestia* reported how the 7000 inhabitants of the small town of Bragin, almost fifty miles north of Chernobyl, said goodbye to their children and stayed at home to decontaminate their own houses.[54] They scraped four inches of topsoil from the streets and yards, and laid new asphalt on all the roads, squares and school playgrounds, cleaned their wells, and worried how to flush the radiation from the peat bogs that surrounded their homes.

The slowness of the evacuation programme goes some way to explaining the reluctance of the Soviet system to release the information. At almost all costs, they did not want to be faced with the prospect of trying to evacuate a city the size of Kiev, with its 3 million people. Even the city of Gomel, with about 300,000, would have imposed terrible strains. The evacuation of the 100,000 people in the first two waves led to a series of complaints in the Soviet press about poor facilities, delays in distributing food and clothing, gross overcrowding and poor organisation, which led to many officials being fired. And throughout the crisis, the authorities were desperate to avoid any kind of public panic.

There were some cases. The Ukrainian minister of health admitted that some people had gone to hospital after poisoning themselves by drinking iodine in the hope that this would ward off radiation. Others gave themselves alcoholic poisoning by believing the widespread legend that vodka mixed with red wine was a sovereign remedy against radiation.[55] And from the beginning of May, almost as soon as the government admitted that the accident had happened, the parents of Kiev mobbed the train stations to buy tickets to get their children out of the city. Day after day at Moscow's Kievsky Voksal, the main terminus for the trains from the Ukraine, the carriages pulled to a halt to release hordes of children. As the people of Kiev were being warned not to buy or eat food in the open air, to sluice out their flats with water to get rid of the dust, and saw their homes and streets being washed down several times a day, the parents' concern was understandable.[56]

It is an open question how much better the West might have

done, faced with a similar disaster. The inherent secretiveness of the nuclear power industry around the world was graphically emphasised by the leak on 4 May at the West German reactor at Hamm, a leak that was kept secret until the end of May, while increases in local radiation were attributed to the fallout from Chernobyl. After Three Mile Island and the constant scandals at the British nuclear power complex at Sellafield, Western nuclear technology could hardly claim much superiority. And mass evacuations place intense strains upon any social system.

The main difference is almost certainly that the Western media would have been told more than the world ever learned about Chernobyl. But as the crisis went on, the Soviet media itself began to give it saturation coverage in the press and on television. There were interviews with the firemen, the construction workers and the scientists, and an increasing number of long and detailed feature articles which sought not to reassure the readers, but to probe the failures and mistakes of the evacuation programme. By the end of May, there was little doubt that the policy of *glasnost* had been revived in the Soviet press. On 30 May, Alla Pugacheva and a number of other Soviet rock groups gave a huge concert for Chernobyl in Moscow's indoor Olympic stadium, in a deliberate echo of the West's Band Aid charity rock concerts for the African famine victims. Bands who had hitherto led a shadowy, underground existence, not authorised to release records by the state recording monopoly, were suddenly given a stamp of official approval. The heavy-metal band Kruiz, with their dog collars and metal chains swinging from their belts, and the almost-punk band Bravo played for Chernobyl and helped to convince the world that with its rock musicians and young rebels and charity concerts, the Soviet Union was a society not all that different from their own.[57]

But, of course, it was *different*, and the differences had been forcibly thrust down the world's throat during the first weeks of Chernobyl as the radiation cloud drifted across the Soviet border and into northern and western Europe. The silence from Moscow stretched out so long, and the later prevarications strained so much international credulity, that Mikhail Gorbachev's brave new image was irretrievably damaged. When the Soviet leader finally broke his silence, almost three weeks after the explosion, his televised address to the nation on 14 May barely began the long slog back to credibility. He gave only the sketchiest account of the explosion and had nothing but praise for the rescue workers and technicians involved, even while Soviet newspapers were already printing the first accounts of a purge of local officials. He had no word of apology, or even regret, to those European neighbours he had been wooing politically as inhabitants of 'our common home of Europe' for the cloud of radiation that had drifted across them.

Yet the speech was, in some ways, a typically impressive performance. Gorbachev's problem was to hold the line for his attempt to rebuild a foreign policy of détente against the hawks in the military and the party who claimed that it was impossible to reach any accommodation with the Reagan administration. His moratorium on nuclear testing and his grandiose scheme for world-wide nuclear disarmament by the year 2000 had met with no response from Washington, and he used the Chernobyl disaster to try again. 'It is another sound of the tocsin, another grim warning that the nuclear era requires a new political thinking . . . The accident at Chernobyl showed again what an abyss will open if nuclear war befalls mankind,' he said. He made some eminently sensible proposals for increasing international cooperation in nuclear energy, increasing the role and powers of the IAEA and a 'system of prompt warnings and supply of information in the event of accidents or faults at nuclear power stations . . . and an international mechanism for the speediest rendering of mutual assistance when dangerous situations emerge.'[58]

At the Warsaw Pact meeting in Budapest in June, he put forward further proposals for 25 per cent cuts in conventional weapons and forces in Europe, and promised to cooperate in the negotiations of an effective agreement of verification of the reductions.[59] Although still sceptical, the West listened, and noted that in spite of and yet somehow also because of Chernobyl, the arms control negotiations were back on track. Gorbachev followed up the Budapest proposals at the Geneva talks with American negotiators, suggesting a new package that would permit the Americans to continue laboratory testing of their Star Wars technology, so long as both sides agreed to abide by the 1972 Anti-Ballistic Missile Treaty for another fifteen years. And he suggested new limits to strategic weapons, of 1600 launchers and a maximum of 8000 warheads for each side. The medium-range missiles in Europe, and even the long-range cruise missiles, could be left on one side for further negotiation, he added. It was a pragmatic offer and it signalled that whatever the doubts of his hawks, Gorbachev remained in complete control.[60]

Chernobyl had been a disaster that threatened to derail Gorbachev's plans for internal reform and international détente when his regime was barely a year old. It did not, partly due to the luck that sent the initial burst of radiation so high that it dispersed, partly due to the skill and courage of his nuclear technicians who prevented the worst case of a meltdown, and partly because of the inherent strengths of the Soviet system he had inherited. In spite of its ponderous bureaucracy, its slowness to react, once in motion it is a formidable machine. The evacuation and medical services did a reasonable job, and the decontamination procedures seem to have been efficient enough.

There will be imponderable long-term consequences. One of the first decisions made was that Chernobyl would not derail the plan to increase the country's reliance on nuclear energy, although the need to increase safety systems, and to build containment shells around the RBMK reactors, would impose heavy new costs.

The impact on short-term food supplies was ruthlessly minimised. Contaminated milk that in any other country would have been thrown away was simply sent for processing, on the grounds that the radioactive Iodine-131 isotopes present would have decayed into harmlessness by the time the resulting cheese, butter and dried milk reached the consumer.

According to the American expert Dr Gale, something like 100,000 people would have to be monitored for the rest of their lives, and many of them could expect to die early from radiation-induced cancers.[61] The decision to go ahead with the harvesting of grain from the Ukraine and Belorussia will mean that millions of people will be ingesting some low-level radiation in their diet. Quite simply, medical science does not yet know what the effects will be as the radiation enters the food chain, seeps into the meat, into the earth and the water table.

There seem to have been few internal political effects. Although Chernobyl is located in the Ukraine, and the cloud of radiation drifted across Belorussia, Latvia and Lithuania, which are at once the most religious and the most nationalist of the Soviet republics, there has been little sign of outrage against Moscow for inflicting the nuclear danger upon them. There had been tremors in the past, with short-lived demonstrations in Lithuania against the siting of nuclear power stations, but this seems to have been less a revulsion against nuclear power than a nationalist reaction to the siting of the stations, with a resultant influx of thousands of Russian construction and technical workers in one of the last predominantly Lithuanian areas.[62]

The government's commission of enquiry submitted its own report to the Politburo on 16 July, and the main findings were released in a Politburo statement on 20 July.[63] It claimed that the tragedy had cost twenty eight lives, some 2000 million roubles, and contaminated 368 square miles of land around the plant. The main blame was attached to six senior officials, at the plant and in the regulatory ministries and state committees, who had been involved in 'gross breaches of regulations' in permitting unauthorised experiments with 'turbo-generator regimes. . . conducted when the reactor was side-lined for planned repairs at night. . . proper supervision was not organised when those experiments were carried out, nor proper safety measures taken. . . Irresponsibility, negligence and indiscipline led to grave consequences.' This was, for the Soviet state, a staggeringly frank series of admissions, but it characteristically raised more new questions than it answered: on the nature of those experiments, whether human error had been solely to blame, whether technical failures had also played their part. The main implication of the report was to exonerate the basic design of the reactor, and thus to put the planned expansion of Soviet nuclear power back on course. By blaming human error, Moscow had refused to accept the possibility of a systems failure.

The main political fallout of Chernobyl may well be a psychological one. The Soviet Union is perhaps the last society on earth to share that old Victorian faith in science as progress, to revere its scientists and accord the members of its Academy of Sciences the kind of status which protected the dissident Academician Dr Andrei Sakharov for so long. The country has now learned of the nuclear menace which lurks behind the men in white coats. It may not have lost its faith in science, or in the materialism which remains the psychic bedrock of the Soviet creed. But the Soviet people have been introduced, and this is something that they share in immediate experience only with the Japanese, to the concept of nuclear dread. If anything can alleviate this almost subliminal effect, it will be the message being rammed home in the media that the system worked, that it faced the nuclear nightmare and coped. In Soviet mythology, the vast concrete sarcophagus in which the Chernobyl reactor is being entombed may one day come to rival the mammoth statue of the Motherland, sword in hand, that towers over the old battlefield of Stalingrad. Another monstrous challenge that was faced and withstood.

The construction of such mythology began within a month of the explosion with the poet Andrei Voznosensky, a man of Gorbachev's generation, who published a poem in *Pravda* entitled 'Thoughts on Chernobyl'. It read:[64]

> God is in a man who,
> Though irradiated,
> Went into the object,
> Who put out the reactor fires
> Having burnt his skin and his clothes.
> He did not save himself.
> He saved Kiev and Odessa.
> God is a helicopter pilot
> Who saved and is saved,
> And Dr Gale, born in the year of Hiroshima,
> The man who flew over to Russia.
>
> We will find out later,
> Who is guilty
> And where is the poisoned fruit of the knowledge.
>
> When the robot failed to switch off the tragedy,
> A man stepped into that radiant block.
> We both stayed alive, you and I,
> Because that was a real man.

15

The West's Real Interests and Realpolitik

It remains an open question whether or not Mikhail Gorbachev will achieve his ambition of transforming the Soviet Union into a post-industrial economy by the year 2000. Certainly, the possibility cannot be ruled out. Even a partial success, which would allow the Soviet defence industries to match the American Star Wars programme, or end the Soviet reliance on imported grains, would have a dramatic effect on international politics.

Gorbachev's relative youth and his ease with television combine with his personal attractions and commitment to reform to make him the most formidable Soviet leader the West has had to face since the nuclear stalemate began. He forces us to confront the question: does the West really want to see an efficient Soviet Union? Do we yet comprehend the implications of the world's biggest and most resource-rich nation coming under dynamic new management?

The great-man school of history has long been derided. World affairs and modern economies are too complex to be much affected by the impact of one individual, however talented. But during the 1980s the West saw for itself the way that a political leader can transform a nation's mood. America entered the decade still caught in the dismal, almost fatalist grip of the post-Vietnam syndrome, and chastened and frustrated by the hostage-taking in their Iranian embassy. Whatever the merits or dangers of President Reagan's policies, his charm, his media skill and his cosy optimism have steered the American temper from gloomy introspection to a renewed self-confidence. Perhaps it took such a master of the medium to teach us how far television has led the citizen as audience to identify the nation with its political leader.

We are returning not just to the trappings but to the symbolism of monarchy. The narrow focus of the television lens leaves little room for other, lesser figures. If the dissemination of the printed word and newspapers helped publicise a wider range of opinions, and helped undermine the dominance of monarchs, television has the effect of concentrating public attention on the solitary figure of the head of state. It has happened in the United States, and it is happening in Western Europe. We should not be surprised that a similar focus of the national identity is evolving in that highly televised country, the Soviet Union. The Gorbachev television roadshow in London, Paris and Geneva was something unique for Soviet viewers. They saw a new, thrusting leader stepping confidently and capably onto the world stage. After years of sick old men in the Kremlin, it was a revelation. Ronald Reagan has shown how the monarchs of the television age can change a nation's mood, can bring about what seems in retrospect a miraculous psychological cure. Soviet society is not so different from that of the West.

How should the West respond if Gorbachev succeeds in injecting his own self-confidence into the Soviet body politic, if the managers are left free to manage and the farmers to farm and the workers given real incentives to work? The first priority is to think seriously about the implications. So far, there is little sign of that happening. The dominant trend in Western assessments of the Soviet Union is to take the view that the system is doomed and that it will be our task, in the words of US Senator Daniel Moynihan, 'to manage Soviet decline'.

The influential American political commentator George F. Will paid a brief visit to the Soviet Union at the time of Gorbachev's party congress in 1986, noted the lack of neon lights in Moscow, and drew some gloomy conclusions from the absence of this 'symbol of the crackling energies of capitalism'.[1] He should have gone to Murmansk, the Arctic city of long, long nights, where bright colours are held to have a therapeutic value, and which is in consequence the neon capital of the Soviet Union. In one of a series of articles for the *Washington Post*, Will concluded that the Soviet Union is 'a Third World country with first-rate rockets, at the disposal of a collective mind that never ever rises to the second rate'. This was a bold judgement at a time when American rescuers were dragging the wreckage of the Challenger space shuttle from the Atlantic and shortly after the Russians had successfully launched a permanent space station. Not only the rockets are first rate; so are the brains that design them and the cosmonauts who man them. Will's series would have been so much provocative comment were it not for two things: the way in which it typified so much Western thinking about the prospects for the Soviet Union, and its prescriptions for what the West should do. His articles ended:

> Policy should be: no detente, and more of the Reagan doctrine of increasing the cost of Soviet empire by supporting insurrections at its margins.

This, in effect, seemed to be the governing principle behind American policy in the months that followed the Geneva summit. The resistance forces in Afghanistan and Angola were equipped with advanced 'Stinger' anti-aircraft missiles. The president fought tooth and nail with Congress to get money for the Nicaraguan Contras. Gorbachev's proposals for a long-term, phase-by-phase nuclear disarmament programme were bluntly rejected; his unilateral moratorium on nuclear testing was punctuated by the repeated blasts of American testing in Nevada; and the Libyan allies were swatted from the sky and rocketed and bombed on land.

The determination of the Reagan administration to proceed with the Strategic Defence Initiative seemed aimed not only at constructing a futuristic anti-missile shield over America, but at driving the Soviet economy into bankruptcy. Certainly it was perceived in precisely this way by Mikhail Gorbachev. During his post-summit press conference at Geneva, Gorbachev went out of his way to stress that this point had been raised during the two leaders' private talks. He said that he had reminded President Reagan that neither the USA nor Hitler's Germany had been able to outspend or outstrip the Soviet Union in an arms race in the past. Nor would it happen in the future.[2]

The implicit threat in the SDI programme was rather more subtle. If it did not overwhelm the Soviet economy, the Americans believed, it could at least distort it, so that the investment and research and production skills on which Gorbachev relies to improve the civilian economy would have to be conscripted into military use, thus postponing interminably the better life that Gorbachev has promised the Soviet people.

Well, maybe. But the Soviet economy is too vast and too complex an industrial organism for safe prediction. A crash Soviet research and production programme in Star Wars technology would not only suck resources from the rest of the economy, it would also eventually create new resources which could leak back into the civilian sector. This is what happened in the American economy, where the technology and computing skills developed in the space programme and the defence sector quickly found their way into the broader economy. The compartmentalisation and secrecy of the Soviet system may delay that process but they will not stop it. It would be dangerous to rule out the possibility that an arms race in space could actually benefit the Soviet economy.[3] And attempts to exert American leverage on Soviet industry have backfired before. The classic example followed the embargo on selling American compressors to help pump oil through the Siberian pipelines. The Russians made their own compressors, faster than anyone had anticipated, and if not as sophisticated as the American originals, they were cheap enough to undercut them on world markets.

There is an almost inherent tendency in the West to underestimate the technical and productive capacity of the Soviet Union, in defiance of a great deal of evidence. The Russians have not only proved their capacity regularly to catch up with American technical leaps, as in the case of MIRV warheads or ballistic submarine missiles; they have also on occasion revealed that there is method to their apparent backwardness. In 1976, Western aviation experts mocked the MiG–25 Foxbat fighter after examining the example brought to Japan by defecting Soviet pilot Lieutenant Viktor Belenko. The plane's avionics were so backward, it was reported, that they relied on vacuum tubes and valves rather than transistors. It was only two years later that the US air force began assessing the impact of the EMP (electro-magnetic pulse) unleashed by a nuclear blast on delicate modern electronics. They found that even a small air burst would cause a vast communications blackout, unless transistorised equipment was specially shielded. Vacuum tubes, on the contrary, would continue to function.[4]

The real danger of an American policy aimed at distorting the Soviet economy, however, is that ultimately the West knows so little about it. For eight years, from 1976–84, the CIA and the Department of Defense and NATO continued to insist that the Soviet defence budget had been growing at a constant rate of between 5 and 8 per cent a year, depending on whose estimate one accepts. They were all wrong, or so they all agreed in 1984, when they scaled down their estimate of the budget's annual growth rate to 2 per cent or less. Perhaps the revised estimate was wrong too.[5]

The American decision to impose the Siberian pipeline embargo, which was taken at the height of President Reagan's denunciation of the 'evil empire', was based on the assumption that the Soviet energy crisis had uncovered the jugular vein of the Soviet economy. The CIA had reported that Soviet oil supplies were running out, and the (incorrect) assumptions about the Soviet defence burden suggested to the Washington computers that the Soviet economy could crash without the hard currency that would come from energy exports to the West. The strategy may have been brilliant but its premises were mistaken. The defence estimates were wrong, and so were the assessments of oil reserves.

This sequence of events is troubling, when one remembers what is at stake in an attempt deliberately to destabilise the economy of a rival superpower. But more profoundly depressing is the lack of feel, the absence of any real understanding of Soviet life, that can be detected in the statements and the thinking of so many Western leaders. A policy that is based on inaccurate facts is bad enough, but at least the facts can be corrected. An entire approach to the Soviet Union that is founded not only in ignorance but in a refusal or reluctance to understand is more dangerous because more deeply rooted, and much, much harder to change. A great deal of the responsibility for this situation can be laid at the Soviet Union's own door. Its traditional secrecy, its suspicion of foreigners, the heavy hand of the KGB in dissuading its own people from simple human contact have played a dominant role in perpetuating Western ignorance. When the Soviet Union does try to show itself off to the West, it focuses on its Potemkin villages, manufacturing an artificial impression of how it believes it ought to be.

To its credit, the West is attempting to improve matters. Or at least Western television crews, Western journalists who try to describe and convey a sense of Soviet life, have started on the long, hard road of dismantling myth. Sadly, in the process, we have helped to erect some myths of our own. The constant preoccupation of Western journalists in Moscow in the 1970s with the dissident movement, brave and honourable as it was, gave Western readers what seems in retrospect to have been a highly inflated sense of the dissidents' importance in Soviet life. The dissidents were always few, and there was no single movement. There were the Jews who wanted to leave, the liberal humanists like Sakharov and the idealist Marxists like Medvedev who wanted to stay and see the system reformed from within. And there were the arch-nationalists and the religious militants who wanted to build a Russia that few Western liberals would admire.

The presence of the Western press in Moscow grew sharply with detente in the 1970s, when it became easier to work from Moscow as a news base. The journalists who dominated the West's perception during the decade were gifted men, and Hedrick Smith of the *New York Times* and Robert Kaiser of the *Washington Post* wrote bestselling and excellent books which were pillaged and half plagiarised by a generation of thriller writers and film and television producers looking for local colour to flesh out their own second-hand fictions.[6] But while that generation of journalists produced good books, they have left the West's view of the country locked in a time capsule. They were describing Brezhnev's Soviet Union, which is as different from the current Soviet reality as Carter's or Nixon's America is from that of Ronald Reagan.

The Soviet Union in the mid-1970s had barely begun to produce the private car in any real numbers. Colour television sets were rare, and the demographic and social changes which have since proved so important were barely discernible. Brezhnev dominated a quite specific era in Soviet history, a time when official corruption was commonplace and almost accepted, when the novelty of access to Western ideas and goods and people that came with detente was causing a series of strange ferments in Soviet life. It was a period when Soviet resources still seemed inexhaustible, and the West, battered by the OPEC price rise and by the defeat in Vietnam, was vulnerable and alarmed. Dissidents were gaining in confidence, holding press conferences and seeming more widespread, more united and more of a significant social force than they ever really were.

Things are different now. The novels the West reads, our images of Soviet life, the justifiably embittered memories of the exiled Jews whom we now have as fellow-citizens in the USA, in Europe and in Israel, remain rooted in the Brezhnev period. Yet there are few places more critical of the Brezhnev years than Gorbachev's Moscow.

The new perspective from the Soviet capital rendered all the more bizarre the sudden Western fashion in the mid-1980s to produce novels which dealt with the theme of imminent Soviet collapse, through army coup, or popular uprising, or a mixture of both, guided and sustained by the wisdom of a tough American president who believed that the Soviet system was destined for the dustbin of history.[7] Novels are feeble enough clues to the mood of a nation, but the way in which their plots chimed with the prescriptions of influential columnists such as George F. Will certainly alarmed intelligent Russians.

It should be clear from this account that the Soviet Union is not facing imminent collapse, that it is even a fairly stable system, capable of change and improvement, and that it now has an intelligent leadership with a well-thought-out programme of reform. But if this view is wrong, and the Soviet system is about to implode, then before applauding or encouraging that process, we ought to think through its implications.

A collapse of Soviet authority would almost certainly involve the dissolution of the multinational Soviet state. Not all the minority peoples would want to escape the rule of Moscow, but some might do so. What would happen then? Iran would doubtless be interested in carrying its Muslim fundamentalism to its Islamic brothers in Soviet Central Asia, whether or not they were keen to receive it. Iran would certainly seek to reunite the Azerbaijani nation, currently divided by the Soviet border, and such an ambition would probably incite Turkey to recover its lost Armenian lands.

The Baltic states would probably seek independence, and there would be some in Belorussia and the Ukraine who would seek to join them. Unrestrained by the presence of Soviet armies, the countries of Eastern Europe would proclaim their freedom, and doubtless then set about recovering the national lands and minorities lost when the Red Army redrew the frontiers in 1945. East Germany would want to recover old Prussia, now behind Soviet borders, and the Oder-Neisse territories from Poland. Poland in turn would want its old lands in the Ukraine and Belorussia, while Hungary and Romania have a border dispute of their own. Even if a general war over Eastern European frontiers could be avoided, the collapse of Soviet authority in Eastern

Europe would mean the reunification of Germany. The continent of Europe would be faced once again with that German domination which it fought two world wars to prevent.

In the Far East, a truncated Russian state would be hard put to hold its huge Siberian hinterland. The Chinese have never recognised the current frontiers, which, they hold, were inflicted on them by the unequal treaties imposed in Tsarist days. The Japanese maintain their claim to the Kurile islands, and no doubt recall their prewar dominion over half the island of Sakhalin and their Manchurian empire. A Chinese and/or Japanese attempt to fill the Siberian vacuum left by Soviet collapse would transform the current balance of power in Asia and the Pacific.

So, taking the long view, it can be argued that the West has a direct interest in maintaining the physical and territorial integrity of the Soviet state. Its collapse would mean, at best, chaos and an immediate European crisis when faced with a united Germany; at worst, a general war.

There are dangers in such predictions, simplistic and wildly hypothetical as they may be. But we must learn to think ahead, because we are now faced with a Soviet Union which has begun to map out its own progress into and beyond the year 2000. Barring accidents, the Soviet Union now has a leader who can expect to be in power into the next millennium, and still be less than seventy years of age. He has drafted, published and started to implement an economic strategy for the next fifteen years, with clear goals. He has presented to the world a detailed and controversial scheme for universal nuclear disarmament by the turn of the century.

The countries of Western Europe have no choice but to address their minds to the future. The world is transforming about them, and the Atlantic alliance on which they have depended since 1945 is changing its nature. This is not because of any short-term political event, the ups and downs of peace movements, or even the placing and withdrawal of missiles. In 1980, for the first time, the amount of American trade with the nations of the Pacific exceeded that across the Atlantic. Simultaneously, the east coast states of America, traditionally Europhile, cosmopolitan and not isolationist, have been losing their old numerical dominance of the American political scene. The largest pluralities of recent years were won by two California-based American presidents, Nixon and Reagan. For the past six elections, the presidential candidates have come either from the West or the Midwest, or from the old South. The last Europhile American president from the old north-eastern political heartland was John Kennedy. The days of mass European emigration are over. The new citizens of the United States come from Latin America and from the Pacific rim.

Meanwhile, Europe's trade with its Soviet neighbour to the east continues to grow, and the trading relationship is locked into the long-term future through energy deals and the Soviet natural gas flowing down the pipeline from Siberia. In 1985, the Soviet Union's biggest trading partners were, in order, West Germany, Finland, Italy and France. Japan followed behind.[8] This is a matter of trends, not of raw figures. West German trade with the Soviet Union still falls short of its trade with the USA. The pattern, however, starts to change sharply when Eastern Europe is included; the overall trend of East–West trade on the European continent is growing more than twice as fast as Europe's trade with the USA, and even more rapidly when the currency fluctuations which distort American trade figures are allowed for.

The point is not that the Atlantic alliance is in trouble but that the deeper currents which have given that alliance meaning have been steadily shifting. The American balance of trade and political power is moving towards the Pacific, while Europe's trade edges towards the east. While the Soviet military and political threat to Western Europe continues to give the alliance cohesion and purpose, the nature of that threat is also altering. Domestic communist parties no longer carry any great electoral weight in Western Europe, except in Italy, where the party professes a communism which has little in common with that pursued in Moscow. And whereas NATO is a genuine military alliance, the Warsaw Pact looks to be something of a military fiction. It would be a bold Soviet commander who relied on the loyalty of Polish troops in any battle that was not defending Polish soil. Russian officers on leave, and most Soviet officials in private, acknowledge that the only ally on whom they place any military reliance is East Germany, and even then only on condition that the Russians are not facing German troops.

The transformations that are under way in Eastern Europe are clearly crucial to the future development of the Atlantic alliance and its relations with the Soviet Union. The detente years of the 1970s, which were meant to bring a lasting improvement in Soviet–American relations, in fact made their most enduring impact upon Eastern Europe. They gave the Hungarians the room to experiment with a cautious return to private enterprise, and the Romanians took the opportunity to slip out of the military responsibilities of Warsaw Pact membership. The Lutheran church in East Germany began to speak with an increasingly independent and dissenting voice; and on the subject of Soviet missiles based on their soil the East German government was prepared to listen, and even discreetly to sympathise.[9] With hindsight, the dominant symbol of the changes afoot in Eastern Europe was not so much the emergence of the Solidarity movement in Poland as the fact that Soviet tanks did not roll in to crush it.

Until the detente years, Soviet rule in Eastern Europe rested on the bayonets of the Red Army. Outbreaks of independence were crushed in East Berlin in 1953, in Hungary in 1956, and in Czechoslavkia in 1968. In Poland in 1981, it was left to the Polish army to impose military rule, while the Russians stayed in their barracks. The difference was not entirely academic; a Russian intervention would probably have meant great bloodshed. General Jaruszelski persuaded the sceptics in Moscow to let him apply a Polish solution to a Polish problem, and, convinced that the only alternative would be Soviet troops, the Polish people reluctantly but realistically acquiesced. When the Polish army imposed martial law, it looked like the same old tanks and troops advancing to impose Moscow's will, except in different uniforms. In retrospect, it looks rather different. The last precedent for Soviet military intervention in Eastern Europe is now almost twenty years old. And there was no ringing reassertion of Moscow's authority at the subsequent party congress of 1986, as there had been at the congresses that followed Prague, Budapest and East Berlin. In fact, what Gorbachev said carried a surprising echo of the speeches made by the toppled Czech leader, Alexander Dubček, in the Prague Spring of 1968:[10]

> Today, it is especially important to analyse the character of the socialist way of life on the basis of the development of several countries, rather than of one country. A considerate and respectful attitude to each other's experience, and the enjoyment of this experience in practice, constitute a huge potential for the socialist world . . . We do not see the diversity of our movement as a synonym for disunity, much as unity has nothing in common with uniformity, hierarchy, interference by some parties in the affairs of others, or the striving of any party to have a monopoly over what is right . . . One of socialism's

advantages is its ability to learn: to learn to prevent collisions of the interests of different socialist countries, harmonise them by mutual effort, and find mutually acceptable solutions even to the most intricate problems.

It would be unwise to take this at face value, or to suggest that it heralds a new era for Eastern Europe. It is too soon to tell. But the rhetoric of Moscow's political supremacy has changed, and this may be reflected in practice. One reason for the change may be the fact that the economic shifts which the detente years brought to Eastern Europe at last gave the satellite nations some significant cards to play in their relations with Moscow. They had become desirable trading partners in their own right and, in some key areas, technologically more advanced. The Soviet Union's need to take advantage of Eastern European skills added a new dimension to the relationship. Ironically, this too was prompted by Western attempts to put pressure on the Eastern-bloc economies. It was the NATO embargo on the export of modern technology and computers to the Soviet Union which made Moscow turn to its Eastern European allies, and it was the freezing of loans by the Western banks during the debt crisis which encouraged Eastern Europe to respond.

The future of Soviet authority over Eastern Europe will depend upon Gorbachev's success in reforming his own country, and upon the return of a new detente. Since neither reform nor detente is certain, the threat of repression will remain. We may not have seen the last of the tanks in Prague and Budapest. But to send in the tanks would be an admission of something worse than failure, an admission that the Kremlin is no more than a warped modern version of those Bourbons of whom it was said that they had remembered nothing and forgotten nothing. It would make a mockery of Gorbachev's efforts to play to world opinion, to improve the grim image that he inherited; and the importance he attaches to image was evident in his speech to the party congress:[11]

We are watched by both friends and foes. We are watched by the huge and heterogeneous world of developing nations. It is looking for its choice, for its road, and what this choice will be depends to a large extent on socialism's successes, on the credibility of our answers to the challenges of our time.

Perhaps the greatest single surprise of Gorbachev was his awareness of the role of the media and his capacity to exploit it. After the success of his televised walkabouts in Moscow and Leningrad, and his performance on French television in Paris, the Americans might have predicted that their own incomparable publicity machine might meet its match at the Geneva summit. But they failed to anticipate it, and they were ambushed by the most professional effort of political marketing that the Soviet side had ever mounted. Days in advance of the summit's opening, and before the White House press corps reached Geneva, Soviet spokesmen were giving daily briefings at the Geneva press centre, dominating the story for those journalists who had begun to arrive. Immediately after the summit finished, while Reagan was catching a plane to Brussels to brief the NATO leaders before returning home to Washington, Gorbachev was giving a two-hour press conference which was screened in full in Western and Eastern Europe, and which allowed his version of the summit almost to monopolise the media.

Gorbachev's main concern in foreign policy throughout the first year in office was to haul the Soviet Union back towards the moral high ground and away from the pariah status it had won with the invasion of Afghanistan and the imposition of martial law in Poland. The unilateral moratorium on nuclear tests and the nuclear disarmament proposals were aimed not just at the USA but at world opinion. The sheer flurry of offers and the new skill with which they were launched and presented, served to camouflage the weakness of his hand. His objective was to stop or at least control the American Strategic Defence Initiative, and he had little with which to bargain, save the force of his argument, the charm and novelty of his personality and the new professionalism of the Soviet media.

Clearly, Gorbachev's campaign against Star Wars was a matter of absolute priority for the self-interest of the Soviet state. But he deployed arguments against the programme which reinforced suspicions that he was speaking from a genuine personal concern so deep that it amounted to obsession. At Geneva, at the party congress, in his television speeches and in his dialogues with foreign leaders, he kept returning to the point that the combination of computers with nuclear weapons and access to space forced mankind to develop a new kind of thinking. At the congress he warned:

The modern world has become much too small and fragile for wars and policy of force. It cannot be saved and preserved if the thinking and actions built up over the centuries on the acceptability and permissibility of wars and armed conflicts are not shed once and for all, irrevocably ... The world will no longer depend upon the intelligence and will of political leaders. It may become captive to technology, to technocratic military logic.

Whether or not the West believes in Gorbachev's sincerity, we can appreciate the force of his argument. We know that, in all likelihood, he will still be leading the Soviet Union while the West sees three or four new American presidents. And each new American and French president, German chancellor, British or Japanese prime minister can expect to hear the same case put, the same dilemma posed, to them as leaders, and to their electorates. We have now lived in the nuclear age for forty years without a major war between the powers. But then, as Gorbachev said at Geneva, it only needs one: the first nuclear war will be the last.

Whatever the West's eventual response to Gorbachev's proposals for disarmament, we are compelled as fellow citizens of the planet to consider his case and to examine our own motives for doubting it. So far, the rejections of Gorbachev's plea for a nuclear test ban and of his proposal for a staged programme of nuclear disarmament have been delivered with dismaying speed. It is as if any idea emanating from Moscow is prejudged or, rather, condemned in advance, as though polluted by its very source.

We all know why. The Soviet Union steps onto the international stage like some actor whose name has been made by playing the villain. It is not simply Afghanistan and Poland and the tanks in Prague. Great Powers have always upheld their influence and defended their empires in terrible ways. For every Afghanistan there is a Vietnam. It is not simply the Gulags and the persecution of a Sakharov, a Solzhenitsyn, a Shcharansky. It is that the Soviet system seems unable to examine itself honestly, to tell the truth about Stalin and what he did to them, the good and the evil alike.

The United States often appals and exasperates its citizens and its allies alike, but it nonetheless examines its own record and its own conscience for the world to see. When its troops commit an atrocity, or its president conspires to conceal a felony, its press will scavenge and scour and expose. There are few people who find this openness harder to comprehend than the Russians, who continue to maintain that Nixon was toppled not for Watergate but because he was the detente president who had to be stopped. And while the Russians cannot understand the West's cast of mind, we find it almost impossible to make the leap of faith required before we can trust a system so closed, so secretive, so unable to admit that it has been wrong and, above all, so reluctant to give its own people access to the national memory.

Somehow, this gap must be bridged. The West has to go beyond its archetypes of Soviet commissars and Gulags and try to assess how far the place has changed; to understand the force and scope of the social revolution which has produced the educated Soviet leadership of Gorbachev's time. The Soviet Union remains a country of which we know desperately little; until we know more, we have little right to make judgements, still less to dismiss its proposals as inherently suspect. For when the Russians read what we think and say about them, when they assess the prejudice of vision and reluctance to learn which underpins so much of Western thinking about the Soviet Union, they are encouraged to keep their own minds closed. We remain trapped inside our images of one other, each unable to recognise that a society deserves to be judged by its aspirations as well as by its faults; by its capacity for change as well as by its past misdeeds. We, and they, deserve better.

16

Change and a Restless Future

This chapter is being written in the autumn of 1986, some eighteen months after Mikhail Gorbachev came to power. In that brief period, the capricious pendulum that is Western public opinion has swung back and forth from admiring curiosity to something like disillusion. After the sad parade of sick old men in the Kremlin, his relative youth and evident charm and energy produced a wave of interest and of optimism in the West, a wave which crested at the Geneva Summit. But the disaster at Chernobyl saw the pendulum swing sharply back again. The honeymoon was over, and the traditional image of the Soviet Union as a churlish, secretive and semi-competent system could flourish once more. More than that, Chernobyl threw into question the entire strategy behind Gorbachev's hopes of economic reform. His constant stress on scientific and technical innovation as the panacea for the lumbering Soviet economy sat unhappily with the catastrophe at Chernobyl, a place that was supposed to symbolise the cutting edge of Soviet technology.

But the story of Chernobyl, gruesome and frightening as it was, did not end with the explosion and its immediate aftermath. The programme of damage limitation was, by any standards, an impressive feat of organisation and technical ingenuity. The rogue reactor was brought under control, and four months after the disaster, at a gathering of the world's nuclear power experts in Vienna under the auspices of the IAEA, academician Valery Legasov presented the authoritative Soviet account. The report ran to three hundred pages, and was accompanied by a video film of the molten core, shot from a helicopter hovering over the very jaws of the spewing reactor. The consensus of the Western experts was that the Soviet version was persuasive and admirably full.[1] It confessed to a catalogue of almost wilful mistakes by the plant technicians who deliberately over-rode a series of safety devices while running an experiment to find out how long the turbines could continue to produce electric power after the reactor was shut down. By Soviet standards, the report was a dramatic example of the new policy of *glasnost*, or openness about events that society had traditionally kept secret.

It was followed within ten days by another example of *glasnost*, when the Black Sea cruise ship *Admiral Nakhimov* sank after a collision with a cargo ship. Over eight hundred people were saved, but almost four hundred were lost. Previous disasters of this kind, from air crashes to train collisions, had gone unreported by the Soviet media, but the sinking of the cruise ship was given the kind of saturation coverage in the Soviet press that such a tragedy would provoke in the West. There were interviews with survivors, including a rather shy account from a honeymoon couple, and endless stories on the rescue operations. *Pravda* ran a feature on the divers in the salvage operations, an ironic contribution to the new policy of *glasnost* from the newspaper which, under the old rules, had failed to report the deaths of construction workers who were erecting the new *Pravda* offices.[2]

It is important to keep this in perspective. Freedom of the press was not breaking out across the Soviet Union: simply, the straps of the straitjacket were being loosened slightly, to allow the press to report the corruption and bureaucracy, and air the criticism that the Kremlin found useful. This amounted to a subtler form of media management. Otherwise, the Soviet press remained unchanged. The commentaries in the various papers on international events remained identical in tone and barely distinguishable in phrasing. Independent judgement was not encouraged. When Nick Daniloff, the American correspondent of *US News & World Report* was arrested on transparently trumped-up spy charges, *Pravda* not only declared him guilty even before formal charges had been laid and before the trial, it had the gall to accuse the Americans of 'making a hullaballoo' over the affair to distract attention from Soviet peace proposals.[3]

But, for the Soviet media, and for its public, the policy of *glasnost* was change of a tangible kind, and it was being pushed from the very top.

While on a tour of the Soviet Far East just before the cruise ship disaster, Mikhail Gorbachev had made a speech on economic reform which bluntly said: 'there is nothing more potent than the force of public opinion, if only it can be realised. And it is only realised in conditions of criticism and self-criticism and wide publicity . . . One should go to the people, consider their opinions, meet them and keep them informed. And the tougher the going gets, the more frequently one has to meet them, to stay with them at the moment when this or that task is being solved.'[4]

On that same Far Eastern tour, Gorbachev spoke in the strongest terms so far of the scale of his reform programme. Just as Western cynics were beginning to note that 'reform' was not the word which came often to Gorbachev's own lips, he told a party conference in Khabarovsk that the reforms and changes planned 'are tantamount to a real revolution in the entire system of our social relations'.[5]

It is the peculiar nature of Soviet society that makes a speech by Gorbachev so important. The planned economy is, in effect, a command economy, and the exhortations and instructions from the top of the Politburo are meant to be put into effect by the whole apparatus and control machinery of the Soviet system. This may be the goal, but it is very far from the reality of Soviet life. The commands from the top get distorted, bungled and ignored on their way down the chain. And there have been times, when listening to yet another Gorbachev speech on reform, that one is reminded of Shakespeare's Glendower, who vowed to 'summon spirits from the vasty deep'. But, as Hotspur replied, would they come in answer to the call?

The vast inertia of the Soviet system has confounded reformers in the past, and to many observers, Gorbachev's obsession with economic reform doomed his entire vision to failure. Any reform that required greater initiative and more personal responsibility in the economic sphere, while maintaining the rigid party control over political life which actively discouraged popular initiative, was simply not going to work. And it was the view of some of the canniest Soviet watchers, among them M. Jean-Bernard Raimond, the French Ambassador to Moscow who was promoted to Foreign Minister, that the Gorbachev plan amounted to no more than that, to promote economic reform less for its own sake, than to buttress and continue to legitimise the party's weakening grip on political life. Economic change was the price that had to be paid to keep the political system the same.[6]

It is a thoughtful and intriguing argument, and it is one that at least some powerful senior officials seem to share. In July 1986, a curious document was leaked to two Western journalists in Moscow: to me as the *Guardian* correspondent, and to Mr Steve Hurst, the veteran correspondent of NBC-TV who had earlier served as Moscow Bureau Chief of the Associated Press News Agency. It was titled 'To the Citizens of the Soviet Union', and was signed by an unknown group calling themselves the Movement for Socialist Renewal. Couched in the language of a loyal opposition, its seventeen pages began with a powerful critique of the backwardness of much of the Soviet economy, and the failure of the party leadership to build an adequate defence capacity. It went on to argue the need to integrate economic and political reform, and to stress that without freedom of speech, the press and assembly, and an end to state persecution for political beliefs, economic reforms by themselves would find little response from the people. Above all, the manifesto argued, the country needed a degree of political pluralism, the freedom for alternative political organisations to present their different programmes to the citizens, all within the framework of a socialist and Soviet system.[7]

The manifesto was leaked from senior official sources, whose identity and eminence persuaded the two journalists that the document was genuine. Internal evidence, from the quality and range of information at the disposal of the authors of the manifesto, also argued that it came from people with unusual and privileged access to statistics and official data. The document was dated November 1985, some eight months before the date of the leak, and at a key moment in the Kremlin's own internal debates on reform. The 27th Party Congress was due to be held in the following February; the drafts of the new party programme and of the new economic guidelines for the rest of the century had just been published; and, to the despair of many official reformers, those draft documents did not go nearly as far as they had hoped. Much of the manifesto came from the position papers and memoranda that had been spilling from think-tanks, academic institutes and party organisations while the draft party programme was being drawn up.

The *Guardian*'s publication of the document almost in full, and the simultaneous broadcast on NBC's primetime TV news in America, stirred enormous interest and controversy in the West. The *Guardian*'s own account stressed that 'it remains possible that the leak of this document is a deliberate provocation, concocted by anti-reform groups in the Soviet Union who are seeking to discredit the Gorbachev reform strategy by linking it to an openly political programme which threatens the Communist Party and its monopoly of power'.[8]

It is impossible ever to be sure of the authenticity of such documents in the Soviet Union. One has to know one's sources, and decide how far to trust them, and look for corroborative evidence. In the case of the manifesto, the KGB showed considerable interest even before publication. My colleague Steven Hurst of NBC-TV was allowed to go through customs and immigration on his way out of Moscow Airport with his copy of the manifesto, before being belatedly stopped by the KGB. This is highly unusual. They seemed to know what they were looking for, and confiscated the document.

The official Soviet response was oddly muted. Foreign Ministry spokesman Gennady Gerasimov neither denounced the document as a fabrication, nor dismissed it out of hand. 'It was written by some kind of authors who want to reshape our society', he told a Moscow press conference immediately after publication, 'I have to say that it is provocative and anti-socialist in that it challenges the leading role of the Communist Party.'[9]

Vladmir Kalugin, a commentator for the Novosti Press Agency, argued in the Western press that 'it is clearly the product of those who wish to use the open self-criticism of Soviet society, its frank exposure of its own shortcomings, to smear the socialist system and Marxism-Leninism. It is the work of those who wish to undermine the real, practical reforms now being undertaken in all areas of Soviet society, who still hope that the Soviet Union can be nudged back to capitalism and that the Communist Party can be split and disintegrated.'[10]

The ambiguities in those two Soviet comments are intriguing. They do not, as is the common practice, attribute authorship to the CIA nor to any of the usual Soviet exile sources. There is even a hint in Kalugin's comment that it was written by anti-reform groups within the Soviet Union. Perhaps the most interesting Soviet comment, albeit an indirect one, came from Mikhail Gorbachev, who referred in a major speech the week after the document was published to 'articles' published in the West casting aspersions on the changes in progress in our country, trying to set the nation and the leaders of the party at loggerheads'.[11]

But he continued in that speech to party activists in Khabarovsk to pin his own colours even more firmly to the mast of reform. He attacked the conservatives who 'fail to see what this process of renewal is all about, and regard it as a virtual denouncing of our foundations, a disavowal of our principles'. And although he spoke in general terms, he went on to define the sphere of his reform much more broadly than he had done in the past. 'The current restructuring covers not only the economy, but all other aspects of social life – social relations, the political system, the cultural and ideological sphere, the style and methods of the work of the Party and all our cadres. Restructuring is an all-embracing word. I would equate the words "re-structuring" and "revolution",' he said, in the first public call from a Soviet leader for a new Soviet Revolution since 1917 had first brought the Soviets to power.[12] And he was at pains to stress that he was not simply talking in generalities. The process of reform, he argued, was ongoing, its scope increasing as it went on. 'The further we go along the road of restructuring, the more obvious its complexity becomes, and the fuller the tremendous scale of the work ahead is revealed. We are coming to see with increasing clarity the extent to which many ideas about the economy, management, social issues, statehood, democracy, education and moral standards are lagging behind today's, not to mention tomorrow's, requirements.'

This was a remarkable speech at any time. In the week after the publication of the manifesto, it seemed quite specifically to relate to the manifesto's arguments. 'Our party, government and economic personnel must learn to work under the conditions of extending democracy', he went on. 'The People's desire to participate in the management of public and state affairs is natural. Everyone must realise this, adjust one's thoughts and approaches . . . for there is nothing stronger than the force of public opinion when it is able to be realised. And it is realised only when there is criticism, self-criticism and broad publicity.'

While Gorbachev was making his contribution to the debate, Soviet experts in the West were subjecting the manifesto to close analysis. Inevitably, opinions varied. The mainstream view, as represented by the research staffs of Radio Liberty after exhaustive comparison with other political samizdats, was that 'almost certainly, it is a genuine document, probably written by members of the middle-level intelligentsia (people with a technical background).'[13]

The key question that remains is not the authenticity of the document, which now seems widely accepted to have come from Soviet sources, within the think-tank intelligentsia and from the traditions of the loyal dissidents like Roy Medvedev and/or Andrei

Sakharov, but on the precise status of its authors and distributors within the system. For obvious reasons, neither of the two Western journalists familiar with the identity and status of the sources is at liberty to reveal them. We can say only that the leak was planned and deliberate, and came from official sources currently holding very senior executive posts within the Government, rather than from academics.

One of the factors that persuaded us that the document was genuinely what it purported to be, a statement from reformers within the system, was the gap of eight months between its being written in November 1985, and its leak to us in July of 1986. A dissident document would almost certainly have surfaced very much faster if only because dissident circles have more familiarity with the Western press, and ways to reach it. The gap was also significant because the document claimed to have been written at a key phase during the internal debate on reform, between the publication of the relatively tame draft new programme for the Communist Party, and Gorbachev's seminal speech to the Party Congress the following February.

Official Moscow was flooding itself with paper and ideas in those months that were made heady by the coming to power of Mikhail Gorbachev, and his promise that real and fundamental reform was now on the agenda. Few Soviet officials doubted that reform was needed, but there were enormous differences between the maximalist and the minimalist wings over just how much was required. As Gorbachev asserted his authority in that first summer after coming to power, and publicly let it be known that the draft party programme he had inherited from Chernenko had been rejected and a new document was under way, the maximalists were convinced they had won the argument. But their disappointment at the caution of the draft programme that appeared in October led to the composition of the manifesto of the Movement for Socialist Renewal.

In the event, the party programme that was to emerge from the 27th Party Congress went further than the disappointing draft, and Gorbachev's own speech went very much further still, embracing many of the proposals for economic reform that the manifesto had argued. Since the Party Congress, Gorbachev's advocacy of *glasnost* in the Soviet media and his encouragement of criticism suggested that he was aware that economic change had to be buttressed by some reform on the political front. But whatever kind of reformer Gorbachev eventually proves to be, he is a politician in a hazardous environment. There are pressure groups and vested interests in great estates of the Soviet realm, from the military to the individual republics, from the advocates of heavy industry to the new priests of high technology. Their conflicting demands on the national budget have to be arbitrated, their own political weight assessed and accommodated. In the rhetoric of reform, Gorbachev has gone further than any previous Soviet leader, and there is a constant danger that his very vehemence could yet provoke a conservative consensus among some of those with vested interests against him. It happened to Kruschev, and could yet happen to Gorbachev if the new Party Congress in 1991 does not see some clear indication that his strategy has begun to work.

My own guess, and it can be no more than that, is that he will succeed partially, enough at least to ensure his own political survival, and to keep the Soviet Union from falling irreparably behind the West in the key technologies of the Arms Race. The new freedom for farms to sell surplus produce on the open market should increase the harvest and cut food shortages, although it will need a sharply improved distribution and retail system to make a dramatic difference. The showcase factories and the high-tech sector will get the investment and the top-level administrative attention to ensure their progress as planned, and the arrival of the Bam, the second Trans-Siberian railroad, should sharply increase the potential to exploit the vast wealth of Siberia. Against this must be set the collapse of the world oil-price, with its consequent fall in the hard-currency earnings the Soviet Union needs to import Western grain and technology.

But this is to look simply at the economy, and as many Western critics and the authors of the manifesto of the Movement for Socialist Renewal agree, that is only one part of a complex equation. The political life of the Soviet Union equally needs reform. And there are signs of movement here, not only in the rhetoric of Gorbachev's speeches on the need for more public participation in government, but also in practice. On the eve of Gorbachev's Far Eastern tour in the summer of 1986, the Supreme Soviet and the Central Committee issued a joint resolution which gets to the heart of the crisis in local government.[14] On paper, local government is in the hands of the local soviets. In fact, they have no resources of their own to carry out the building programmes and improve the retail and public services for which their constituents clamour.

In the city of Komsomolsk-on-Amur, on the Chinese border,

Gorbachev spelt out the problem. Local people had complained to him about the poor water supply, the shortages of children's clothes and of fresh fruit and vegetables, the slow housing programme and overcrowding of schools and sports stadiums and other public facilities. Although the local soviet is technically responsible, all of the required investment funds are channelled to the local factories and production enterprises through the relevant ministries in Moscow. Since a plant manager's bonus and his job depend on fulfilling the ministry's plan, the needs of the local community have a low priority. The local soviet may propose, but only the separate factory administrations actually dispose of the funds.

The new joint resolution announced three reforms. First, new laws are to be enacted to spell out the rights and duties of local industries and soviets in respect of one another. Second, the degree to which the local soviet's plans are fulfilled will be taken into account in assessing the performance of each factory. And most important, the soviets are to be given the material means and economic leverage they have been lacking. As political reforms go, this is modest enough, but if it works, it could have a disproportionate effect on the way ordinary Russian people live, and on the way they feel about the responsiveness and thus the potential of their local government and soviets.[15]

Perhaps even more striking, in the light of the manifesto's call for more political pluralism, was the appearance in the orthodox Soviet press of well-argued articles that admitted the limitations of Soviet elections, and called for radical improvement.

'As a rule only one candidate is nominated at election meetings,' ran the article in the new section titled 'Our Democracy' in *Literaturnaya Gazeta*. 'Each of us knows that these meetings are often very slow, the discussions very formal, and they arouse no interest among the public.' The article went on to suggest that not one, but several candidates be discussed at nomination meetings, and that even a choice of candidates could be presented on the ballot paper.

'Western propaganda often asserts that a single candidate is a sign of the inevitable excesses of the one-party system', it went on. 'But a one-party system need not preclude a choice among candidates. Why then not change things to ensure that not one, but several candidates be put forward, to give us a chance to pick the best? Not only their positive qualities could be discussed, but also the things that have to be changed. The educational implications of this for our democracy are obvious.'[16]

For the official media, and the weekly organ of the writers' union with a circulation of over 3 million, *Literaturnaya Gazeta* counts as a heavyweight in the Soviet press, this was exploring new and controversial territory. It did, however, give powerful reinforcement to the view that the manifesto accurately reflected the ideas and concerns and reforms being discussed in the top echelons of the Soviet system. *Literaturnaya Gazeta* would never otherwise have published it.

So the link between economic and political reform has not entirely been lost on the Soviet leadership. But that is not the whole point. The real weakness of the argument that says economic and political reform will depend on one another is that an entire dimension of the argument has been lost. Certainly an economic revolution has now been officially launched, and a political revolution is now desperately overdue. But the theme of this book has been that Gorbachev himself, and the generation that has risen with him, embodies a social and cultural revolution that has been under way in the Soviet Union since the Kruschev era. In 1940, on the eve of war, two-thirds of the Soviet population were classed as rural dwellers. Twenty years later, in the Kruschev years, just over half of the population lived in the rural areas. In 1986, the proportion of rural dwellers fell below one third.[17]

It is, in effect, an urban society, and an educated one. And after the long and terrible blood-letting of revolution and civil war and famine and the Nazi invasion, it has had forty years of peace in which to rebuild a social system that is not so very different from that of developed nations in the West. It is tempting to say that the years of peace have produced something approximating to a Western class system, because there is a large and visible middle class, a whole range of prosperous and booming professional classes, and a large and embarrassing gap between the privileged classes and the ordinary working poor. There is a confident and increasingly assertive intelligentsia, and there are the *nouveaux riches*; there are prosperous peasants and free-wheeling blue-collar workers who head for the Siberian oil fields to become wealthy: there is a growing drug problem among alienated young people: there is organised crime and there are booming holiday resorts.

The grim old Soviet shops are being replaced by supermarkets, selling, among other things, pre-cooked TV dinners. Some Moscow streets are becoming pedestrian precincts, and the occasional video-hire shop is opening, reflecting the very much larger black market in

Western movies that has scores of private flats turned into make-shift underground cinemas in the eighties. Increasingly stylish new Soviet cars are appearing on the streets, replacing the old-fashioned box shapes that made Moscow's thickening traffic jams into a kind of time machine, taking one back to the Western designs of the sixties. And the Soviet young people, who are emotionally quite uninvolved in the great events of war and purge and revolution which shaped their elders, look and behave increasingly like their counterparts in the West. They listen to the same music, wear the same jeans and track shoes, and experiment with the same drugs.

This is not the kind of society that Stalin or Kruschev or Brezhnev set out to build, but it is the social mix that has emerged in spite of the Five-Year Plans and the grandiose exhortations to produce a 'New Soviet Man'. The social revolution which has happened in the years of Mikhail Gorbachev's adulthood, and which still goes on, was the unplanned pre-condition of the new mood of reform which Gorbachev has now promised. He is not only a classic example of that social change, but also its beneficiary.

In trying to assess the implications of this, we come up with a thump against the mysteries of the Soviet system. Were this a Western society, we could say (and ironically, we could use Marxist analysis to do it) that the growing economic power of a new social class will eventually be translated into political power. I suspect that is also true, although at a much slower rate, in the Soviet system. But we do not really understand the system well enough to draw a precise relationship between the new social formations of the last forty years and the current shape of political forces. What we can say is that a fundamental change of generations has taken place, that Gorbachev and the men who have risen to power and prominence with him are, with the notable exception of Yegor Ligachev, men who came to maturity after Stalin's time, and whose adulthood has been shaped by the long, slow and still incomplete convalescence from that trauma.

And the question is not simply whether Gorbachev's government can produce an efficient and modernised Soviet economy, in spite of the constraints on political reform that the party will doubtless impose. To put it that way is to fall into the Communist Party's own trap, to assume that the decisions and policies adopted by an authoritarian central government will in and of themselves determine the future course of Soviet society. If the long social revolution which produced the Gorbachev Generation and the complex social system of today tell us anything, it is that a command economy cannot always deliver what was demanded, and that a totalitarian society cannot always produce the social structure that was intended.

This is the wild card in the Soviet pack. Social change has its own momentum and its own logic, quite apart from the decisions taken in the Kremlin, and is steadily transforming Soviet society in its own unpredictable way. The classic example of this is the campaign through which the decisions of a generation of planners and agronomists and party officials to reverse the flow of the Siberian rivers was opposed, and ultimately confounded, by an unprecedented mobilisation of public opinion that finally found in the Kremlin a new and sympathetic leadership.

And it is this, rather than the full panoply of the state and superpower itself, that is 'The Waking Giant' of the title of this book. The book was conceived and begun, I should add, some time before Mikhail Gorbachev achieved power. It had become clear to me, during my first year in Moscow, that there was a sense of energy and change in Soviet society that seemed to be coming from below, rather than from the moribund leadership of Konstantin Chernenko. Many things in the Soviet Union and, indeed, in this book, have changed since the coming of Gorbachev, but the title has remained. The difference now is that the sense of energy and change and possibility that I felt surging in the country has been matched by a similar energy and purpose at the top. This is still a transitional moment. The Giant is stirring, rather than standing. What will happen when it fully awakes remains to be seen. The one thing of which I am sure is that it will.

Postscript

Writing a book about a contemporary political event always runs the risk of being overtaken by events. To write about Gorbachev's Soviet Union is almost a hopeless task. The pace of change is now so fast and so unprecedented that a book is outdated as soon as it is written. But in the broad analysis of the kind of change Gorbachev was trying to bring about, the political and economic priorities he had established, this book holds up reasonably well. To the surprise of most Western experts in Soviet studies, whose familiarity with the stagnant years of Brezhnev had left them with little confidence that any real and fundamental reform was feasible, Gorbachev has announced a commitment to political democracy, legalised small-scale private enterprise, begun to free political prisoners and has dismantled the mechanisms of literary and artistic censorship.

The revolution he promised has certainly begun, and in the spring of 1987, Moscow could lay claim, for the first time since the early 1920s, to being one of the most exciting, innovative and lively cultural centres in the world. In January, at an exhibition hall in the city's Red Guard district, those members of the Artists' Union who had been censored or banned from showing their works for years, were suddenly invited to present their most daring canvases to the public. Day after day, thousands of Muscovites trekked out to the Kashirskaya Metro station to attend the most remarkable art show the city had seen in living memory, as almost every artistic genre the West had explored for decades was made available to a Soviet public all at once. Pop-art jostled with religious primitives, abstract expressionism jarred against conceptualist joke-sculptures, op-art with brutalist realism. There were canvases which cruelly carica-tured the inconography of the Soviet state, its medals and its busts of Lenin, its prison garb and its rockets.[1]

That exhibition was followed by another near the huge Zil automobile plant in Eastern Moscow, where a newly formed group calling themselves the Avantgardists staged a multi-media situationist show. An experimental rock band called Central Russian Hills (a pun which could also be translated as 'average Russian attitudes') played amid the canvases of the rot of the old Roman Empire, which was presented in a way which highlighted the similarities to the decadence of the Soviet empire. One statue, a jackbooted man in a chair with a bathroom shower for a head and a grimy washbasin for a belly, ran through all the rooms. From its anus snaked an endless, excremental trail, a plastic tube some sixty metres long, stuffed with the throwaway packaging of what passed in Moscow for the consumerist society.[2] There were plastic milk cartons, empty toothpaste tubes, packets of porridge and cigarettes and bottles of wine and vodka, copies of TV and theatre guides. It led towards a wall covered with what looked like the usual Soviet portraits of socialist heroes, although carelessly and crudely drawn. But then you looked more closely, and wondered what Colonel Gadafy and Ayatollah Khomeini were doing in the Pantheon with Che Guevara and Karl Marx. There was a scrawled poster at the entrance which read 'Forgive any accidental bad taste in what you see. We are only just winning the right to make mistakes, and learn to choose between the good and bad'.

Meanwhile, at the Satyr theatre, Nicholas Erdman's play *The Suicides* was getting its first performance since being banned in 1930. Slava Spesitsev was running the rehearsals for a play based on Gingiz Aitmatov's controversial new novel of drug addiction and a young man's search for spiritual salvation, *The Executioner's Block*. New studio-theatres were opening to perform experimental drama. Fyodor Burlatsky was working on a new play *1927*, based on Lenin's political testament, which had warned the party against electing Stalin its leader. *Novy Mir* was publishing the text of Mikhail Shatrov's new play *The Brest Peace*, whose main roles included Trotsky, Kamenev, Zinoviev and Bukhanin – victims of Stalin whose role in history had been condemned to silence for fifty years.[3]

After a speech by Mikhail Gorbachev which warned 'There should be no blank spots in our history',[4] the state Encyclopaedia publishing house announced that its new edition of the encyclopaedia of the 1917 Revolution would for the first time contain entries on all of these heroes of the Revolution who fell foul of Stalin. The leading historian Yuri Afanyasev, brother of the editor of *Pravda*, called for 'a full historical re-assessment of Stalin's role in our history'. The editor of *Novy Mir* announced that Pasternak's *Dr Zhivago* would at last be published in the long-suffering land where it was written. And perhaps most striking of all, Anna Akhmatova's *Requiem*, the most powerful poetic statement on Stalin's purges, was published in the March issue of *Oktyabr*.[5]

Banned even when Akhmatova herself was rehabilitated in the 1960s, *Requiem* was a poem of and for the mothers of the purge victims, and it specifically compared their grief to the role of Mary at the crucifixion of Jesus. Akhmatova had begun her career as a poet even before the Revolution, and married the poet Nikolai Gumilev, who was shot by firing squad as a counter-revolutionary in 1921. Her long friendship with the poet Osip Mandelstam ended when he was sent to his death in the camps in 1938. Her own son was also sent to the camps and her poem, written between 1935 and 1940, is a desperately moving lament for an entire generation of Soviet intellectuals who fell victim to Stalin's persecution. It was the time they call the 'Yezhovschina', after Nikolai Yezhov, head of the NKVD secret police until he himself fell victim in 1939. Her preface to the poem begins:

I spent seventeen months in prison queues during the Yezhovschina, and one day, I was picked out. The woman standing behind me, her lips blue, standing with the rigidity we all shared in those times, whispered to me. We all whispered then. She did not know me.

'Can you ever describe this', she asked.

'I can', I replied.

And what might have been a smile appeared on what used to be her face.[6]

But the cultural event which had the most impact was the feature film *Pokayaniye*, 'Repentance', made in Georgia by Tinghiz Abuladze two years earlier. A Fellini-like exploration of the surreal horror of life under a dictatorship, it was intended to have a universal appeal. The villain, Varlam, wore a black shirt like Mussolini, sported a toothbrush moustache like Adolf Hitler, and wore a pince-nez, like Lavrenti Beria, Stalin's most evil henchman. But sequence after sequence in the film left few in the audience in any doubt that the real target was Stalin himself. There were Varlam's balcony speeches, his insistence to visitors who protested at the destruction of a cathedral that he was building 'a paradise on earth', and the awful randomness of his terror. There is one shattering scene where the wives of prisoners haunt the local lumber yard in the hope of seeing a message or just a name carved into the tree trunks by their husbands, working in the distant forestry camps. And there are still Soviet women who remember doing that in Stalin's time. But perhaps the most remarkable feature of the *Pokayaniye* phenomenon was the way it was deliberately encouraged by the state. In Stalin's home republic of Georgia, it was not only shown in every cinema, it was screened on the state TV network. In Moscow, every cinema in the city seemed to be showing it at once, every billboard seemed dominated by advertisements for what became something of a catharsis for Stalinism.

And there were other films being screened, which not only showed how much creative skill had been damped down in the Soviet state, but made other powerful political points of their own. There was *Plumbum*, which attacked one of the most powerful myths of the Stalin era, the glorification of the odious child Pavel Morozov, who informed on his own parents to the secret police. There was Panfilov's sympathetic film about Jewish emigration, *Thema*, made ten years earlier but only now cleared for general release. It won the Golden Bear Prize at the Berlin film festival in 1987. There was Askoldov's remarkable film *Commissar*, of a woman Bolshevik organiser in the civil war who has an illegitimate baby by her lover, and abandons it to the care of the poor and unwilling family on whom she has been billeted. Banned for twenty years, while Askoldov's name was excised from the Soviet film encyclopaedia, it is still a moving and daring film that makes the simple point that the Bolshevik revolutionaries were human, rather than saints.

Even more striking, for its explicit probing of modern Soviet life, was a documentary made in Latvia called *Is It Easy To Be Young*; perhaps the first honest statement of youth alienation. It began with a riot at a rock concert, followed the fate of the teenage vandals through the courts, explored the world of Soviet punks and drug addiction, and then turned to the growing social problem of the Afghan war veterans. It looked at the cripples, learning to live without legs at Army convalescent centres, and at the 'heroes' who refused to wear their medals. The importance of this documentary was that it put into focus one curious feature of the cultural thaw under Gorbachev. So much of it was to do with the Soviet past, opening up the history books, that at times it seemed as if Moscow were in a time machine, reliving the Kruschev thaw. Arguments raged over the same issues, whether or not to publish *Dr Zhivago*, and were led by many of the same people, like the poets Yevtushenko and Andrei Vosnosensky, the angry young men of the sixties who were now twenty-five years older.

In October 1986, Vosnosensky organised a curious evening at the Manezh, the old riding school of the Tsars, just across the street from the Kremlin, that is now the city's main art exhibition hall. Vosnosensky had arranged a rock concert, combined with a poetry reading and a discussion. There was no entry charge, no police control on the doors, and the place was packed when Vosnosensky said that he believed rock musicians were the poets of today, and that all art had a right to be heard and seen so that people could decide which was good and which was bad. He was howled down by an audience of punks and hippies and heavy metal fans, who demanded to know who had given him the right to make artistic judgements. Other hecklers said that Vosnosensky was doing well, writing sycophantic poems for *Pravda*, but what of the other poets of the early sixties who had been sent into exile or imprisoned or crushed by the system. What of them? The generation gap seemed to yawn in the shadow of the Kremlin.[7]

And there were other divisions. When a society too long held down starts to feel its bonds loosening, there is no guarantee that only wholesome things will emerge. Shortly after the Manezh evening, Moscow's heavy metal fans, in their chains and black leather, gathered at a Palace of Culture attached to an electrical factory for a rock concert with the band Ariya. While the band played, the hall was surrounded by gangs of youth toughs, known as *Liuberi*, who proceeded to beat up the fans as they came out. Eventually, the police commandeered buses to drive the battered heavy metal fans away. The *Liuberi* were fiercely patriotic working class kids from the outer suburbs, and bore some striking similarities to the British skinheads who used to hang around the fringes of extreme right-wing groups like the National Front. Known as *Liuberi* from the Moscow satellite town of Liubertsi where the cult began, they went in for body-building, swore off drink and drugs, and loathed the pampered youth of Moscow with their access to Western clothes and cigarettes, their fondness for Western rock music and crazes. These *Liuberi* were officially blamed for the attacks on Jewish demonstrators and Western newsmen in the Old

Arbat shopping street in February, a claim that few of the journal-ists took seriously.[8] But there were teenage thugs among those who taunted and punched the Jewish refuseniks who were demonstrat-ing on behalf of the imprisoned dissident Josef Begun. They shouted anti-Semitic slogans, including 'Hitler did not get enough of you'. A week later, they were back again, fighting students from Moscow University who were holding a demonstration of their own in protest at the 'militarism' of the *Liuberi*.

The fact that this was reported on Moscow Radio, and the *Liuberi* phenomenon explored at great length in the Soviet press, pointed to the very real changes that the *glasnost* policy was making in the way the Soviet public was allowed to perceive the world around them. The concept of openness was being stretched by the journalists themselves, to include open debates on policies that had hitherto taken place behind closed doors. The current affairs weekly *Moskovskii Novosti* published a straightforward argument between the foreign affairs commentator Alexander Bovin and the academic Yevgeny Primakov on whether or not there was any point in negotiating with a US Administration bogged down and dis-credited by Irangate.[9] The press began to explore the nature of the bureaucratic and party opposition to the Gorbachev reforms, most notably by Bovin writing in *Novaya Vremya*, warning, 'we are underestimating the depth and scale of the resistance . . . Twice in my lifetime they have thrown us back, succeeded twice in barring the way to long overdue and urgently needed reforms'. He was referring specifically to the failure of Kruschev's de-Stalinisation campaign in 1956, and to the abortive Kosygin reforms of the 1960s. The opposition, Bovin indentified as 'our homegrown bureaucratic Soviet socialist conservatives'.[10]

Hitherto taboo subjects began to emerge in the press, from homosexuality to prostitution to abortion, and on TV the advent of *glasnost* was even more striking. New discussion programmes, such as *12th floor*, invited Ministers and senior officials to take phone calls from the public. We saw the Minister of Justice agreeing that Soviet laws were out of kilter with the rights guaranteed under the Constitution, and promising that at long last, an official book of Soviet laws would be published for the public to consult. We heard a high official of the Ministry of Education facing a barrage of criticism on the state of Soviet teaching, and replying plaintively, 'Comrades, any society gets the schools it deserves'. On the youth programme *To 16 and Older* we heard young *Liuberi* claiming that the passion for Western clothes and styles and music among trendy young Muscovites reminded them of the eighteenth-century British slavers heading for Africa with cargoes of cheap glass beads and mirrors.

Glasnost had developed its own momentum. If originally it had been conceived as a more palatable and professional way for the party leadership to get its message across to the Soviet public, it had now become something rather different. Perhaps the classic example of the former was the way that *Pravda*, by publishing several stories on the harassment of a Ukrainian journalist, finally succeeded in having the head of the local KGB brought to book. The editor of *Soviet Miner*, who had been working on an exposé of police corruption in the city of Voroshilovgrad, was imprisoned for thirteen days on charges trumped up by the local KGB, his home illegally searched, and an official cover-up began. As *Pravda* began writing about the scandal, the first heads to roll were two low-level procurators, the state's investigating attorneys. But finally in January, in a signed front-page article in *Pravda*, KGB chief Viktor Chebrikov announced that the regional KGB chief had been fired for 'infractions of Soviet legality'. This was clearly a public statement about the role of the KGB which had been approved at the highest levels.[11]

But beyond the news the party wanted people to know, was a new acceptance that the people should be allowed to say and publish things on their own behalf. Throughout the years of Soviet power, the state had insisted on a monopoly over the printed word. In March of 1987, both the Writers' Union (run by Vladimir Karpov) and the State Printing Authority, now run by the reforming former editor of *Sovyetskaya Rossiya* Mikhail Nenashev, agreed to back the establishment of a private printing co-operative.[12] Owned by its shareholders, and facing the commercial risk of bankruptcy, the co-op called *Vest* was in the business of publishing first novels from unknown authors, re-printing books that had long been out of print, and making their own judgements on what books to publish. The venture depended on the support of established writers like Bulat Okudzhava and Fazil Iskander, but the scheme had been devised and was run by a group of young writers.

The official support for the newly-fashionable idea of co-ops made them into a highly visible symbol of the Gorbachev reforms. There was Moscow's first co-op restaurant on Kropotkinska Street, the co-op hairdressers in Tallin, the co-op art gallery in Bitza Park, the Ornament co-op in Moscow's Eletrichesky Street which hired out a range of services from computer specialists to car mechanics, from art consultants to language teachers. Outside the high-priced free markets, the collective farms would send lorries loaded down with fresh fruit and vegetables and sell them direct to the public from the back of a truck at dramatically lower prices. These were important developments, but they remained symbols, isolated examples of the potential of the Gorbachev reforms, rather than any sudden and widespread transformation of the face of Soviet life. The queues remained outside the slovenly state shops, the quality of consumer goods remained pitiful, although at least the press was now openly admitting it, with one remarkable claim that the biggest single cause of fires in the home was the tendency of Soviet-made colour TV sets to explode.[13]

The process of changing the course of a country as vast and as set in its ways as the Soviet Union was never going to be easy. And it was made more difficult by the political problem that Gorbachev faced. He had come to power with a mandate for economic reform, but it was clear from his speeches in his first year in office that this was not going to be enough. Gorbachev kept talking of the need for economic change to be buttressed and guaranteed by changes in cultural and social life, stressing that the economy did not exist in a vacuum. And in the autumn of 1986, this debate within the higher reaches of the party focused upon the single issue of political reforms and democratisation. On 1 October, Soviet TV screened a speech by Mikhail Gorbachev to a conference of social scientists in which he said that 'an acute uncompromising struggle of ideas' was in progress in the Soviet Union. The old ways of doing things were struggling against the need for 'profound and revolutionary changes in Soviet society'.[14]

Gorbachev needed the agreement and support of the party machine for such a dramatic new reform. In particular, he needed the authority of a full plenary meeting of the Central Committee. This plenum was first scheduled to take place in October. When it finally began, the following January, Gorbachev confirmed that it had been postponed three times. Evidently, its themes had been the subject of an intense debate, of which perhaps the first public sign had been the leak to the *Guardian* and NBC in the previous July of the Manifesto for Socialist Renewal. That document had called for choices between candidates and between political programmes at elections, for secret ballots, and had insisted that the Soviet economy and system were in a state of deep crisis which could be resolved by the introduction of radical political reforms.

Gorbachev's speech to the Central Committee echoed that manifesto to a remarkable degree. For the first time, he used the word 'crisis' to define the current state of affairs, and then went on to stretch his mandate for economic reforms into the controversial new area of political change. He called for a choice between candidates at elections to the soviets, the country's regional councils and national parliaments, and for secret ballots at elections of party officials, all the way up to the Politburo. Party members should be able to propose anyone for election, and not be limited to the candidates suggested by the party apparat. 'We need democracy like we need air to breathe,' he said. 'Democratisation is not just a slogan, but the very essence of the national reconstruction we are living through'.[15]

This is not democracy as the West would understand it. 'Socialist democracy has nothing in common with permissiveness, irresponsibility and anarchy. What I have in view is an organic combination of democracy and discipline, of independence and responsibility, of the rights and also the duties of every citizen', he said. And he insisted that this did not mean dismantling the fundamental principle of party control through 'democratic centralism' under which, as he put it, 'decisions taken by the party supreme bodies must be carried out by the rest, even if they do not agree. But with all the importance of control from above, it is of fundamental importance in the conditions of democratisation of society to raise the level and effectiveness of control from below, so that each executive and each official feels his responsibility to and his dependence upon the electorate', he said. 'The main thing is to strengthen all instruments and forms of real control by working people . . . because a house can only be put in order by someone who feels that he owns the place'.[16]

The first real sign of the new system came at the RAF car factory in Latvia, the source of most of the country's minibus vehicles. An old-fashioned design with a poor reputation for reliability and quality, and an apparent inability to produce any spare parts, the plant was a classic example of most that was worst about the Soviet economy in the Brezhnev years. It was decided to hold an open election among the workforce for a new director, and dozens of hopeful candidates applied from all over the country. The final short-list, selected by a group of factory workers and executives, came to the plant and spent three weeks studying the problems, talking to the staff and discussing schemes for renovation and fresh investment. The short-list was whittled down to two men, Sergei Gorbunov, deputy director of an industrial complex in Pskov, and Viktor Bossert, director of a plant in Omsk. It was not all smooth going. There were allegations of arm-twisting from some of the shop floor workers, who complained they were not being allowed to campaign for Gorbunov. But on the whole, it was a remarkably impressive performance, thoroughly covered by the Soviet media.[17]

It was not just this flowering of elections and *glasnost* that gave Moscow in early 1987 a feeling akin to that of the Prague spring of 1968. Some, at least, of the political prisoners began to come home. The process had begun the previous year with the sending abroad of two of the best-known prisoners, Anatoly Scharansky and Yuri Orlov. Then came the tragic death in prison of Anatoly Marchenko and, just in time for the West's Christmas news bulletins, came the release from his exile in Gorky of the Nobel Laureate Dr Andrei Sakharov, after a long phone call from Mikhail Gorbachev. In that conversation, Dr Sakharov had asked the Soviet leader to free those who had been detained under Article 70 of the law, the clause which made 'anti-Soviet agitation and propaganda' into a criminal offence.[18]

Gorbachev's reply came in January, with the announcement of a full-scale judicial review of the cases of nearly three hundred prisoners, and a review of Article 70 itself. It was a confused process, with official Foreign Ministry spokesman Gennady Gerasimov claiming that one hundred and forty prisoners had been released, after giving undertakings not to engage in anti-Soviet activity in future. By contrast, Soviet human rights groups late in March said they could only identify ninety-three such prisoners, and that few of them had given any undertakings at all. One said simply that he had agreed with the procurator before his release from prison that Mr Gorbachev's speeches meant that 'it is now the duty of every Soviet citizen to engage in principled criticism of the Soviet system'.[19]

But the confusion surrounding the releases, and the brutal attacks on the demonstrators demanding the release of Josef Begun in the Moscow shopping street of Old Arbat, and on the Western journalists present, did untold damage to Mr Gorbachev's improving image in the West on the eve of the Soviet Union's biggest propaganda junket for years. The Moscow Peace Forum saw eight hundred Western politicians, film stars, writers and celebrities come to discuss the issues of peace at Soviet expense. The serious purpose behind it all was to spread yet further the message that Mikhail Gorbachev had tried to convey during the Reykjavik summit, that the Soviet Union was now determined to change the very basis of the arguments over disarmament. Rather than continue with the traditional arms control process, which had done little more than regulate the pace at which the numbers of missiles grew, Gorbachev proposed direct and dramatic cuts. He bushwhacked the Reagan negotiators at Reykjavik who had not come at all prepared for the vast and tantalising package that Gorbachev had to offer. He proposed first to accept President Reagan's original 'zero-option' deal on medium range missiles in Europe, the Soviet SS-20s and the US Cruise and Pershings. Secondly, he offered to leave the French and British nuclear forces out of the equation, and not raise the other difficulty about the US forward bases, as the Russians describe the US nuclear airbases in Western Europe. Third, he offered 50 per cent cuts in both US and Soviet strategic arsenals within five years, with an eventual commitment to their total abolition. The price he wanted in return was an American commitment not to stop research into the Strategic Defence Initiative, but to contain it within the tight confines of the laboratory, and not to 'take the arms race into outer space by the deployment of a new generation of weapons'.[20]

The talks at Reykjavik failed, in that they did not produce an agreement. But Gorbachev later claimed, with justice, that they had succeeded in putting the arms race itself, and East–West relations generally, into a remarkable new context. However utopian it may seem, one of the superpowers was insisting on putting full-scale nuclear disarmament on to the international agenda. The Reykjavik proposals put flesh on to his repeated calls for 'new thinking in the nuclear age' and sketched out his own vision of that 'integral and in many ways interdependent world' which he had described in his address to the 27th Party Congress the previous year.

In his long TV address to the Soviet people after the Reykjavik talks, he said that the Soviet proposals had come after an unprecedented process of consultation within the Soviet governing élite, among the military, the academics, the diplomats and the party, and with the Warsaw Pact allies. The debate had covered not simply the small print of the Reykjavik offer, but something more fundamental, the basic ideological concept of the purpose of war. Lenin had defined peaceful co-existence with the capitalist world as a way of buying time to wage the international class struggle by other and more subtle means than straightforward war.

In Brezhnev's last years, an important debate within the ideological élite began to surface in Moscow, whose main thrust was that the coming of nuclear weapons meant that this concept had to be re-thought: that the inevitable threat to all life on the planet in the event of a nuclear exchange meant that war had become unthinkable, that there were now no political objectives that could justify such a war. Its first sign was a highly controversial article in the heavyweight theoretical journal *Voprosy Filosofii* by Georgy Shahnazarov, who was one of Brezhnev's foreign policy aides, and a senior figure in the party secretariat.[21] It read:

> In the nuclear age, war can no longer be considered as a means for achieving political objectives . . . there are no political objectives which could justify the use of means that might lead to nuclear war.

This article was followed by a debate of increasing intensity as the Old Guard and the new thinkers of the Soviet foreign policy establishment argued over what was, after all, one of the key components of Lenin's testament, his interpretation of long-term relations with the capitalist world. Gorbachev made his own sympathies plain enough in his speech to the party congress, but in February of 1987, at an International Peace Forum convened in Moscow, he nailed his colours to the mast. He described the long debate within the Soviet leadership 'before we saw things as they are, and became convinced that new approaches and methods are required for resolving international problems . . . we came to conclusions that made us review something that once seemed axiomatic, since after Hiroshima, war, at least world war, ceased to be the continuation of state policy by other means'. And Gorbachev went on to stress 'this is no one-off adjustment of position, but a new methodology for international affairs . . . military doctrines must in future be purely of a defensive nature'.[22]

The long legacy of Western suspicion, the presence of Soviet troops in Afghanistan and in Eastern Europe, the constant headlines in the Western press on human rights and the plight of Jewish refuseniks combined into a massive burden of doubt that Gorbachev found desperately difficult to overcome. Having turned down his proposals at Reykjavik, the US administration then broke the limits of the SALT-2 agreement limiting strategic nuclear arms, by allowing the expansion of their B-52 bomber fleet armed with Cruise missiles above the levels permitted by the Treaty. Almost simultaneously, the American government challenged that cornerstone of arms agreement, the Anti-Ballistic Missile Treaty of 1972, on which the Soviets were depending to keep the deployment of Star Wars technology under some form of control.

The sense of frustration in Moscow became palpable, as each new Soviet initiative was greeted with renewed Western suspicion. For Gorbachev, who had his own military men and hard-liners to convince of the wisdom of his strategy, the Western lack of response was galling. After eighteen months, and clearly under pressure from his generals, he abandoned his unilateral moratorium on nuclear testing, and began a new series of nuclear explosions at the Semipalatinsk testing grounds.[23]

Gorbachev made yet another concession, offering to accept the original Western proposals of a 'zero option' on medium range missiles in Europe, removing all the Soviet SS-20s in exchange for the US Cruise and Pershing missiles based in Europe. Again the Western doubts lingered, with fears that the Soviet superiority in conventional arms and short range missiles could now become more telling. It became clear that Gorbachev had come to power with a thoughtful strategy on the inter-relation between his domestic reform programme and his foreign policy. He had assumed that his dramatic early reforms on *glasnost* in the press, elections and cultural thaw and human rights, would receive such an enthusiastic response in the West that they would give him a foreign policy success. At best, he had hoped for the kind of breathing space through a new détente that would give him the momentum and the time to push through the hardest part of the internal reform programme, the overhaul of the bureaucracy, the party machine and the economy. And having understood this, the Western leaders were in no mood to help. Indeed, some of them saw it as a way of forcing more concessions from a Soviet leader desperate for their support.

This was not simply a vindictive determination to make Gorbachev pay for the sins of Brezhnev. It was rooted in the tangled history of the détente process of the 1970s. The Soviets reckoned they had kept their part of the bargain, by releasing two hundred and fifty thousand Soviet Jews. The West's hard-liners maintained that the decade of détente had been used to increase Soviet strength while making few domestic changes that could encourage the West to trust the Kremlin in the future. Mr Gorbachev was left in no doubt of the difficulty of convincing Western leaders of his goodwill when Britain's Prime Minister Margaret Thatcher, who had been dubbed 'The Iron Lady' by the Soviet press, arrived in Moscow for a formal visit at the end of March.

In her speech at the Kremlin banquet held in her honour, she was blunt. 'The extent to which you, the Soviet government, meet the commitments which you have freely undertaken in the Helsinki Final Act will determine how far other countries will have confidence in your promises on arms control', she said. 'The Soviet Union's readiness to withdraw its armies from Afghanistan with the shortest possible delay will have a crucial part not only in the future of Afghanistan, but also in deciding how others see you, and whether they trust or fear you, and make their plans accordingly'.[24]

In short, whatever promise there might be in the Gorbachev reforms, the Soviet Union was still on probation. Ironically, on the day that Mrs Thatcher had arrived in Moscow, the leader of the World Jewish Congress, Mr Charles Bronfman, had been promised that some eleven thousand Soviet Jewish refuseniks would be granted exit visas in the course of the year. And while Mrs Thatcher was in Moscow, she received some personal knowledge of the new policies on human rights, lunching with the most eminent dissident of them all, Academician Dr Andrei Sakharov, and taking breakfast with Mr Josef Begun, who had been released from his prison camp only a month before.

The Western pressure was paying off. At least, that is how it seemed to Mrs Thatcher and to the Reagan White House, which was wondering how many more concessions might be squeezed from Mr Gorbachev before arranging a new US–Soviet summit in Washington. The question remained, how stiff a price domestically was Mikhail Gorbachev having to pay for these concessions? After two years in power in the Kremlin, and having caught the world's imagination as a new and inspiring breed of Soviet leader, Mr Gorbachev was discovering the limits of power. The economy was not responding as it should. The crisis in the oil and coal and gas industries, trying to exploit new reserves from ever more remote areas at a steadily-increasing cost, had been exacerbated by the disaster of Chernobyl and its implications for the Soviet nuclear power programme. The programme was not stopped, but it was delayed as new safety technologies had to be inserted into the RBMK power stations of the Chernobyl type. The establishment of a new independent quality control system to check the output of Soviet factories was essential in the long term. But in the short run, it had a devastating effect on worker morale and on the production statistics. Gorbachev himself admitted that the dislocations had been so bad at some factories that there had been 'work stoppages', which sounded like a euphemism for strikes, as the workers saw their pay packets halved when their bonus payments were stopped.[25] But the appalling quality of Soviet goods was emphasised by a report in *Izvestia* on the proportions of output rejected as unfit in a series of factories around the country. In the factories of Uzbekistan, 73.8% of goods were rejected, and 71% in Kirghizia, and 69.4% in Moldavia.[26]

'Our national growth rates for the past few years would have been much lower if we took the quality of the goods produced into account', conceded Professor Vladimir Kostakhov, the deputy head of research at Gosplan, the central planning board. 'This is part of a general problem with our statistics. We do not have enough data even on how we produce our statistics. There is not enough data on production. Frankly, we often do not know what we produce in the Soviet economy. Generally, we are not satisfied with the statistics we have, and on which we rely'.[27]

This was not just a devastating admission of the feebleness of real control over the Soviet economy by the very organisation that was meant to plan it, it also pointed to the enormous task that lay ahead of Gorbachev and his reforming administrators. And there were increasing signs that many of the administrators at his disposal were less than keen on his ideas. In speech after speech, he warned of bureaucrats 'who cannot learn to work in the new way'. In his speech to the January plenum, he warned of the 'red tape and irresponsibility in the work of ministries and departments which carry out the party and government resolutions. The staff of ministries and departments appears to be a captive of old regulations and instructions, acts by inertia and refuses to give up its prerogatives'.[28] The main message of that January plenum was that the party itself needed a thorough reform, an infusion of new blood into its hierarchy through secret ballots and open nominations for candidacies to party positions. The real extent of the party's internal problems became dramatically apparent just before Christmas, when one of Brezhnev's last cronies on the Politburo,

Dinmukhamed Kunayev, was toppled from his perch as party chief of the southern Republic of Kazakhstan. In part because of the difficulty of finding a Kazakh replacement from a local party that had been thoroughly re-shaped to Kunayev's will, and partly because the Russian population of the Republic slightly outnumbered the native Kazakhs, he was replaced by Moscow's own choice, a middle-aged Russian of Gorbachev's own generation, Gennady Kolbin.

The Kazakh capital of Alma-Ata erupted into riots that killed at least two people, saw dozens of injuries, mass arrests and shops looted. The police were attacked and cars set on fire. The university and several academic institutes were barricaded, as students and Kazakhs took the streets 'incited by nationalist elements', in the words of the official TASS news agency.[29] This challenge to Moscow's authority was given some tacit support by the local party hierarchy, which had good cause to fear the inevitable purge of the new man from Moscow. Kazakhstan had become corrupt under Kunayev, with the tight-knit tribal system of the Kazakh clans breeding nepotism within the party.

Within a month of taking over, Gennady Kolbin gave a press conference to the Soviet press in which he claimed that up to 30 per cent of the Republic's food supplies, and four out of five new flats built in Alma-Ata, were being creamed off by the local party élite for their personal use or for families and friends.[30] The familiar tales of Soviet corruption, of private hunting lodges and lavish domestic staffs appeared again in the press, exposed at last when it was safe to do so. But the Kazakh riots had other and deeper roots, in a traditional nationalism that Moscow had too long ignored or misunderstood. It was a warning to Mikhail Gorbachev not only of the rot within the party, but of the fragility of the bonds which held the world's largest multi-racial state together. It also reminded many observers, Soviet and Western alike, of the old saw which claims that an authoritarian state is at its most vulnerable when the controls begin to be relaxed. If the Gorbachev reforms unsettled the party bureaucracy in Moscow, it sent alarming tremors into the various reaches of Moscow's empire, into the traditionally Muslim Republics of the Soviet south, and into an eastern Europe where the local party bosses had spent years repressing people for saying the kind of things that Mikhail Gorbachev was now urging in Moscow.

A desperate amount of responsibility hung on the lonely shoulders of Gorbachev. The leader of the Argentine Communist

Party talked to him in the Kremlin, and came out to tell a waiting press conference that Gorbachev had confided his fears that a new cult of personality was coalescing around him, that he had to struggle against attempts to deify him. 'I am not a God', he told his guest.[31] And by refusing to allow the Soviet press to acknowledge his birthday, or the anniversary of his accession to power, he tried to keep the old adulation at bay. Steadily, but still slowly enough to emphasise the limits to his power, he brought his own men into the highest ranks. Alexander Yakovlev, the US-educated propaganda chief, became a candidate member of the Politburo, alongside the energetic new Moscow party chief Boris Yeltsin. His old colleague Georgy Razumovsky, and his former Moscow University law school classmate Anatoly Lukyanov were promoted to secretarial rank in the central committee, which was clearly emerging as Gorbachev's chosen instrument of executive authority. But the obstacles to change were daunting. The delays in convening the January plenum were one sign, and Gorbachev's call for an extra-ordinary party conference was another. Such a conference could give Gorbachev the opportunity to push through the changes in the party rule book that had eluded him at the 27th Party Congress, and to give full legal backing to the party reforms he demanded in his speeches. It was the permanent structure of Soviet society that Gorbachev wanted to change, not simply to introduce spasmodic changes by personal fiat. The frankness with which he viewed and condemned so much of the Soviet past, and the passion he brought to the strategy of change, suggested that the Soviet Union might have produced its most impressive leader since Lenin. Certainly he shared with Lenin a fundamental sense of idealism about socialism as a doctrine, and as a vehicle for the improvement of mankind. Gorbachev remained a believer, in spite of the repressions of Stalin and the rot of the Brezhnev years. Western politicians who said glibly that the Gorbachev reforms were bringing capitalism back to the Soviet Union were quite wrong. His goal was to perfect social-ism, not to dismantle it.

But this involved some highly creative reinterpretations of what socialism actually meant. At the crucial Central Committee plenum in June, which voted for the introduction of NEM (the New Economic Mechanism), Gorbachev stressed, 'There should be no upper limit on the amount of money an honest Soviet worker is allowed to earn.'[32] The main thrust of the NEM, according to Gorbachev's economic adviser Professor Abel Aganbegyan, was to leave 70 per cent of the Soviet economy free of state interference or control over the next four years. The state's direct role in the economy was to be limited to the defence sector, to strategic goods like oil and gas and gold, and to specific contracts the state would make with industry. But the rest, which Aganbegyan estimated at 70 per cent of GDP, would be made up of factories, farmers and consumers trading freely among themselves, while the once-all-powerful State Planning Board would be reduced to a strategic role.[33]

The NEM immediately invited comparison with Lenin's New Economic Policy, a return to small-scale private enterprise to help the country recover from the ravages of revolution and civil war. But the Gorbachev economic reforms went further. In a major speech in the Arctic city of Murmansk in October 1987, Gorbachev warned the Soviet people that the state could no longer afford to subsidise food prices at a cost of 9,000 million roubles a month, and that prices were going to have to rise sharply.[34] At the same time, Gospriemka, the new state quality control board, was squeezing the take-home pay of Soviet workers by rejecting goods as they came off the factory production lines. That meant that plan targets were not met, and consequently the usual wage bonuses were not paid.

'You need to understand who gains from these reforms, and who loses', commented Tatyana Zaslavskaya, the most influential female economist in the country. 'The losers are those who cannot increase their output, the elderly, the badly educated, the passive in spirit. But the young, the educated and the energetic people gain – the active people in the society.'[35]

Gorbachev stressed repeatedly that there was no alternative to the NEM, but was clearly aware of the political risks he was running, promising at the June plenum that there would be no deliberate policy of unemployment, and stressing in Murmansk that price rises would come only after public consultation. His position was strengthened in the autumn by the first clear success for his diplomatic policy, the agreement reached in Washington in September 1987 to remove all medium- and shorter-range nuclear missiles from Europe. It was the first substantive achievement of his 'new thinking for the nuclear age', and it paved the way to a summit meeting with President Reagan.

On the eve of the 70th anniversary of the 1917 Revolution, Gorbachev could claim that the main components of his reforms were in place. But difficulties loomed ahead. Although the process of de-Stalinisation had gone so far that the magazine *Ogonyok* was able to print the Ministry of Defence's own list of the victims of Stalin's purges in the officer corps, the effective number two in the Politburo, Yegor Ligachev, publicly complained at the way *glasnost* was being used to stress 'the negative aspects of our past'.[36] When Dr Yuri Afanasiev opened his Institute of State Archives to a series of public lectures on Stalin, at which long-secret supreme court documents on the purges were read aloud, he came under attack from orthodox historians. But if the campaign to unlock the secrets of the Soviet past found increasing resistance to looking at the purges of the 1930s, they found fascinating new areas to probe.[37] In October, Mikhail Shatrov's new play *On and On and On* went into rehearsal at the Moscow Arts Theatre, with the actress playing the role of Rosa Luxemburg reading these lines from the most prestigious stage in Soviet theatre: 'Without general elections, without unrestricted freedom of press and assembly, without a free struggle of opinion, life dies out in every public institution, in which only the bureaucracy survives ... we can go further. Such conditions must cause a brutalisation of public life.'[38]

Shatrov's play examined events around the 10th Party Congress, held in March 1921, when the Red Army was crushing the sailors' uprising at Kronstadt and a huge peasants' revolt in Tambov. That was the party congress which introduced NEP, and which also banned faction within the party. For most Western historians, this was the moment that free debate died out within the party. But suddenly this was the period that had begun to fascinate the Soviet intelligentsia. The September issue of *Novy Mir* carried a novel about one of the survivors of Kronstadt, and the October issue of *Yunost* published the long-banned novel of Elizaveta Drabkina, titled simply *Kronstadt*, an agonising reappraisal of the way the Bolsheviks had turned on the very revolutionary sailors who had put them into power in 1917.[39] And Fyodor Burlatsky was completing his new play, *1927*, about the party congress at which Stalin consolidated his dictatorial grip. The cutting edge of de-Stalinisation was shifting from the familiar ground of what Stalin had actually done in the 1930s to the events of the 1920s which allowed him to seize power in the first place. This was much less known territory, and far more intriguing, because it began to raise the question of Lenin's own responsibility for the nightmare which was to overtake the country under Stalin.

But even as the intelligentsia plunged into these debates, and flocked to the first-ever exhibition of Marc Chagall's paintings, and to the Hermitage Group's exhibition of the banned Soviet modern art of the 1970s in their new premises on Profsoyuznaya Street, there was an uncertain, even a fearful mood developing. It was expressed best by the Ukrainian writer, Vladimir Drozd, writing in *Literaturnaya Gazeta*: 'You have to understand my fear, fear for myself and for my family. For we all feel behind us the hot breath and the narrowed wolfish eyes of those who do not want *Perestroika* ... they get together in the evenings and late at night, cursing everything new that has already come or is coming into our life. Our every mistake or miscalculation, and even natural disasters please them to an incredible extent.

'"See what your reforms lead to," they sneer. I will go further. They take note of all of us who today speak in favour of our social reformation, and they make lists of our names, to be used when their time comes.'[40]

The growing alarm among even Gorbachev's most passionate supporters stemmed from their realisation that the eventual benefits of his economic and political reforms would take years to achieve, and those years would see increasing political risks as price rises and industrial dislocation and redeployment tested the patience of the Soviet working class.

But the long legacy of Soviet history was perhaps his greatest problem. His economic programme depended on the Soviet people rediscovering an initiative and creativity that had been carefully repressed for the seven decades of Soviet power. His political reforms depended upon the flowering of a sense of personal responsibility and civic duty that had been officially discouraged since Lenin's death. Like all revolutions, his *Perestroika* was a gigantic step into the unknown, a great risk that depended, at root, upon a gamble that the Soviet people had themselves developed and matured and been educated into a readiness for the course on which he had embarked. In its implications for the Soviet Union, and for the rest of us, Gorbachev's revolution promises to be as profound, and may yet prove as dramatic, as that astonishing year of 1917.

Martin Walker, Moscow, November 1987.

Notes

Introduction (*pages xi–xxix*)

1. *Sunday Times*, London, 16 June 1985.
2. *Guardian*, London, 29 May 1985.
3. *Vremya*, Soviet television news, 16 May 1985.
4. R. Gorbacheva, 'Emergence of new characteristics in the daily lives of the collective farm peasantry'. Thesis submitted to the V. I. Lenin Pedagogical Institute in Moscow, under supervision of G. V. Osipov, 1967.
5. Geoffrey Hosking, *A History of the Soviet Union*, page 415, Fontana, London, 1985.
6. See also *Social Sciences*, Vol. XVII, No. 1, 1986, pages 174*ff*., Academy of Sciences, Moscow.
7. See Roy Medvedev, *Let History Judge*, Spokesman, London, 1976; Anton Antonov-Ovseyenko, *The Time of Stalin*, Harper and Row, New York, 1981; Alexander Solzhenitsyn, *The Gulag Archipelago*, Fontana, London, 1975.
8. *Narodnoye Khozyaistvo SSSR*, 1983 and 1984, Tsnentralnoye Statisticheskoe Upravleniye, Moscow, 1984, 1985. See also *The USSR in Figures for 1984*, page 79, Finansy i Statistika Publishers, Moscow, 1985.
9. *The USSR in Figures for 1984*, page 252.
10. *Pravda*, 12 February 1986.
11. *Pravda*, 26 February 1986.
12. *Izvestia*, 3 October 1985.
13. *Literaturnaya Gazeta*, 15 May 1985.
14. Author's observation.
15. *Trud*, 4 April 1986.

1: The Rise of Mikhail Gorbachev (*pages 1–23*)

1. Alec Nove, *An Economic History of the USSR*, pages 174*ff*., Pelican, London, 1982 (revised edition).
2. Yuri Moshkov, *Zernovaya problema v gody sploshnoi kollektivatsii*, page 215, Moscow University, 1966.
3. Nove, *An Economic History*, page 180.
4. Official biography of Mikhail Gorbachev, introduction to *A Time*

for Peace. Speeches by M. Gorbachev, Richardson and Steirman, New York, 1986.

5. *Stavropolskaya Pravda*, 6 February 1979.

6. Y. Zaitsev and A. Poltorak, *The Soviet Bar*, pages 52*ff.*, Foreign Languages Publishing House, Moscow, 1959.

7. For Mlynar's account of his student days with Gorbachev, see *L'Unita*, Rome, 9 April 1985.

8. Ed. V. Tarras, *Handbook of Russian Literature*, page 469, Yale University Press, 1985.

9. Personal accounts to author. See also *Guardian*, London, 17, 18 and 19 February 1986.

10. See Archie Brown, 'Gorbachev, new man in the Kremlin', in *Problems of Communism*, May–June 1985, USIA.

11. Nove, *An Economic History*, page 333.

12. Nove, *An Economic History*, page 365.

13. *The Road to Communism, Documents of the 22nd Party Congress*, page 625, Foreign Languages Publishing House, Moscow, 1962.

14. *The Road to Communism*, page 589.

15. Brown, 'Gorbachev, new man in the Kremlin'.

16. Brown, 'Gorbachev, new man in the Kremlin'. See also Christian Schmidt-Hauer, *Gorbachev, The Path to Power*, pages 59*ff.*, I. B. Tauris, London, 1986; Zhores Medvedev, *Gorbachev*, pages 60*ff.*, Blackwell, Oxford, 1986.

17. Official biography of Mikhail Gorbachev.

18. Official biography of Mikhail Gorbachev.

19. *Izvestia*, 10 February 1983.

20. *Ekonomicheskaya Gazeta*, supplement No. 9, 1978, page 1.

21. Byrne, Cole, Bickerton and Malish, 'US–USSR Grain Trade'. Paper submitted to the Joint Economic Committee of the US Congress for *Soviet Economy in the 1980s; Problems and Prospects*, 2 Vols., US Government Printing Office, Washington DC, 1983. See Vol. 2, pages 60*ff.*

22. Anton Malish, 'The Food Program: a new policy or more rhetoric?' Paper submitted to US Congress for *Soviet Economy in the 1980s*, Vol. 2, pages 41*ff.*

23. Brown, 'Gorbachev, new man in the Kremlin'. But see also Zhores Medvedev, *Gorbachev*, page 109, for a slightly different view.

24. *Literaturnaya Gazeta*, 10 April 1985.

25. Author's interviews. Lithuania, 1984. Crimea, Georgia and Latvia, 1985.

26. Author's interview. Lithuania, 1984.

2: The New Generation of the Party Leadership (*pages 24–37*)

1. *Velikaya Otechestvennaya Voyina, 1941–5*, page 750. *Sovyetskaya Entsiklopediya*, Moscow, 1985.

2. *Velikaya Otechestvennaya Voyina, 1941–5*, page 387.

3. *Velikaya Otechestvennaya Voyina, 1941–5*, page 224.

4. See Archie Brown, 'Leadership Succession and Policy Innovation', in *Soviet Policy for the 1980s*, pages 232–5, Macmillan, London, 1982.

5. Interview with V. Afanyasev, *Pravda* editor, 9 October 1984, Asahi Shimbun, Tokyo.

6. A. G. Rahr, *Biographic Directory of 100 Leading Soviet Officials*, pages 9–10, Central Research, Radio Liberty, Munich, August 1984.

7. Press conference given by G. Aliev, Moscow, 27 February 1986.

8. Vladimir Solovyov and Elena Klepikova, *Yuri Andropov, A Secret Passage into the Kremlin*, pages 192–3, Hale, London, 1984.

9. Rahr, *Biographic Directory*, pages 52–3.

10. Solovyov and Klepikova, *Yuri Andropov*, pages 100–21.

11. Solovyov and Klepikova, *Yuri Andropov*, pages 82*ff*.

12. Christian Schmidt-Hauer, *Gorbachev, The Path to Power*, page 98, I. B. Tauris, London, 1986.

13. Private information to author from central committee source. See also Zhores Medvedev, *Gorbachev*, page 146, Blackwell, Oxford, 1986.

14. Zhores Medvedev, *Gorbachev*, page 146.

15. Interview with V. Afanyasev, 9 October 1984, Asahi Shimbun.

16. *Kommunist*, No. 3, February 1984.

17. Michel Tatu, *Le Pouvoir en URSS*, page 551, Editions Bernard Grasset, Paris, 1967.

18. Private information to author from Tomsk party source.

19. Private information to author from Uralmash source.

20. *Prava*, 6 March 1986.

21. Henri Troyat, *Ivan le Terrible*, pages 128–9, Librairie Flammarion, Paris, 1982.

22. *Pravda*, 11 December 1984.

3: The Economic Experiment (*pages 38–52*)

1. Geoffrey Hosking, *A History of the Soviet Union*, pages 363–4, Fontana, London, 1985.

2. Hosking, *A History of the Soviet Union*.

3. David Lane, *Soviet Economy and Society*, pages 15–16, Blackwell, Oxford, 1985.

4. Lane, *Soviet Economy and Society*; and author's interviews, Strume factory, Riga, 1985, and Bratsk factory complexes, Irkutsk Oblast, 1985.

5. Author's interviews. See also *Izvestia*, 20 July 1985.

6. Hosking, *A History of the Soviet Union*, pages 389–90.

7. *Pravda*, 28 March 1977.

8. *Sotsialistichiski Trud*, No. 1, 1983.

9. Author's interviews, Zil factory, January 1986. See also *Guardian*, London, 22 January 1986.

10. *Pravda*, 20 May 1985. Article by V. Parfenov.

11. Author's interviews, Vilnius, 1984.

12. See P. Hanson, 'Success Indicators Revisited' in *Soviet Studies*, Vol. 35, No. 1, January 1983; and *Pravda*, 29 August 1979.

13. Author's interviews, Ust-Ilimsk, 1985.

Notes

14. Author's interview with Nina Romanovna Zima, Ust-Ilimsk party secretary, 1985.

15. For the Liberman debate, see *Pravda*, 9 September 1962; *Pravda*, 17 August 1964, article by Academician Trapeznikov; and *Pravda* editorials for 12 October 1964 and 13 January 1965.

16. *Pravda*, 27 December 1980. See also *Sovietskaya Kultura*, 4 January 1986, article by Professor Vladimir Kostakov.

17. George G. Halliday, 'Western Technology Transfer to the Soviet Union'. Paper submitted to US Congress for *Soviet Economy in the 1980s: Problems and Prospects*, Vol. 1, page 523. US Government Printing Office, Washington, 1983.

18. *Ekonomicheskaya Gazeta*, No. 45, November 1980.

19. P. Hanson, 'Success Indicators Revisited', pages 10–11.

20. A full English translation of the report is printed in *Survey*, Vol. 28, No. 1, 1984, together with an expert commentary by P. Hanson.

21. See note 20.

22. M. S. Gorbachev, *Political Report of the CPSU Central Committee to the 27th Congress of the CPSU*, 25 February 1986, page 43, Novosti, Moscow, 1986.

23. Author's interview with Professor Oleg Bogomolov, Moscow, 1986. See also *Guardian*, 19 February 1986.

24. Gorbachev, *Political Report*, page 15.

25. Gorbachev, *Political Report*, page 40.

26. Gorbachev, *Political Report*, page 40.

27. Gorbachev, *Political Report*, page 36.

28. Gorbachev, *Political Report*, page 51.

29. Gorbachev, *Political Report*, page 45.

30. Gorbachev, *Political Report*, page 27.

4: The Technology Revolution (*pages 53–68*)

1. *SSRV v Tsifrakh (v 1984 godu)*, pages 70*ff.*, Finansy i Statistika, Moscow, 1985.

2. Marshall I. Goldman, *USSR in Crisis*, pages 122*ff.*, W. W. Norton, New York, 1983.

3. *Guardian*, London, 12 July 1985.

4. *Guardian*, 12 July 1985; and personal interviews with TASS photographers.

5. See *Soviet Military Power*, 110–3; US Department of Defense, 1986,

6. *Soviet Military Power*, 110–3; and Michael Alexeyev, *Military Expenditures and the Soviet Economy*, Radio Liberty Research, RL 120/85, Munich.

7. *Sotsialistichiskaya Industria*, 28 March 1986.

8. *Pravda*, 11 December 1984.

9. *Pravda*, 11 December 1984.

10. See *Business Week*, 11 November 1985.

11. Author's observation.

12. *Business Week*, 11 November 1985.

13. Author's observation.

14. Author's observation.
15. Author's observation.
16. Author's observation.
17. Martin Cave, *Computers and Economic Planning: the Soviet Experience, passim,* Cambridge University Press, 1980; *Soviet Economy in a Time of Change,* pages 524–51, Joint Economic Committee of US Congress, Washington, 1979; and eds. R. Amman and J. Cooper, *Industrial Innovation in the Soviet Union,* pages 212–41, Yale University Press, New Haven, 1982.
18. Eds. Amman and Cooper, *Industrial Innovation,* page 218. See also, for an account of the Lysenko tragedy, ed. H. Salisbury, *Anatomy of the Soviet Union,* pages 276–98, *New York Times,* New York, 1967.
19. M. S. Gorbachev, *Political Report of the CPSU Central Committee to the 27th Party Congress of the CPSU, 25 February 1986,* page 48, Novosti, Moscow, 1986.
20. Eds. Amman and Cooper, *Industrial Innovation,* page 235.
21. Eds. Amman and Cooper, *Industrial Innovation,* page 227; *Business Week,* 11 November, 1985; and author's interviews with Gosplan, February 1986.
22. Eds. Amman and Cooper, *Industrial Innovation,* page 231.
23. *Pravda,* 26 November 1985.
24. See, for example, *Ekonomicheskaya Gazeta,* No. 16, 1985, report on the central committee colloquium; and *Pravda,* 13 July 1985, article by Professor A. Aganbegyan.
25. Gorbachev, *Political Report,* page 40.
26. *Economist,* London, 30 May 1981.
27. *US News and World Report,* 1 October 1984. See also *L'Expansion,* Paris, September 1985.
28. Gorbachev, *Political Report,* page 32.
29. Gorbachev, *Political Report,* page 32.
30. Quoted in *Business Week,* 11 November 1985.

5: Why the Time is Right *(pages 69–84)*

1. *SSSR v Tsifrakh (v 1984 godu),* pages 67 and 70–9, Finansy i Statistika, Moscow, 1985.
2. Even before he became general secretary. See, e.g, *Pravda,* 11 December 1984.
3. 'Along with the arms race being forced on us, the biggest of our objective difficulties.' M. S. Gorbachev, interview with *L'Humanité,* Paris, 8 February 1986.
4. Alexander Guber, *Intensified Economy and Progress in Science and Technology,* page 5, Novosti, Moscow, 1985.
5. *Guardian,* London, 20 April 1985.
6. Alec Nove, *An Economic History of the USSR,* page 333, Pelican, London, 1982 (revised edition).
7. J. C. Dewey, *USSR in Maps,* page 46, Hodder and Stoughton, London, 1982.
8. Ed. A. Hewett, 'Near-term prospects for the Soviet natural gas

industry, and implications for east–west trade'. Paper submitted to US Congress for *Soviet Economy in the 1980s: Problems and Prospects*, Vol. 1, page 394. US Government Printing Office, Washington, 1983.

9. *SSSR v Tsifrakh*, pages 112*ff*.

10. *SSSR v Tsifrakh*, pages 56–7.

11. *Information Moscow*, autumn–winter 1985, published by V. and J. Louis.

12. *SSSR v Tsifrakh*, pages 222–3.

13. Author's interviews. See also David Lane, *Soviet Economy and Society*, pages 178–80, Blackwell, Oxford, 1985.

14. *SSSR v Tsifrakh*, page 216.

15. *SSSR v Tsifrakh*, page 224.

16. *Pravda*, 9 November 1985.

17. Thane Gustafson, 'Soviet Energy Policy'. Paper presented to US Congress for *Soviet Economy in the 1980s*, Vol. 1, page 440.

18. *Sovyetskaya Rossiya*, 16 April and 16 May 1985.

19. Hewett, 'Near-term prospects . . .' in *Soviet Economy in the 1980s*, Vol. 1, page 401.

20. Hewett, page 402.

21. Hewett, pages 404 and 451; and *Pravda*, 11 August 1981.

22. Hewett, page 407.

23. Author's interviews with holidaying oil and Arctic workers, Black Sea coast, 1985.

6: The Party and the Twenty-seventh Party Congress (*pages 85–101*)

1. *Yezhegodnik SSSR–86*, page 89, Novosti, Moscow, 1986.

2. *The CPSU: Stages of History*, page 86, Novosti, Moscow, 1986 (revised edition).

3. Ed. E. Crankshaw, *Khrushchev Remembers*, pages 64–70, Little Brown, Boston, 1970.

4. *The CPSU: Stages of History*, page 86.

5. *Kommunist*, No. 9, 1985.

6. *Sovyetskaya Kultura*, 6 February 1986.

7. *Pravda*, 14 July 1985; and *Pravda Vostoka*, 23 January and 1 February 1986.

, 9. *Kommunist*, No. 11, 1985.

10. *Rules of the CPSU*, page 40, Novosti, Moscow, 1986.

11. *The CPSU: Stages of History*, pages 93*ff*.

12. *The CPSU; Stages of History*, page 105.

13. T. H. Rigby, *Communist Party Membership*, page 386, Princeton, 1967; see also Bohdan Harasymiw, *Political Elite Recruitment in the Soviet Union*, page 119, St Antony's/Macmillan, London and Oxford, 1984.

14. *Selskaya Zhizn*, 17 June 1985.

15. See Michael Voslensky, *Nomenklatura*, *passim*, Bodley Head, London, 1984.

16. Voslensky, *Nomenklatura*; but see also Harasymiw, *Political Elite Recruitment*.

17. *Sovyetskaya Rossiya*, 19 April 1985.
18. *Pravda*, 5 April 1983.
19. *Sovyetskaya Rossiya*, 14 June 1985.
20. *The Road to Communism, 22nd Congress of the CPSU*, pages 502–8, *passim,* Foreign Languages Publishing House, Moscow.
21. *The Old Bolshevik, Bratsk Station*, Yunost, Moscow, 1965.
22. Author's interview, February 1986.
23. *Literaturnaya Gazeta*, 9 April 1986.
24. *Rules of the CPSU*, page 13, Novosti, Moscow, 1986.
25. *Rules of the CPSU*, page 17.
26. *Rules of the CPSU*, note 2b, page 10.
27. *Rules of the CPSU*, rule 58, page 33.
28. *Rules of the CPSU*, rule 28, page 19.
29. See analysis by Michel Tatu in *Le Monde*, Paris, 10 March 1986.
30. Tatu, *Le Monde*, 10 March 1986.
31. *Pravda*, 27 February 1986.

7: Foreign Policy: No More Need to Bluff (*pages 102–23*)

1. Ed. G. Segal, *The Soviet Union in East Asia: Predicaments of Power*, page 9, Heinemann, London, 1983.
2. George Vernadsky, *A History of Russia*, pages 67*ff.*, Yale University Press, New Haven, 1961.
3. Vernadsky, *A History of Russia*, pages 61*ff.*
4. Geoffrey Hosking, *A History of the Soviet Union*, pages 104*ff.*, Fontana, London, 1985; see also Bernard Pares, *A History of Russia*, pages 501*ff.*, Methuen, London, 1955 (revised edition).
5. W. S. Churchill, *Collected Speeches*, page 107,, Hodder and Stoughton, London, 1965.
6. See, for example, *Soviet Military Power*, 1985, chapter 7, 'Global Ambitions', *passim*, US Department of Defense, Washington DC.
7. *Pravda*, 27 April 1986.
8. The most sober and balanced assessment of Soviet demographic trends is available in Ann Hegelson, 'Demographic Policy', in eds. Brown and Kaser, *Soviet Policy for the 1980s*, pages 118*ff.*, St Antony's, Oxford, 1982. See also *Soviet Economy in the 1980s: Problems and Prospects*, Vol. 1, pages 265–322, US Government Printing Office, Washington DC, 1983.
9. Martin Walker, *Powers of the Press*, appendix (each paper's coverage of Iran), page 374, Quartet, London, 1982.
10. Hugh Seton-Watson, *The Russian Empire*, page 61, Clarendon Press, Oxford, 1967.
11. Albert Seaton, *Horsemen of the Steppes*, pages 159*ff.*, Bodley Head, London, 1985.
12. Seton-Watson, *The Russian Empire*, page 442.
13. M. S. Gorbachev, *Political Report of the CPSU Central Committee to the 27th Party Congress of the CPSU, 25 February 1986*, page 13, Novosti, Moscow, 1986.

Notes

14. Marshall I. Goldman, *USSR in Crisis*, page 126, W. W. Norton, New York, 1983.
15. Cited in A. Cockburn, *The Threat*, page 247, Hutchinson, London, 1983.
16. *Velikaya Otechestvennaya Voyina, 1941–5*, page 215, *Sovyetskaya Entsiklopediya*, Moscow, 1985.
17. *Soviet Military Power*, 1985, page 107, US Department of Defense, Washington DC.
18. *Morskoy Sbornik*, Ministry of Defence, Moscow, 1971.
19. *Guardian*, London, 12 December 1985.
20. *Soviet Military Power*, 1985, page 107.
21. *Guardian*, 16 April 1986.
22. *Guardian*, 12 December 1985.
23. See Brown, *Problems of Communism*, USIA, Washington DC; Gromyko's official biography; and *Knizhka Partiinovo Aktivista*, page 12, Politizdat, Moscow, 1984. The best single modern study of Gromyko's foreign policy is to be found in *World Power, Soviet Foreign Policy under Brezhnev and Andropov*, by my *Guardian* colleague Jonathan Steele, Michael Joseph, London, 1982.
24. Private information to the author from Soviet foreign ministry source.
25. Private information to author from British, Indian and US diplomatic sources.
26. A. Gromyko and V. Lomeiko, *Novoye Mishlenniye v Yadernyi Vek*, Mezhdunarodniye Otnosheniye, Moscow, 1984.
27. Christian Schmidt-Hauer, *Gorbachev, The Path to Power*, page 105, I. B. Tauris, London, 1986.
28. Schmidt-Hauer, *Gorbachev*, page 104.
29. Schmidt-Hauer, *Gorbachev*, page 146.
30. Schmidt-Hauer, *Gorbachev*, page 146.
31. See, for example, *Mezhdunarodnaya Zhizn*, Vol. 12, 1985, pages 108*ff.*, and Vol. 2, 1986, pages 57*ff.*, Obshchestvo Znaniye, Moscow.
32. *Pravda*, 8 April 1985.
33. *Literaturnaya Gazeta*, 26 June 1985.
34. See *Guardian*, 24 July 1985 and 4 March 1986.
35. *Guardian*, 10 June 1986.
36. Soviet television press conference, 13 January 1985; and *Guardian*, 14 January 1985.
37. *Time* magazine, New York, 5 September 1985.
38. *Guardian*, 22 November 1985.
39. *Pravda*, 31 December 1985.
40. *Pravda*, 16 January 1986.
41. Gorbachev, *Political Report*, pages 77–8.
42. Gorbachev, *Political Report*, page 23.

8: The Armed Forces: the Struggle for Cash (*pages 124–38*)

1. *Estimated Soviet Defence Spending*, CIA SR 78–10121, Washington DC, June 1978, and CIA SR 78–10002, January 1978, and subsequent years. See also *Soviet Military Power*, 1985 and 1986, Department of Defense, Washington DC. See also Joint Economic Committee of the US Congress, *Soviet Economy in the 1980s: Problems and Prospects*, Vol. 1, pages 287–351 *passim*, US Government Printing Office, Washington DC, 1983.

2. *Los Angeles Times*, 13 September 1982.

3. *Guardian*, London, 5 December, 1981.

4. Author's interviews with British and American military attachés, Moscow.

5. Leonard Schapiro, *The CPSU*, page 420, Vintage Russian Library, New York, 1960.

6. Roy Medvedev, *Khrushchev,* pages 118–19, Blackwell, Oxford, 1982.

7. *Velikaya Otechestvennaya Voyina, 1941–5*, page 222, *Sovyetskaya Entsiklopediya*, Moscow, 1985.

8. Roy Medvedev, *Khrushchev*, page 123 and pages 136–7. For subsequent expansion, see *The Military Balance, 1981–2*, International Institute of Strategic Studies, London.

9. A. G. Rahr, *Biographic Directory of 100 Leading Soviet Officials*, pages 224–7. Central Research, Radio Liberty, Munich, August 1984.

10. *Pravda*, 22 October 1976.

11. *Soviet Economy in the 1980s*, Vol. 1, pages 131–2.

12. *Military Expenditures of the Soviet Union and its Prospects for the Future*, NATO Scientific and Economic Committee, Brussels, January 1984. See also *Guardian*, 15 June 1984.

13. *Guardian*, 7 June 1977, and 12 November 1984. See also A. Cockburn, *The Threat*, pages 68–9, Hutchinson, London, 1983.

14. Cockburn, *The Threat*, page 65.

15. *Sovyetskaya Voyennaya Entsiklopediya*, pages 555–65, Moscow, 1979.

16. *Kommunist*, No. 10, October 1981.

17. *Pravda*, 7 November 1981. For an illuminating account of the entire debate, see G. G. Weickhardt, 'Ustinov versus Ogarkov', in *Problems of Communism*, Vol. XXXIV, 1, January–February 1985, pages 77–82, USIA, Washington DC.

18. Ogarkov, *Always Ready to Defend the Fatherland*, Voyennizdat, Moscow, January 1982.

19. *Serving the Country*, Voyennizdat, Moscow, May 1982; and *Pravda*, 12 July 1982.

20. *Pravda*, 22 December 1982.

21. *New York Times*, 17 March 1983.

22. *Krasnaya Zvezda*, 9 May 1984.

23. *Krasnaya Zvezda*, 18 May 1983.

24. *Pravda*, 28 November 1984.

25. Joint Economic Committee of the US Congress, *Soviet Economy in*

the 1980s: Problems and Prospects, Vol. 1, pages 287–96. US Government Printing Office, Washington DC, 1983.

26. *Air Force* magazine, New York, March 1986.

27. *Guardian*, 12 December 1985.

28. *Guardian*, 25 June 1985.

29. *Soviet Military Review*, No. 4, 1985. Krasnaya Zvezda, Moscow.

30. Simyonov gave a press conference on his trip to Geneva, two days before the Reagan–Gorbachev summit began. See *Tribune de Genève*, 18 November 1985.

31. *Literaturnaya Gazeta*, 28 August 1985.

32. P. Kruzhin, *New Cadres Policy in the Soviet Army?*, Radio Liberty Research, RL 388/85, Munich.

33. M. S. Gorbachev, *Political Report of the CPSU Central Committee to the 27th Party Congress of the CPSU, 25 February 1986*, page 78, Novosti, Moscow, 1986.

9: Soft Repression: the Future of the KGB (*pages 139–53*)

1. Roy Medvedev, *Khrushchev*, pages 61–9, Blackwell, Oxford, 1982. For increasing role of KGB in 1986, see *Sovyetskaya Kirgizia*, 25 January 1986; and Radio Liberty Research, RL 83/86, Munich.

2. Roy Medvedev, *Khrushchev*, page 137.

3. Leonard Schapiro, *The CPSU*, pages 414–21, Vintage Russian Library, New York, 1960. See also *The Dethronement of Stalin*, pages 10–20, full text of Khrushchev's speech to 20th Congress of the CPSU, published by the *Manchester Guardian*, Cross Street, Manchester, June 1956.

4. Roy Medvedev, *Gorbachev*, page 138.

5. Roy Medvedev, *Gorbachev*, page 135.

6. See Edward J. Brown, *Russian Literature Since the Revolution*, pages 250–1, Harvard University Press, 1982 (revised edition).

7. .Ed. Peter Reddaway, *Uncensored Russia*, text of *Chronicle of Current Events*, pages 53–61, Jonathan Cape, London, 1972.

8. Ed. Reddaway, *Uncensored Russia*, pages 95*ff*.

9. See, for example, the deeply unpleasant writings of the 'anti-Zionist' Lev Korneyev, such as *The Class Essence of Zionism*, Kiev, 1983; his articles in the military newspaper *Krasnaya Zvezda*, 25 September 1980, and in the Leningrad journal *Neva*, No. 4, 1978.

10. *Guardian*, London, 10 July 1985.

11. Vladimir Solovyov and Elena Klepikova, *Yuri Andropov, A Secret Passage into the Kremlin*, pages 92–3, Hale, London, 1984.

12. Solovyov and Klepikova, *Yuri Andropov*, page 106.

13. A. G. Rahr, *Biographic Directory of 100 Leading Soviet Officials*, pages 190–2, Central Research, Radio Liberty, Munich, August 1984.

14. Solovyov and Klepikova, *Yuri Andropov*, page 105.

15. Solovyov and Klepikova, *Yuri Andropov*, pages 107–12.

16. Zhores Medvedev, *Andropov*, page 65, Blackwell, Oxford, 1983.

17. Rahr, *Biographic Directory*, pages 34–6.

18. *Pravda*, 28 February 1986.

19. *Kommunist*, No. 7, July 1985.
20. *Literaturnaya Gazeta*, 3 October 1984.
21. *Guardian*, 15 November 1985.
22. Author's interviews with Svetlana Alliluyeva and Erakli Ochiauri.
23. *Guardian*, 19 September 1985.
24. Zhores Medvedev, *Andropov*, page 139.
25. Zhores Medvedev, *Andropov*, page 120.
26. *Pravda*, 29 May 1985.
27. See, for example, *Pravda*, 13 February 1986.
28. Author's interview.
29. *Prisoners of Conscience in the USSR*, page 53, Amnesty International, London, 1975.
30. Hugh Seton-Watson, *The Russian Empire*, Clarendon Press, Oxford, 1985. Page 625 claims 683 death sentences carried out by Stolypin's courts-martial, but see pages 611 and 615 for evidence of many more shot out of hand.
31. *Guardian*, 12 June 1985.

10: Changing Soviet Lifestyles (*pages 154–75*)

1. Author's interview.
2. Kathleen Berton, *Moscow, an Architectural History*, page 223, Macmillan, New York, 1977.
3. See, for example, *Literaturnaya Rossiya*, 21 April 1986, for a case in which the official involved was shot.
4. Author's observation and interviews, Mxheta.
5. M. S. Gorbachev, *Political Report of the CPSU Central Committee to the 27th Party Congress of the CPSU, 25 February 1986*, pages 52–3, Novosti, Moscow, 1986.
6. *Nedelya*, 7 October 1985.
7. Author's interview.
8. *Izvestia*, 14 April 1986.
9. *Literaturnaya Gazeta*, 29 August 1984.
10. *Izvestia*, 18 April 1985.
11. Author's observations, Moscow, 1984–6.
12. Author's interview with Professor Oleg Bogomolov, February 1986.
13. Author's observation.
14. *Sovyetskaya Rossiya*, 7 June and 23 July 1985; and *Vechernaya Moskva*, 20 May 1985.
15. *Sovyetskaya Rossiya*, 25 September 1985.
16. *Literaturnaya Rossiya*, 21 April 1986.
17. Gorbachev, *Political Report*, page 52.
18. Author's interviews.
19. Author's observation, and interviews with Livanov.
20. Author's observation, April 1986, Malyi Gruzinski, Moscow.
21. Author's observations, Bitza Park, 1984–6.
22. Author's observation and interviews, Riga, April 1986.
23. Author's interviews with Djemma Skulme and others, Riga, April 1986.

24. Author's observation, and attendance at *Cyrano de Bergerac* concert, Riga University, 22 April 1986.
25. Author's interviews, Riga.

11: The Woman's Lot (*pages 176–87*)

1. Author's interviews with Moscow diplomatic corps.
2. *Pravda*, 7 March 1986. For Furtseva's career, see Michel Tatu, *Le Pouvoir en URSS*, pages 143–4, 160–1, 550, Editions Bernard Grasset, Paris, 1967.
3. *SSSR v Tsifrakh (v 1984 godu)*, page 15, Finansy i Statistika, Moscow, 1985.
4. *Cambridge Encyclopaedia of Russia and the Soviet Union*, page 381, Cambridge University Press, 1982.
5. *Cambridge Encyclopaedia*, page 382; and *SSSR v Tsifrakh*, page 7.
6. Eds. Carola Hansson and Karin Linden, *Moscow Women*, page 189, Allison and Busby, London, 1984. See also *Cambridge Encyclopaedia*, page 381. See also ed. T. Mamonova, *Women in Russia*, page xviii. Blackwell, Oxford, 1984.
7. *Narodnoye Khozyaistvo SSSR (v 1983 godu)*, page 5, Finansy i Statistika, Moscow, 1984.
8. *Cambridge Encyclopaedia*, page 381.
9. *SSSR v Tsifrakh*, pages 36–7.
10. Hedrick Smith, *The Russians*, page 179, Sphere, London, 1976; and author's interviews.
11. Smith, *The Russians*, page 180. See also ed. Mamonova, *Women in Russia*, page xix.
12. Author's interview, Moscow, 1985.
13. *Cambridge Encyclopaedia*, page 396.
14. Author's interviews, Moscow, 1985.
15. Author's interviews, Dom Modi, 1985.
16. Author's interview, RSFSR ministry of health, December 1985.
17. See *Daily Telegraph*, London, 21 December 1984; and Christian Schmidt-Hauer, *Gorbachev, The Path to Power*, page 9, I. B. Tauris, London, 1986.
18. *Daily Mail*, London, 31 March 1986.
19. See *Kommunist*, No. 12, 1985, and *Sovyetskaya Rossiya*, 25 December 1985.
20. *Guardian*, London, 7 March 1986.
21. *Kosmonavtika, Malenkaya Entsiklopediya, Sovyetskaya Entsiklopediya*, page 450, Moscow, 1968.
22. Ed. Mamonova, *Women in Russia*, page ix and *passim*.
23. Ed. Mamonova, *Women in Russia*, page 272.
24. Ed. Mamonova, *Women in Russia*, pages 236–44.
25. *Novy Mir*, 9, 1969.
26. Ed. Mamonova, *Women in Russia*, pages 208–9.
27. M. S. Gorbachev, *Political Report of the CPSU Central Committee to the 27th Party Congress of the CPSU, 25 February 1986*, pages 57–8, Novosti, Moscow, 1986.

28. Schmidt-Hauer, *Gorbachev*, pages 53–7.

12: The Sons of the Elite (*pages 188–205*)

1. A. G. Rahr, *Biographic Directory of 100 Leading Soviet Officials*, page 53, Central Research, Radio Liberty, Munich, August 1984.

2. David Shub, *Lenin*, page 35, Pelican, London, 1966 (revised edition).

3. Adam Ulam, *Lenin and the Bolsheviks*, page 583, Fontana, London, 1969.

4. See M. S. Gorbachev, ' . . . the institution of a progressive inheritance tax', in *Political Report of the CPSU Central Committee to the 27th Party Congress of the CPSU, 25 February 1986*, page 52, Novosti, Moscow, 1986.

5. Kevin Klose, *Russia and the Russians*, pages 299*ff.*, W. W. Norton, New York, 1985.

6. See Zhores Medvedev, *Andropov*, page 65, Blackwell, Oxford, 1983.

7. Klose, *Russia and the Russians*, page 304*ff.*

8. Klose, *Russia and the Russians*, page 293; and eye-witness accounts from Taganka actors.

9. TASS, 19 March 1986.

10. Author's interview with Vladimir Karpov.

11. *Novy Mir*, No. 9, September 1985; and author's interview with Yevtushenko.

12. V. V. Karpov, *Polkovodets*, Sovyetski Pisatel, Moscow, 1985.

13. E. J. Brown, *Russian Literature since the Revolution*, page 230.

14. Yuri Bondarev, *Vibor, The Choice*, Raduga, Moscow, 1984.

15. Author's observation. The book was published in Britain by Virago in 1985.

16. Vladimir Solovyov and Elena Klepikova, *Yuri Andropov, A Secret Passage into the Kremlin*, page 244, Hale, London, 1984.

17. Michael Voslensky, *Nomenklatura*, page 101, Bodley Head, London, 1984.

18. Hedrick Smith, *The Russians*, page 68, Sphere, London, 1976.

19. Svetlana Alliluyeva, *Twenty Letters to a Friend*, letter 19, pages 212*ff.*, Harper and Row, New York, 1967.

20. This story was being deliberately leaked in Moscow in the summer of 1985 by known KGB sources and by reputable Soviet journalists. It surfaced, among other places, in the *Sunday Times*, London, 16 June 1985.

21. Author's observations; and Voslensky, *Nomenklatura*, page 101.

22. Author's observation.

23. *Pravda*, 11 December 1984.

24. *Literaturnaya Gazeta*, No. 51, 1985, gave a partial account of the speech. The full text was published in the *New York Times*, 18 December 1985. Current quotations are from the author's own copy.

25. *Pravda*, 12 February 1986.

26. Author's interview with Afanyasev, 2 March 1986.

Notes

27. *Pravda*, 12 February 1986.
28. Aliev press conference, Foreign Ministry press centre, 27 February 1986, and *Guardian*, London, 28 February 1986.
29. *Sunday Times*, 16 June 1985.
30. *Sovyetskaya Kultura*, 1986, 3 April 1986.
31. *Guardian*, 25 June 1986.
32. *Guardian*, 1 July 1986.
33. *Vremya i Mi*, No. 41, 1979, page 176, Tel Aviv.

13: The Return of History (*pages 206–22*)

1. Author's interview with curator of the Stalin Museum, Gori, December 1984.
2. Roy Medvedev, *Let History Judge*, pages 48*ff.*, Macmillan, London, 1972.
3. Isaac Deutscher, *Stalin*, page 416, Pelican, London, 1966. See also Anton Antonov-Ovseyenko, *The Time of Stalin*, Harper and Row, New York, 1981; Antonov-Ovseyenko's father was put in charge of the purges in Spain, and was himself purged by Stalin on his return to Moscow.
4. Alexander Solzhenitsyn, *The Gulag Archipelago*, *passim*, Fontana, London, 1974.
5. See notes 3, 4 and 5 above for references.
6. Zhores Medvedev, *Andropov*, pages 51–2, Blackwell, Oxford, 1983.
7. Author's observation, Zvyezdi Gorodok, April 1986.
8. Roy Medvedev, *Khrushchev*, pages 259–60, Blackwell, Oxford 1982.
9. *Krasnaya Zvezda*, 14 February 1942. See also *Sobranie sochinenii*, Sovyetski Pisatel, Moscow, 1966–70, Vol. 1, page 271. Translation by the author.
10. See note 9.
11. Vasily Belov, *The Usual Thing*, 1966, and *Carpenters' Stories*, 1968.
12. Vasily Shukshin, *Kalina Krasnaya*, 1973. The film made from the book won the state prize.
13. Valentin Rasputin, *The Last Days*, 1970, *Live and Remember*, 1975, *Farewell to Matyora*, 1976.
14. Author's interview with Archimandrite Alexei, Danilovsky monastery, Moscow.
15. *The Cambridge Encyclopaedia of Russia and the Soviet Union*, page 131, Cambridge University Press, 1982.
16. Author's interview with the Metropolitan Alexy of Tallin, Chancellor of the Moscow Patriarchate.
17. Message of the Holy Synod, Moscow, 7 February 1986; and press conference, Moscow, 8 April 1986.
18. See note 17.
19. Cited in Alexandre Bennigsen, 'Mullahs, Mujahedin and Soviet Muslims', in *Problems of Communism*, Vol. XXXIII, 6, November–December 1984, pages 28*ff.*

20. Bennigsen, 'Mullahs, Mujahedin and Soviet Muslims'.
21. *Cambridge Encyclopaedia*, pages 308–9.
22. W. M. Mandel, *Soviet but not Russian*, page 161, University of Alberta Press, Edmonton, Canada, 1985.
23. General P. G. Grigorenko, *The Grigorenko Papers, passim*, C. Hurst and Co., London, 1976.
24. V. I. Lenin, *Collected Works*, Vol. XXXVI, pages 605–6, Progress Publishers, Moscow, 1966.
25. *Pravda*, 22 December 1982.
26. *L'Humanité*, Paris, 8 February 1986.
27. Author's interview with Roy Medvedev.
28. *Sovyetskaya Kultura*, 15 April 1986.

14: Chernobyl (*pages 223–45*)

1. *Newsweek*, 12 May 1986, page 19, article by Zhores Medvedev. See also papers presented to the Joint Economic Committee of the US Congress, *Soviet Economy in the 1980s: Problems and Prospects*, Vol. 1, pages 474*ff*, US Government Printing Office, Washington DC, 1983.
2. *Newsweek*, 12 May 1986.
3. *Newsweek*, 12 May 1986. See also Zhores Medvedev, *Nuclear Disaster in the Urals*, London, 1978.
4. Nikolai Ryzhkov, *Economic Guidelines*, pages 38–9, Novosti, Moscow, 1986.
5. *Soviet Economy in the 1980s*, Vol. I, pages 474–8.
6. *Literaturnaya Ukraina*, March 1986, Lyubov Kovalevska.
7. *Soviet Economy in the 1980s* Vol. I, page 488.
8. *Soviet Economy in the 1980s* Vol. I, page 488.
9. *Newsweek*, 12 May 1986, page 14.
10. Author's interviews. See also Roy Medvedev, *Il Messagero*, Rome, 18 May 1986.
11. Soviet TV, 14 May 1986. See also Novosti transcription, Moscow, 1986.
12. IAEA press conference, Moscow 9 May 1986.
13. *Sovyetskaya Rossiya*, 8 May 1986.
14. *Sovyetskaya Rossiya*, 8 May 1986.
15. Press conference given by Dr Gale, Moscow, 5 June 1986.
16. *Pravda*, 14 June 1986.
17. Reuter's tape, datelined Kiev, Charles Bremner, 8 May 1986.
18. *Sovyetskaya Rossiya*, 8 May 1986.
19. Press conference given by Boris Scherbina, Moscow, 6 May 1986.
20. *Krasnaya Zvezda*, 7 June 1986.
21. *Pravda*, 2 June 1986.
22. *Pravda*, 2 June 1986.
23. Scherbina press conference, 6 May 1986.
24. *Pravda*, 14 June 1986.
25. *Sovyetskaya Rossiya*, 10 June 1986.
26. *Time* magazine, vol. 127, No. 19, page 7.

Notes

27. Author's interviews, Swedish diplomats.
28. *Der Spiegel*, Hamburg, 15 May 1986.
29. TASS statement, 28 April 1986.
30. *Newsweek*, 12 May 1986.
31. IAEA press conference, 9 May 1986.
32. Gorbachev TV address, 14 May 1986.
33. IAEA press conference, 9 May 1986.
34. Scherbina press conference, 6 May 1986.
35. Gale press conference, Moscow, 15 May 1986.
36. *Krasnaya Zvezda*, 7 June 1986.
37. Associated Press, 12 May 1986.
38. *Pravda*, 30 May 1986.
39. Dr Ilyev, press conference, Moscow, 3 June 1986.
40. *Guardian*, 8 May 1986.
41. Gorbachev TV address, 14 May 1986.
42. TASS, 2 May 1986.
43. Author's interviews, US diplomatic sources.
44. Scherbina press conference, 6 May 1986.
45. UPI, 29 April 1986. See also *Guardian*, 26 May 1986.
46. *Guardian*, 13 May 1986.
47. Author's interviews.
48. Author's interviews, Charles Bremner, Reuter bureau chief.
49. IAEA press conference, 9 May 1986.
50. TASS, 13 May 1986.
51. Scherbina press conference, 6 May 1986.
52. *Pravda*, 4 June 1986.
53. Author's interviews, French TV correspondents.
54. *Izvestia*, 14 June 1986.
55. Author's observation. Also Reuter, 8 May 1986.
56. Author's observations, Kievsky Voksal. Also *The Times*, 5 June 1986.
57. *Guardian*, *Daily Mail*, *Daily Express*, London, 31 May 1986.
58. Gorbachev TV address, 14 May 1986.
59. *Pravda*, 11 June 1986.
60. *Pravda*, 17 June 1986.
61. Gale press conference, Moscow, 5 June 1986.
62. Author's interviews, Riga.
63. *Pravda*, 20 July 1986.
64. *Pravda*, 3 June 1986.

15: The West's Real Interests and Realpolitik (*pages 246–59*)

1. G. F. Will, *Washington Post*, 10 March 1986.
2. *Moscow News Supplement*, No. 48, 1985.
3. See, for example, report on a conference on 'Soviet Military Spending' at the Russian Research Centre of Harvard University, 14 February 1985. Published in Radio Liberty Research, RL 120/85, Munich.

4. A. Cockburn, *The Threat*, pages 15 and 223, Hutchinson, London, 1983.
5. *Guardian*, London, 15 June 1984.
6. Hedrick Smith, *The Russians*, Sphere, London, 1976: R. J. Kaiser, *Russia, the People and the Power*, Atheneum, New York, 1976.
7. This flurry of novels included *The Fall of the Russian Empire*, *Moscow Rules*, *Moscow Spring*, etc.
8. TASS, 31 March, 1986.
9. Christian Schmidt-Hauer, *Gorbachev, The Path to Power*, pages 146–8, I. B. Tauris, London, 1986.
10. M. S. Gorbachev, *Political Report of the CPSU Central Committee to the 27th Party Congress of the CPSU, 25 February 1986*, page 81, Novosti, Moscow, 1986.
11. Gorbachev, *Political Report*, page 80.

16: Change and a Restless Future (*pages 260–71*)

1. *Time* magazine, 24 August 1986.
2. See for example *Izvestia*, 2 September 1986 and *Pravda*, 5 September 1986.
3. *Pravda*, 8 September 1986.
4. 'Restructuring is urgent', text of speech at Khabarovsk, 31 July 1986 by M. S. Gorbachev, published by *Novosti*, 1986, page 28.
5. *Ibid.*, page 6.
6. *Le Monde*, 14 September 1986.
7. The full text of the manifesto was carried in the *Guardian*, 23 July 1986.
8. *Guardian*, 22 July 1986.
9. *Guardian*, 25 July 1986.
10. *Guardian*, 28 July 1986.
11. *Pravda*, 1 August 1986. See also full text of speech in 'Restructuring is urgent', *Novosti*, 1986.
12. *Novosti, ibid.*
13. Radio Liberty Research Bulletin, Munich, No. 31 (3392) RL 282/86 and 283/86.
14. *Moskovskii Novosti*, 10 August 1986.
15. *Ibid.*
16. *Literaturnaya Gazeta*, 17 September 1986.
17. *SSR V Tsifrakh, Finansy i Statistiki*, Moscow, 1985, page 5.

Postscript (*pages 272–89*)

1. *Guardian*, 12 February 1986. See also the author's 'Moscow Diary', *New Statesman*, 20 February 1986.
2. Author's observation.
3. *Novy Mir*, Moscow, April 1987.
4. *Moskovskii Novosti*, 6 March 1987.

Notes

5. *Oktyabr*, Moscow, March 1987.
6. Translation by the author.
7. *Moskovskii Novosti*, 25 January 1987.
8. *Guardian*, 13 February 1987.
9. *Moskovskii Novosti*, 25 January 1987.
10. *Novaya Vremya*, 9 February 1987.
11. *Pravda*, 9 January 1987.
12. *Moskovskii Novosti*, 15 March 1987.
13. *Sozialisticheskaya Industria*, 28 March 1986.
14. TV programme *Vremya*, 1 October 1986.
15. TASS, 27 January 1987.
16. 'Re-organisation and Party Personnel Policy', speech by M. S. Gorbachev to the January plenum, 27 January 1987, published by *Novosti*, Moscow, page 27.
17. *Novaya Vremya*, 2 March 1987.
18. *Guardian*, 22 December 1986.
19. *Guardian*, 18 February 1987.
20. *Pravda*, 23 October 1986.
21. *Voprosy Filosofii*, July 1984.
22. 'For the sake of preserving human civilisation', speech to the International Forum, 16 February 1987, published by *Novosti*, Moscow, 1987, pages 8, 12.
23. *Guardian*, 6 February 1987.
24. *Pravda*, 31 March 1987.
25. TASS, 27 January 1987.
26. *Izvestia*, 26 March 1987.
27. Author's interview, 25 March 1987.
28. TASS, 27 January 1987.
29. TASS, 18 December 1986.
30. *Moskovskii Novosti*, 25 January 1987.
31. Press conference of Athos Fava, Moscow press centre, 4 March 1987. See also the *Guardian*, 5 March 1987.
32. *Pravda*, 26 June 1987.
33. Press conference, Dr Abel Aganbegyan, Moscow, 26 June 1987. See also *Guardian*, 27 June 1987.
34. *Pravda*, 2 October 1987.
35. Dr Zaslavskaya's interview with the *New York Times*, *Time* and Radio Liberty Research was published in full by Radio Liberty, Munich, RL 365/87.
36. *Ogonyok*, 18 June 1987. Ligachev's speech was published in *Pravda*, 6 March 1987.
37. *Guardian*, 11 May 1987. See also *Nauka 1 Zhizn*, Moscow, Volume 9, 1987, which published the lectures in full.
38. Author's interview with Mikhail Shatrov. See also *Guardian*, 13 October 1987.
39. *Novy Mir*, Vol 9, 1987. *Yunost*, Vol 10, 1987.
40. *Literaturnaya Gazeta*, 30 September 1987.

Index

Index

Index

Glushkov, Academician 64
Goldstein, Isai and Grigori 64
Gorbachev, Andrei 2–3
Gorbachev, Irina xvi, xvii, 182
Gorbachev, Mikhail and agriculture xxvii,
    2–3, 17–22, 65
  and Andropov 14–15, 30
  anti-corruption drives xxvii, 92, 150
  and the army 132–3, 137–8
  and bureaucracy 65
  and Chernobyl 226–7, 231, 236, 241–2
  and Communist Party xxvii, 22–3, 88,
    94, 97, 100–1
  and culture 203, 205
  disarmament proposals 120–2, 242,
    248, 253, 257, 258
  early days 1–4
  and economic reform 22, 39, 49–52, 56–70
    passim, 95, 101, 170, 253, 261–2, 264
  foreign policy, personal control of 107,
    114–23, 257
  freedom of the press, 261–3
  and incentives 15–16, 19–22, 59, 170
  industry, strategy for 64–7
  and international relations 107, 111–12,
    115–23, 137, 242–3
  and KGB 153
  law studies xvii, xix, 4–6
  and *Nomenklatura* system 13–14,
    93–4, 101
  party work 3, 6–23
  personal political manifesto 37, 256–8
  and Politburo 17, 57, 101
  and post-industrial economy 72, 97, 246
  product of social revolution xviii, xx-
    xxi, xxviii
  and professional classes xv-xxv
  second degree (in agronomy) 14
  and service sector xxvii, 161
  on Stalinism 220, 222
  television personality xvi, 119–20 246,
    256–7
  tour of Moscow xiv-xv
  and United States 120–3, 248
  and Warsaw Pact countries 116–17,
    255–6
  and women's status 186–7
Gorbachev, Raisa xvi-xvii, 8, 15, 176,
    182–4, 205
  influence of xxiv, 183, 187
Gorbachev, Oksana xvi, 183
Gordievsky, Oleg 149
Gorshkov, Admiral Sergei 100, 108–11,
    124, 127, 133
Gosplan 45, 62–3, 64
Grechko, Marshal 109, 126, 127
Grekova, I: *Ship of Widows* 197
Grigorenko, General 219
Grishin, Viktor xiv, 33, 198
Gromyko, Anatoly 114–15, 199, 201
Gromyko, Andrei 25–6, 31, 32
  foreign policy 112–17, 119–20
Gulayev, General 133
Gvishiani, Dzhermen 199

health care 69

Henry, Ernst 209
history, refusal to confront xix, 208, 210,
    220–2, 237, 258–9
hoarding 38–9
Honecker, Erich 116
Hoover, J. Edgar xx
housing problem 179
Hungarian uprising 124

incentive systems 15–16, 19–22, 41, 45,
    ^6–7, 77
industrialisation xxii, 11, 71, 79, 87, 95,
    97, 207
industry 39–47, 69
  brigade system 46–7
  computer industry 60–6
  defence industry 55–8
  industrial base, transformation of 58
  investment in 80, 81
  lack of software skills 54
  and managerial responsibility 40–3
  productivity 41, 45–7, 69, 70, 81
  quality of production 39, 46, 55, 63
  relocation 71–2, 97
  self-financing 43–4
  slowness in absorbing new technology 45
  territorial-production complexes (TPCs)
    43–4
Institute for the Study of the US and
    Canada 113, 201
intelligentsia 190, 203–5, 209–10
International Atomic Energy Agency
    (IAEA) 227, 231, 237–8, 242, 260
invasions of Russia 102–3, 104–5
Iran 105–6
Iskander, Fazil 197
Islamic fundamentalism 105–6, 108, 217,
    252
Israel 127, 130–1
Italy 220–1, 254
Ivan the Terrible xiii, xxviii, 36
Ivanovsky, General Yevgeny 124, 133
Izvestia xx, xxv, 17, 164, 240

Japan 103, 117, 137
Jaruszelski, General 255
Jews 151
  in Communist Party 90
  emigration of 142, 151, 251

Kaiser, Robert 251
Kandinsky, Wassily 189
Kantorovich, Leonid 64
Kapitsa, Pyotr 209
Kapivsky, Anatoly 154–5, 157–60
Karpov, Vladimir 194–7, 204
Kennedy J. F. and Jacqueline xix-xx, 254
KGB (Committee for State Security) 36,
    100, 139–53, 184–5
  anti-corruption role 143–6, 149–50,
    153
  arrest powers, limited xvii-xviii, 140
  humiliations 148–9
  and internal dissent 26, 37, 40, 140–2,
    151
  prestige increase 150–3
  security policy 67–8

312

Index

Index

314

Index

315

*"If you've never bought a book about rock and roll, no matter —
this is the one you've been waiting for."* PLAYBOY

The True
Adventures
of
THE ROLLING
STONES

Stanley Booth

IT LEAVES NO STONE UNTURNED:

*"Stanley Booth gets closer to the essence of the Rolling Stones
and their world than any previous author. It is the only book
about the Stones I would recommend both to the general reader
and to the most devoted fan."*
Robert Palmer NEW YORK TIMES

"Easily the best study of Mick, Keith and Co." TIME OUT

0 349 103577   ABACUS NON-FICTION   £3.95

Beyond the Dragon's Mouth
SHIVA NAIPAUL

Shiva Naipaul brings together autobiography, fiction and journalism, in a classic collection ranging from the streets of Port of Spain to the streets of London, Liverpool and Hull, from Iran on the eve of the Shah's fall to Moroccan misadventure, from Bombay to the Seychelles and the jungles of Surinam, and from the funeral of a Pope to the dens of Rastafarianism. It's retrospective which shows Naipaul in all his varied moods, highlighting his marvellous feel for people and places.

'Shiva Naipaul has powers of observation, let alone expression, which are enviable . . . [his writings] have a classic quality, and if they are still read in a hundred years, they will be read with pleasure.' *Peter Levi, Spectator*

'This is a rich collection . . . how admirable a writer he is.'
Anthony Burgess, Observer

ABACUS FICTION/TRAVEL   0 349 12493 0   £3·95

Also by Shiva Naipaul in Abacus paperback:

A HOT COUNTRY
BLACK AND WHITE

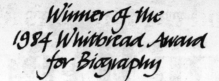

*Winner of the
1984 Whitbread Award
for Biography*

T·S·ELIOT

PETER ACKROYD

'Excellent . . . Ackroyd's biography is scrupulous in maintaining the principle that what we are told about the life must increase our understanding of the work. He has an extraordinary power of entering the mind of his subject. *Stephen Spender, Observer*

'A major biography . . . the result does justice to the complexity of Eliot's genius, and builds up a commanding case for the unity of life and work. We are unlikely to have a better biography of Eliot for many years.' *John Carey, Sunday Times*

'This brilliant account of Eliot's life turns a wealth of detailed research into a fluent narrative that is consistently engrossing and contains insights into every aspect of the man's literary output.' *Ian Hislop, Books and Bookmen*

'Perceptive and assured . . . the fullest and most plausible portrait yet achieved.' *Frank Kermode, Guardian*

'I can't praise this book highly enough. It is a model of how to write a biography' *A. N. Wilson, Harpers and Queen*

ABACUS NON-FICTION/BIOGRAPHY   0 349 10061 6   £4.95

Also by Peter Ackroyd in Abacus paperback:

**THE LAST TESTAMENT OF OSCAR WILDE
THE GREAT FIRE OF LONDON**

THE MARCH OF FOLLY

FROM TROY TO VIETNAM

BARBARA W. TUCHMAN

Twice winner of the Pulitzer Prize

From the distinguished American historian whose work has been acclaimed
around the world, THE MARCH OF FOLLY is a major new book that
penetrates one of the most bizarre and fascinating paradoxes in history: the
persistent pursuit by governments of policies contrary to their own interests.

Across the march of thirty centuries, Tuchman brings to life the dramatic events
which constitute folly's hallmark in government: the fall of Troy, symbolic
prototype of freely chosen disaster; the Protestant secession, provoked by six
decades of spectacularly corrupt Papacy; the British forfeiture of the American
colonies; and America's catastrophic thirty year involvement with Vietnam.

NON-FICTION   0 349 13365 4   £4.95

ARTHUR AND CYNTHIA KOESTLER
Stranger on the Square

In March 1983, the bodies of Arthur and Cynthia Koestler were discovered in their home at Montpelier Square. He was 77, she was 55. They had committed suicide. Arthur Koestler had been suffering severely from Parkinson's Disease and leukaemia. Cynthia, his wife and former secretary, had devoted her life to him: this was her final, tragic sacrifice.

After their deaths, their friend and literary executor Harold Harris found a manuscript – a kind of joint autobiography – among their papers. It constitutes an intimately revealing glimpse into the life of one of the greatest philosophers of this century – his drinking, his violent tempers, his promiscuity and, above all, his brilliance. It is also a moving testament to the incredible devotion of Cynthia Koestler, who expressed the literal truth in her suicide note, 'I cannot live without Arthur.'

ABACUS FICTION   0 349 12124 9   £2.95

Also available in ABACUS paperback:

FICTION

THE HOTTENTOT ROOM	Christopher Hope	£3.99 ☐
BANANA CAT	Christopher Hood	£3.99 ☐
GOD HELP THE QUEEN	Geoffrey Cush	£2.99 ☐
LEAN TALES	Gray/Kelman/Owens	£3.99 ☐
REDHILL ROCOCO	Shena Mackay	£3.50 ☐
HEAVENLY DECEPTION	Maggie Brooks	£3.95 ☐
I WISH THIS WAR WERE OVER	Diana O'Hehir	£3.50 ☐
WELCOME STRANGERS	Mary Hocking	£3.95 ☐

NON-FICTION

IN THE LABYRINTH	John David Morley	£3.99 ☐
SON OF "IT WAS A DARK AND STORMY NIGHT"	Scott Rice	£2.99 ☐
THE WAKING GIANT	Martin Walker	£4.99 ☐
IF THIS IS A MAN/ THE TRUCE	Primo Levi	£3.95 ☐
FORESTS IN BRITAIN	Thomas Hinde	£4.95 ☐
HOMAGE TO QWERTYUIOP	Anthony Burgess	£4.95 ☐
MOVE YOUR SHADOW	Joseph Lelyveld	£3.95 ☐

All Abacus books are available at your local bookshop or newsagent, or can be ordered direct from the publisher. Just tick the titles you want and fill in the form below.

Name _____

Address _____

_____

Write to Abacus Books, Cash Sales Department, P.O. Box 11, Falmouth, Cornwall TR10 9EN

Please enclose a cheque or postal order to the value of the cover price plus:

UK: 60p for the first book, 25p for the second book and 15p for each additional book ordered to a maximum charge of £1.90.

OVERSEAS & EIRE: £1.25 for the first book, 75p for the second book and 28p for each subsequent title ordered.

BFPO: 60p for the first book, 25p for the second book plus 15p per copy for the next 7 books, thereafter 9p per book.

Abacus Books reserve the right to show new retail prices on covers which may differ from those previously advertised in the text elsewhere, and to increase postal rates in accordance with the P.O.